THE ART OF RE-ENCHANTMENT

The Art of Re-enchantment

MAKING EARLY MUSIC IN THE MODERN AGE

Nick Wilson

OXFORD
UNIVERSITY PRESS

Oxford University Press is a department of the University of Oxford.
It furthers the University's objective of excellence in research, scholarship,
and education by publishing worldwide.

Oxford   New York
Auckland   Cape Town   Dar es Salaam   Hong Kong   Karachi
Kuala Lumpur   Madrid   Melbourne   Mexico City   Nairobi
New Delhi   Shanghai   Taipei   Toronto

With offices in
Argentina   Austria   Brazil   Chile   Czech Republic   France   Greece
Guatemala   Hungary   Italy   Japan   Poland   Portugal   Singapore
South Korea   Switzerland   Thailand   Turkey   Ukraine   Vietnam

Oxford is a registered trademark of Oxford University Press
in the UK and certain other countries.

Published in the United States of America by
Oxford University Press
198 Madison Avenue, New York, NY 10016

This volume is published with the generous support of the AMS 75 PAYS Endowment of the American Musicological Society, funded in part by the National Endowment for the Humanities and the Andrew W. Mellon Foundation

© Oxford University Press 2014

All rights reserved. No part of this publication may be reproduced, stored in a
retrieval system, or transmitted, in any form or by any means, without the prior
permission in writing of Oxford University Press, or as expressly permitted by law,
by license, or under terms agreed with the appropriate reproduction rights organization.
Inquiries concerning reproduction outside the scope of the above should be sent to the
Rights Department, Oxford University Press, at the address above.

You must not circulate this work in any other form
and you must impose this same condition on any acquirer.

Library of Congress Cataloging-in-Publication Data
Wilson, Nick, 1966–
The art of re-enchantment : making early music in the modern age / Nick Wilson.
pages cm
Includes bibliographical references and index.
ISBN 978–0–19–993993–0 (hardback : alk. paper)—ISBN 978–0–19–993994–7 (electronic text)   1. Music—Great Britain—History and criticism.   2. Performance practice (Music)—Great Britain.   I. Title.
ML285.W55 2013
781.4'3—dc23
2013010514

9 8 7 6 5 4 3 2 1
Printed in the United States of America
on acid-free paper

This book is dedicated to Mary, Flo, and Jake—everyday, my source of (re-)enchantment.

Contents

Preface   ix
Acknowledgments   xv

PART ONE | MAKING EARLY MUSIC
1. Introduction   3
2. Seven Ages of Early Music   19
3. Transcending Text & Act?   37

PART TWO | MAKING EARLY MUSIC WORK
4. A Tale of Two Authenticities   57
5. Shake, Rattle and Roll   76
6. Holding History in Their Hands   93
Early Music in Early Music (illustrations)   110

PART THREE | MAKING EARLY MUSIC PAY
7. Spinning Out Early Music   123
8. Jumping on the Old Band Wagon?   140
9. Everything to Play for   157

PART FOUR | MAKING EARLY MUSIC IN THE MODERN AGE
10. The Thief Who Came to Dinner   177
11. The Ineluctable Ore of the Authentic   196
12. The Art of Re-enchantment   212

Notes   229
References   261
Index   279

We are the music-makers,
And we are the dreamers of dreams,
Wandering by lone sea-breakers,
And sitting by desolate streams.
World-losers and world-forsakers,
Upon whom the pale moon gleams;
Yet we are the movers and shakers,
Of the world forever, it seems.
ARTHUR O'SHAUGHNESSY[1]

I don't like nostalgia unless it's mine.
LOU REED

Preface

I HAVE BEEN making music all my life. There is nothing particularly unusual about that. Music, after all, is a universal human pursuit, practiced by peoples of all ages, cultures, and backgrounds, and enjoyed in every corner of the world. But I have also been lucky enough to earn my living from making music—and this *is* out of the ordinary. Making music became my job; it was what I did both at work and play. It was within this professional context that debates concerning how to perform *early music* first began to have serious personal relevance for me. As a young music undergraduate I had been introduced to "historically informed performance" (HIP) in theory at least, but it was only when I was actually performing, and getting paid for it, that HIP moved beyond mere academic inquiry and began to really matter. My professional operatic debut in the early-1990s was in a fully staged reworking of Monteverdi's (1607) opera *L'Orfeo*, for a regional touring company. I played the title role, Orpheus, the archetype of the enchanted singer, who could "charm all living things, even stones" with his music. Looking back, this was probably about as far removed from "authentic performance" as one could conceive of at the time. My famous Act III recitative *Possente spirto*, for example, was sung not to the echoes of cornetts, sackbuts, and harps, as originally scored, but to the distinctively 20th-century accompaniment of a pair of saxophones and a bank of synthesizers. Nevertheless, we *were* performing Monteverdi's opera, and we *were* deeply committed to making it work for our audience. Moreover, what successes we managed to achieve can largely be put down to our ability to reconcile a fundamental dilemma that has confronted *all* of the musicians featured in this book: how to do justice to the inherent meaning and value of "old" music, whilst also making it "new," relevant for our own time, and in keeping with the exacting demands of the contemporary classical music profession and its audience; in short, how to "re-enchant" art?

As we shall see, now-familiar musicological arguments concerning the nature of "authentic performance" have tended to reinforce a dualistic opposition between those who favor the "old" and those extolling the "new." There appears to be little or no room for compromise. But, of course, in allowing practice to be our instructor, we find that it is precisely in the unfolding relationship between old and new (constraint and freedom, text and act) that authenticity properly understood is to be found. The implications of this insight are far-reaching, and form the backdrop for what follows.

First and foremost, this is a book about the British early music movement (hereafter Early Music). It documents, explains, and reflects upon an extraordinary and revolutionary cultural phenomenon that has grasped classical music performance and shaken it to its core. What makes Early Music so distinctive is its particular approach to re-enchanting art, based as it is on the intention (broadly speaking) to perform music of earlier times in such a way as to recreate the sounds of the original performances, rather than according to the standard "traditional" practices generally cultivated later on (largely in the 19th century). Early Music's impact has been phenomenal. Its popularity and appeal would surprise even those who blazed the trail for what was to come. Forty years on, the evidence of Early Music's transformative influence is to be found in concert halls across the world, and in a library's worth of recordings. And yet the movement's demonstrable success has not been without controversy. Early Music has provoked heated debate, and for good reason—it has had a substantial impact on peoples' livelihoods, after all. Difficult questions remain. Long after the movement was compelled to throw open its doors to detailed and searching scrutiny, its foundational ideology of authentic performance continues to divide opinion. If, as some have suggested, authentic performance is ultimately an impossible dream, an illegitimate claim, where does this leave historical performance today? Putting aside arguments over the legitimacy of HIP, did Early Music's performer-scholars actually possess the skills necessary to achieve their uncompromising agenda? Was interest in historically informed performance just another facet of the burgeoning heritage industry? Was the exploitation of early music little more than a commercial ruse, a means of making money by profit-driven record companies? And, more broadly, what does this specific case of cultural production reveal about the integral relationship between high culture and the market? By providing an in-depth history and analysis of the early music movement in Britain from the 1960s through to the present day, this book seeks to provide answers to these and other related questions.

I have been spurred on in the belief that unless the evidence was documented soon, Early Music would either be forgotten as little more than a curious historical anomaly,[2] or be subject sometime in the future to a revisionist history (with or without a happy ending). Such is the extent of Early Music's contemporary mainstreaming that it is all but taken for granted as "just how old music is performed these days." As my inquiry progressed, it became increasingly clear that beyond mere description, this remarkable phenomenon also demanded explanation. What has made such a task all the more interesting is Early Music's deeply contradictory nature, and the harder I looked, the more contradictions I found. The movement's reliance on recordings to disseminate early music, for example, is just one of the most obvious *in*-authentic practices of the "authenticity movement." The implicit challenges of even partially recreating the premodern (a world before Enlightenment and capitalism) in modernity (a world of rational logic and bureaucratic organization) are manifold, to say the least. So although my focus is very much on the continued development of a specific cultural movement in Britain, it has also been necessary to engage with a far wider set of ideas and practices, contemplating forms of knowledge that go beyond the purely cognitive and rational—and in the process, questioning the perceived value of art and authenticity in contemporary life.

My approach to writing this book has, of course, been bound by "the limiting constraints of discursive communication,"[3] but it is, I hope, as much a celebration of my felt experience and passion for early music as it is a product of my (social) scientific knowledge of the movement. Such a position, as will become clear, is consistent with my emerging conception of authenticity. For a decade I made my living from singing, performing with a number of the early music groups and ensembles discussed here. I also worked in arts administration, experiencing first hand the harsh realities but also the rewards of putting on concerts, festivals, and other cultural events. Since 2000 I have been employed as a researcher and educator, lecturing on subjects relating to cultural and arts management, entrepreneurship and cultural production, arts-based learning and education, and critical realist philosophy. My doctoral research, *Explaining Labour Market Emergence: The Case of Early Music Performance in the UK*, was completed at Kingston University in 2007. However, it is simply as a human being that I consider myself best qualified to engage with my subject.

The book is timely because 2013 is a year of Early Music anniversaries. It is 60 years since Nikolaus and Alice Harnoncourt founded Concentus Musicus Wien, arguably the continental period instrument ensemble that has had most influence on the modern-day Early Music revival not just in Britain but worldwide. More importantly, in the context of this study of British, largely London-based, early music performance, it is also the 40th anniversaries not only of several of the most prominent professional early music ensembles, including the Academy of Ancient Music, The English Concert, The Tallis Scholars, and The Taverner Choir, Consort & Players, but also the *Early Music* journal dedicated to matters relating to historical performance.[4] It is 25 years since Nicholas Kenyon convened a symposium on the theme of "Authenticity and Early Music" (1988) at the Oberlin Conservatory of Music; the specialist magazine *Early Music Today* is 20 years old; and finally, it is 18 years since Richard Taruskin published *Text & Act*, a book that challenged the movement to look at itself and its practices with a much more critical eye.

Any one of the chapters in this book could have been extended to include far more commentary, discussion, and anecdote, and I have had to learn how to make some substantive editing decisions of my own. As Robert Donington notes in his introductory chapter to *The Interpretation of Early Music*, "To recover something of what direct tradition can no longer convey to us, our best and indeed almost only recourse is to read what the actual contemporaries of the music had to say about it."[5] And so, I have chosen to focus on the first-hand accounts of many musicians, producers, promoters, record company executives, and others, whose ideas and practices have been so influential. I count myself lucky to have met and talked with many of the movement's "movers and shakers." This has been hugely stimulating, sometimes daunting, but always inspiring. Whilst many early musicians would no doubt prefer their music "to do the talking," they have nonetheless proved themselves remarkably insightful interlocutors. Over and above the 40 or so interviews, the book draws on an extensive survey of performers and instrument-makers, which I undertook in 2003, as well as secondary data from archive material, essays, articles, record covers, program notes, and broadcasts. The outcome, I hope, is a book primarily informed and shaped by those people who were, and are very much in the thick of it, at the heart of the early music revival.

While focusing on the period from the 1960s through to the present day, the analysis embraces earlier influences, and acknowledges the seminal role(s) of such pioneers as Arnold Dolmetsch, Wanda Landowska, August Wenzinger, Arnold Goldsbrough, Alfred Deller, George Malcolm, Edgar Hunt, Walter Bergmann, Denis Stevens, Thurston Dart, and Robert Donington. There will no doubt be other individuals who have not been given the credit in this book that their contribution deserves. Such are the constraints of inquiring into this highly complex set of activities and events that my account will necessarily remain partial at best. Such partiality also extends to the book's geographical focus. On purely practical grounds, it became necessary to limit the scope of analysis to the *British* early music movement. The vast majority of the many individuals who took part in research for the book were based in Britain and saw this as their primary place of work. But more importantly, there is a strong case for arguing that British Early Music displays characteristics that make it stand apart from related developments in Austria, Holland, Germany, the United States, and elsewhere; for example, the emergence of a distinct and separate labor market for early music performers in Britain (as discussed in Chapters 4 and 5). The geographical boundaries of my inquiry are, however, necessarily blurred at the edges.

I could not have completed this book without the support of colleagues, friends, and family, and a period of study leave from my everyday role as a lecturer at King's College London. It was here in 1964 that Thurston Dart, pioneer and authority on the interpretation of early music, became the university's first professor of music, succeeded in the mid-1970s by Howard Mayer Brown, a key contributor to Early Music debate. More recently, Laurence Dreyfus was professor of music, and the Music Department still boasts eminent historical musicologists, Daniel Leech-Wilkinson and Cliff Eisen amongst them. Whilst Dart had a sign above the entrance to his office that read "Abandon counterpoint, all ye that enter here," my own department has the somewhat more prosaic notice "Culture, Media and Creative Industries." Labels apart, I believe that my motivations are broadly the same as those of my illustrious predecessors. This work is first and foremost about the value and meaning of music, in practice, not just in theory. To paraphrase that great visionary of musicology Wilfrid Mellers,[6] "[early] music does not create or realise itself, but is always the result of people doing things together in particular places and times. To understand [early] music is to understand the men and women who make it, and vice versa." This, then, is the story of the early music-makers, those men and women who through their extraordinary (and everyday) practices, have brought solace, surprise, joy, and enchantment, and who continue to be responsible for "making early music in the modern age."

Acknowledgments

ACKNOWLEDGMENTS ARE USUALLY written at the very end of a book project; but, of course, I could not have even moved beyond the first page were it not for the generous support given to me by so many, and in so many ways. I would like to extend my particular thanks to those early music-makers who have contributed through being interviewed, including Robert Bailey, Clifford Bartlett, Jane Beeson, John Bickley, Kate Bolton, Alison Crum, Laurence Cummings, Robert Deegan, Richard Edgar-Wilson, Marion Friend, Sir John Eliot Gardiner, Maureen Garnham, Paul Goodwin, Helen Gough, Christopher Hogwood, Claire Holden, Annette Isserlis, Heather Jarman, Sir Nicholas Kenyon, Colin Kitching, Christopher Lawrence, Raymond Leppard, Catherine Mackintosh, Sir Roger Norrington, Daniel Pailthorpe, Andrew Parrott, Simon Perry, Andrew Pinnock, Trevor Pinnock, Clare Salaman, Chris Sayers, Lucie Skeaping, Bernard Thomas, Felix Warnock, Jeremy West, Richard Wood, and those many other individuals who have provided written correspondence, informal chats, and discussions. Thanks, too, to all the early music performers and instrument-makers who took part in my survey of British Early Music in 2003.

My perspective on this story of Early Music has been profoundly influenced by my own experience of working alongside many (early) musicians, teachers, managers, and agents over the years. It is difficult to single out individuals, but I am bound to mention here Dietrich Fischer-Dieskau, who I was lucky enough to study with as a young tenor in Berlin, and who showed me that interpretation and authenticity *could* be natural companions (how could I not be enchanted as he sung Schubert's *Danksagung an den Bach* to me in his sitting room, the miller's daughter—*"zur Müllerin hin!"*—being almost literally conjured up out of thin air?). In my work on critical realist philosophy, I have had the privilege to attend regular seminars and talks given by Roy Bhaskar and other scholars at the International Centre for Critical Realism, based at the Institute of Education. I am particularly indebted to Roy for his encouragement, and for helping me to believe in the value of my own ideas. Special thanks also to Steve Fleetwood, who was very supportive of my work early on. So, too, Lee Martin for many hours of conversation and exploration in our ongoing research on creativity and entrepreneurship—long may this continue. Thank you, too, to my editorial team at Oxford University Press, especially Suzanne Ryan, Adam Cohen, Jessen O'Brien, and Mary Jo Rhodes, and three anonymous reviewers who have provided an invaluable mix of critical and encouraging feedback on both proposal and completed manuscript. Thanks also to my former colleagues at Askonas Holt Ltd for putting me in touch with various artists with great speed and efficiency; Toby Bennett for his insider's knowledge in contacting various record companies; Wendy Pank, and Mike Ellis (Slipperyfishes) for technical assistance in producing figures and illustrations.

I am particularly grateful to King's College London Archives, for permission to use quotations from the Morrow Collection (ref: K/PP93); and to all those individuals and institutions that have granted permission to reproduce the adverts from early editions of *Early Music* (including BBC Proms Publications; Bernard Thomas of London Pro Musica; John Bryan; National Early Music Centre; MDS (Hire & Copyright) Ltd; Oxford University Press; Anthony Rooley; Schott Music Ltd; Sotheby's; The Early Music Shop; Zuckerman Harpsichords International). Every effort has been made to contact contributors and to provide accurate copyright acknowledgments, and where for any reason my version of events is incorrect, or I have made any omissions, I apologize.

The support of colleagues both at Kingston University and now at the Department for Culture, Media and Creative Industries (CMCI), King's College London, has been crucial to my completing this project. Particular thanks to Harvey Cohen for his encouragement and wise counsel throughout; Andy Pratt and Ros Gill for providing helpful feedback on drafts of the book proposal; all my colleagues at CMCI for ongoing collegial support; Laura Speers and Birgit Wildt for thought-provoking, often challenging conversations under the guise of PhD supervisions; and my former-colleagues at Kingston, especially Mark Hart, John Kitching, David Stokes, Martha Mador, Catherine Gurling, Rob Blackburn, Miguel Imas, and Pam Kiernan.

I am, of course, extraordinarily lucky to have so many friends, family, and supporters cheering me on from the touchline (too many to mention individually here). They have been very generous in giving me a "space to play" with my ideas, which has sometimes meant that I turned down invitations, parties, holidays, table tennis (sorry, Matthew), and doing the washing-up. Heartfelt thanks to my mother Jane Wilson for, amongst so much else, being the first to read and comment on the completed draft; my father Philip Wilson, who I like to think would have been very proud; Alison Hall, Richard Wilson, and Sarah Wilson for always "being there" for me (a special note of thanks to Richard for his detailed and very knowledgeable review and feedback on final drafts); Jennifer Barnes, Sam Wilson, Clara Wilson, Nigel Hall, Emma Hall, and Benjamin Hall, who provided photographic inspiration for an early mock-up of the cover; Ben Parry, Kathryn Parry, Mark Allan, Sara Byers, Gareth Hancock, Mark Le Brocq, who over the years have shared my enchantment with music; Christopher Shackle for always encouraging, hugely informed, and characteristically sage advice; Shahrukh Shackle, Emma Shackle, and all those who have had to put up with me talking about "the book" for so long. Finally, a huge thanks to my wonderful, loving, and long-suffering family: Mary, Flo, and Jake Wilson. I really could not have done this without you.

Nick Wilson (May 2013)
Kingston upon Thames

THE ART OF RE-ENCHANTMENT

PART ONE
Making Early Music

Mountain peaks do not float unsupported; they do not even just rest upon the earth.
They are the earth in one of its manifest operations.
JOHN DEWEY[1]

What we think...or what we believe is, in the end, of little consequence. The only consequence is what we do.
JOHN RUSKIN[2]

1

Introduction

INTRODUCING EARLY MUSIC

"Once upon a time, in a land far, far away..."

It is a truly remarkable thing to be able to perform and listen to music composed hundreds of years ago. It is perhaps yet more remarkable that we should continue to want to. Our world is a very different one to that of our musical forebears they did indeed "do things differently there."[3] But, as the ethnomusicologist John Blacking observed, "music that was exciting to the contemporaries of Mozart and Beethoven is still exciting, although we do not share their culture."[4] Despite being written off by many as peripheral to society's needs, "old" music steadfastly finds its place in the modern age, not as some long-since dead museum piece, but as an altogether living art. We continue to be moved and enchanted, whether attending live concerts or listening to recordings. Music, it seems, has the capacity to transcend time and culture.

This book is about our ongoing transformational relationship with the music of the past, and specifically with what has come to be known as "early music." The term covers a variety of interests, but at its core is a deliberate attempt to recreate the sounds of an original performance for music of earlier times. During the 1950s and '60s early music denoted music primarily of the Medieval and Renaissance periods, and usually no later than 1640.[5] By the early 1970s it referred to music composed in the Baroque era or earlier.[6] By the early 1980s, however, early music performances of works by Mozart, Haydn, Beethoven, and other Classical or early Romantic composers were increasingly frequent. In practice, early music now can take in almost any music written up to the 20th century where a historically appropriate style of performance is reconstructed on the basis of surviving instruments, treatises, and other evidence. But "early music" has also become shorthand for a particular approach to the performance of classical music, where its "interpretative tradition"[7] has been interrupted or lost. Here, the question of "authenticity," relating principally to the composer's intentions, as well as the performance conventions of the day, assumes a primary significance. Those involved in championing this approach have frequently been referred to as pioneers of the early music "movement" (Early Music). Their activities, involving "authentic performances" on "original instruments," played in a "period style" have now become more widely labeled as "historically informed performance" practice, or HIP for short.[8]

Above all else, this book is testament to a group of people who not only saw the possibility of an alternative approach to making classical music (and this in itself is a remarkable starting point), but who went on to make it happen. For most of us, bringing about a substantive change is something we might talk about, dream about, but usually spend most of our time just moaning about. Few actually get round to doing anything. We don't think there is any point. We believe that there is no alternative to the status quo, and so tend to give up before even starting. It is easy to see how those interested in the historical performance of older repertoire could have felt just the same. The classical music profession, with its traditions derived extensively from ideas, beliefs, and practices developed during the 19th century, had become somewhat stuck, and performance innovations were few and far between. Early Music faced the challenge of seeking to overturn not just the cultural status quo, but the commercial one to boot. In contrast to the bygone age of patronage, courtly music, and sacred ritual, when much of the early music was written, making Early Music in the modern age has required competing with other musicians in an unforgiving market context for work. Early music has been repackaged, marketed, and commodified. To survive, professional early musicians have had to ensure that their market offering was more attractive than that of their competitors. Their very livelihoods depended upon it.

It is no hyperbole to claim that Early Music has been the most important and far-reaching cultural development to influence the classical music profession in modern times. In bringing its influence to bear, however, it has divided opinions. Like with the "Marmite effect," there are those who love it and those who can't stand it. The latter group sees early music performers as a bunch of "beardy weirdy"…"cranky, tree-hugging bed-wetters."[9] Over the years, there has been little love lost between some professional classical musicians and specialist historically informed performers (early musicians). Early Music has provoked strong reactions, fostered deep resentments, and spawned controversy, whilst at the same time capturing hearts and beguiling audiences, performers, instrument-makers, and critics alike. For some, the very idea of Early Music is no more than art "memorialized in a melancholy recollection of past artistic periods,"[10] a deeper manifestation of classical music's "celebration of the 'sacred history' of the Western middle classes."[11] For Lindholm (2008) Early Music's success has been attributable to the fact that it "meets the yearnings of the shrinking classical music audience, which maintains a defensive moral posture of unswerving loyalty to the standards of the past."[12] He suggests that Early Music's approach to authentic performance will continue to be challenged by "musicians who want to assert their own genius, and believe they know the music in their hearts, not in their heads."[13]

This brings me to a central theme of the book, which is about overcoming separation. Most obviously, Early Music has required surmounting the temporal and spatial boundaries that detach us from our past. The challenges of "knowing" just how 17th-century composers would have heard their works performed, let alone whether this conformed with their "intentions," for example, are far from insubstantial. As we shall explore, the process of making early music in the modern age has required those involved (often unknowingly) to overcome separation at a deeply personal level, reconciling different "parts" of themselves that usually get treated as wholly separate domains, such as their musicianship, scholarship, craftsmanship, management, leadership, cultural entrepreneurship, and all that which constitutes "professional" as opposed to "amateur" music-making. In this process of integrating head and heart, what is revealed is a deeper truth about human *being*. For all of us are every day involved in reconciling opposites that, in strict logic, are irreconcilable. Writing in 1973 the British economist E. F. Schumacher observed how "In macro-economics (the management of whole societies) it is necessary always to have both planning and freedom," whilst "in microeconomics (the management of individual enterprises)…it is essential that there should be full managerial responsibility and authority," whilst also being "a democratic and free participation of the workers in management decisions."[14] We need not look too hard to find this contradictory nature of the economy mirrored in our cultural life (culture and the economy are, after all, embedded in each other). Classical musicians, for example, are daily faced with a profound dilemma. On the one hand, they are required to *re*-create musical works, maintaining faithfulness to their musical heritage, and performing in line with deeply held traditions and guild-like standards of quality. On the other hand, they are expected to create something different and distinctive with each and every performance, always having something new to say. The ability to transcend these two apparently competing positions is a basic requirement of the classical music profession. However, for many of those opposed to Early Music, this tension has been perceived as a potentially catastrophic fault-line—the incitement for head to rule over heart, and for mere academic scholarship or dogma to hold sway over the "authentic" musical concerns of all involved.[15] For others, and I will argue this includes the vast majority of those I have met and interviewed in the course of putting together this book, it is the root and cause of that which keeps classical music alive. It is the spark that reignites classical music, or to borrow a turn of phrase from Martha Graham, "a blessed unrest that keeps us marching and makes us more alive than the others."[16] It is the constant wrestle between being and becoming, the possibility of re-enchantment every time the performer steps out onto the stage to perform a musical work.

THREE MAIN AIMS

The book has three main aims. The first of these is to document the cultural history of the early music movement in Britain from 1960 onward. Simply put, this looks at what happened when, and who was involved. Although interest in matters of historical performance has motivated a wide variety of early music activities at least as far back as the 18th century,[17] the scale and scope of what took place in the latter half of the 20th century is of a different order to anything that had gone before. The story of Early Music tells of a remarkable journey. It starts with a small group of musicians championing the right to perform classical music in an altogether different way to the mainstream, and ends, in the present, with the principles and practices of HIP all but universally accepted as a performance norm, with historical performance courses and specialist teachers at all the major music colleges, and with early music recordings and broadcasts widely available in Britain and across the world.

The second aim is to explain just *how* Early Music provided an alternative to the classical music mainstream. This involves unearthing the many day-to-day practical challenges and inherent tensions involved, and considering how these were overcome, both at an individual and collective level. What is most striking about this inquiry is how it brings our attention to the variety of human practices involved, extending well beyond the purely musical or performance-based discussions, which dominate existing literature on early music performance. Where others might focus exclusively on the music itself, the history of early music performance, or the debates and issues that characterize "authenticity" as it is realized in performance,[18] here we examine the phenomenon of Early Music as a set of positioned practices. This requires an interdisciplinary study of causality and a particular concern in seeing the bigger "joined up" picture, including explaining how those involved made their living from early music, how they made it work, and how they made it pay. In the process, attention is brought to the confluence of cultural entrepreneurship, developments in recording technology, instrument manufacture, publishing technology, and the readiness of the market, together with the particular musical and aesthetic motivations, talents, and actions of a small group of musicians when given an opportunity to "play," as just some of the conditions for the development of a demonstrably successful artistic and commercial industry.

The third aim of the book is even broader and more ambitious in scope; for building on our emergent understanding of Early Music, I seek to cast fresh light on the entirely pivotal relationship between "doing art" and "being authentic" in a world where the intrinsic meaning and value of art is all too readily overlooked. To state my purpose more boldly, what is envisaged here is nothing short of a reappraisal of the underlying value of *art* and *authenticity* in contemporary life; a call to arms, if you like, to re-energize public conversation and debate concerning the central importance of these aspects of human practice in all walks of life, not just in the context of (high) cultural production.

This book's explicit focus on "re-enchantment" responds to the pervasive level of "disenchantment,"[19] disconnection, division, and split (hence *in*-authenticity) that characterizes the world we live in, and so, too, the context within which we make early music in the modern age. The root cause of much of this separation and alienation can be traced back to the Enlightenment—a cultural movement that has had an extraordinary and unquestionably beneficial impact on human life. As David Atkinson notes, "we might say that (in the West at least) the birth of all that is modern science, all that is modern (social) moral and legal practice, and all that is autonomous (modern) art can be seen as stemming from the autonomous logics arising from this great division of thought."[20] The dividing of reality into separate spheres of existence—instrumental, moral and aesthetic—is as visible today as it was when Kant penned his three critiques (of *Pure reason, Practical reason,* and *Judgment*) in the final decades of the 18th century. Such is the contemporary dominance of the autonomous logic of rationalism (clearly evident in the political economic practices of neoliberalism), however, that even our societal discourses of art and authenticity have succumbed to a "kind of madness."[21] Under this instrumental logic, art is valued more often than not for its potential to be useful in the market e.g., providing jobs, stimulating regional productivity, contributing to a sense of national self-worth, and so on, rather than for its inherent meaning and value (its enchantment), which of course lie beyond our powers to explain.[22] Equally, rational man has come to distrust the notion of authenticity, believing it to be a rhetorical device employed all too often as a means of justifying vested self-interest. As Steven Poole observed in a recent essay on our culture's obsession with authenticity, "The self-appointed guardians of authenticity...want desperately to believe that they are at the top of the labour pyramid."[23] Furthermore, "the authenticity fetish disguises and renders socially acceptable a raw hunger for hierarchy and power." Such a belief, albeit written more with high-end brands and "artisanal" coffee shops in mind than historical performances of Bach or Handel, would surely not be out of kilter with the views of many of HIP's detractors over the years. But as I will argue in the course of this book, the story of Early Music, with its very particular focus on authentic performance and re-enchanting art, offers us an altogether more positive and emancipatory take on the value of both authenticity and art. Just as we cannot be fully, i.e., authentically, ourselves without allowing space for art in our lives, so we cannot truly bring art into our lives without acting with authenticity. As we shall see, the ongoing, everyday practice of this unfolding dialectic has been (and remains) altogether central to making early music in the modern age.

SEVEN RHETORICS OF EARLY MUSIC

The first, most important task for any social scientific research is to (re-)conceptualize the object of study. A useful starting point is to review what people have had to say about Early Music. This reveals (at least) seven "rhetorics," which offer not just a distinctive take on the historical performance of classical music, but also betray certain vested interests. The term *rhetoric* here denotes "a persuasive discourse, or an implicit narrative, wittingly or unwittingly adopted by members of a particular affiliation to persuade others of the veracity and worthwhileness of their beliefs."[24] These partial abstractions capture the main theories and beliefs that will be probed more deeply over the coming chapters.

Each rhetoric is framed around a dualistic opposition, such as that between "authentic and inauthentic," or "amateur and professional" (see Table 1.1). Such oppositions

TABLE 1.1.

The seven rhetorics of Early Music

No.	Rhetoric	Dualistic opposition
1	Revolutionary	culture vs. counterculture
2	Amateur	amateur vs. professional
3	Commercial	master vs. slave
4	Dogmatic	text vs. act
5	Creative	work vs. play
6	Modernist	disenchanted vs. enchanted
7	Authentic	authentic vs. inauthentic

always involve a lived out power struggle between individuals and groups holding particular, and contradictory, interests. For example, the countercultural objectives of the early music movement were at odds with the cultural mainstream; the motivations of the professional early musician have not always accorded with those of the amateur; and the views of the historical musicologist as to how a particular musical work *should* be authentically performed have not always sat comfortably with the commercial concerns of the specialist early music record label.

(1) Revolutionary

Early Music has been nothing if not revolutionary. "In the 1960s, it is doubtful whether a movement could have had credibility if it did not have an element of protest and revolution about it. A mainspring of HIP in the 1960s was a rejection of the status quo."[25] With this observation, Bruce Haynes accurately captures Early Music's links to the so-called "postmodern turn." In line with other new social movements (NSMs) of the time, such as the feminist and gay rights movements, Early Music provided a voice for the identity-less (early music composers and modern-day professional performers overshadowed by the veneration of "stars"), and sought to counter the alienation of the market. Sir John Eliot Gardiner, founder of the Monteverdi Choir and Orchestra, describes himself as "a member of a generation that has pioneered, and has in a way traversed musical terrain that no previous generations have done."[26] He goes on to say, "it has been a radical, epoch-changing moment in cultural history." Sir Nicholas Kenyon (formerly editor of *Early Music,* controller of BBC Radio 3, director of the Proms, and currently managing director of the Barbican) agrees: "it was genuinely revolutionary, in the sense that it caused a radical step change; that is certainly what it brought about in orchestral practice."[27]

Classical music is founded upon a set of composed musical works (the canon), which over time have become sanctified as timeless things of beauty—worthy of their place in the "imaginary museum of musical works."[28] Before HIP, conventions governing how one should perform these pieces were almost as strict as the harmonic rules that first came to delineate the tonal "work" from about 1600 onward. The foundation of classical music is harmony, meaning "agreement of feeling, or concord." The ability to work *with,* as opposed to *against,* is, of course, epitomized in our perception of the 19th-century symphonic orchestra—a group of skilled practitioners working together to produce the apogee of classical music. So, too, the way we learn to perform classical music has been based on a system that "conserves" culture in music conservatories. There are heavily prescribed ways of playing instruments, in accordance with stylistic norms that have come down to us through the route of teacher-pupil instruction. Individualized tuition remains at the very heart of music colleges today.[29] The circumstances in which we consume classical music are also based on a conservative model of reception—the 19th-century adoption of concert halls; the maintenance of canonic repertoire; the adulation of performers and composers as "maestros," "divas," and "superstars." Despite popularizing trends, such as the radio station Classic FM and cross-over charts, classical music in Britain is still regarded as the epitome of high art or high culture, as elitist, for the gray-haired rather than the young. Confronting such entrenched perceptions and their underlying power relations, as Early Music was bound to do, represented a major challenge, to say the least. And yet, the very act of performing music, whether "new" or "old," is always a revolutionary one. For however true to the composer's supposed intentions one might seek to be, there is always a very human longing to do something different, something new, something revolutionary.

(2) Amateur

One of the most fascinating aspects of the emergence of Early Music in Britain in the 1960s is the role played by the amateur. The classical music mainstream had become deeply entrenched in contemporary society, with classical music "belonging" very much to the professional musician. The increasing dominance of the profession effectively severed traditional ties with everyday music-making. By the late 1960s, something of a gulf had opened up between performing classical music "just for fun" or as part of the ritualized marking of the passing of the seasons, and the serious "business" of classical music concert performance—a gulf that very much remains to this day, despite the temporary in-roads made by amateurs in the early music field.

Though characterized as an ideological movement born out of a scholarly obsession with recreating the past, Early Music appealed to amateur musicians, not least because it offered an exciting "new" world of sound. There was also the possibility of getting close-up and personal with the fascinating instruments that produced these sounds. In the infant years of the early music revival, early really meant "early." A whole array of bizarre Medieval and Renaissance instruments—cornetts, crumhorns, dulcians, nakers, rebecs, regals, sackbuts, and many other "buzzers and whiners" dating at least as far back as the 14th century[30]—suddenly let loose on an otherwise fairly conventional audience, conjuring up altogether "other" times. The sound of a familiar Bach concerto played at baroque pitch on period instruments prior to many of the "original" instruments being mastered was shockingly new. This aural landscape was genuinely exciting for many musicians who had come to feel classical music performance had reached something of a dead end. The performances and subsequent recordings of Medieval, Renaissance, and early Baroque music by the likes of Michael Morrow's Musica Reservata and David Munrow's Early Music Consort of London (founded "to present authentic and uninhibited performances"[31]) in the 1960s were crucial in catalyzing interest in historical performance. But more than this, amateur musicians quickly found themselves being able to "join in," as copies of old instruments became increasingly widely available, through the likes of The Early Music Shop. Before long it was possible for enthusiasts to construct affordable historical instruments from DIY kits, encouraging an even closer allegiance with this form of music-making. Such "early adopters" of early music were central to its subsequent success—forming its audience and fan-base, though ironically also hastening its subsequent professionalization (as discussed in Part II) and associated reduction in terms of repertoire covered (see Part IV). It is striking how little instrumental music from the Middle Ages, for example, now finds its way both into the concert hall and across the airwaves.

It would be wrong to imply that amateur musicians began their love affair with early music only in the 1960s. There had been considerable interest in previous decades, not least because music-making in general was much more commonplace in the domestic context. Looking back to the first decades of the 20th century, the extraordinary, pioneering work of Arnold Dolmetsch as performer, instrument-maker, and scholar is nonetheless characterized as "amateurish." Dolmetsch's work was met with "the patronising indifference of the majority of the music profession."[32] He was surrounded by largely amateur musicians and musical instrument-makers at his Haslemere workshop, but what they were doing was regarded by many as just too specialized for its time, too cut off from the professional music mainstream.[33] The word "amateur" is strongly divisive. Whilst etymology reminds us that its meaning is derived from having a love of something (*amator*—"lover"), there is an enduring connotation of enthusiasm matched by lack of technical proficiency. Amateurs are often contrasted with professionals not just because the latter earn money from their work, but because they are skilled and have reached a level that the former can only dream of. The unfolding story of Early Music warns us against jumping to any such simplistic conclusions.

(3) Commercial

Whatever the artistic merits of authentic or historically informed performance, there is no denying that Early Music proved itself very successful in business and financial terms, as well as being a major influence on the way we perform classical music. By the mid-1980s "a huge industry connected to the revival of early music and HIP was blossoming."[34] Those involved in the 1980s and '90s were part of a "golden age" of lucrative performances and multiple series of recordings. In seeking to account for this commercial success we need to unravel the link between this specific form of cultural production in which the economy is ostensibly disavowed,[35] i.e., where making classical music and making money are considered practices to be largely kept apart, and yet where the forces of capitalism (a system in which money chases more money) profoundly influences and, to some extent, molds the everyday practices and thinking of classical musicians.

The primary opposition exposed by this "commercial" rhetoric is that between culture (art) and the market (commerce). The perceived division between art and commerce mirrors the division of labor within the classical music profession. At one end of the spectrum we find the performers and instrument-makers cast as intrinsically motivated musicians and craftsmen, guided by lofty ideals and worthy interests. At the other end are the managers and promoters, agents, and distributers, whose concern for the bottom line is characterized in terms of extrinsic motivation and the promise of monetary reward. The relationship between these two groups is dictated by power: managers ("masters") wield power *over* artists ("slaves").[36] It is easy to see how the logic of this rhetoric quickly leads to the conclusion that Early Music was really about the music industry exploiting early musicians, as a way of selling more records.

The analysis in this book paints something of a different picture, however, not least by recasting some of Early Music's pioneers, including both musicians and those working for commercially motivated promoters and record companies, in the guise of cultural entrepreneurs.[37] Crucially, such individuals proved themselves to be adept at communicating their message, persuading others in the industry to come around to their way of thinking about early music performance.[38] However, they also remained true to their primary and overriding desire to share with others this music's capacity to entertain, enlighten, and enchant.

(4) Dogmatic

For those critical of Early Music, its dependence on scholarship and textual research has been construed as an overreliance on knowledge at the expense of other essentials of musical performance. As I discuss in Chapter 3, the principal voice in this respect has been that of Richard Taruskin, himself a musician, period performer, and musicologist. His book *Text & Act* (1995), which is a collection of previously published essays, explores many of the challenges and contradictions that lie at the heart of Early Music's pursuit of authentic and historically informed performance. Taruskin was not the first to draw attention to the "utopian" nature of authenticity in musical performance. Leading musicologists and musicians on the Continent had written on the subject of being faithful to the musical work ("werktreue") at least as far back as the 1950s and '60s (e.g., Adorno, 1967a [1951]; Fischer, 1957; Wiora, 1967).[39] Finding the right balance between scholarship and performance is clearly a central issue, as indicated in this quotation by Nicholas Kenyon, from a birthday tribute to the Academy of Ancient Music's founder, Christopher Hogwood:[40]

> The bringing together of scholarship and performance is something that absolutely lies at the heart of what you would call the early music revival, because

it has needed people who were scholars in their own right; but there were very few people who have it in the right balance... that balance between being a performer who can bring music to life at the moment when it happens... and the scholar, in a thoughtful and reflective way, to decide what is the best way to perform something.

The primary problem with Early Music according to the rhetoric discussed here is that it is prescriptive and rule-bound. Detractors would say that Early Music was overly dogmatic, leaving little space for the performer to respond to the music itself. The "scholar-performer" is parodied as someone more interested in preserving the past according to rules laid down in a dusty old treatise than in bringing a long-forgotten piece of music back to life. "All this music-making by the book is a bit pitiful... for all I know their players may take a pinch of snuff during the pauses before the last chords."[41] Such a dismissive position is compounded yet further for its critics given the belief that the dogma on which performance practices are modeled is itself flawed.

(5) Creative

It is highly characteristic of Early Music that whilst some espoused the dogmatic rhetoric, accusing early musicians of being too rule-bound, others regarded their activities as in some way overly creative.[42] Far from performing according to the rigorous scholarship of historical musicology, they were, in fact, just "making it up." Certainly, there is ample evidence to suggest that those involved in performing early music were indeed "inventing," or re-creating historical performance practices. Daniel Leech-Wilkinson has convincingly argued that much of the scholarship on which performance of Medieval music was based, was in fact the product of personal ideology, musical taste, and the persuasive personalities of scholars involved.[43] The conductor and founder of the Academy of Ancient Music, Christopher Hogwood, discussing his motivation to move away from the sort of repertoire performed by the Early Music Consort of London toward later music of the 17th and 18th centuries, notes "Although the whole world thought that this type of music-making had a musicological foundation, the very opposite was the case: we had to do a lot on 'feeling', because there was insufficient basis and definite proof of the way in which music was made in the middle ages."[44] Elsewhere, as the performer and academic John Potter candidly observes, "The fact is, we all made it up."[45] The big question, of course, is just how much license *should* authentic performers have to be creative?

Creativity has been defined as "the ability to produce work that is both novel (i.e., original, unexpected) and appropriate (i.e., useful, adaptive concerning task constraints)."[46] Straightaway we see the paradox of referring to Early Music, a movement concerned with the recreation of the "old," as creative, i.e., giving rise to the "new." What is highlighted here is the sense in which creativity is very much a boundary phenomenon,[47] flourishing at the edges of things and in-between spaces—between old and new, authentic and inauthentic, amateur and professional, and so on. Given the particular focus on the teleological nature of professional music-making, where there is the goal of earning a living (making early music *pay*), it is helpful here to highlight the dualistic opposition between work and play. Early musicians, in common with artists in general, do not work 9am to 5pm. Much of their "work" (rehearsal and practice, learning of new instruments, reading of treatises, listening to recordings, and so on) happens in their "free-time." Here we are reminded of the vocational nature of professional work; indeed, all music-making is rooted in an amateur, i.e., domestic, embedded, and integrated context, pursued for the love of it. Crucially for our understanding of Early Music, the creative rhetoric reminds us that this was a project born of imagination as much as evidence. Those involved had to hold a "play space" open, where it would be possible to experiment, to play with a creative approach to the performance of classical music; a means of providing an alternative; a way of *making* it work and pay.

(6) Modernist

Though the subject of modernity (not to be confused with modernism) has courted much controversy (not the least of which has been over when exactly it started, and whether or not we are still in it), my use of the term "in the modern age" in the book's subtitle denotes the post-Enlightenment world that has come to be dominated by the economic system of capitalism. For Max Weber (1905) the key concept that defined this modernity was what he termed "the disenchantment of the world."[48] Two aspects can be highlighted: "secularization and the decline of magic," on the one hand, and "the increasing scale, scope, and power of the formal means-ends rationalities of science, bureaucracy, the law, and policy-making" on the other.[49] Given this background and what has been said already about Early Music from the dogmatic rhetoric's perspective, it is not difficult to understand why Adorno, amongst others, regarded the early music movement as "part of a wider cultural malaise in the wake of the depersonalising forces of industrialism and late capitalism."[50] As Morgan, writing in the late 1980s, expressed it, "Concern for historical authenticity represents an unmistakable symptom of the present situation of our musical culture, a situation characterized by an extraordinary degree of insecurity."[51] The "modernist" rhetoric reverberates with this reflexive anxiety, as attention is cast on the "authentic self" in musical performance, coupled with a characteristically *in*-authentic context for such activity.

From the early 1980s onward Early Music found itself facing a rising tide of critique, culminating in several articles by Richard Taruskin. The crux of Taruskin's argument was that "Historically authentic practices... embodied a whole wish list of modern(ist) values, validated in the academy and the marketplace alike by an eclectic, opportunistic reading of historical evidence."[52] According to this rhetoric Early Music was doing something altogether "new" under the label "old," a form of "modernism in disguise" as John Butt puts it.[53] For Lindholm, "novelty is twinned with the recognizable and traditional, so that audiences can hear something new while convincing themselves that they are listening to something old."[54] This modernist charge was problematic for Early Music protagonists on at least two levels. Firstly, there was more than a hint of moral outrage, the implication being that early music performers were hoodwinking the audience, cheating them even. The best that could be said for Early Music, falling short of downright subterfuge, was that those involved were acting hypocritically. Secondly, the equally damning alternative view suggested that those involved were unaware that this was what they were doing. Here the charge was one of naiveté, reinforcing the notion of the early musician as an inept enthusiast, rather than practiced professional. Whichever interpretation was favored, the modernist rhetoric drew attention to the fact that Early Music was not what it said it was.

(7) Authentic

Finally we come to the most central of the rhetorics of Early Music—that of authenticity and authentic performance. Over and above the heated debates concerning the veracity of authenticity claims themselves, it is the implied criticism of mainstream classical music performers that counts for much of the vitriol and ire that has been leveled at Early Music over the years. For its detractors, Early Music has been anything but authentic. In itself, this is bad enough. But what has been even more difficult to bear for many classical musicians is just what it has meant for their own music-making; for it was *their* authenticity as musicians that appeared to be coming most under threat. In effect, the "authenticity movement" waged a two-pronged assault on the authenticity of the classical musician. The first line of attack was the very idea that musicians' behaviors and practices should be governed by "dogmatic" performance guidelines. As Raymond Leppard warned, "to put performances therefore into rigid, factual straitjackets is fatal."[55] The second assault on the classical musician's authenticity came in the form of a no less insidious enslavement—here replacing the musical score as "master" with the market. Early musicians' "authentic practices" were compromised on a variety of levels just by the process of "working." Firstly, performing "authentically" when those involved were being paid for it, rankled, to say the least. It is easy to see why some would no doubt have preferred Early Music to remain strictly an amateur affair. Secondly, there has been frequent allusion to the idea that the rhetoric of authenticity was no more than a tool, a marketing ruse to sell records. As Haynes commented, "there was a time when 'AUTHENTIC' sold records like 'ORGANIC' sells tomatoes."[56] Furthermore, "if they were described as 'authentic' when they were really 'an attempt to be authentic', it seemed like quibbling." Thirdly, what really angered many of those working in the classical musical establishment in the 1970s and '80s, was when professional period instrument orchestras and ensembles were engaged to perform concerts in leading venues and festivals, at their expense. In the early days of the revival, insult was added to injury when players who, even by their own admission, were not yet technically competent on their instruments, were amongst those being hired for HIP concerts. Learning to play "old" instruments with different bowings, fingerings, embouchures, and so on could not happen overnight. This was a battlefield of ideas being played out in the very real, highly competitive world of professional classical music-making.

In more recent years, since the critique spearheaded by Taruskin, there has been a marked retreat from using "authenticity" as a legitimizing discourse for Early Music. "Gone forever is the favorite slogan: 'First recording in the original version!'"[57] To some extent this mirrors the wider philosophical trajectory of the times. The prevailing postmodern sentiment is scornful of any view that seems to claim the "one true way." As Raymond Leppard wrote in 1988, "There can be no reason why, for example, a Haydn opera composed for Esterhazy should not be performed in a much larger modern theatre. But to insist in such surroundings on the tiny band that Haydn used may so diminish its effect as to cause the venture to fail."[58] The rhetoric of "authenticity" has largely given way to that of "HIP." As Fabian observes, "Nowadays it is more customary to speak of 'historically informed performances' and avoid any reference to authenticity."[59] An important question remains as to whether this has resulted in our understanding of authentic performance as a real embodied practice, being compromised by our theories of what we can (or more accurately, can't) *know* about it.

A CRITICAL REALIST INTERVENTION

Useful as these rhetorics are in helping to define a movement, they can only provide at best a partial account. We need to move beyond discourse[60] and clarify the underlying causal mechanisms that explain how the movement emerged. This requires adopting an approach that can explain a social world comprised of different things (people, institutions, rhetorics, and so on) and undergoing a continuous process of change. Critical realism is ideally suited to the task.

Central to critical realist philosophy is the belief that the world exists independently of us and our investigations of it.[61] Things and processes exist in the world "independently of their identification by human beings."[62] This philosophical position is clearly significant for what it tells us about the existence of musical works and our knowledge of them, as well as how they change over time through the process of repeated performance and discussion. A key aspect of my approach is the primacy afforded to the level of human practice. John Ruskin's words at the opening of this chapter remind us about the consequence of what we *do*, over and above what we think or believe. The musical work is theorized not as merely a socially constructed entity, a concept that gained currency at a particular time in history,[63] but as a phenomenon that is reproduced and transformed through the situated actions and practices of musicians, instrument-makers, musicologists, promoters, publishers, broadcasters, record company executives, teachers, audiences, and critics, with real causal impact on all those immediately involved, as well as on subsequent generations. This, as I will argue, has an important bearing on our understanding of authentic performance.

Critical realist applied research also encourages the researcher to seek explanation in terms of the widest possible set of explanatory and causal factors. We can explain a given phenomenon in terms of a multiplicity of mechanisms "potentially of radically different kinds...corresponding to different levels or aspects of reality."[64] My own explanation of Early Music is cast in terms of a potentially wide and complex set of causal mechanisms, which are not restricted to the performance realm alone. Crucially, music-making must be conceptualized in such a way that aspects of cultural production, consumption, and distribution are explored without stripping out the central protagonist—music itself.[65] A key feature of this book is that it encourages us to take more seriously that part of our lives, which we get in touch with inter alia, through the experience of performing and/or listening to music, but which otherwise remains beyond our powers of rationalization to explain in full. The mysterious, the ineffable, the spiritual, the enchanted—these are ubiquitous aspects of human being, yet for reasons already touched on they do not feature in many of our attempts to explain the world as we experience it. Later phases of critical realism, i.e., dialectical critical realism[66] and meta-Reality,[67] offer the philosophical tools that can at least begin to help us bridge this gap, drawing on the argument for the nondual nature of the "truth of reality."[68] Whilst it is beyond a book such as this to engage more directly and comprehensively with such philosophical argument, it is important, nonetheless, to acknowledge the meta-theoretical foundations on which this discussion of "re-enchantment" is built. My aim in what follows, therefore, is to be maximally inclusive—not just for the sake of it, or to call myself a critical realist, but rather because I believe this is quite simply the best way to achieve a better understanding of the complex and multilayered phenomenon that is Early Music.

THE STRUCTURE OF THE BOOK

In keeping with the book's call for overcoming separation, the intention throughout is to provide a "joined up" as well as maximally inclusive account of Early Music. Nonetheless, it has proved useful to structure the book's overall message by thinking in "parts." The book divides simply into four parts, each comprising three chapters, focusing on a different facet of "making early music in the modern age."

Part I, "Making Early Music," provides an introduction to the book's main themes, debates, and characters. There is a mix of theoretical, historical, and descriptive content, forming the foundation for later in-depth analysis. Chapter 2 is an overview of the life course of early music's revival, loosely following the developmental logic of what I refer to as the "Seven Ages of Early Music." We are introduced to the key players, and the dimensions of Early Music as it has unfolded over the last 40 years or so. Chapter 3, "Transcending Text & Act?" responds directly to Taruskin's critique of Early Music, revisiting key concepts, including the musical work, and werktreue. This is important for putting forward a foundational justification of Early Music's interest in authentic performance, which I describe in terms of "dispositional (historical) authenticity."[69] The emphasis here is on determining the *possible* conditions of performance at the time a musical work was composed, rather than seeking slavishly to recreate any particular aspect of an historical event. Building on Taruskin's observations, the chapter also prepares the ground for later discussion of authenticity as a core human capability.

In Part Two, the emphasis shifts to consider the professionalization of early music performance. Here the concern is with "Making Early Wusic *Work*." Of course, the very idea of making music "work" will be anathema to many. Work, after all, is something most of us have to do, not something we choose to do. And yet, behind every historical performance, every Urtext edition, each carefully crafted musical instrument, lie hours and hours of work. As all musicians, performers, artisans, and artists know, either intuitively or through bitter experience, it is only after countless hours of committed work that what appears to be spontaneous right action happens at all. Chapter 4, "A Tale of Two Authenticities," introduces an important distinction between what is termed Authenticity$_1$, i.e., a focus on historical performances of Medieval, Renaissance, and early Baroque repertoire, and Authenticity$_2$, relating to the performance of Baroque, Classical, and later musical styles. Chapter 5 examines key aspects of the early musician labor market, and brings the development of Early Music up to the launch of the Orchestra of the Age of Enlightenment in 1986. Chapter 6 refocuses attention toward other professionals at the heart of the early music movement—the editors, publishers, and instrument-makers, whose "hands-on" work has been critical, but often rather less obvious, to Early Music's success.

As much as the early music revival is about the music, the instruments, the authentic performance practice(s), and the people involved, it is also a remarkable case of new economic activity in the cultural sector. Early Music has made a sizeable contribution to the British cultural economy, created jobs, paid for mortgages, given a decent standard of living for many, and provided an additional source of income for many more. The three chapters comprising Part III, "Making Early Music *Pay*," constitute a causal explanation of this emergent story of artistic and commercial innovation and cultural entrepreneurship. The market for early music was created and sustained through the actions of particular individuals, endowed with certain skills, attributes, and behaviors, working under particular conditions. "Making" in this context refers to a range of practices including but not limited to steering, negotiating, persuading, dealing, acting, and performing. This part of the book explains this from within a theoretical perspective that can take account of the transformational and emergent nature of social reality. Chapter 7, "Spinning Out Early Music," considers the role of three knowledge-producing institutions—universities, music colleges, and the Arts Council. Chapter 8 looks at the role of the BBC and of commercial record companies through the lens of three "world views" in music (*art, folk,* and *commercial*). We are challenged to think again about a more joined up view of these often quite separate discourses of value in music. In Chapter 9, "Everything to Play For," the role of Early Music's musical directors as cultural entrepreneurs, leaders, managers, and employers is explored. This analysis is guided primarily by (cultural) entrepreneurship theory, with some reflections from the literature on "play" offering an alternative take on the distinctive individual character of their early music activities.

The final part of the book, "Making Early Music *in the Modern Age*," brings the Early Music story up to the present day with a "balance sheet" of the movement's achievements and a discussion of the "mainstreaming" of historically informed performance

(Chapter 10). The last two chapters then turn more directly to the third of my over-arching aims, as I raise issues relating to the role of art and authenticity in our lives today. The focus in Chapter 11 is on authenticity *in the modern age*. Here, I highlight a range of false beliefs (so-called "TINA formations") that have their source in the capitalist mode of production, and which in the eyes of its critics at least, have rendered Early Music an otherwise "in-authentic" project. The chapter explores the deeply embedded challenges of making early music in spite of the "disenchantment of the world." It is striking to note the general level of disinterest in disenchantment's "other," i.e., enchantment; and yet, contrary to general opinion, the pre-modern concepts of enchantment and magic continue to play a fundamental, albeit hidden, part in our lives. The book's final chapter seeks to bring the many strands of this analysis together around "the art of re-enchantment." Early Music is explained as a process of re-enchanting classical music, and in so doing reveals further clues as to why the movement took off when it did. Turning then to the wider context of (doing) art, attention is drawn to the need for reconnection—with nature, knowledge, cultural entrepreneurship, capitalism, and authenticity. Most crucially, "making early music in the modern age" shows us that it is only through developing our transformational capability to reconcile the apparently contradictory, whether this is old vs. new; amateur vs. professional; art vs. science; culture vs. commerce; or head vs. heart, that we will really find authenticity. Our universal challenge as artful human beings can then be expressed in the form of an intriguing paradox: we need to allow space for (doing) art in our lives in order to become fully, i.e., authentically, ourselves; but equally, we need to be prepared to act with authenticity if we are indeed to bring art more fully into our lives. Learning to live this unfolding dialectic is the art of re-enchantment.

> All the world's a stage,
> And all the men and women merely players:
> They have their exits and their entrances
> And one man in his time plays many parts,
> His acts being seven ages.
> WILLIAM SHAKESPEARE *As You Like It*[1]

2

Seven Ages of Early Music

INTRODUCTION

Credit for familiarizing the term "early music" in British musical culture, along with much else besides, must go to the charismatic musician, musicologist, and radio presenter David Munrow. In choosing, in 1967, the Early Music Consort of London as the name for his newly-formed specialist period performance group, and coincidentally having a hand in the naming of the Early Music Shop launched a year later, Munrow had effectively hit upon a workable Anglicization of "Alte Musik," which already held considerable currency in Germany and other European countries.[2] By the early 1970s the historical performance gauntlet had been thrown down, forcing the classical music establishment in Britain, as elsewhere, to question much that it had otherwise simply taken for granted.

There are clear grounds for beginning this study of Early Music in the latter part of the 20th century; but, of course, this is a story that can be tracked back considerably further. As Howard Mayer Brown observes, there is evidence of musicians in the late Middle Ages copying out troubadour songs from original manuscripts composed years earlier.[3] The historical musicologist Friedrich Blume argued that the early music movement really stemmed from the Bach revival, sparked off by Mendelssohn's 1829 performance of the *St. Matthew Passion*.[4] Three years later, François-Joseph Fétis held his influential series of "historical concerts" at the Paris Conservatoire. Writing in 1983, Laurence Dreyfus describes the cultural phenomenon of Early Music as a late 20th-century ensemble of social practices relating to the performance of older repertories of Western classical music. Elizabeth Roche (1989) criticizes Harry Haskell's (1988) history of *The Early Music Revival* for being "too simplistic" in suggesting that "everything that has happened in this field within the last 150-plus years can be seen as part of a definable 'early music movement.'"[5] Whether Early Music is seen to embrace a long tradition of historically informed performance practice or is exclusively related to a more modern-day commercial phenomenon divides opinion. Nonetheless, as a cultural movement offering an alternative to mainstream classical music performance, Early Music unquestionably gained a particular prominence and foothold in the market from the 1960s onward, and in terms of its impact this was of a qualitatively different order to anything that had gone before.

Interest in authenticity (understood broadly as the extent to which a performance faithfully recreates—or tries to re-create—the music as the composer would have intended it) has tended to surface as a reaction to the prevailing musical currents of the day. Alte Musik in early 20th-century Germany, for example, denoted a rejection of the "overheated emotionalism of the age of romanticism and the increasing secularism of the age."[6] The musicologist and conductor Paul Sacher established a chamber orchestra in 1926 in Basle specifically to explore and perform pre-classical[7] and modern repertories, such was his antipathy toward 19th-century music. He followed this up seven years later by opening the Schola Cantorum Basiliensis—the first institution to develop a formal curriculum for training musicians in older performance techniques.[8] After the Second World War, whereas early music in Germany, Switzerland, and Austria was chiefly the province of amateurs and academics, Paris became home to the "first great virtuoso" to specialize in the music of the 17th and 18th centuries—the Polish-born harpsichordist, Wanda Landowska.[9]

In Britain, the roots of the early music movement are most usually traced back to the influential activities of Arnold Dolmetsch (1858-1940), who made his own instruments, introduced the recorder to the UK, and performed works by early composers on the instruments for which they were written.[10] As Howard Mayer Brown notes, "it was Arnold Dolmetsch more than anyone else who was committed to the idea that performers should try to play music in the way its composers intended. He, more than anyone else, is the founding father of the 'cult of authenticity.'"[11] However, despite Dolmetsch's relative successes, he remained a somewhat isolated figure within the musical life of his times. Something of a maverick, he was admired by many but regarded as an outsider by the classical music establishment. The sense in which Dolmetsch had to fight against the status quo is powerfully relayed by Robert Donington, himself one of Dolmetsch's most illustrious pupils:[12]

> What many thousands of active musicians across the world now take for granted had to be conceived with rare vision and fought for with rare tenacity when Arnold Dolmetsch embarked on his half-century of uncompromising crusading, way back in the 1880s... [N]ow the world of music is so resonant with the results of it that not one enthusiast in a thousand knows that it all pretty much began, as such movements must, in a single man's visionary initiative.

Donington's praise for Dolmetsch attributes causality to the actions and "visionary initiative" of this pioneering individual, rather than any more general societal or structural change. This is an attractive proposition, and certainly Dolmetsch's contribution to early music, especially in Britain, should not be underestimated. The fact remains, however, that the modern-day revival of early music did not "take off" for at least another 20 years after Dolmetsch's death.

In the years prior to the Second World War increasing numbers of musicians became interested in the "problems" of performing early music. Brown describes them as having "an open, eager, and perhaps slightly naïve attitude towards questions of authenticity."[13] Though halted by the War, the activities of musicians, particularly in England, America, and the Netherlands, picked up again quickly. Performer-musicologists like Edward Dent, Boris Ord, and later, Thurston Dart at Cambridge as well as Jack Westrup at Oxford had considerable influence on generations of students. In America, the activities of two men in particular (Paul Hindemith and Noah Greenberg) represented the forefront of early music performance. Another American, Thomas Binkley, established the "Studio Der Frühen Musik" in Munich in 1959. Further significant developments in Germany included the growth of the Moëck Verlag und Musikinstrumentenwerk, which had been founded in 1925 as a center for making recorders and many other historical wind instruments; the influential (nonperiod) groups such as the Münchener Bach-Chor (1954) and the Bach-Collegium Stuttgart (1965); and later, Reinhard Goebel's Musica Antiqua Köln (1973). In the Netherlands, the early music movement was spearheaded by the virtuoso players Gustav Leonhardt (harpsichord), Frans Brüggen (flute and recorder), and the Kuijken brothers (violin, flute, recorder, viola da gamba, and baroque cello). These early music performers were very active in the establishment of the distinguished early music program at the Conservatory in The Hague. Meanwhile, in Austria, Nikolaus Harnoncourt cofounded the Vienna Viola Da Gamba Quartet (1949), together with Eduard Melkus, Gustav Leonhardt, and Alice Hoffelner (whom he was to marry), and later the Concentus Musicus Wien (1953). By the early 1970s, Harnoncourt and Leonhardt had embarked on a landmark project together to record all of Bach's cantatas for the record company Teldec. This carefully researched series of recordings featuring period instruments and an all-male choir marks a decisive turning point, most notably in regard to historical performance practice's expanding claims to core classical music repertory.

By the 1960s there were three different types of early music performance going on in Britain.[14] To begin with, professional ensembles of various sizes, playing on modern instruments, were performing music by the likes of Bach, Vivaldi, Handel, and their contemporaries, very much as an integral part of their standard repertoire. In the main, there was only limited interest in performance practice per se (i.e., an explicit concern for how the composer would have heard the music performed).[15] Neville Marriner's Academy of St. Martin in the Fields, and the Goldsborough Orchestra (which later became the English Chamber Orchestra (ECO)), stand out as hugely important precursors of the early music movement; for they offered historically aware, stylish, refined, scaled-down performances, in contrast to the large-scale professional concerts also popular at the time—one thinks particularly of Bach's choral works performed by massed chorus, e.g., with the Three Choirs Festival (pre-1719), the Birmingham Triennial Music Festival (1784-1912), or The Bach Choir (founded 1875), with modern orchestral players. Meanwhile, a relatively small group of amateur musicians was experimenting with period instruments, forming ad hoc ensembles with like-minded enthusiasts. Many of these amateurs were highly educated professionals (academics, doctors, teachers) for whom early music performance represented an intellectual as well as an aesthetic pursuit, a hobby, not a job or career. Much of their playing was based on their own musicological and archival research; some also made their own instruments. Finally, a number of professionally-trained classical musicians were branching out into early music, working with their own period instrument groups, consisting of three or four players, sometimes a few more. Over a short period of time, early music performance began to prove itself both artistically and commercially, as the musicologist and performer John Butt observes:[16]

> Particularly fascinating was the fact that a huge industry connected to the revival of early music and HIP [historically informed performance] was blossoming just down the road in London...The movement was dominated by a handful of scholar-performers directing versatile vocalists and instrumentalists who learned the historical styles and techniques more or less 'on the job.'

Butt's observations about the "movement" very much set the scene for this present study. Firstly, there is recognition that Early Music has become more than just a parochial approach to performing classical music; indeed, it represents a sizeable commercial phenomenon (a "huge industry"). Secondly, those involved in the early days of the revival were performing in a HIP manner without any formal didactic channels for training in just how to do this. Thirdly, the domination of the early music movement by a "handful of scholar-performers" begs further examination. How exactly did such a small group of people come to have such a major influence on the classical music profession?[17] Writing in the late 1980s, Nicholas Kenyon remarked that "No change has more profoundly influenced the development of our music-making during the last two decades than the growth of the historical performance movement."[18] With the benefit of hindsight, it is hard to disagree with Kenyon in his assessment of the central importance of Early Music on the classical music profession. But the question remains, *how* did this all come about?

SEVEN AGES OF EARLY MUSIC

Before explaining Early Music's remarkable rise in more detail, we need first to get a better sense of who was doing what and when. Figure 2.1 presents an overview of professional early music group formations over the last 40 years or so in Britain.[19] Two aspects of this activity are worth highlighting. First, there is an immediately obvious rise and fall in the number of formations, with a distinct peak in activity during the late 1970s to early 1980s. Second, underlying this trend is a less prominent pattern of heightened activity, with clusters of particularly influential new formations occurring (approximately) every 7 years.

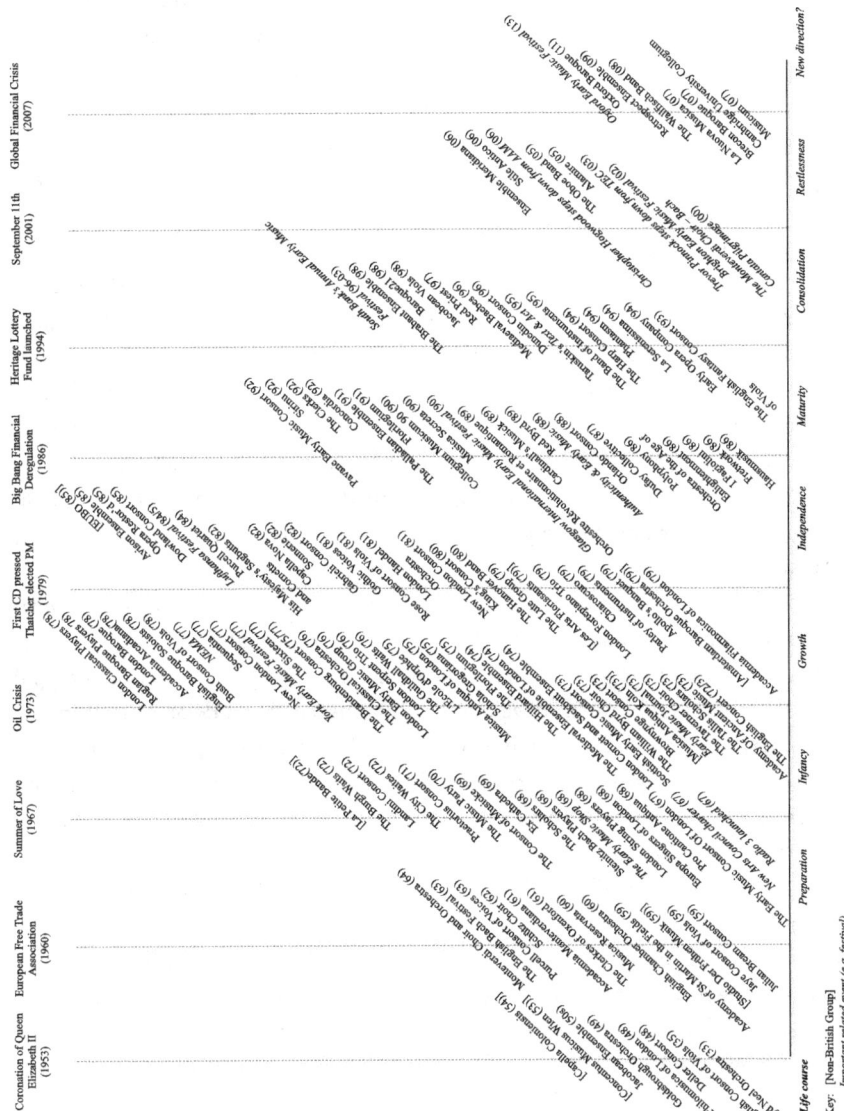

FIGURE 2.1 The Early Music Life Course

It is interesting to speculate as to the cause of this clustering effect. Although demand-side influences are important when it comes to promoters and record companies' vested interests, i.e., in sustaining support for breakthrough artists, to the point where they would be unlikely to look elsewhere for other "new kids on the block" within the same area, they do not usually appear to influence the decision to form an ensemble in the first place.[20] On the supply side, attention could be brought to the distinctive context of the university or music college, where many such groups were formed. It seems plausible to suggest that new ensembles find it harder to break through, folding before they come to the public's attention, when existing groups are either still resident or, at the least, remaining firmly in the collective consciousness of those living and working within such institutions.[21]

It is intriguing to review this pattern of formations in terms of the underlying logic of human development, though in doing so I would seek to avoid the anthropomorphic implication that cultural movements somehow take on the characteristics of individual human beings (it should also be observed that not all of the phases are of strictly 7 years' duration). Figure 2.1 refers to the stages in terms of phases of the human life course. The idea of human development unfolding in a number of stages (often 7) is deeply embedded in our cultural mythology. Coincidentally, the number 7 also held special significance for one of the key figures in Early Music—Thurston Dart, who, being as "superstitious as he was intellectually acute,"[22] believed that his career operated in 7-year cycles (he died aged 49). My own model in what follows, complete with illustrative typology and phase descriptions (which begin each section), takes inspiration from Jaques's monologue[23] in Shakespeare's *As You Like It,* as well as archetypal models of childhood and human development. Of these, the work of educationalist Rudolf Steiner, who founded the Steiner Waldorf schools in 1919, is the most widely known. He held that 7-year cycles continued throughout life.[24] He would therefore have linked Shakespeare's "puking infant" to the 0–7 year period, the "whining schoolboy" 7–14, the "lover" 14–21, and so on.

We cannot properly consider each of the phases without taking into account the broader socioeconomic context (see also Figure 2.1). Unfortunately, providing a causal link between macro- and micro-levels of analysis is never a straightforward task. Discerning between necessary and merely contingent causal factors is difficult, to say the least. For example, although on the face of it the burst of early music activity around 1973 seems to be entirely coincidental to the deepening economic meltdown that resulted from the oil crisis of that year, this might overlook the fact that peoples' faith in mainstream institutions, including those within classical music, was being shaken in the trickle-down from world events. Equally, it is fascinating to reflect on the shifts in political power and ideology taking place across many European countries in the 1970s and '80s, and to ask what sort of impact the progression toward free-market neoliberalism—that deeply embedded culture in which market functioning is the "*overwhelming* priority for social organization"[25]—might have had on the level of private sector funding for early music projects during this period. At the very least, we need to bear in mind the motivating, enabling, and constraining influence of such structural conditions on the activities and practices of those involved.

PREPARATION (PRE-1967)

Without wishing to stretch the literary metaphor too far, Shakespeare's puking infant did not arrive into the world without prior notice; there were signs. Some of the leading exponents in the lead-up to early music's revival have already been introduced, including such figures as Arnold Dolmetsch, Wanda Landowska and Thurston Dart. The performances of scholar-musicians in Basle, Vienna, and The Hague during the 1950s were pivotal. Certainly, it is far from unreasonable to suggest that it was the Austrians (Harnoncourt) and the Dutch (Leonhardt, Brüggen, Bylsma), not the British, who were the real "pioneers" in this field. "English period instrument specialists followed them after a 10–20 year time lag" suggests Andrew Pinnock (former early music officer at the Arts Council).[26] One notable exception is Michael Morrow, the founder of the group Musica Reservata in 1960. In interviewing performers and other early music experts for this research, it was striking how often they mentioned Morrow's approach to early music performance as representing something really new, distinctive, and highly original. As Catherine Mackintosh, formerly leader of the Academy of Ancient Music and later the Orchestra of the Age of Enlightenment, put it, "Musica Reservata was the most exciting and original early music group—ever! Full stop."[27] In Morrow's obituary notice, David Fallows commented, "He remains for me the clearest case of what they call an original."[28] Clifford Bartlett, a lynchpin figure in making new editions available to performers, recalls:[29]

> Then the sudden break was Musica Reservata in the late 60s. They were enormous events. You could put on a medieval programme and fill the QEH, which you wouldn't do now. [Michael Morrow] was not a conductor. He was a man with good ears—a concept of the sound he wanted. That's what was so good about Reservata—they broke away, a completely different style of singing, influenced if anything by Balkans. Some musicology behind it, and a lot of intuition and guts, and the desire to do something revolutionary and have a complete break.[30]

Andrew Parrott conducted Musica Reservata in the mid-1970s. He recalls: "One of the most important experiences I had during these years was as conductor for Michael Morrow's Musica Reservata. It was a crazy, eccentric and ground-breaking group, and a tremendous window into pre-Baroque repertoire."[31] To those who said "why bother" with early music, Morrow's reply was, "Music only exists in terms of its style."[32] As J. M. Thomson eloquently put it, Morrow "was a musical apostle of a highly distinct nature whose precepts influenced (and ruffled) a multitude."[33] John Sothcott (a cofounder of Musica Reservata) remembers Morrow being far from pedantic about the instruments he was to use. "The spirit and the style of the performance were everything."[34] Most significantly, Sothcott recalls, "Michael's reason for attempting performances, by fair means or anything else, was to bring the music to life for its own sake and, as he often said, so that he could hear it. He was in no way a careerist performer and perhaps never really understood those who were"[35] (and here perhaps is a critical point of difference between Morrow and the younger Munrow, who played with Musica Reservata on several occasions). Anyone who has listened to a Musica Reservata performance or recording, and particularly the singing voice of Jantina Noorman, will even today recognize something quite distinctive in terms of the sound-world being conjured up in their performances. This pioneering group, at least, was no mere copy of Harnoncourt or Leonhardt's approach to HIP.

There were other incipient stirrings happening in the mid-1960s in Britain, and probably the most notable of these was the then student John Eliot Gardiner's project of putting on Monteverdi's *Vespers* at King's College Cambridge—in his words, "to some extent an act of hubris" at the time. The event is significant on a number of levels. For Gardiner himself it marked the beginning of his own musical pilgrimage, and the launch of the Monteverdi Choir (and later the Monteverdi Orchestra)— "For me it was a defining moment, a clear indicator that this was the direction my life should take."[36] He describes founding the Monteverdi as an "anti-choir" insofar as it was "a deliberate reaction to the polite, euphonious Oxbridge choral sound of the time, by encouraging its members to sing with far more colour, passion and intensity than they were used to." Gardiner recalls how the event gave him "the desire to train as a conductor, and the motivation to study music in as wide a way as possible, including historical performance practice." He adds "I was very aware not only of my own technical shortcomings, but also those in the nascent early music movement, which still had a slightly amateurish feel to it." More widely, the concert brought together a whole range of interested parties: among the performers were David Munrow (who led the recorder consort), Christopher Monk and Donald Smithers (cornetti), Andrew Davis, Simon Preston, and members of the future King's Singers. In the audience were Thurston Dart (Philomusica's founder, and professor of music at Cambridge at the time, and later at King's College, London, where he invited Gardiner to study as a postgraduate in 1966); Raymond Leppard (Trinity College, Cambridge); and George Malcolm (harpsichordist and ex-music director at Westminster Cathedral).

INFANCY (FROM C. 1967)

Infant (0-7 years):
During these foundation years we are moved by instincts, and heavily dependent upon the nurture we receive from our environment. We learn to say 'I' and recognize ourselves, as standing apart from our parents.

1967's "summer of love" signaled the rise of hippie subculture. What started in San Francisco quickly moved to other countries, including Britain. It is perhaps rather more than just a coincidence that the acronym for historically informed performance (HIP), which has gained prominence over the more problematic label "authentic," is also the root of the word hippie ("hip" or "hep," denoting awareness). Though early music performers have been criticized for being overly self-conscious about their performances of classical music, a more empowering explanation sees their concern with authentic editions, instruments, and performance techniques as displaying a greater *awareness* of the limitations of the notation system and instrument manufacture, and perhaps a greater concomitant awareness of their potential. This focus on "awareness" has some scientific backing, too. Psychology-based research by Kernis and Goldman[37] highlights awareness (i.e., knowledge of one's positive and negative traits, values, needs, and preferences) as the first of four components in a "multicomponent conceptualization of authenticity."

To the extent that we can sensibly talk of any single year as marking the "birth" of Early Music in Britain, it would surely have to be 1967. For it was in this year—the 400th anniversary of Monteverdi's birth—that David Munrow together with Christopher Hogwood launched the Early Music Consort of London. It was also the year that Michael Morrow's Musica Reservata gave their ground-breaking performance at the Queen Elizabeth Hall in London (on July 2). John Thomson remembers this South Bank concert very well: it was "an unforgettable occasion when we felt that early music had at last taken off in London."[38] At about the time Michael Morrow was forming Musica Reservata, David Munrow was undergoing an altogether different epiphany in his musical development—having flown off to Peru during his year off to teach English, he amassed a small collection of Bolivian flutes and other assorted wind instruments, which on return he taught himself to play (he had learned the bassoon at school). After studying English at Pembroke College, Cambridge, he became a lecturer in early music history at the University of Leicester, before setting up the Early Music Consort. Although Munrow was to die tragically young, committing suicide in 1976 aged only 33, he had by that time recorded more than 50 albums and given many performances with his own Consort and with Morrow's Musica Reservata, amongst others. He had also presented 655 editions of the Radio 3 program *Pied Piper*, which was the conduit for many to learn about (early) classical music in the late 1960s and early 1970s.

Munrow's unbridled energy and enthusiasm for performance, together with his "showmanship" and virtuosic technical skills on a host of wind instruments, is legendary. Christopher Bishop, Munrow's producer for EMI, recalls how he "was the most tremendous fun to work with."[39] "He mucked about all the time. He was great fun." His playful music-making was "jolly, clever, and full of life. It just had *it*." But at the same time, he was so professional and absolutely disciplined. He would stay up all night to write out the parts, as he wouldn't trust other people to do it for him. He used to do all the copying by hand; nothing was printed. As Bishop recalls, "he was so full of energy, it was terrifying!"

Just as Morrow sought "to bring the music to life," so Munrow relished the challenge of playing all sorts of Medieval and Renaissance instruments, and communicating the joys of this music to as many people as he could. As anyone who has ever tried to play a sackbut, cornett, regal, or crumhorn would know, they are far from easy instruments to master. The physical challenges involved remind us that part of the fascination of early music comes from the very immediate, tangible, embodied pleasure one can get from performance itself. One of Christopher Bishop's abiding memories of Munrow is seeing him (as much as hearing him) perform—"I can see his red face puffing away," Bishop recalls.

In an echo of Donington's words about Dolmetsch, David Munrow's part in the early music revival has been described as "decisive." Writing at the time of Munrow's untimely death in 1976, Howard Mayer Brown suggests:[40]

> The special quality that set David Munrow apart, or so it seems to me, was a rare combination of abundant musical talent, the energy and skill to organize and lead other people, and an uncanny ability, given only to a few great teachers, to convince large numbers of people that what was important and attractive to him should also be attractive and important to them.

The decisive influence of Munrow and how his activities impacted on the direction of early music performance is a theme taken up further in Chapter 4. Here we see a growing distinction between Medieval, Renaissance and early Baroque, and later repertoires, as interest in "authentic" performance began to be played out in markedly different ways for all those involved.

GROWTH (FROM C. 1973)

Whining schoolboy (7-14 years):
In the second phase, we learn to create an inner world of our own—a world of imagination, essential for navigating through the turbulent world of adolescence. In this period our abilities in the outside world are tested, as we become better able to share with others.

Moving into the early 1970s, we come to the launch of the most prominent early music groups that have formed the nucleus of the professional early music scene in Britain over the last 40 years. Two of the founding music directors, Christopher Hogwood and Andrew Parrott, were already familiar faces with regular appearances for the Early Music Consort and Musica Reservata, respectively. Hogwood had been a founder member of Munrow's group, having first met him whilst at Cambridge. He also played with Musica Reservata on occasion. Parrott's connections at Oxford were instrumental in his later involvement with Musica Reservata, conducting the group in the mid-1970s in place of John Beckett. Peter Phillips founded The Tallis Scholars whilst he too was at Oxford—where he studied Renaissance music with David Wulstan and Denis Arnold. Trevor Pinnock, who founded The English Concert, was the only one of this "class of '73" who was not an Oxbridge graduate. This is a theme that warrants further study, as the Oxbridge connection, and what it says about necessary social, cultural, and educational capital[41] to set up an early music ensemble, is an integral feature of this story. The sheer number of Oxbridge graduates involved at all levels of early music performance is remarkable, though not at all at odds with the wider British cultural elite—British arts and comedy in particular. The majority of leading figures, and many others who were involved to a less prominent degree, studied and/or taught at either Oxford or Cambridge (see Figure 2.2).

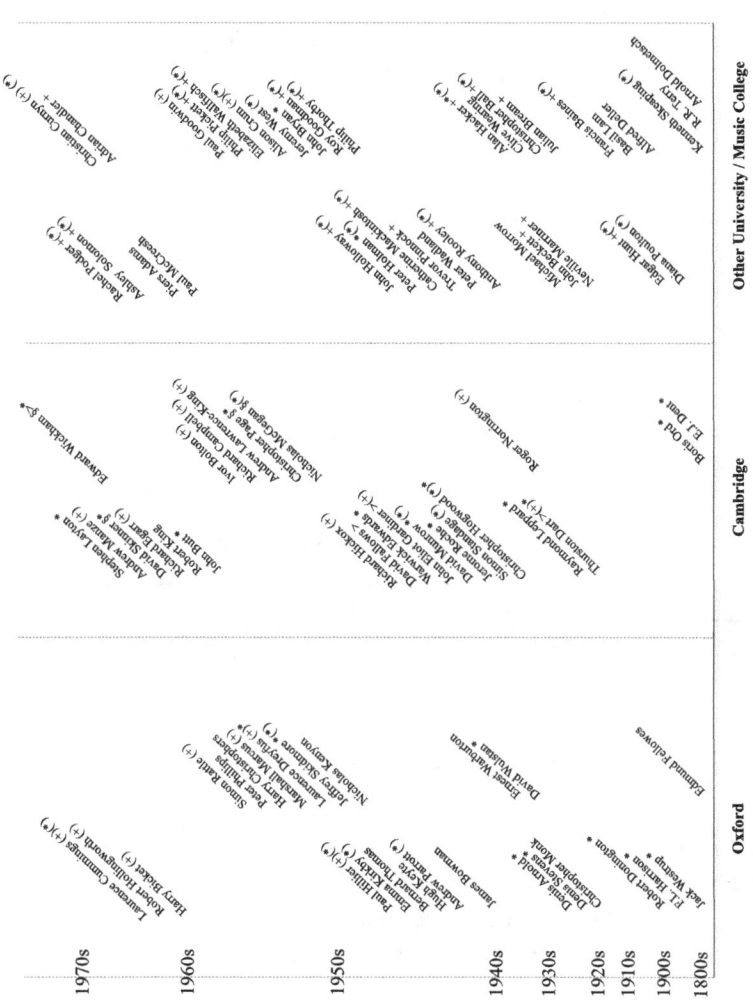

FIGURE 2.2 Leading Early Musicians' Education & Training

In the case of The English Concert and the Academy of Ancient Music, both Pinnock and Hogwood had been regularly performing with smaller groups prior to the establishment of the orchestras we know so well today. Trevor Pinnock recalls that his group The Galliard Harpsichord Trio, which had performed widely for over six years in local music clubs and regularly at the newly-built Purcell Room on the South Bank, just got to a point where change was needed: "I did feel that we were at the end of a road, and I knew of new developments, Harnoncourt and Leonhardt, and I knew there was something further, but I didn't know what it was. I wanted to find out."[42]

Hogwood, too, harbored desires to form an ensemble a little bit bigger than a chamber group (an economically viable size), for which there was work from the music clubs and the BBC. As Hogwood recalls, "the evidence of Harnoncourt and Leonhardt, both here and in Amsterdam, showed that bigger groups could be put together...and the reason we knew that was that we heard the recordings."[43] Here again, we can clearly see the pivotal influence of the continental pioneers. It is also at this point that the involvement of the record companies became decisive:

> We had a conversation with somebody who worked at Decca—Peter Wadland—who had the job of re-packaging an existing label (L'Oiseau-Lyre). He persuaded the people who hold the budget at Decca to take a risk in allowing him to pay for just one record; and we got players together.[44]

Whilst individual movers and shakers like Hogwood and Pinnock were clearly central to what was to unfold, the impetus for Early Music's success resulted to a large degree from intense collaboration with like-minded commercial record executives, and, of course, the first wave of early musicians who performed in their groups.

INDEPENDENCE (FROM C. 1980)

Lover (14-21 years):
During the third phase we become self-conscious. Focus falls on our emotions as new interests develop. This is a time characterized by searching for life purpose, and testing of boundaries. We undergo physical, emotional, moral and mental change and conflict, as we begin to break free from parental influence.

Moving into this third phase of Early Music, we see a very active pattern of early music groups being founded. Gothic Voices, His Majestys Sagbutts and Cornetts, the Rose Consort of Viols, and the Gabrieli Consort, amongst others, were establishing a name for themselves in earlier repertoire. Meanwhile, there was a growing contingent of period instrument ensembles that focused on Baroque repertoire, including the English Baroque Soloists, London Baroque, Raglan Baroque Players, the Parley of Instruments, the King's Consort, and the London Handel Orchestra. It was not long before these and other groups, notably Norrington's London Classical Players, The Hanover Band under the direction of Roy Goodman, the Academy of Ancient Music, The English Concert, and later Collegium Musicum 90 under Simon Standage and Richard Hickox, began pushing at the boundaries of "early music," performing later repertoire still.

The parallels with the life cycle outlined (under "lover") above are striking. The repertoires of Classical and then Romantic music are themselves redolent of an interest in more emotionally diverse musical experiences. The rhetorical Baroque gives way to the passion and angst of later musical styles. It is not surprising that proponents of HIP found themselves in sometimes heated discussion about what was or wasn't suitable for the Early Music "makeover." By the early 1980s, the academic question of how late early music should go had been overtaken by practice. The success of recordings such as the Academy of Ancient Music's complete Mozart symphonies (1979 onward) demonstrated that the tide was not to be turned. The launch of the compact disc (CD) in the early 1980s then provided a hugely significant boost, as the movement began in earnest to assert its independence.

The "testing of boundaries" associated with this phase of development inevitably involved a degree of internal competition. The pool of professional players from which the HIP ensembles were drawn in the initial years was very small. This inevitably led to diary clashes, when performers would be forced to choose between competing loyalties. Even by the 1980s the level of formal training available in early music performance at the music colleges remained modest. A "second wave" of young players was about to come through seeking careers in HIP, but opportunities remained relatively scarce.

Also at about this time, some historical musicologists began to challenge perceived wisdom over the use of instruments with Medieval vocal music—the so-called "English *a capella* heresy" as Howard Mayer Brown dubbed it.[45] Old HIP "truths" were being questioned from the inside; the uniformity of view that on the face of it characterized this single cultural "movement" was coming under threat from internal wrangling and division. Nowhere is this increasing "self-consciousness" more evident than in relation to the writings of Richard Taruskin, whose essays published in the early 1980s characterize a period of deep and sustained reflexivity for Early Music. The authenticity and resolve of the historical performer was to be sorely tested by these now publicly aired views.

MATURITY (FROM C. 1986)

Soldier (21-28 years):
In the cycle that follows we fully enter into adulthood. This is our 'coming of age'. Faculties of insight, intuition and judgment are central. Sparks of interest that were awakened in previous phases now get developed along more definite lines. Any issue not faced up to at this time will likely require attention at some later date.

Amidst the new groups formed around 1986, the setting up of the Orchestra of the Age of Enlightenment (OAE) demands particular attention; for this group, more than any other, heralded the "growing up" of the early music movement, challenging not just the status quo of the classical music mainstream but also its early music "parents." The founding of the OAE speaks volumes about the state of early music performance by the mid-1980s. The orchestra was an idea born out of the performers' own frustrations with the limitations of the HIP scene. From the outset the orchestra emphasized its collective credentials, giving all the players a say in its decision-making, though one of its cofounders has suggested that this was more a pragmatic response to the particular circumstances of hastily assembling an orchestra for its first performance than a principled stand. It is striking, nonetheless, that this was the first time that such an organizational policy, wholly in keeping with the underlying HIP principle of democratic control, had been acted out on such a scale within the movement.

As a professional early music instrumentalist in London in the mid-1980s, you generally "belonged" to one or more groups—typically Hogwood's Academy of Ancient Music, Pinnock's English Concert, Norrington's London Classical Players, or Gardiner's English Baroque Soloists (to a lesser extent this was also true of early music singers). Though there were generally high levels of loyalty for what many performers considered "family" units, there was also a growing dissatisfaction with the way things were heading. Ten to fifteen years after setting up, many performers were searching for new avenues, new directions and opportunities. A key unfulfilled aim was to play with other leading HIP directors, such as Leonhardt or Harnoncourt, from the continent. Under the current scheme of things, this was just not possible.

By this time, Early Music's founder-directors were increasingly building their own careers in the wider musical mainstream. Alongside performing regularly with their individual HIP ensembles, they were branching out into other territories, working with (early and modern) orchestras and groups abroad. Not surprisingly, this gave rise to a further legitimate concern on behalf of some of the early musicians that they had effectively helped to secure the reputations of their founders, but were now themselves in danger of being left out in the cold. There was a growing desire to claim back control, both artistic and financial.

Probably the single most important development, which catapulted the OAE to success, was its cause being taken up by the now world-renowned conductor Simon Rattle at Glyndebourne Festival Opera in 1989. As a condition of Rattle's conducting the Da Ponte trilogy of Mozart operas at Glyndebourne, he insisted on bringing in the OAE (formerly, orchestral accompaniment was provided by the London Philharmonic Orchestra). The arrival of the OAE onto the musical scene is also significant, therefore, in marking a coming together of the hitherto separate classical music mainstream and early music fields, in such a way as to have a decisive impact on its subsequent trajectory. Early Music had "come of age"; but with the benefit of hindsight one might already be asking "at what price?" This was already a very different early music scene to the one that Michael Morrow or David Munrow would have recognized in the mid-1960s.

CONSOLIDATION (FROM C. 1993)

Judge (28-35 years):
It is often felt that creative individuals seem to make their greatest advances during these years. A possible contributory cause for this is that the association centers of the brain come to their peak efficiency at about thirty-five years of age.

One can point to the latter half of the 1990s as being a time of consolidation for the established professional groups and ensembles, accompanied by a decline in the number of influential *new* early music groups being formed. The continuing trend to advance the repertoire going under the HIP treatment saw some period instrument orchestras fully embrace works from the Romantic and late Romantic periods. The OAE and Gardiner's Orchestre Révolutionnaire et Romantique (set up 25 years after the Monteverdi Choir) now performed Brahms, Berlioz, and Bizet. Groups being formed at this time were doing so against the backdrop of a very established early music scene in Britain and abroad.[46] Music colleges now employed dedicated, salaried staff, some of whom were themselves players from the class of '73. For the first time in Britain, early music was being taught as a fully legitimate strand of conservatoire education. Younger (second and third) generations of performers were also establishing themselves in early music and its continuing training: Laurence Cummings assumed responsibility as head of Historical Performance at the Royal Academy of Music (1997); and Ashley Solomon was appointed professor of flute and recorder at the Royal College of Music (1994), becoming head of Historical Performance a few years later.

At a wider level, 1994 marked an important shift in British cultural policy, with the introduction of the National Lottery in November of that year. The arts were beneficiaries as one of the five "good causes" (the others being sport, charity, national heritage, and a millennium fund). From a public funding perspective, the Lottery offered a watering-down of the "long-recognized division between professional and amateur artists"[47] as community and other amateur groups were now eligible for funding. Arguably, this also represented the potential abolition of any hierarchy of art forms within funding,[48] since Lottery awards were judged on the strength of the bid rather than by genre. With no access to detailed records, however, it remains open to speculation whether this had any significant bearing on the activities of amateur early musicians across the British Isles—particularly amongst the National Early Music Association's (NEMA) regional fora. Having said this, there were certainly occasions when large-scale cultural initiatives had a positive impact on regional early music provision. In particular, the popular Glasgow International Early Music Festival, under Warwick Edwards (who had founded the Scottish Early Music Consort in 1973) was launched in 1990, as part of Glasgow's year-long celebrations as Cultural Capital of Europe.

By 1995 (the year of Taruskin's *Text & Act,* and Kivy's *Authenticities*), the explicit use of "authenticity" as a promoting discourse for Early Music was disappearing from PR leaflets and program notes. Even with the benefit of hindsight, however, it is hard to ascertain whether this had any direct effect on what those involved were actually doing. Perhaps the deepest level of consolidation at this time was in respect of the recording industry's interest in early music as a lucrative commercial opportunity, and the impact this had on the breadth and depth of repertoire now recorded. As Nicholas Kenyon observes,[49] the period instrument movement provided a "perfect match" for the latest recording technology.

RESTLESSNESS (FROM C. 2000)

Slippered pantaloons (35-42 years):
During this period we experience a desire to share whatever we have learned in life with others. Many philanthropic acts are undertaken, as individuals 'give back'. But there can also be some sense of impending crisis as we look back and question the value of our achievements.

The weeks and months after September 2001 saw a retrenchment in the amount of work being made available to early music ensembles. The level of touring of classical music groups in general slowed, also hitting the early music scene. Even before 9/11, however, the musical establishment, including big record companies like Deutsche Grammophon (DG), had been getting anxious. John Eliot Gardiner's ambitious Bach Cantata Pilgrimage, in which every one of Bach's Cantatas was performed on the appropriate feast day in the millennium year, was originally intended to be recorded by DG, though in the end they only recorded 4 out of the 59 Cantata programs given; but all but one of the others were recorded live for archival purposes. It was five years later, having listened to all the pilgrimage "takes" that Gardiner and his wife Isabella decided to set up their own record label, Soli Deo Gloria (SDG), named after Bach's appending of these initials to the end of each of his Cantata scores, and to issue these recordings commercially. Somewhat tongue in cheek, SDG has been taken by some journalists to stand for "sod DG!" after it had pulled out of the deal and reduced its commitment (though Gardiner himself asserts "that this was only suggested to me afterwards"[50]).

Elsewhere, there were positive signs that Early Music was "giving something back." The new National Centre for Early Music, "an educational resource" housed in a converted church in York, opened its doors for the first time in April 2000. Early Music's pioneers were also increasingly keen to share more widely what they had learned themselves. For example, as principal conductor of the Stuttgart Radio Symphony Orchestra, Sir Roger Norrington was in a position to encourage modern orchestral players to explore "pure tone" performance (i.e., eschewing vibrato) across a broad range of repertoires. Norrington has described his approach more generally in terms of "Evidence-Based" Performance (EBP).[51] EBP is motivated by the underlying belief that "tradition is laziness," i.e., that the response "we usually do it like this" is not a sufficient justification for its continuance. Of course, such a position is not just held by advocates of historical performance practice. It is fascinating to chart the rise of "Evidence-Based" approaches in other domains (notably the medical field and policy development), in the years toward the turn of the millennium.[52] Regardless of context, a key challenge for all "evidence-based" approaches is to ensure the appropriate balance when basing one's actions on "facts" and "knowledge." As Etzioni (1968, 1993) suggests, the vision should be of a society where analysts and experts are "on tap but not on top"—a society that is active in its self-critical use of knowledge. Interestingly, another key development in the early noughties saw some of Early Music's own experts (performer-scholars) stepping back from their groups so as to allow the next generation of younger musicians to be "on top." Notable amongst the class of '73, Trevor Pinnock stood down from The English Concert in 2003, and Christopher Hogwood from the Academy of Ancient Music in 2006.

NEW DIRECTION? (2007 ONWARD)

Second childishness (42-49 years):
In this seventh stage we often undergo some major change. Very often, we seek a new direction in life—a new beginning. Unresolved aspects of life come to the fore, and this can, of course, be very unsettling (if not ultimately fruitful) for those involved.

Bruce Haynes's book *The End of Early Music* was published in 2007. Though the book is not as pessimistic as the title might suggest, it marks a taking stock. In fact, 2007 was a year still full of early (and not so early) music. The York Early Music Festival celebrated its 30th year; Harry Bicket took over the helm from founder-director Trevor Pinnock at The English Concert; the Orchestra of the Age of Enlightenment really did come of age, with a 21st birthday concert at the Royal Festival Hall; and the Monteverdi Choir and John Eliot Gardiner's Orchestre Révolutionnaire et Romantique, continued to push the HIP boundaries as they immersed themselves in Brahms's symphonies and choral works, on tour.

At the time of writing this book there are rumors that the current season of the Lufthansa Festival of Baroque Music, in London, will be the last to enjoy the support of its title sponsor (Lufthansa have been "on board" this flagship festival for the last 28 years).[53] As I discuss in more detail in Chapter 10, there is much to celebrate, even if the balance sheet of Early Music's achievements is not unequivocally positive. So what next for early music? It is increasingly difficult today to distinguish between, say, the specialist period instrument orchestra and the chamber orchestra. Both operate on similar economic models, competing for work with each other from festivals and promoters. Arguably, this is just how it should be—the period instrument orchestra returning to its origins, having grown out of such groups as the Boyd Neel Orchestra, the Philomusica of London, the Academy of St. Martin in the Fields, the Goldsbrough Orchestra, and the English Chamber Orchestra. There is today a very significant level of overlap in terms of the players involved in "historical" performances, with a mix of specialist and modern players. This, at least, is the case for Baroque repertoire and later. We see another story altogether with Medieval and Renaissance music. Whilst interest in early vocal music has flourished, with many specialist young groups coming to prominence in recent years (e.g., The Cardinall's Musick, The Clerks, and Stile Antico), early instrumental music has remained somewhat out of the spotlight, despite the continued presence of established groups such as the Rose Consort of Viols, Fretwork, and His Majestys Sagbutts and Cornetts, which celebrated its 30th anniversary in 2012.

On the back cover of *A very short introduction to early music*, written by Thomas Forrest Kelly (2011), Christopher Hogwood congratulates the author on what he sees as "a very astute recognition that present ideas could soon seem as dated as those of Beecham and Stokowski—or Mozart and Mendelssohn." Whilst this will no doubt be proved right in some respects, we must surely do what we can now to understand and *explain* the early music movement, how it came about, and how those involved managed to make it work and make it pay (whilst continuing to allow its music to enchant us). I pick up on this task over the next few chapters, but first we return to the case for and against authenticity in musical performance. In particular—is authenticity in performance a matter of legitimate interest for performers today, or is this, as some have suggested, yesterday's story?

> Do we really want to talk about 'authenticity' any more? I had hoped a consensus was forming that to use the word in connection with the performance of music—and especially to define a particular style, manner, or philosophy of performance—is neither description nor critique, but commercial propaganda, the stock-in-trade of press agents and promoters.
>
> RICHARD TARUSKIN[1]

> The authentic work of art instructs us in our inauthenticity and adjures us to overcome it.
>
> LIONEL TRILLING[2]

3

Transcending Text & Act?

INTRODUCTION

"And then I started the opening bars of the Mozart *Requiem* and there was an electric atmosphere of new music. I can only describe it like that...it was something totally new."[3] This is how Trevor Pinnock recalls a recent performance he was conducting in Salzburg. Pinnock is far from alone, of course, in drawing attention to that sense of old music being altogether fresh and exciting, as if it had been composed only this morning. But how might we explain this trans-temporal phenomenon? How can a musical work that we've performed and listened to sometimes hundreds of times over, engage or perhaps even shock us as if it was a wholly new discovery? In this chapter I begin to formulate the answer to this question, and in so doing present a fundamental justification for the practice of authentic performance.

Writing in 1978, the early musician and scholar Michael Morrow drew a distinction between authenticity "in its real sense and in the contemporary cult meaning of the word."[4] Describing authenticity as "a convenient catchpenny commercial label"[5] (one is put in mind here of Adorno's critique of the alienating nature of the "culture industry"), Morrow was scathing about the authenticity claims of modern early music performances: "What then about all these first modern really authentic performances proclaimed by the record companies and so many concert handbills? Nonsense...This is not authenticity." For Morrow, authenticity could only mean "the real thing."[6]

Understanding just what the "real thing" is has proven a stubbornly enduring problem. The list of philosophers and social commentators who have devoted time and effort to addressing this problem of authenticity is long indeed (Plato, Aristotle, and Socrates, through to Hegel, Adorno, and Sartre). The notion of the authentic "self," and what this means in terms of an individual's capacity for self-realization, is a subject each of us has a singular interest in, of course. But "personal authenticity" cannot really be grasped without also taking into account the nature of our wider relations with society. As Marshall Berman put it, "seekers of authenticity are just beginning to learn a fact of life...that whoever you are, or want to be, you may not be interested in politics, but politics is interested in you."[7]

Much of the writing on authenticity in the arts and cultural production has focused on the relational nature of this distinctive societal context, whether in terms of Adorno's "assembly line,"[8] Harker's "sausage machine,"[9] Hirsch's "systems model,"[10] Becker's "art worlds,"[11] or Peterson's "production of culture perspective."[12] For Adorno, the culture industry's imperative to make money effectively nullified the authenticity and "originality" of the non-commodified cultural good.[13] Whilst an art work might still be deemed to possess *nominal* authenticity, i.e., its origins, authorship, or provenance are correctly identified, "ensuring that an object of aesthetic experience is properly named," it was bound to cede a deeper level of *expressive authenticity*—"a true expression of a society's values and beliefs."[14] As Negus suggests in the context of the popular music industry, once the music "had left its origins and been subject to the culture industry it...lost any authentic link to non-commodified forms of expression."[15] Determining just what scope there has actually been for "authenticity," given Early Music's subjection to the same commercial logic as the rest of the culture industry, is clearly a central question for this book.[16]

Authenticity has been written about extensively in the context of the performing arts in general,[17] the aesthetics of music,[18] popular music,[19] hip-hop,[20] blues,[21] and country music;[22] but there is something particular about the context of early music that makes the question of authenticity all the more central.[23] For in this context, "authenticity" is referred to explicitly by those involved, and by its critics, to determine what individuals do, and which individuals should do it. Authenticity is not just an interesting and supportive concept in theory, but also an integral premise of what early music is.[24]

Within the field of historical performance, Arnold Dolmetsch is credited with introducing the "cult of authenticity"[25] in the early years of the 20th century. "Authenticity" was slow to take any sort of hold, with no clear consensus emerging as to what exactly the word meant.[26] At the end of Morrow's 1978 article on authenticity and musical performance, he asks "So where does this leave us today? I really would like to know—and I have no doubt that somehow, somewhere, somebody will only be too anxious to explain to me how simple it all really is."[27] A couple of years later that "someone" was the musician and musicologist Richard Taruskin.[28] Whilst his motives were "exposing the conceptual constraints that prevented 'historical performance' from being truly historical,"[29] Taruskin cast doubt on the whole "authenticity" project, suggesting that "talk of authenticity might better be left to moral philosophers, textual critics, and luthiers."[30] As we shall explore shortly, Taruskin's argument was that early music performers weren't really being authentic at all in their practices: it was impossible to know what the composer's intentions were, and early music performance was really about how modern performers *wanted* it to sound. After all, as Hennion and Fauquet later put it, "Nothing is more modern than an historical approach to an old repertoire."[31]

The response to Taruskin's onslaught was one, understandably, of some soul-searching and defensive posturing. The singer Nigel Rogers wrote in *Early Music* in 1984, "My immediate reaction was to wonder whether the early music movement was trying to destroy itself."[32] Clifford Bartlett noted, "The early musician is particularly sensitive: he welcomes the critic's attention, hoping not only for praise for himself, but also for support for the concept of early music."[33] However, the critical cat was out of the bag, and it wasn't long before authenticity had become something of a taboo word. Sir John Eliot Gardiner no doubt now speaks for many when he says, "I really dislike the term 'authenticity,'" adding that "any sincere, coherent music-making is surely authentic in its own terms."[34] As Claire Holden remarks, "In the years since Taruskin first voiced his objections to the claims of the HIP movement, period instrument ensembles have been shamed into all but abandoning the authenticity label."[35] Twenty-five years after Taruskin's views were published in Kenyon's volume *Authenticity and Early Music* (1988), perhaps it is now time to go over some of the central arguments with a fresh perspective.

THE "AUTHENTICITY MOVEMENT" CRITIQUE

Although Taruskin directed his attack at several different facets of the so-called "authenticity movement," the main thrust of the critique concerned the relationship between notated musical score and live performance (the *Text & Act* of the title of his collected essays, published in 1995). Working out how to respond to this, however, begs further philosophical puzzle-solving. After all, conventional wisdom would have it that to perform music "authentically" requires there to be something to be authentic toward. Authenticity is a "dimension word,"[36] a term "whose meaning remains uncertain until we know what dimension of its referent is being talked about."[37] In this context, the referent in question is the "musical work." Notwithstanding the undisputed epistemological challenges involved in "knowing" anything about how music was actually performed in the past, about which Taruskin, amongst others, has had much to say, two levels of conceptual difficulty arise from this focus on the musical work. The first is the challenge of accounting for its existence without reification, and determining what relationship musical score and performer have to this object. The second concerns the normative question of how musicians *should* act in relation to the musical work—the extent to which they should be "faithful" to it in their performing.

Lest this discussion of the musical work appear somewhat abstruse, far removed from the real-world practices or interests of the music profession, it is worth briefly commenting on the case of Hyperion Records being taken to court in 2004 by the musicologist Dr. Lionel Sawkins over an alleged copyright infringement. At issue was Dr. Sawkins' claim that his editions of the 17th- through 18th-century French Baroque composer Lalande's music constituted the production of new musical works that, in turn, warranted copyright protection. As the High Court judge concluded in his judgment: "To succeed in this action Dr Sawkins has to establish that each of his editions is an original musical work within the meaning of s.1(1) of the 1988 Act...What the 1988 Act does not do is to define what is meant by music in the definition of a musical work, and it seems to me that this is what this case is really about."[38] Although Mr. Justice Patten found in favor of the claimant, landing Hyperion Records with a bill of approaching £1 million, the legal ruling on what constitutes a "musical work" should not perhaps be taken as the final word on the matter.

THE PROBLEM OF THE "MUSICAL WORK"

Musical works are generally thought of as being sound structures that are indicated by their composers.[39] However, composers and musicologists, to say nothing of practicing musicians, record companies, and judges, disagree over exactly what features (if any) "apart from the sonic profile of its instances"[40] comprise such works. Taruskin's complaint with early music performers is that they held an idealized notion of the musical work that turned ideas into objects, and put objects in place of people. The musical work was "something wholly realized by its creator, fixed in writing, and thus capable of being preserved."[41] So how then have philosophers sought to explain the musical work in such a way as to overcome this "essentialist modernist fallacy, the fallacy of reification?"[42]

The answer it seems is, with some considerable difficulty, weighed down with "a mountain of metaphysical baggage."[43] Lydia Goehr outlines four different types of theories.[44] The *Platonist* view treats musical works as always already existing "universals." According to this theory, the job of the composer is more to "discover" rather than "create" the work in question. The *Aristotelian* view is similar, but here works are considered essences (typically sound structures), belonging to other things, rather than as distinct in their own right. The *nominalist* approach attributes no abstract existence to the musical work but rather treats them *as if* they exist. Under this view the musical works are no more than linguistic place-holders (labels or types). A performance of a specific musical work (say the Academy of Ancient Music performing Handel's *Messiah*) is then considered as a token of this particular type. The musical score (or score-copy) is considered as a means for producing such a token of a type. Finally, the *idealist* analytical perspective treats the musical work as if it is an imaginary thing existing in a person's head.[45] The *Messiah* is then no more than an idea or ideas formed in Handel's mind.[46]

None of these perspectives would seem to provide a wholly convincing answer to Taruskin's reservations about reification. In her response to the perceived limitations of these theories in 1992, Lydia Goehr gave prominence to the "work-concept" as opposed to the "musical work." Goehr's thesis, characteristic perhaps of a gradually emerging wider "new musicology," replaced aesthetic transcendence with a historically and socially constructed analysis. Her theory, which Taruskin enthusiastically supported in his Foreword to the 2007 revised edition, entails what she describes as a historically based ontology[47] of the musical work. Goehr's main claim is "that the work-concept began to regulate musical practice at the end of the eighteenth century."[48] In other words, at around the time Beethoven was composing the *Eroica Symphony* (No.3), musical production began to be understood in terms of "the use of musical material resulting in complete and discrete, original and fixed, personally owned units. The units were musical works."[49] Goehr famously remarks that "Bach did not intend to compose musical works."[50] For in his time, pieces of music were very much crafted in terms of their (one-off) functional or ritual purpose and context, rather than as individually tradable "units" in their own right.[51] Of course, one implication of this perspective is that authenticity in performance becomes something of a "non-issue," since repeat performances were never even envisaged in a world of spontaneous and socially embedded music-making. But this would be to ignore the reality of what has happened, with Bach's music as with so many others.

THE PROBLEM OF "WERKTREUE" (FAITHFULNESS TO THE WORK)

All performances are necessarily the emergent outcome of competing demands, or in Peter Kivy's (1995) terms, "authenticities." Kivy helpfully distinguishes between three concepts of historical authenticity, before adding in what he refers to as "the other authenticity," i.e., "personal authenticity." Depending on one's attitude toward historical performance, the musician is more or less obliged, therefore, to remain faithful to (up to) four different kinds of potentially conflicting authenticities: *authenticity of intention*, i.e., "the historical authenticity of performance one achieves when following as closely as possible the performing intentions of the composer";[52] *authenticity of sound*, i.e., "duplicating as closely as possible the way a performance of the work in its own time would have sounded";[53] *authenticity of practice*, i.e., "reproducing as closely as possible the performance practice prevailing in the historical period of the composition being performed";[54] and *personal authenticity*, i.e., the esteem accorded the performer's individual expression, or for Kivy "something close...to originality."[55] Clearly, the notion of authenticity carries with it a burden—the burden to perform music as the composer would have intended or expected it, given the performance conventions of the times—the so-called "intentional imperative."[56] This imperative is implicit in Koopman's working definition of authentic performance as "the performance of music on period instruments, using rules of performance practice from the same period, according to the ideas developed at that time as skilfully and as accurately as possible."[57] This commitment and faithfulness to the musical work and/or the composer's intentions, as far as these are fallibly understood,[58] can indeed have the look and feel of an act of reverence and preservation. The key question for the performer is then to determine just how much liberty they have to "skillfully and accurately" *interpret* the musical work.[59]

E. T. A. Hoffmann famously wrote "The genuine artist lives only for the work...He does not make his personality count in any way."[60] For Taruskin such a "Romantic notion of the autonomous transcendent artwork entail[s] a hierarchized, strictly enforced split between emancipated creators, beholden (in theory) to no one but the muse, and selfless curators, sworn to submission."[61] Early music performers are cast as powerless "selfless curators," bound to preserve rather than to fully realize their own "authentic" selves as performers. The power balance is very much tipped in favor of the composer—a somewhat unfashionable idea in the late 1960s, just at the very time that Roland Barthes was declaring *The Death of the Author* (1967). Anyone familiar with Ton Koopman's powerful performances, along with those of so many of his period performer colleagues, however, would have great difficulty in reconciling these views.

It is especially difficult to disentangle the problem of the musical work and its associated work-concept from that of the musician's "fidelity" toward it, when the musical score, i.e., the "text," is mistaken for the musical work itself. Taruskin's argument is that Werktreue has in fact been reduced to just this kind of text fidelity—faithfulness to the score, rather than any other quality. He contrasts the "straight" performer—for whom he has little or no time, with the "crooked"—"the real artists among performers," whose "subjective imaginings"..."claim [his] heart."[62] A particularly troubling consequence of the Werktreue position according to Taruskin is a sense of the performer becoming invisible due to being "bound scrupulously to carry out the masters' intentions for the sake of their glory, their own lives pledged to a sterile humdrum of preservation and handing-on."[63] Again, as any performer will attest, this strikes at the very core of the performing act. To the extent that the performer is bound to seek a form of personal authenticity through performance,[64] we must conclude that either early music performers are just not "authentic," i.e., genuine, performers at all, or this interpretation of events, and our understanding of the relationship between the performer and the musical work need reexamining. On the evidence available, it is the latter of these two options that seems most convincing.

SOME ISSUES WITH THE "AUTHENTICITY MOVEMENT" CRITIQUE

Looking back, there is no question that Taruskin blew the wind out of Early Music's ideological sails. Over and above some initial rhetorical positioning, there has actually been precious little critical response to Taruskin in these years since the publication of *Text & Act*. But then we must be careful not to ignore the practical response that has been played out on stage—to use Taruskin's own phrase, "letting the music speak for itself."[65] Certainly, it is Taruskin's voice that has remained very much the dominant one in contemporary debate concerning historical performance. His once outspoken views have been all but appropriated within HIP orthodoxy, although often at the level of tacit acceptance rather than wholehearted approval. With the benefit of hindsight, Taruskin's critique has unquestionably done more good than harm. It has given rise to an increasingly self-aware, reflexive cultural movement that now conspicuously avoids making any grand claims concerning the authenticity or historical accuracy of its performances. Nicholas Kenyon notes that "although it appeared undermining to the early music purists, it in fact helped to start building bridges in what had been a very polarized situation by showing that neither side was 'right.'"[66] It would be easy to stop there. It is enough, we might conclude, to recognize Taruskin's contributions within this niche field of early music, and have done with it. But I think this would be a mistake. There are at least two areas of unfinished business that continue to demand our attention. Firstly, Early Music has fought shy of defending its ideological position on authentic performance, whilst continuing to pursue it on a practical basis, both on and off the concert platform. The analytical case for seeking (historical) authenticity in performance *at all*, needs (re-)asserting with greater clarity (not simply to defend or promote the particular interests of those involved in HIP, but rather to provide fresh insights concerning the performance of classical music). Contrary to what some might think, Taruskin's ideas provide a strong basis for doing this. Secondly, we should be looking to draw out the wider implications of this debate—transcending *Text & Act*, if you will. At issue is our understanding of "doing art" and "being authentic" in all walks of life, not just in the performance of "old" music. For these are fundamental features of humanity that have been largely squeezed out of societal discourse by other apparently more immediately pressing concerns. We need to cultivate a public "play space" where these issues can be discussed and shared as rigorously, but also as openly and passionately as has been the case in Taruskin's own writings. The "art of re-enchantment," as it is introduced in the final Part of the book, seeks to get just such a conversation under way. For the rest of this chapter, however, it is to the first of these goals that we now turn.

i) An Ahistorical and Totalizing View of the "Authenticity Movement"

The very notion of there being an "authenticity movement"—an organized cultural movement unified by its advancement of authenticity as a common goal—is one that tends to go unchallenged. Understandably, it is the word "authenticity" that has received all the attention. It is revealing to note that it was not actually until Taruskin's *Early Music* article of 1984, published as part of a series of essays on the "limits of authenticity," that the idea of there being an "authenticity *movement*" received any sustained and explicit coverage in print. In fact, Taruskin explains that he had himself come across the term in a recent *New York Times* review of one of his own concerts, with his choir Cappella Nova. Looking through archive copies of *Early Music* one finds that the first reference to a "movement" of any kind was not until 1975, the year of the Dolmetsch Festival's golden jubilee, and two years after the journal's launch. Thereafter, only a scattering of "movements" appear, with the first mention of the "early music movement" not until 1977, in a piece by Nicholas Kenyon on the York Early Music Week.[67] Kenyon suggests that the York event was "Highly significant for the future direction of the 'early music' movement," on account of its "lack of ties with the hothouse parochialism of London's music-making." However, in his 1984 article, Taruskin uses the word "movement" no less than thirteen times. There are several references to "*our* movement," thus signaling the sense in which this is a critique from the inside—an informed and friendly "critical other" rather than a hostile outsider. And yet, as the article progresses, there is also an increasingly antagonistic stance toward the "movement." The reason this is worth noting, perhaps, is because it reflects a somewhat ahistorical account of what Taruskin (after Trilling) defines as, a "concerted effort of...a segment of a culture to achieve authenticity."[68] To the extent that there was (of course) an emergent "movement" advocating authenticity in performance, it does not seem to be the case that it ever explicitly did this on its own behalf. One suspects that this is, in part, a reflection of the heterogeneity of the beliefs and practices of those involved at the time. There were, perhaps, "fifty shades" of authenticity, not just the one being alluded to. In retrospect, there is also something ironic about the case for the "authenticity movement" being first made, according to Taruskin, by a music critic for the New York Times, rather than from within its fold.

At the heart of Taruskin's critique, of course, is the assertion that the movement "reflects modernist assumptions about how *all* modern music should sound."[69] The use of the word "all" here is totalizing in a way that suggests that the "movement" was also strategically calling for its approach to be adopted by everyone, across the board.[70] With the benefit of hindsight, Taruskin's totalizing critique—the charge that the authenticity movement felt it held a monopoly over acceptable performance practice—appears an "aunt sally" argument.[71] Though it is undeniable that there have been some over-inflated claims made on behalf of authentic performance, notably in the late 1970s and early '80s when the movement was reaching its commercial high-point, and that some early music purists no doubt implied that theirs was "the only show in town," this is not a view shared by the vast majority of early music performers, either then or now.

ii) A Lack of Reflexivity in a Modernist Critique

The basic charge before Early Music was that their practices embodied "a whole wish list" of modernist values.[72] In this context, Taruskin's call for "liberation" on behalf of the performer, such that their freedom in "choice of action and creed"[73] could be restored, was (and remains) compelling. But if we pause for a moment to consider such a viewpoint more carefully, we can see how it betrays a less than neutral position. Early Music is critiqued for *not* being the very things that a 19th-century Romantic view of "art" might hold dear: in place of the genius, the early musician is cast as rule-bound performer; inspiration is replaced by calculation, i.e., as to what makes an "authentic" score and/or performance; the craft-like skills of the early music performer (playing on the "right" instruments) are celebrated over and above spontaneity; and Early Music is about imitating (models of performance) rather than originality, copying rather than creating, paid work rather than the freedom to play.[74]

That early musicians were partly motivated by contemporary ideals seems beyond doubt. However, it is never wholly clear which of the subsequent failings of the movement are considered most heinous: authentic performers were not doing what they said they were doing; they *were* doing what they said they were doing; they weren't doing what they said they were doing, and knew that; or what they were doing gave rise to something creative, and thus in keeping with modern(ist) rather than historical values? On the one hand, Early Music's devotees stand accused of being overly preoccupied with the "text," giving undue emphasis to the musical score at the expense of the performance "act." On the other hand, Taruskin's comments about authenticity and the market also cast the early musician as something of an instrumental pawn in a bigger game of selling records and making money. "Authenticity," in this case, becomes little more than a strategic tool or marketing ruse. The "authenticity movement" is guilty of being too dogmatic and somehow too creative at the same time.

Interestingly, the vast majority of commentaries on "authentic performance" put forward following Taruskin's influential interventions (including both supportive and rather more critical works by historically informed performance's leading musicologists and exponents[75]), have been characteristically postmodernist, or at the very least, broadly "liberal" in their perspective.[76] It is particularly striking that "authenticity" has given way to the rather equivocal "historically informed performance" (HIP)—a much more acceptable term to many. Authenticity, after all, infers a "right" way of doing things, i.e., very much in line with the modernist's penchant for grand narrative, and this is wholly at odds with postmodern academia and cultural practice characteristic of the late 1960s onward. However, neither of these approaches suffices to explain why or how it was that the early music movement has proved to be so successful. The third of the three issues (and the most important) now prepares the ground for answering these questions.

iii) An Irrealist Position

The barb of Taruskin's critique remains largely at an epistemological level, where what we can *know* about historical performance is really the central issue. In this respect, Taruskin raises important qualifications, which practitioners and theorists have taken much account of. However, his ontological position is perhaps rather less clear. To the extent that he has most openly supported Goehr's social constructivist position, whilst also being openly hostile to the "notion of the autonomous transcendent artwork,"[77] it is this meta-theoretical position that is the focus of my attention here. Goehr's historical ontology is distinctive for its inclusion of an embedded historical perspective—something that analytical philosophers could be accused of previously overlooking. However, in focusing so closely on the work-concept, something of the "historical" baby gets thrown away with the "ontological" bath-water. Goehr herself rather lightly dismisses ontology as being less relevant to her project. As a consequence, her theory of the work-concept tends toward an irrealist position where its existence and associated causal powers are held to operate within the level of discourse alone. The problem with this is that musical works and musical "work" are all too real in an embodied and material sense (how else is music "produced?"). Reality is not exhausted by or through language, though this is the largely unwitting implication of much postmodernist theorizing. It is this very problem that prompted Nicholas Cook to describe Werktreue—understood as an unswerving commitment to the musical score—as something akin to religious fundamentalism. For Cook, "Fundamentalism arises from the false belief that language can circumscribe and contain reality, from which it follows that what cannot be said does not exist."[78]

Goehr's views on the centrality of the work-concept are in themselves highly persuasive. The weight of evidence that people only started referring to musical works from around the beginning of the 19th century is compelling. For Goehr this is linked to the rise of the Romantic ideal and the glorification of the individual. She is careful to avoid making any grand claims for the "presence or absence of the work-concept as a regulative concept,"[79] referring rather to "a certain standardization to which the work-concept submits as the surrounding practice becomes more standardized." As such, the link between capitalistic "work" and the "work-concept" remains under-theorized. Although the capitalistic logic of economic production is implicit throughout Goehr's essay, including in the focus given to the changing social status of composers ("The Beethoven Paradigm"), there is only passing reference to the standardizing capitalistic structures and institutions (not under the control of the composer) that have been instrumental in reproducing and transforming musical work(s) over time.

If the claims for the work-concept are so important (as indeed they are), we can and should see them in an ontological light. The musical work is not neatly replaced by the work-concept in some ontological side-stepping maneuver, but it is itself partly constituted by the work-concept. This has a significant bearing on our understanding of musical works, how they have been performed, discussed and written about over time, how they change over time by virtue of these different practices, and therefore just what the concept of "authentic performance" entails from this critical realist perspective, as we shall now see.

THE (NOT SO) IMAGINARY MUSEUM OF MUSICAL WORKS

This immanent critique of Goehr's position is motivated by a belief (however fallible) in the need to pay more attention to epistemology's "other," i.e., ontology; discourse's "other," i.e., social and natural practices; as well as "the Other," (understood here in the sense of a spiritual dimension to our lives, not necessarily involving religious belief). Though my primary interest is within the domain of cultural musicology, this perceived "lack" is characteristic of much theorizing in the social sciences more broadly today. My approach is very much motivated by the intention to provide a more "practically adequate"[80] explanation.

Musical works exist and are real; they are dependent upon, but not reducible to the ordering of sound structures, and their reproduction through performance; they possess emergent properties that are causally generative, and they have an impact on human beings. Musical works endure over time and through space, but only as the result of human practice (most notably, but not only performance), and not as an unchanging essence of the original. We can think of the musical work, e.g., Handel's *Messiah*; Bach's *Brandenburg Concerto No.2*; *Three Blind Mice*; and *Happy Birthday to You* as the enduring form of music in a social, relational, sonic, and necessarily emergent context. Singing *Happy Birthday to You* at a children's birthday party in Lewisham, London in 2013 holds quite different meaning and is an altogether different experience to a rendition amongst friends in Louisville, Kentucky, in 1898.[81] Our appreciation and enjoyment of the musical work (regardless of whether it carries with it any extra-musical narrative or text) is always contingent upon our place in the world. As Elizabeth Upton (2012) observes, all modern performers of early music (likewise their audience) have "been shaped by their experience as listeners to the music of their own time."[82]

It is important to stress that the musical work is not just the score, and not just the performance. Given the potential complexity of analysis, there is clearly a danger here of commentators talking at cross purposes, and this has been a contributory factor in some of the confusion that arises in this area. One way of understanding the difficult-to-grasp relationship between these things is to view them from the perspective of the semiotic triangle, comprised of signifier, signified, and referent.[83] In modernist and postmodernist theorizing, the referent is effectively overlooked (since ontology is not accepted), and this leaves the musical work looking like an "ontological mutant."[84] Applying the semiotic triangle to our terms, the score is the signifier, the performance is the signified, and the musical work is the referent (though this model can also be applied at other levels of analysis, such as treating the musical score as the referent).[85] The main point to emphasize in analytical terms is that the whole (the musical work) is greater than the sum of the parts (the score, performance, sounds, instruments, etc.). Musical works are complex and emergent systemic phenomena.[86]

MUSICAL WORKS ARE REPRODUCED AND TRANSFORMED THROUGH HUMAN PRACTICE(S)

Much of the disagreement over the existence of musical works can be put down to a mistaken belief that they are either historical constructions (see Goehr 2007) or the product of some eternal, unchanging essence, i.e., musical essentialism.[87] I would argue for an alternative emergentist view, which is to conceptualize the musical work as always and only existing through human practice, so avoiding some notion of eternal existence or reification (i.e., giving musical works powers that are independent of any human involvement). Not only is the musical work *reproduced* through human action (principally, but not exclusively through being performed), it is also *transformed* through practice, so it is not "unchanging." This, of course, is fundamental to our enjoyment of the "living" art of music, and of (re-)discovering it as if it were "new." Such a view allows for the socially constructed nature of performing and listening to music. Shared beliefs about musical works do indeed influence our views as to what is or isn't authentic.[88] However, we also need to take account of the properties and powers of musical works that exist by virtue of their being what they are (I discuss the implications arising from this "natural necessity" in the final section of the chapter).

To recap, musical works *only* endure if related human practices are enacted (including musical scholarship, editing, performance, critique, sale, recording, practice, etc.); they cease to exist if no one performs the "music," talks about it,[89] analyzes the original score, remembers it, and so on (until it is "discovered" again at a later date). This position recalls John Dewey's statement concerning when a work of art is "actually, not just potentially, a work of art": "As a piece of parchment, of marble, of canvas, it remains (subject to the ravages of time) self-identical throughout the ages. But as a work of art, it is recreated every time it is esthetically experienced."[90]

Musical works are dependent upon the potential relationships between many different agents and structures, including the performing musician, audience, musicologist, editor, publisher, promoter, record company, critic, and so forth. It follows from what has been said so far that in reviving "early music," those involved were, through their many practices, breathing new life into musical works that to all extents and purposes had otherwise ceased to exist—they were no longer recalled, known about, discussed, critiqued, and, most importantly, performed.

MUSICAL WORKS ARE DEPENDENT UPON (BUT NOT REDUCIBLE TO) THE DIALECTICAL RELATIONSHIP BETWEEN PERFORMING MUSICIAN AND MUSICAL WORK

The range of human practices relevant to the reproduction and transformation of the musical work clearly extends beyond that of performance per se—and this is an especially important point to emphasize in the context of this book's subject. All the same, it is the performing musician, first and foremost, who is the central figure in our story. Understanding the dialectical nature of this relationship between musician and musical work is paramount—not least because prevailing perspectives have tended toward a view of reality as being purely positive and present.

Perhaps the best way of explaining what I mean by dialectical here is in terms of "being and becoming" (product and process). Bhaskar (1993) states that any entity contains within it, as part of its being (product), the process that constituted it (becoming). This process can be thought of as both "becoming and begoing."[91] As Norrie puts it, "we are existentially constituted by what is now apparently absent because past."[92] Furthermore, the "present as a future is mediated by, or event dependent upon the presence of the past."[93] Both musical work and performer are then individually constituted by what is apparently absent and past. Bach's *Mass in B Minor* would not *be* the *Mass in B Minor* without it having been composed (then possibly re-composed) and then performed (on multiple occasions), recorded (variously), discussed and written about (in program notes, reviews, books, etc.) in the past. Similarly, Gustav Leonhardt only became the great musician that he was by virtue of his past performances and experiences of performing, to say nothing of all the life-experiences that made him, including his love of fine wine and fast cars, and his staunch Protestant faith. Although Leonhardt himself declared "authenticity" to have no place in music, it is difficult not to read into his distinctive and successful career in early music what Kivy (1995) refers to as "personal authenticity." The intrinsic qualities of the performing musician constitute their biggest constraint and enabler—we can't escape being the person we are. But more than this, there is also a dialectical dimension to the relationship *between* musician and musical work, i.e., between Leonhardt and Bach's *Mass in B Minor*. For in the process of bringing the musical work into being (which changes it), the musician (and audience) is also changed. Gustav Leonhardt, together with his fellow performers, brought the *Mass in B Minor* into being through their legendary performances and recordings. These early musicians were transformed by the experience, as was the audience and the musical press who heard and wrote about it subsequently; so, too, (I argue) the musical work that is the *Mass in B Minor*.

One of the important aspects of thinking of this relationship in dialectical terms is to draw attention to the effect of the musical work on the performing musician, without reifying the musical work itself. As a musician one is molded through this dialectical relationship with musical works. Of course, this is mediated in a variety of ways—reading scores, performing works, hearing others, making and selling recordings, persuading broadcasters to commission programs, or teaching up-and-coming students in master classes (I prefer the term "musician" rather than "performer," since the musician does much more than just perform). Each of these practices is characterized by a relational quality, involving engagement with some kind of "other." There is an enabling aspect to this relationship, certainly; but there is also a constraining side, and one of the big questions already aired in this chapter concerns the extent to which the musician is free to take liberties in performing and interpreting according to the personal tastes and requirements of their authentic selves. After all, as Richard Schechner says, performance isn't "in" anything, but "between."[94] A dialectical reading of this crucial relationship between performer and musical work, as well as the sense in which this dialectic is disclosed (a "showing doing"[95] to the audience through performance) also focuses on the possibility, indeed the requirement, for personal and historical authenticity to be kept in balance. It is this balance that is really at stake for all those seriously engaged in performance of any music.

Our philosophical beliefs concerning the nature of the musical work carry with them some important implications. For example, the emergentist position I have outlined here supports the "thick"[96] view (as expressed by Mr. Justice Patten in the Hyperion vs. Sawkins court case) that a musical work "includes items such as the figuring of the bass, ornamentation and performance directions" as opposed to being "limited for copyright purposes to the notes on the score."[97] In fact, my position goes further in recognizing the role of many more human practices (including most notably that of performance) in reproducing and/or transforming the musical work over time. On this basis, one might question why it is that performers, who also put in hours of "effort, skill and time," are not similarly entitled to copyright protection—indeed, nearly all early music performers who have helped swell the coffers of record companies and musical impresarios have been "bought out," their contributions to iconic recordings garnering worldwide prizes and praise measured in just a few hundred pounds. I can't help but agree with Peter Phillips, the director of The Tallis Scholars and a music editor himself, who said: "All the music I perform has to be edited, or we couldn't read it. But copyright should be there...to reward creativity, not scholarship or diligence. How much an editor did or did not write should never be asked and judged upon during a million-pound lawsuit involving a small and innovative recording company."[98]

WHAT DOES THIS MEAN FOR AUTHENTIC PERFORMANCE?

The argument so far presented maintains that musical works are not unchanging essences, but are reproduced and transformed through human practice. Musical works change over time, through their performance, but also as a result of being edited, recorded, written about, discussed, and commodified. On one level, every new performance is an opportunity for a fresh discovery. For the performer, this quality of music to be "alive" transforms a science into an art. But the argument is not yet complete. One crucial step remains. For musical works *cannot* be changed too much, or they become different works altogether. It is here that we come to see the motivation of the authentic performance movement in a fresh light. For in accepting the inherent possibilities for change, early music practitioners argued that we should also accept the legitimacy of striving to perform a musical work according to those conditions that brought it into existence; those that made it possible to *be*. This is the principle of "dispositional (historical) authenticity," which holds that music's inherent meaning and value is always dependent upon, though not reducible to, the compositional act. Over and above the notated music, this reflects a composer's temporally and spatially situated knowledge and experience of performance practice (i.e., the instruments available, how they were played, notation used, performance venues, etc.). Whilst it would be preposterous to suggest that those involved in Early Music have thought explicitly in the theoretical terms used here, dispositional (historical) authenticity nonetheless represents a foundational justification for the practice(s) of authentic performance. To better explain this now, I summarize seven key features arising from the preceding discussion, highlighting relevant implications for our understanding (see Table 3.1).

First, having established the existence of the musical work, it is clear that performing authentically is, at least, a legitimate position to strive for, even though this will always remain relative rather than absolute in quality.

Second, the position presented does allow for a reasoned commentary as to what is or is not authentic. As Davies says, "Because it is essentially implicated in a work's performance, authenticity is an ontological requirement not an interpretative option."[99] To perform any musical work, we have an obligation to a minimal level of authenticity, otherwise in effect we will be performing another piece of music, and so doing under false pretenses. Over and above this minimal level of authenticity, however, it is also clear that performing Monteverdi's *Possente Spirto* on synthesizer and saxophones is clearly not authentic—even if we can all agree that Monteverdi may have been fascinated by this sound-world, and that there is nothing "wrong" about playing

TABLE 3.1.

Understanding dispositional (historical) authenticity

No.	Feature of musical works	Implications for authentic performance
1	Real existence	Authenticity claims are legitimate, but relative
2	Geo-historically specific	Conditions of possibility trump realization
3	Transformed over time	Dependent on dialectic with performer
4	Cannot be fully notated	The score alone is inadequate
5	Practice-dependent	Non-performance issues also important
6	Natural necessity	Authentic performance sounds different
7	Inherent meaning & value	Re-enchanting music matters

music on any instrument at all. The fact remains that when Monteverdi composed, there were certain geo-historically-specific conditions of possibility that determined (to some extent at least) what the musical work created *could* be. The foundation of dispositional (historical) authenticity is the philosophical perspective that argues for the ontological, epistemological, and logical priority of the *possible* or potential over the actual or realized. For the performer this means asking questions about what must have been possible to perform the musical work at the time and place, rather than what were the actual conditions of any first performance, what the piece sounded like, or what the composer's intentions actually were. (There have been ample discussion pointing out the limitations of these approaches—see for example Kenyon, 1988; Kivy, 1995, 2002; Jackson, 1997; Taruskin, 1995.) Whilst at first glance, this might look similar to Kivy's (1995) *sonic* and *practical* authenticities—the implied focus being on physical conditions of performance—there is an important distinction to be drawn between establishing the conditions that determined just what it was possible to perform, and seeking to replicate a given or predetermined outcome. Furthermore, dispositional (historical) authenticity is not just concerned with sound and performance practice, but embraces aspects of Kivy's other authenticities too (including "personal authenticity").

Third, though we understand the musical work as existing and enduring through the years, it is not an unchanging "essence." It is transformed over time. The focus on composition of classical music (by canonical composers) has given rise to the myth that music endures endlessly, and that performance is somehow just the physical re-expression of the music. But, the musical work is always the product of a dialectical, i.e., changing relationship with the performing musician, and indeed with the constantly evolving tastes and expectations of modern listeners. As a consequence, there will always be an ontological gap (to say nothing of an epistemological gap) between us and the "original" musical work as it was composed (this is the case regardless of the date of composition).

Fourth, the musical work cannot be fully notated through a score. The conventions of performance that are passed on through practice, tuition, and performance are also important in transmitting a musical work and allowing the performer to perform it, rather than what would potentially amount to another musical work. Instead of presenting Early Music as a dogmatic movement, which advocates restoration for its own sake (typical of what Scruton (1997) refers to as "the museum culture"), its underlying purpose can be re-expressed much more positively, as drawing attention to the fact that the transmission of the musical work is *not* detailed exhaustively by the score alone.

Fifth, a musical work is to some extent made "new" every time it is performed; every time it is reviewed; every time we buy tickets to go and hear it; every time we listen to it through our mp3 player or on an old gramophone record. Crucially, the practices involved in the reproduction/transformation of the musical work are not confined to performance. *All* related practices, including scholarship, market activities, and the mediating use of technology, are involved in shaping what the musical work actually is (and becomes) over space and time.

Sixth, by virtue of attributing real powers to the musical work, the musician, and the relations between them, we can also begin to talk of the truth of these things as distinct from the truth of propositions about them. Musical works, by virtue of being what they are, have natural necessity, or what philosophers refer to as "alethic truth"—the truth about things.[100] Sound structures have their effect, in part at least, by virtue of their causal powers, which we can think of as tendencies to produce corresponding effects (such as those we experience when listening to music). In turn, these powers result from the mechanisms or processes involved in structuring sound. We *tend* to have a complex emotional, affective, embodied response to particular sounds, regardless of what anyone tells us about them (though this is not to deny that what people tell us makes a difference). Authentic performance makes music *sound* different—and early musicians have been first and foremost driven by questions of musical sound rather than dogma for its own sake. I would argue that playing on "old" instruments in an "historically informed style" is not just a distinctively different practice to playing on modern instruments, but the sounds produced, and their effects on us, the listeners, are different too, by virtue of being what they are. Natural necessity is important—but not the whole story. Countervailing tendencies will impact the music, too (the most authentic performance one could otherwise conceive of may not "work" if played as background music in a shopping mall). This is a practice beyond the immediate control of musicians. Of course, what we "do" with musical works matters.

Does authentic performance give better performances? Leaving aside what "better" actually means (and ignoring the obvious statement that world-class exponents will generally give "better" performances than beginners), the answer must be—not *necessarily*. Clearly, we need to exercise considerable caution before making any grand claims on behalf of historical authentic performance per se. This said, the authentic performance (always understood in relative terms) will be the performance that strives to disclose the alethic truth[101] of the original musical work as conceived, and/or modified, by the composer, in their time and space. Composers are intuitively aware of what "works," composing with certain performance conventions, instruments, and sounds in mind—this is, in part, what marks them out as composers, after all. Very often they write with particular instrumentalists and singers in mind. The "true" work is only ever expressed through the relation between musician(s) and the composer's intentions, as they are fallibly perceived (for composers *always* had intentions even if we don't "know" what they were). It is not the notes, the instruments, the performing style, or the musician that constitutes the truth; it is the emergent relationship between all of them, which we experience as "music." Sir Roger Norrington puts the musician's perspective very eloquently: "we are playing the music *now*, for modern audiences. But that cannot be an excuse for not being intensely interested in *then*, and in what the composers may have hoped for in performance. And even if we don't (can't?) get it right, at least we are taking the past seriously. Each previous era had its own way of doing things; in the end this is ours. But it's not borrowed from a grey tradition of dread respectability; it's carefully considered, and often joyful."[102]

Seventh, what is being suggested here also rests on the premise that being *is* enchanted. In other words, there is inherent meaning and value in being, though we may not be able to express this through rational discourse (I provide much more discussion of this perspective on enchantment in Chapters 11 and 12). This is a profoundly important idea for music, Early Music, for this book's focus on the social practices that make authenticity work, and, of course, for human beings in general. Life and music are enchanted. Meaning is not *just* socially or historically constructed (though all social activity is of course mediated by human beings). This is why art matters. The common saying that art makes life worth living is a reflection of this. But art is not here some mystical transcendent essence that lives apart from our concretely embodied flesh and blood. A much more immanent and everyday understanding of transcendence is envisaged.

The position I have outlined focuses the spotlight on the lived relationship between the performing musician and the musical work, giving rise to music. Crucially, this signals that our understanding of the (professional) musician must embrace a wider set of practices than just performance. Musicians are also scholars, professionals, entrepreneurs, negotiators, leaders, workers, consumers, audience members, and so on. They must perform multiple, and sometimes contradictory, roles. In recognizing this we are alerted to the exciting potential of seeing authenticity in a new way—not as an impossible ideal, but rather in terms of the emergent, lived-out strategy each one of us is engaged in everyday, as we seek to reconcile different aspects of ourselves and our relations with the world around us. It is here that I believe we can see real potential for building on these ideas concerning authenticity. For what amounts to an emergent consensus on authenticity in musical performance, a topic that owes a considerable debt to Taruskin's *Text & Act*, has not yet done full justice to the contribution made by Early Music to our understanding of authenticity more generally as it relates to art and life. Nowhere is this relationship more central than in the world of "work"—and it is to this domain that we turn in the next Part of the book.

PART TWO

Making Early Music *Work*

It was the best of times, it was the worst of times, it was the age of wisdom, it was the age of foolishness, it was the epoch of belief, it was the epoch of incredulity, it was the season of Light, it was the season of Darkness, it was the spring of hope, it was the winter of despair, we had everything before us, we had nothing before us, we were all going direct to heaven, we were all going direct the other way.

CHARLES DICKENS *A Tale of Two Cities*[1]

The dulcimer-strumming flower children have been overtaken by a newer generation of trained professionals. It is no longer enough to dress in ruffles and to brandish thirty odd-shaped musical objects at the public; people can now hear those instruments played well, by men and women in street clothes.

JOEL COHEN[2]

4

A Tale of Two Authenticities

INTRODUCTION

Artistic revolutions "rarely happen overnight." So wrote Nicholas Kenyon in March 2011 on the occasion of the debut performance of New York's newest period instrument ensemble.[3] What had started many years before "as an eccentric, irrelevant outsider in cultural life," went on to provoke a "radical shift in performance styles," transforming "attitudes towards tradition" and bringing about "major changes in orchestral practice."[4] But, of course, this revolution was only made possible by the courage of many of those involved in making Early Music *work*, i.e., taking the sometimes bold decision to do it as a job. It is to this unfolding process of professionalization that we now turn.

On the surface, the professionalization of Early Music entails an extraordinary transition from being merely a handful of "obscure enthusiasts"[5] operating within a "fringe movement"[6] all the way through to a "huge industry"[7] where those involved got paid for their services and made a decent living. Probing a little deeper, however, we see this is something of a simplification. For example, in her study of professional classical musicians (surprisingly, one of very few contemporary studies on the subject), Dawn Bennett observes, "Far from making a living by making music, the majority of musicians finance music making by making a living."[8] The precarious nature of this kind of creative labor is typical of the cultural industries in general[9] and has been characteristic of the music profession for centuries. To understand when exactly Early Music was professionalized we could follow text-book advice and see when those involved were able to pursue *a full-time occupation*; when *specialist education* was available through music college and university; and when local and national *associations supporting* the profession were drawn up, with regulating codes of *professional ethics* and licensing laws.[10] With the launching of professional freelance orchestras such as the Academy of Ancient Music and The English Concert in

1973, a full-time career in early music performance became a realistic prospect for some. Doubts remained, however, as to whether there was really a future in it. John Bickley, former chairman of the Early Music Network and founder-director of the music agency Magenta Music (who represented the Hilliard Ensemble, The Clerks of Oxenford, Ton Koopman, and the Amsterdam Baroque Orchestra, amongst others) remembers thinking "would this interest in early music continue—was it just a flash in the pan?"[11] 1973 was the year that the Guildhall School of Music & Drama launched its specialist program in early music. Oxford University Press's *Early Music* journal was also founded that year. The Early Music Centre was launched in 1976 under the directorship of Anthony Rooley; the York Early Music Festival was established in 1977; and the first conference devoted to early music (*The Future of Early Music in Britain*) was held in May 1977. An outcome of this conference was the setting up of the National Early Music Association in 1978. Whilst professional ethics were not explicitly on the conference's agenda, topics discussed were largely focused on "ways and means to improve the lot of the early musician, to raise standards in general, and to enhance the role early music plays in musical life."[12] The 443rd edition of *Time Out* magazine in October 1978 devoted its cover story to early music, with the memorable title, "A resounding tinkle." The feature story read, "As harpsichords change hands for a small ransom and plastic crumhorns prepare to hit the market, Renaissance music makes its biggest-ever comeback. We bend an ear to Early Music fever." On the strength of this initial evidence, at least, it appears that professionalization unfolded gradually, only getting fully under way in the early-1980s as Early Music entered its "independence" (see Chapter 2's life course).

We turn now to the question of *how* professionalization took place. A major theme running throughout this analysis is the unrelenting influence of the economic imperative. As the conductor Boyd Neel, writing in 1950, lamented, "The average person has no conception of what it costs to run even a small orchestra," adding, "It is, I suppose, an understandable thing that 'success' should be usually synonymous in the public mind with some sort of financial reward. Little does it know!"[13] Over and above early musicians' principled concern for authenticity, this lack of financial security would invariably impact the choice of instruments actually being used for a given professional engagement. For example, David Munrow noted, "20 instruments is a lot to carry round. Especially when we all live in different places, London, Birmingham, Cambridge and Stratford upon Avon, and, only two of us can drive. We often speculate on the possibility of a weightless harpsichord."[14] Sir Roger Norrington recalls how in 1974 he persuaded Kent Opera to premiere his edition of Monteverdi's opera *L'Incoronazione di Poppea* in Lisbon, on original instruments: "I'd been working there, and they asked me to do an opera; it had never been performed in Portugal ever. I said to the guys 'we'll do this one to a part with original instruments and original voice levels'; no one had ever done that either, and instruments, one to a part—you can't do that in an opera! They said 'we'll take both [instruments], won't we...and then when it doesn't work we'll use our modern instruments'? And I said 'no...we'll just take one set.' They were rather scared, but they just packed the old instruments...so we *had* to play them!"[15]

A second underlying theme concerns the evolving profile of the "early music" actually being performed. For as we shall see, there are distinctive musical, logistical, and business-related challenges in performing Medieval, Renaissance, and early Baroque music (what I term *Authenticity$_1$*), as opposed to repertoire from the (High) Baroque, Classical, and later periods (*Authenticity$_2$*), which was to become increasingly popular. During the 1960s *professional* performance of early music became a prominent feature of the classical music scene, particularly in London. Medieval and Renaissance period music was performed not just by amateur groups, but also at sold-out concerts at London's South Bank and elsewhere around the country, notably by Michael Morrow's Musica Reservata and Munrow's Early Music Consort of London. Elizabeth Roche describes Renaissance dance music as the paramount instrumental form in the 1970s, commenting "enthusiasm has reached almost epidemic proportions; many records of it have appeared, eight in 1972-3 alone."[16] Television programs and plays introduced instruments such as the cornett, sackbut, curtal, dulcimer, the nakers, tabor, and other percussion instruments to a wide audience. The draw of seeing "all those weird instruments"[17] certainly accounted for much of the excitement around Authenticity$_1$ at the time. Record sleeves and inserts reproduced engravings of musical instruments. In turn, this provided extra encouragement for amateur musicians to buy up early music instruments in sizeable numbers.

In Roche's 1979 article for *The Musical Times* focusing on "Early Music on recordings in the last 25 years," she notes "the rise of interest in early music of the early 1970s was primarily in the medieval and early Renaissance areas."[18] She goes on to suggest that the early music revival might well have been "based primarily on anthologies and programmes of dance music"; and "it may be no coincidence that such records show off the exciting sounds of early instruments to best advantage."[19] But with their interest piqued by the "unfamiliar," the early music profession began to set its sights on Baroque and Classical (and later still, Romantic) repertoires. Over the 1970s, Renaissance saltarellos and Medieval ballads faded away, being replaced by something altogether more familiar, but now made different through period performance—the music of Vivaldi, Bach, Handel, Telemann, Haydn, Mozart, and their contemporaries.

The aim of this chapter is to provide not only an analysis of the prevailing conditions for Early Music's professionalization, but to begin to explore how such an upsurge in professional activities was comprised of two increasingly distinct, albeit overlapping, trajectories ("two authenticities").

FROM SEVEN RHETORICS TO SEVEN VANTAGE POINTS

In Chapter 1 seven rhetorics of Early Music were introduced (Revolutionary; Amateur; Commercial; Dogmatic; Creative; Modernist; Authentic). The primary position afforded to the Revolutionary rhetoric remains a dominant theme here. The opening lines of Dickens' novel *A Tale of Two Cities*, quoted at the top of this chapter, are set in revolutionary times. Early Music's story similarly begins at a time of societal change and upheaval. The late 1960s was a "New Age" of questioning and soul-searching, as the role of the individual in society, and society's values, came under a sustained level of scrutiny. A serious alternative to the hard-core avant-gardism of the 1960s was perhaps most eye-catchingly observable in the "Aquarian" fascination with Eastern musical instruments, kaftans, and vegetarian food. As the early music ensemble I Fagiolini's website explains (somewhat tongue-in-cheek) "most of the musicians that seemed to be interested in [early music] (both amateur and professional) seemed to have an alternative lifestyle of knitted yoghurt and wholefood pullovers, living on a diet of nothing but pulses and beans."[20]

By comparison with Dickens' story of Sydney Carton, Charles Darnay, Miss Pross, and Madame Defarge, this was a new kind of "quiet revolution," led predominantly by highly educated middle-class individuals. As Andrew Pinnock (former early music officer at the Arts Council) recalls, "we weren't really allowed in Grammar(y) type schools in the '70s to listen to jazz or world music, so crumhorns were about as fringy as it got!"[21] The revolutionary ethos of the new social movements of 1968 was undoubtedly of a different order to the "old revolutions," built as they were upon the idea of mass uprising by the working-class proletariat. Nonetheless, one can see Early Music as symptomatic of a wider seismic shift in the social landscape of late modernity, with the musical establishment being an obvious target of revolutionary zeal.[22]

To understand more about the revolutionary nature of Early Music's professionalization we need to explore from where the seven rhetorical positions emanated (see Figure 4.1). Here I introduce seven key vantage points (Musical Establishment; Amateur music-making; Instrument-making; Contemporary; Continental Europe and USA; Folk; and University). These can be thought of as collectively representing the

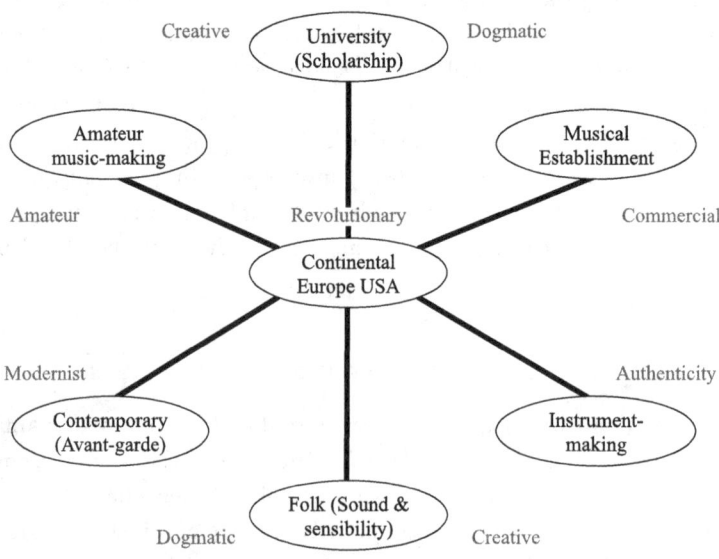

FIGURE 4.1 Seven Vantage Points

pre-existing conditions under which Early Music (and its two distinct trajectories) emerged.

The conceptual positioning of the rhetorics and their respective vantage points in Figure 4.1 seeks to present a complex story, comprised of many overlapping factors and causal mechanisms, in a reasonably manageable way. Little preliminary explanation is needed to elaborate on the connections between the rhetorics and vantage points discussed. At first glance, however, it might seem odd to position *Continental Europe* and *USA* at the center of a model designed to portray the main vantage points of the *British* Early Music scene. Notwithstanding the view that the British version of early music was "imitative" rather than "pioneering,"[23] there is a strong logic to placing the "other" (in this case that which was taking place outside of Britain) at the heart of this revolutionary story. The symmetry of the model captures the dualistic nature of the other six rhetorics discussed. Picking up from the discussion of "dialectic" in Chapter 3, we can understand the *Commercial* in terms of the absenting of the *Amateur*; *Authenticity* (understood here in terms of tradition, etc.) as the absenting of the *Modernist*; and *Creative* as negating the *Dogmatic*. The trajectory of professionalization, and associated distinction between $Authenticity_1$ and $Authenticity_2$, therefore takes us from the left-hand side of the model in Figure 4.2 through to the right-hand side.

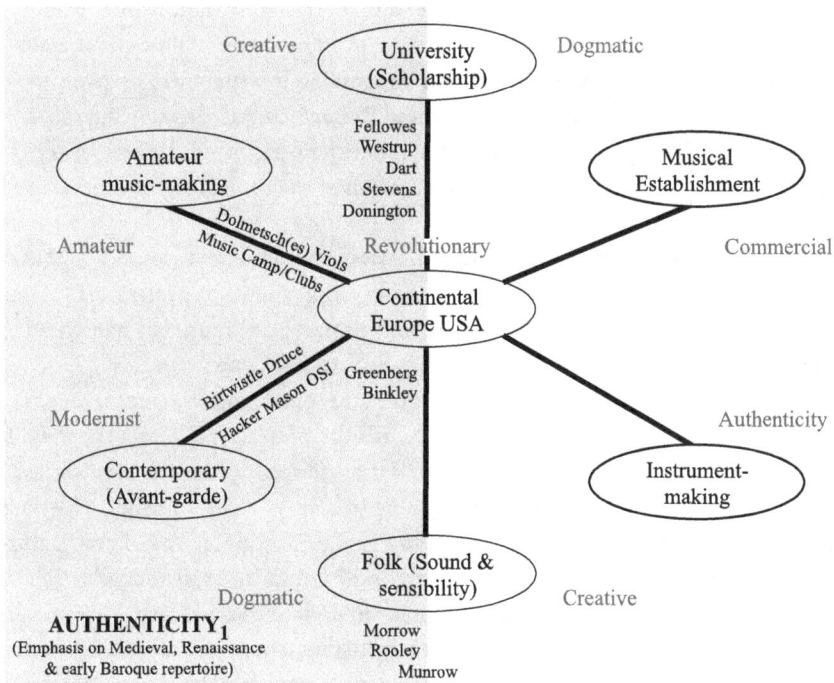

FIGURE 4.2 $Authenticity_1$

MAKING THE UNFAMILIAR FAMILIAR (AUTHENTICITY$_1$)

Early Music's professionalization begins appropriately enough with the amateur. The activities that together make up the early music movement—including an interest in old music, performing techniques, musicological work, and instrument building—"for many years, indeed for most of this century...took place among a small coterie of committed and enthusiastic converts to the cause."[24]

AMATEUR MUSIC-MAKING

The man often credited with launching the early music revival—Arnold Dolmetsch—despite making his living from a mix of professional instrument-making, musicology, and performance, remains (unfairly) tainted by the "amateur" label. With hindsight, history has categorized him "a pioneer before his time."[25] OAE violinist Catherine Mackintosh suggests "The thing about the Dolmetsches was that they attracted amateurs on the whole."[26] Dolmetsch's association with reviving the recorder, introducing it into schools as the instrument so many children toyed with and then quickly forgot, probably has much to do with his overall reputation. Nowhere is Dolmetsch's "amateurism" (in the literal sense of the word) captured more evocatively than in this extract from an article in *The Thursley Chronicle 1991*, by Mary Bennett:[27]

> ...a Dolmetsch concert seemed like a splendid and romantic fancy-dress party. There were false starts; strings broke, people in more-or-less Elizabethan costume produced unfamiliar sounds from unfamiliar instruments, or sang or danced, while the gnome-like figure of Arnold Dolmetsch, with his flowing robes and long white hair, played, expounded, admonished, exhorted, making everyone feel that they were taking part in an occasion of the utmost significance.

By the 1960s the British classical music profession had become a closed shop, with Musicians' Union and Equity agreements forcing employment of professional members only. The divide between the amateur and professional musician had widened substantially as domestic music-making gave way to new opportunities. The early music revival was attractive in the way that it offered something of a retrenchment of this position. The amateur could now mingle with the professional. For a short while at least, both amateurs and professionals found themselves together on more or less a level playing field. When it came to learning how to play "old" instruments, especially those associated with *Authenticity$_1$*, everything was up for grabs. A striking feature of the early music revival, therefore, up until and beyond its professionalization, is the extraordinary contribution made by amateur musicians in respect of performance (purchasing and performing on all sorts of early instruments), performance practice, historical musicology, and editing of musical works. At a practical level, too, interest in original musical instruments and their workings (very much inspired by Dolmetsch) provoked the establishment of specialist societies: for the recorder in 1937; the viola da gamba in 1948; and the lute in 1956, amongst others. Those involved were largely "amateurish in the best sense of the word...there was no cynicism at all."[28] As Kenyon observes, "nothing could have happened so quickly in the professional field" without the "quieter activities" of amateur early musicians.[29]

Summer schools, courses, and music camps have all played a central role in amateur early music-making. Amongst these, special mention must be made of the Dartington Summer School (seen very much as an out-post of the BBC, under the direction of Sir William Glock for more than 30 years), and Bryanston Summer School, where John Eliot Gardiner, aged eight, first met the likes of Imogen Holst and Nadia Boulanger, who would make a lasting impression on him. It is difficult to overemphasize the importance of these courses in terms of providing a vital meeting place and space to play with early music. Another key influence for both Gardiner and Norrington was the opportunity to conduct and perform with the Springhead Ring Choir at Springhead (Gardiner's birthplace), organized by Gardiner's parents. Roger Norrington tutored the 12-year-old Gardiner for a couple of months in August 1956, and it was during this time that Rolf Gardiner offered Norrington the chance to conduct the choir in works by William Byrd and Heinrich Schütz, on tours to Germany and Austria. Gardiner explains, "I am pretty sure that that was how Roger first came across the music of Schütz, which made such an impression on him."[30] Both John Eliot Gardiner and his mother went on to become members of the Schütz Choir, established by Norrington in 1962. Meanwhile, a range of Baroque operas and masques including *Acis and Galatea* (Handel), *Venus and Adonis* (Blow), *Dido and Aeneas* (Purcell), and *Il Ballo Delle Ingrate* (Monteverdi) were performed in the grounds of Springhead, with a mix of professionals coming down from London and boys from the local school, conducted by John Eliot Gardiner from the age of 15 to 20.

Elsewhere, Colin Kitching (OAE librarian and viola player) remembers the influence of Music Camp, run by Bernard Robinson (author of *An Amateur In Music*) at Pigotts, near High Wycombe.[31] Considered by Robinson as the "mainstay of music, the vehicle of its existence, historically and financially, the medium in which it develops,"[32] the amateur music-making that goes on in summer schools and music camps has long provided a critical porous boundary with the music profession. It was at this "powerhouse of amateur music-making," for example, that Kitching met Roger Norrington in 1963, soon after playing viola and undertaking the vital job of fixing performers for Kent Opera, London Classical Players, and later the OAE.

A number of the leading string players in early music orchestras and ensembles of the 1970s and '80s had had their interest in early music first raised through playing the viol (a predecessor to the modern string instruments that we hear in orchestras today). Here again we can trace direct connections back to Dolmetsch and his followers. Marco Pallis, who had helped to fund Dolmetsch's workshop in Haslemere, went on to reconstitute the English Consort of Viols in the 1930s, which was one of the first professional performing groups dedicated to early English music. Catherine Mackintosh, later leader of the Academy of Ancient Music and the Orchestra of the Age of Enlightenment, performed regularly with Pallis's consort, including a tour to

America. She recalls, "I actually made my living playing on the treble viol—if you can believe it, for about two years."[33] A rival group (though here the term "rival" carries with it little sense of competition) was the Jaye Consort of Viols, founded by Francis and June Baines in 1959. As Jane Ryan noted in her obituary of Francis Baines, anyone was welcome to go along to their home in Barnes or at the beginners' course they ran in Chiswick, and have a go. "The fact that amateur viol players still meet regularly in each other's homes for consort playing is largely due to the enthusiasm and love of the music instilled by the Baines over the years."[34] Notable amongst those who sought instruction from the Baines at one time or another are Alison Crum, viola da gamba player with many of the former leading early music groups, including the English Consort of Viols, Anthony Rooley's Consort of Musicke (with Trevor Jones, Polly Waterfield, and Catherine Mackintosh), the Brownynge Consort, the Dowland Consort, the Rose Consort of Viols, and the Musica Antiqua of London; OAE viola player Annette Isserlis; conductor and keyboard player Peter Holman; and publisher Clifford Bartlett (Holman and Bartlett founded the group Ars Nova, which later became The Parley of Instruments). The Consort of Musicke's summer schools under the direction of Rooley in the early 1970s (which later got taken under the wing of the Early Music Centre) also offered an important opportunity for aspiring professionals to meet and play together.

CONTEMPORARY (AVANT-GARDE)

As discussed in Chapter 3, Taruskin's critique of Early Music centered on its taking what amounted to a modernist position on how music really should sound. In this respect there is an obvious link here with the interests of the contemporary avant-garde music field in the 1960s. As David Fallows noted, "I think it is true to say that if you went to a contemporary concert in the '60s you saw the same people as you'd see at a medieval concert...wanting to move away from the standard 19th-century musical fayre."[35]

A key influence for the rising interest in older repertoires also comes through modern composers. Paul Hindemith is often credited with making an important contribution in this respect. He established The Yale Collegium Musicum, shortly after joining the faculty in 1940, very much in the mold of the modern collegium musicum movement that had spread quickly amongst German universities after Hugo Riemann's Leipzig collegium musicum in 1908. As Haskell[36] observes, "Hindemith was neither an antiquarian nor a purist by temperament," but "he realized that only historical instruments could re-create the sound-world of pre-Classical music." In England, the Manchester School of composers, Harrison Birtwistle, Alexander Goehr, and Peter Maxwell Davies, shared an interest in music of the Medieval and Renaissance periods. Under the guidance of their teacher Richard Hall whilst at the Royal Manchester College of Music during the 1950s, this group studied works by the likes of Machaut and Dunstable, which had a profound influence on their compositional style. In turn, they passed on their own interest in a variety of less obvious ways. For example, violinist Catherine Mackintosh recalls how it was Birtwistle who "was the person who introduced me to early music as such."³⁷ (He taught music at her school and wrote music for the school's plays.) Together with clarinettist Alan Hacker, who went on to direct the Music Party (devoted to authentic performance of music from the Classical period), Birtwistle founded in 1965 The Fires of London (originally under the name of the Pierrot Players), a chamber ensemble dedicated to new musical repertoire. Peter Maxwell Davies joined as joint director of the group in 1967, and they were resident artists at the Dartington Summer School for five years. Amongst its players was Duncan Druce, who played baroque violin, viola and viola d'amore with the Academy of Ancient Music, whilst also working as a music producer for the BBC in the late 1960s, and Jennifer Ward Clarke, the cellist who played for The English Concert and Salomon Quartet (together with Simon Standage, Micaela Comberti, and Trevor Jones). A number of early musicians, including the clarinettist Antony Pay, were also members of the specialist contemporary music chamber orchestra, the London Sinfonietta, which was founded in 1968, and commissioned works by the Manchester School and other contemporary composers. Elsewhere, Andrew Parrott was secretary of the Oxford University Contemporary Music Society, with which he conducted *Pierrot Lunaire* (the piece The Fires of London had been first set up to perform). Tim Mason (one of the leading spirits behind the Orchestra of the Age of Enlightenment) regularly played jazz and contemporary music, and founded the Capricorn ensemble in 1973. Players such as Roddy Skeaping, Micaela Comberti, Colin Kitching, and Timothy Kramer also performed with Keith Tippett's innovative jazz band Centipede in 1970. Various others performed with John Lubbock's Camden Chamber Orchestra, which continues to offer a musical experience embedded very much in the community.³⁸

CONTINENTAL EUROPE AND USA

As we have seen, there were significant early music developments taking place in continental Europe and the US that strongly influenced British early musicians. Notwithstanding this book's geographical focus, the early music "movement" appositely denotes a flow of musicians not just from across Europe, but between Europe and the United States. Arnold Dolmetsch traveled to New York on December 27, 1902, where he was introduced to the US early music scene by Sam Franko, violinist, impresario, and founder of the American Symphony Orchestra. During the late 1930s and '40s many musicians and musicologists who had been active in Europe (including Nadia Boulanger (1938) and Wanda Landowska (1941)) emigrated to the United States, taking with them their ideas about how music should be performed. Of those who stayed behind, Guillaume de Van (originally William Devan from Memphis) stands out for his contribution to early music, as head of the Bibliothèque Nationale's music department in Paris.

In the post-war years, opportunities for musicians to travel to England (as much as for British performers to study and work abroad) increased dramatically. It was chiefly through the medium of the sound recording, however, that early musicians were able to influence the performance status quo. Deutsche Grammophon's *Archiv Produktion* was launched in 1947 as a project to survey Western Music from Gregorian chant to Mozart in an "authentic" manner.[39] Other major early music anthologies and collections that followed include HMV's *History of Music in Sound*; Telefunken's *Das Alte Werk*; L'Oiseau-Lyre's *Florilegium*, and EMI's *Reflexe & Electrola* series. It is fascinating to read Elizabeth Roche's (1979) assessment that "the most significant rise of interest in early music in terms of an increasing number of records, adventurous exploration of the repertory, and concentration on most important music—began in about 1954 and reached its peak in 1967."[40] With the benefit of a much longer historical timeline (see Chapter 2), I would argue that the early music revival in Britain, soon to be spurred on by the advances in recording technology and format, was only just beginning to get under way at this time.

Two Americans were particularly influential in the revival of Medieval and Renaissance music in Britain—Noah Greenberg and Thomas Binkley. Like Michael Morrow and David Munrow, Greenberg was largely self-taught. Greenberg, whose group the New York Pro Musica was launched in 1952, had a "common touch" that made him a compelling exponent of the "all-but-unknown" composers whose music he championed. However, as Haskell suggests, "in casting musicological caution to the winds and adopting a more robust, down-to-earth approach to early music, [he] did not lose sight of the manifold problems involved in deciphering and performing old scores."[41] Munrow was strongly influenced by Noah Greenberg's New York Pro Musica.[42] Greenberg was himself inspired to set up his ensemble by fellow American Safford Cape's Pro Musica Antiqua of Brussels (1933).[43] The New York Pro Musica's most well-known work was the Medieval liturgical drama *The Play of Daniel*, which they recorded for Decca's "Gold Label" in 1958. This was broadcast by the BBC in 1959, and the following year the group toured to England, giving a performance in King's Lynn, attended by the composer Benjamin Britten and his partner Peter Pears.[44] In a sad parallel with David Munrow, Greenberg died tragically young, aged just 46.

Thomas Binkley, born in Cleveland, Ohio, was a lutenist and music scholar who came over to Europe to teach at the Schola Cantorum Basiliensis in Basle. Whilst living in Munich, he founded the Studio der frühen Musik (1959). Described as having a "radically different sound,"[45] the Studio der frühen Musik recorded over 50 ground-breaking LPs for Electrola, DGG, and most notably, Telefunken's *Das Alte Werk* label. Their performances were perhaps most distinctive in terms of the extraordinary sense of ensemble achieved. David Fallows describes both Binkley and Morrow as musicians of "fierce conviction about everything they did and a massive sense of fun."[46] This is a powerful combination of essential qualities that characterizes much of what has gone on under the banner "early music" more widely.

FOLK AND UNIVERSITY

Generally speaking, folk musicians and classical musicians do not mix. What cross-pollination there is has tended to involve an appropriation of instruments, sounds, musical idioms, and tunes, rather than musicians directly collaborating together. According to Harker, collections of folk music by the likes of Cecil Sharp, Francis James Child, and Albert Lancaster Lloyd, "chopped up, amended and sometimes...invented" folk songs, leaving out the very *people* who made the folk songs and ballads what they "really are."[47] A rather more promising take on the relationship between folk and classical music can be found in Elizabeth Upton's (2012) analysis of how the "musical identities" of modern-day pop and folk musicians and early music performers have been "shaped by their experiences as listeners to the music of their own time."[48] Upton discusses popular music's appropriation of early music sounds and "pop Baroque" in a surprisingly broad range of cases, from Simon & Garfunkel's *Scarborough Fair/Canticle* (1966), The Doors' *Light My Fire* (1967), tracks from the Beatles' *Sgt. Pepper's Lonely Hearts Club Band* (1967), through to Led Zeppelin's *Stairway to Heaven* (1972), which opens with acoustic guitar and a recorder quartet.[49] In what she describes as a "shared experiential and historical zone for mutual transmission traceable in sonic borrowings across genre borderlines,"[50] Upton then explores how the sounds of popular music (especially non-operatic pop-sounding voices) were appropriated into early music. Central to Upton's argument is what she refers to as "anachronistic dissonance," where certain sounds become unacceptable and "no longer fit with a shared mental image of the past."[51] For the folk musician, of course, that past is inherited from an aural tradition, with music being passed down from one generation to the next by ear. The "authentic" folk performance lives (or dies) through the immediacy of its connection with the sounds and sensibilities of our cultural heritage. The whole trajectory of the classical music profession, including the particular manner in which its musicians have been trained, on the other hand, requires a rather different approach to the pursuit of "authentic performance"—one where scholarship and historical musicology, often acquired at university, also play a vital role.

Notwithstanding their distinctiveness, we can usefully consider both the *Folk (Sound & sensibility)* and *University (Scholarship)* vantage points together here, as they offer two related approaches to joining up with the music of the past. We get a sense of the interplay between the two in practice when looking at Michael Morrow's Musica Reservata, "that extraordinary group"...which "aroused enormous controversy among the early-music coterie."[52] Apparently a broadcast of Yugoslav folk music first "aroused [Morrow's] hypothesis that early music might not sound as then performed, that it might not be just a simplified version of baroque and classical harmonies."[53] An in-house press release for Musica Reservata produced "by kind permission of the British Council" in 1976 sets out Morrow's dogmatic agenda and approach:[54]

> Michael Morrow had very definite ideas about the original performance styles of this music. He believed that it was real, not fairy-tale, music, and that if one played dance music—much of the surviving music is dance music—it should be played strongly and rhythmically as though people were dancing to it; a medieval dance band fulfilled exactly the same functions as a modern dance band. He knew that none of the baroque instruments had been used in the Renaissance or middle ages and that all the earlier instruments were louder and stronger...

Above all, he knew that in some areas medieval instruments such as shawms and rebecs were still in use as folk instruments; in the same areas certain vocal tone qualities were used which might also be survivals from the techniques of the Middle Ages. In this way, the characteristic sound of Musica Reservata was created, and it is by this sound that the ensemble can immediately be recognised...no other group has achieved quite the same bite and attack.... So Michael Morrow had to find singers whom he could persuade to forget all that they had learned; to listen to folk music; to sing absolutely in tune without any vibrato; to develop the same form of attack as the instrumentalists, and all this he did.

Of course, Morrow was far from being the only early musician to seek out repertoire driven by the rhythm and pitch of the dance. David Munrow's recordings often betray a folk crossover, and with his Early Music Consort of London he was certainly no stranger to "folksy bawdiness." Listening to the *Music of the Gothic Era* (1976), for example, one quickly finds traditional labels (folk, classical, etc.) breaking down as the offbeat exuberance of this music "from another age" takes over.

The direct link between scholarship and performance in the modern early music revival can be traced back to the development of collegium musicums and schola cantorums in Germany, Paris, Brussels, and notably, Basle. Central to Paul Sacher's Schola Cantorum Basiliensis was its vision that "early music should not be an elitist pursuit, open only to a guild of professionals, but part and parcel of everyday life."[55] Within Britain it is difficult not to have the impression that a professionally sanctioned and to some extent therefore "elitist" early music was precisely what the university system was fostering in the 1960s, '70s, and indeed since then. As was noted in Chapter 2, an extraordinarily high proportion of early musicians, most especially founder-directors, but also scholar-critics, developed their Early Music credentials whilst studying at either Oxford or Cambridge. Writing in 1993, Christopher Page, himself a fellow of Sidney Sussex, Cambridge, compared the "*a capella* early-music scene in England...to the Whitehall Civil Service, being sustained almost entirely by graduates from the universities of Oxford and Cambridge."[56] He adds, "Here we have an extraordinary influence wielded by two similarly structured and (as it must seem to many) identical educational institutions, neither of which offers anything close to Continental conservatory." Furthermore, "the English choral tradition, with its reliance upon young voices and its tinge of Protestant Englishness, turns the memories and dreams of a social class into sound."[57]

Understanding how any early music would have been performed and how it sounded is challenging, to say the least. When it comes to the music of the Middle Ages, it is particularly problematic, and inevitably involves considerable guesswork. As J. M. Thomson wrote in the editorial to the second volume of *Early Music*, in a piece memorably titled "The Swiss cheese problem," "In early music there are certainly more unknowns than knowns."[58] Those involved in reviving early music in the post-war years (as part of what I refer to as *Authenticity$_1$*), including such figures as Jack Westrup, Thurston Dart, Denis Stevens, and Robert Donington, were inevitably required to interpret "facts" somewhat creatively at times.

MAKING THE FAMILIAR UNFAMILIAR (*AUTHENTICITY$_2$*)

The focus now shifts to explaining the increasingly significant development of *Authenticity$_2$* (see Figure 4.3). Late Baroque and Classical music was regularly being performed alongside earlier repertoire, but during the early 1970s in particular it was to be developed, promoted, and marketed much more intensely, such that the main focus of professional early music, including live performances and recordings, was on this repertoire.

MUSICAL ESTABLISHMENT

It would take a book-length essay to do anything like full justice to the breadth and depth of the classical music profession in Britain in the post-war years. Cyril Ehrlich's (1985) book on *The Music Profession in Britain Since the Eighteenth Century* devotes two chapters to the profession after World War II; Mackerness's (1964) *A Social History of English Music* devotes one chapter to the "modern age." Both are important for highlighting the massive disruption of the war years, followed by a boom in leisure spending that stimulated "phenomenal demand for all kinds of musical enterprise."[59] For my own purposes, discussion of the "musical establishment" (in which those involved

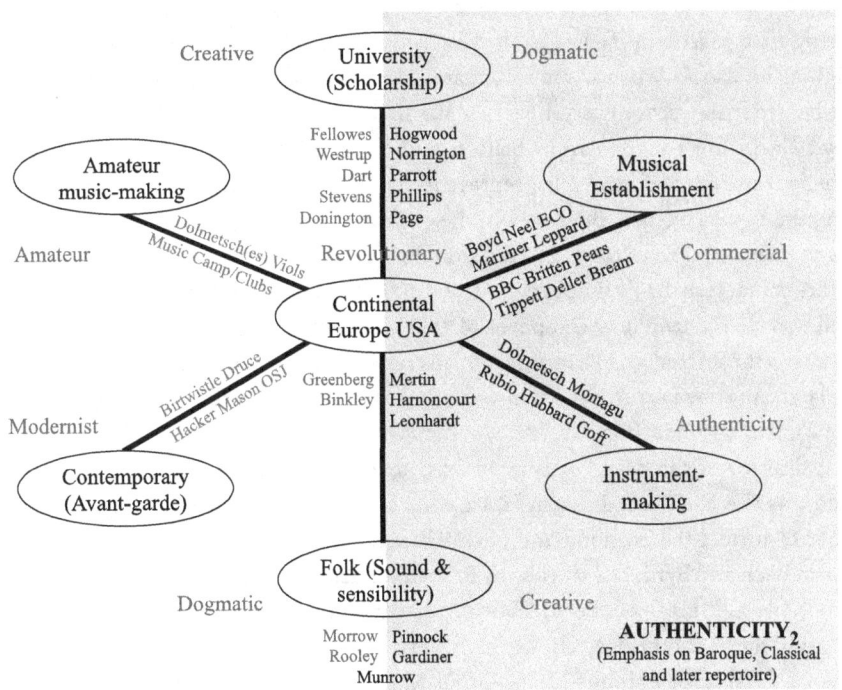

FIGURE 4.3 Authenticity$_2$

make a living from performing) begins by focusing on the conductor Boyd Neel, who was to have a major influence on the development of Authenticity$_2$ in Britain.

Boyd Neel founded the Boyd Neel London String Orchestra in 1932, hiring young aspiring professionals from the London music colleges (the orchestra was renamed the "Boyd Neel Orchestra" the following year). Neel was then working full-time as a doctor at St. George's Hospital, London. Critical acclaim came quickly, and he gave up medicine shortly after the orchestra's debut, signing a recording contract with Decca, and subsequently devoting his life to the music profession. The Boyd Neel Orchestra, with its "modest forces and lithe style," can now be seen to have crucially "anticipated a late-twentieth century trend," as Ehrlich puts it.[60] Certainly the intimate style of this chamber orchestra made a huge impact on audiences and musicians. One notable performer who played with the orchestra was the harpsichordist Thurston Dart. When Neel took up the post of dean of the Royal Conservatory of Music at Toronto in 1952, Dart took over the orchestra, renaming it the Philomusica of London. Neville Marriner, who had first come across Dart whilst they were both convalescing after the war, was later a leader of the orchestra for a while, before he set up his own chamber orchestra, the Academy of St. Martin in the Fields in 1959.[61] Dart was later to become "The Academy's" musicological "father" for performances of early and Baroque repertoire. Later still, upon Dart's death in 1971, Christopher Hogwood, with his knowledge of "Cambridge musicology," took over the editing of scores, until he, too, set up his own period orchestra, the Academy of Ancient Music (AAM), in 1973. Nicholas Kenyon's remarks on the occasion of Hogwood's 70th birthday are telling: "I do think it is important to record how much what he did with the AAM grew out of his experience with groups for instance like the Academy of St. Martin in the Fields, working with Neville Marriner as a continuo player; and I think he also absorbed an enormous amount of Neville's incredible professionalism about how to make recordings...how to make all that work."[62]

Boyd Neel's links to Benjamin Britten and the English Opera Group, as well as Glyndebourne and Sadler's Wells, represent another important point of connection. During the 1950s and '60s, Britten, with his partner, Peter Pears, reintroduced Purcell songs to the recital repertoire. Britten's distinctive arrangements of the accompaniment are characteristically limpid evocations of the time. Their interest in the music of Purcell was shared by fellow composer Michael Tippett, whose cantata *Boyhood's End* was written for Britten and Pears, and which takes its inspiration from Purcell's music. Years later, Andrew Parrott recalls how his Taverner Choir was first "put together for one of Tippett's wonderfully eclectic programmes at the Bath Festival."[63] (Tippett was artistic director of the Bath Festival between 1969 and 1974.) Another close friend of Britten was the composer Imogen Holst (Gustav Holst's daughter), who produced a number of influential editions and performances of early music, as well as writing books on Bach and Byrd. She worked as Britten's music assistant for several years, and later became a director of the Aldeburgh Festival (1956-77). Music festivals, such as Aldeburgh, Bath, Cambridge, Cheltenham, City of London, Edinburgh, Lake District, Lufthansa Festival of Baroque Music, Stour Music, Three Choirs, and Wexford, have provided a vital showcase for the classical music establishment over the years.

Britten formed the English Opera Group (EOG) in 1947, largely to perform his own operas, but the group of British singers (including the likes of Janet Baker, James Bowman, Joan Cross, Heather Harper, Kathleen Ferrier, Norman Lumsden, Peter Pears, Robert Tear) also performed earlier works. Britten wrote the part of Oberon in his opera *A Midsummer Night's Dream* for Alfred Deller, who is credited with reviving interest in the counter-tenor voice, and who founded the Deller Consort in 1948 and the Stour Music Festival in 1962. The EOG was managed for a time by Basil Douglas (formerly, and later in his career, of the BBC). Douglas, together with his secretary and assistant Maureen Garnham, set up an artist management company, becoming Trevor Pinnock's (The English Concert) agent in the early 1970s. Maureen Garnham, whose father (Ben Garnham) was Secretary of the London Choral Society, suggests that the conductor John Tobin's performance of *The Messiah* on March 18, 1950, marked the beginning of a new movement: "John Tobin...was one of the very early pioneers of the early music revival...John said to the Committee, 'I think we are going to have to do a performance of *The Messiah* to get the money in...I've got a few spare days, I might as well go and look at the autograph score in the B[ritish] M[useum]', which he did, and he was looking at the autograph score and various other scores for twenty, thirty years thereafter!"[64] Another connection comes in the form of the guitarist and lutenist Julian Bream, who inspired a generation of players. Bream collaborated with Peter Pears on Elizabethan music, and Britten dedicated his famous *Nocturnal* to him. The celebrated luthier David Rubio made guitars and lutes for Bream, and was based for a while on Bream's country estate.

It is interesting to see how experiments with historically informed performance during the 1960s were often woven into the fabric of the musical establishment at the time. For example, Sir Roger Norrington cites Raymond Leppard's concert of Monteverdi opera extracts with the English Chamber Orchestra (ECO), including two acts of *Orfeo*, in the Royal Festival Hall on October 11, 1960, as "absolutely crucial in showing the possibilities of this repertory."[65] Through Leppard's connections with George Christie, this led to the historic first Glyndebourne performances of *L'Incoronazione di Poppea* a couple of years later. The ECO had itself been founded by Arnold Goldsbrough, who taught Thurston Dart, and is also credited with being a "pioneer" of the early music renaissance.[66] First known as the Goldsbrough Orchestra (1949), it became the English Chamber Orchestra in 1960. Arnold Goldsbrough worked often with Alfred Deller, and had a close collaboration with the German musicologist Ernst Meyer. Together they introduced audiences to many less familiar composers, including Locke, Schütz, Lassus, and Rameau. Goldsbrough also worked with Basil Lam (a central figure in the BBC's music department) on many editions of early music repertoire.

INSTRUMENT-MAKING

In the initial days of the early music revival, the emphasis had to be on obtaining historical instruments at all rather than ensuring they were necessarily the "right" ones. Roger Norrington remembers being hugely impressed by Thurston Dart while at Cambridge: "he talked about the double dot in French Overture, and we were amazed." But, he goes on to add that this was "the beginnings of a lurking idea; nobody actually *did* it. And apart from the odd harpsichord there were no old instruments around at all."[67]

Over time, however, interest in authenticity placed demands on just what instruments were being played. Much of the focus of instrument-making in the 1950s and '60s had been on "improving upon" old instruments rather than reproducing or copying them (one thinks especially of Landowska's famous beefed-up harpsichord that could more easily be heard in a contemporary concert hall setting). This changed after the publication of Frank Hubbard's *Three Centuries of Harpsichord Making* in 1965, which showed with meticulous detail how authentic copies could be made. Interest in authenticity grew in the early years of the 1970s as more and more performers started to experiment on restored instruments or copies made by the likes of Rubio, Hubbard, and Goff.

The history of instrument-making and its role in the wider early music revival also deserves a book in its own right. Chapter 6 provides an overview of the leading characters and major milestones. Before moving on, however, we need to highlight the very practical constraints involved in Early Music's reliance on "original" or "authentic" period instruments, recognizing that this had a significant impact on the professionalization of early music performance. The decision to play on a Baroque or Classical violin as opposed to one's modern violin, for example, carried with it very real logistical implications. It was often impractical to carry multiple instruments to rehearsals and on tour. Decisions, and necessarily compromises, were made (consider, for example, the unfeasible number of different clarinets that the contemporary early music specialist is required to own and master[68]). The standardization of pitch (such that an A =415hz for HIP and 440hz for modern performances) and temperament[69] requires the performer to make choices as to how their instruments are tuned prior to any given rehearsal-period or performance. Today's standardized approach is clearly an uneasy (inauthentic) compromise resulting from the very real difficulty of sourcing instruments that can be tuned as they would have been in the past (e.g., quarter-comma meantone; Bach's well-temperament). Such very practical considerations have had a bearing on what was and what was not done by way of "historically informed performance practice."

CONTINENTAL EUROPE AND USA

The influence of professional musicians from the Netherlands, Vienna, Basle, Paris, Cologne, Munich, and the US on the early development of Authenticity$_2$ in Britain should not be underestimated. A roll call of some of the most familiar names in early music during the 1960s and '70s brings the point home—August Wenzinger, Gustav Leonhardt, Nikolaus Harnoncourt, Noah Greenberg, Thomas Binkley, Reinhard

Goebel, Ton Koopman, the Kuijken brothers, Anner Bylsma, William Christie, Philippe Herreweghe, Frans Brüggen, René Jacobs, Rafael Puyana, René Clemencic, and Jordi Savall. It is remarkable to reflect on the extraordinary progress that had been achieved in the 20 years or so since Harnoncourt had founded the Vienna Viola da Gamba Quartet. After all, in 1949 the study of early music had still been regarded as "an obscure pastime for some lunatics, surrounded by the reputation of dilettantism and without any relevance for concert life."[70]

Attending live performances (where possible) and listening to recordings and broadcasts were the main ways in which musical influence was transmitted. Hogwood, Norrington, and other leading British early music directors and performers talk nostalgically of hearing Harnoncourt and Leonhardt's Bach recordings in particular. Their influence was profound, most significantly for showing that period performances could be achieved on a large scale, with spectacular results. With musicians receiving specialist tuition, often for many years after they have established themselves as performers in the professional arena, the teacher-pupil relation offered a further means of sharing ideas (and people) across national boundaries.

The Swiss-born Dolmetsch, who had himself studied at the Brussels Conservatoire and learned his craft as an instrument-maker from Chickering of Boston and Gaveau of Paris, lived and worked for much of his life in Haslemere, but his influence spread a great deal further than South East England (with performers and instrument-makers coming over to his workshop between 1917 and his death in 1940). Dolmetsch's contemporary, Wanda Landowska, was also a much sought-after teacher at the Paris Schola Cantorum, and at the Berlin Hochschule für Musik, founding the École de Musique Ancienne in 1925 in Paris. The Colombian harpsichordist Rafael Puyana studied with both Landowska and Boulanger, and later he was to teach Trevor Pinnock at Dartington, prior to having his career managed by Basil Douglas. The Dutch harpsichordist Gustav Leonhardt taught many leading players, including Christopher Hogwood, Ton Koopman, Richard Egarr, Philippe Herreweghe, and Colin Tilney. Leonhardt himself, together with Nikolaus Harnoncourt, studied with Josef Mertin in Vienna, and it is indeed intriguing to reflect on the extraordinary influence that this one musicologist and performer has had subsequently throughout the early music field.

FOLK AND UNIVERSITY

As intimated in the previous chapter, "authentic performance" is an area of debate where generalizations are likely to mislead. Nevertheless, we can surely surmise that beyond the ideas and ideologies, the musicology and iconography, the "evidence-based" music-making (as Roger Norrington has referred to it), it was the sound that early music made, first and foremost, that attracted its proponents as listeners.[71] Such a truism is worth highlighting given critics' enthusiasm to condemn early musicians as overly concerned with matters of the head rather than the heart. For Anthony Rooley (founder of the Consort of Musicke and director of The Early Music Centre), performing music is about bringing the soul of the listener face to face with the Divine, in what he terms the "Orphic" approach.[72] For his part, Trevor Pinnock stresses how he "came up very much through the practical side of music-making rather than an academic side," adding "it's the music which leads...I've always been obsessed with sound and creating that."[73] For John Eliot Gardiner as a child, music always seemed "totally naturally connected to the farming year and its seasonal festivities, which my parents and their friends always marked with music of one sort or another—so there was no dichotomy."[74] He explains: "I grew up on a farm...and being actively involved in farming has always been a strong counter-magnet to all the madness and stress of the music profession."

What is perhaps less obvious in respect of Authenticity$_2$'s connection with the folk vantage point is the sense of there being *any* continuous tradition of performance to tap into at all. Early Music, after all, has been defined precisely in terms of its response to an interrupted or lost tradition of performance. But there do seem to be exceptions. The violinist Catherine Mackintosh, for example, recalls having "a sort of road to Damascus discovery" a few years back, when she went to work in a summer school in Moravia. "I heard a Moravian folk group who were also students at this summer school...We had just been doing a whole series of Biber chamber music recordings with the Purcell Quartet...Here it was in exactly the same spot that Biber was. I thought, gosh, instead of trying to recreate something that has become extinct, we should be listening to these guys."[75] It seems plausible that David Munrow thought something similar back in 1960, on being introduced to a vibrant indigenous culture of South American folk music in Peru (he was teaching English there at the time, under the British Council student teacher scheme).

As things panned out, of course, Munrow's musical career was really to take off whilst at university. (Legend has it that he was inspired to pursue his interest in early music only after seeing a crumhorn hanging up in Thurston Dart's room—though it is not clear whether Dart actually possessed one.) Christopher Hogwood recalls how he and David Munrow formed a number of groups whilst at Cambridge: "So nearly everything we wanted to do in early music had no official didactic channel. It did have support; it had support from the Ray Leppards and Thurston Darts, who were paid academics who put their ideas into practice, rather than the paid conservatoire teachers who I think were very much trying to train people to a regular career. Their job was to put you in a job; and it should be a job as secure as their job; a lifetime contract playing in a professional orchestra. There were no professional orchestras or anything to do with period music, so it looked a very dangerous thing."[76]

As has been suggested, the scholarship applied to underpin performance of Medieval and Renaissance repertoires necessitated a degree of inventiveness, to say the least (see Leech-Wilkinson, 2002). John Potter, himself heavily involved in early music performance during the 1970s and '80s, refers to the "charismatic musical pirates who started the movement."[77] These early music pioneers, far from slavishly following the dogma of performance practice, were in fact breaking new ground. He adds, "Munrow, like his near contemporaries Roger Norrington, John Eliot Gardiner, Trevor Pinnock, Christopher Hogwood, Emma Kirkby, the Hilliard Ensemble, Gothic Voices—everyone before early music entered the mainstream in fact—managed to do what they did without the benefit of institutional instruction." Speaking about his integral involvement in Munrow's Early Music Consort, Hogwood himself notes that "Finally my interest in this kind of music became exhausted, because we did not know whether or not what we were doing was authentic. Although the whole world thought that this type of music-making had a musicological foundation, the very opposite was the case: we had to do a lot on 'feeling', because there was insufficient basis and definite proof of the way in which music was made in the middle ages."[78]

Upon Thurston Dart's death in 1971, Neville Marriner called upon Christopher Hogwood to take over the musicology for the Academy of St. Martin in the Fields. Marriner recalls, "But when Christopher came along, he was different. In many ways he was more specific than Bob [Thurston] Dart was. Bob Dart would always say, you know, that an ornament was played the way you feel—it was put there for you to express yourself. Whereas Christopher was much more intent on accuracy as far as this was concerned."[79] Richard Taruskin's scathing attack on the "straight" early music (English) performer was largely directed at Hogwood's performances with AAM.[80] Over and above the specificities of Hogwood's particular approach toward HIP, however,[81] it seems clear that with Authenticity$_2$ came an associated shift toward a *more* dogmatic approach to historical musicology (even if the extent to which this was the case varied enormously). Certainly, the fact that more reliable sources were available for 17th- and 18th-century music is one contributing factor behind the growing interest in Baroque and Classical repertoires at the time.[82]

This "tale of two authenticities" tells of a revolutionary move away from the amateurism that had become synonymous with the activities of Arnold Dolmetsch and his followers, and toward a situation where professional early musicians and classical musicians were effectively competing on a level playing field. Though this transformation came at a cost (Medieval and Renaissahce music ceding much ground to later Baroque, Classical and then Romantic repertoires), the popularity and appeal of the early music movement as a whole enjoyed substantial growth as a result. As we will see in the next chapter, as the opportunities for work multiplied, Early Music's ties with the musical establishment were about to become even stronger.

> The more I work, the faster my money goes. I said shake, rattle and roll.
> BIG JOE TURNER; BILL HALEY[1]

> The epoch-making Mozart *Idomeneo* of 1987 with Simon Rattle, so nearly cancelled for lack of money, turned out to be the way into Glyndebourne and Mozart.
> NICHOLAS KENYON[2]

> It may be relatively unthreatening to exhume trottos and saltarellos of the fourteenth century with vielles and organettos... When you start performing Bach and Vivaldi and Mozart in the "early music" way—well, that is another can of catgut altogether.
> JOEL COHEN[3]

5

Shake, Rattle and Roll

INTRODUCTION

The setting up in 1973 of the Academy of Ancient Music, The English Concert, The Taverner Choir, Consort & Players, and The Tallis Scholars (the class of '73) marked a decisive moment in British Early Music. With Gardiner's English Baroque Soloists (EBS) and Norrington's London Classical Players (LCP) following soon after (1978), period instrument performance had moved from the margins to the mainstream. As Nicholas Kenyon observed, "By the time Hogwood made best-selling recordings of Handel's *Water Music* and *Messiah*, performing both at the Proms in the late 1970s, the bandwagon was well and truly rolling and not much would stand in its way."[4] Annette Isserlis, principal viola with the English Baroque Soloists, remembers this time well: "We led a charmed life...All the groups fitted their diaries around each other, so we got to do most of the recording sessions and concerts. It was a very rewarding time financially: a lot of us bought instruments on the money we made from recordings."[5] For a while, at least, early musicians were enjoying a "golden age."

The principal focus in this chapter is on the early musician labor market.[6] This is the place where making (early) music is transformed into making money. It is where musicians' "labor power" gets exchanged. Whilst we might prefer not to think of musicians as being involved in such a base enterprise (the term "labor power" tends to portray a sense of alienation), such an exchange is absolutely crucial to understanding Early Music and its success. From the economist's perspective, musicians' labor power has the potential to create more value than it does itself command in exchange; it is the source of surplus value from which "exploitative" revenues are derived;[7] it is, in effect, the primary resource for the production of new economic activity. As we shall see, the trajectory of Early Music as it unfolded through the 1980s very much reflects early musicians' growing understanding of the value of their own labor power in an increasingly competitive market for their services.

It is difficult to pin down *exactly* when the British early musician labor market first appeared. At a specific point in time, let us say the 1950s, it did not yet exist. By some later date (the late 1970s), it did. Surprisingly, economists have tended to ignore this kind of transformation, treating labor markets as if they always "just existed." But some explanation is needed. We might start by drawing attention to the influence of pre-existing conditions, including those relating to the seven "vantage points" discussed in the previous chapter. We then need to look at the early musician labor market in terms of its principal agential projects,[8] notably the setting up of new orchestras, ensembles, consorts, and choirs, involving the exchange of early musicians' labor power. Whilst the focus of this Part of the book is on the nature of early music "work," Part III will explore in more detail the social structures (education, public service broadcasting, public funding) and agential properties (enterprising and entrepreneurial behaviors, leadership) that motivated, enabled, and constrained these projects in sundry ways.

Economists have long regarded *artist* labor markets as being distinctive. In a famous passage on "the exorbitant rewards of players, opera-singers, opera-dancers etc.," Adam Smith, writing in 1776, suggested that the rarity of talent and the discredit of employing them in "public prostitution" accounted for their high earnings. He also observed that "in a profession where twenty fail for one that succeeds, that one ought to gain all that should have been gained by the unsuccessful twenty."[9] Rather more recently, Towse suggests that artist labor markets do not work quite like the other labor markets.[10] The primary reason for their distinctiveness is that those involved are held to be highly intrinsically motivated—driven by the love of what they are doing rather than just the pecuniary gain they might expect from "working." As Bennett notes, "classical music performance is a specialist field that demands exceptionally high levels of skill and commitment in preparation for a career that is unlikely to offer participants rewards commensurate with effort."[11] Indeed, for some economists, artists' behavior might be interpreted as anything but rational (see Abbing 2002 for a discussion). It is worth beginning our analysis of the early musician labor market, therefore, by casting a particularly critical eye over the motivation(s) for setting up professional groups, and those comprising the class of '73 in particular.

WAS EARLY MUSIC PUSHED (OR PULLED)?

In reality, there is always something of a balance to be struck between the intrinsically motivated *push*—to follow one's dreams, beliefs, passions and interests, and the market *pull*, which seemingly offers business opportunities to those "alert" enough to take them up.[12] What happens in practice is always the result of a compromise between these two aspects of supply and demand. There are parallels here with the process of innovation, where we can contrast, on the one hand, a technology *push*, in which a new invention is pushed through research and development (R&D), production, manufacture, and sales without the user-need being the primary objective; and, on the other hand, the type of innovation that is based directly upon the user's need, i.e., a market *pull*.[13] What, then, were the push and pull factors behind the setting up of the "class of '73"?

THE CLASS OF '73

1973 was a landmark year for British classical music. It saw the first-ever performance by a British orchestra at the Salzburg Festival, given by the London Symphony Orchestra. For the musical elite, this no doubt eclipsed the more modest activities of a handful of early musicians as they launched their professional ensembles, consorts, and orchestras.[14] But theirs was no mere sideshow; for these musicians were, in fact, providing a radical alternative to the standard classical music offering. The introduction of fully-fledged period instrument orchestras, in particular, is worth highlighting here. (Credit for the first period instrument orchestra in Britain should perhaps go to Andrew Parrott and Peter Holman, who started "The 24 Violins" (albeit a "deservedly" short-lived group according to Parrott) a few years earlier.[15]) The class of '73, together with the EBS and LCP, would form the nucleus of the professional British early music scene in the years to come.

THE ENGLISH CONCERT (TEC)

One common route to the formation of a new organization is when a hobby outgrows itself. In the case of The English Concert, and indeed the Academy of Ancient Music, the "growth" in question was not so much out of initial amateur interest, but rather from an existing professional chamber music ensemble to a larger entity, the size of a small orchestra. Trevor Pinnock, who made his London debut as a harpsichord soloist in 1968, had for some years been playing early repertoire on modern instruments with friends Anthony Pleeth and Stephen Preston, in the Galliard Harpsichord Trio. Speaking about the launch of TEC, Pinnock recalls, "Initially none of the players were 'specialists' although Stephen Preston and Simon Standage were established converts. At this stage our ensemble was free from commercial pressures although our idealism had to be tempered by the realities of families and mortgages; for some years most players earned their living in the parallel modern-instrument world."[16]

None of the musicians involved in those days really harbored the idea that TEC would become the vehicle to a longer-term career in early music. As Pinnock notes, "we didn't think forward. We were very excited by what we were doing; I suppose we all hoped it would grow."[17] Long after the classical music profession had woken up to period instruments, there remained good reasons for reverting to "traditional" i.e., modern, ways. "In those painful moments when things didn't work, you thought 'golly why don't we just chuck the whole thing and go back...'; but then you realized that you couldn't, because you wouldn't be willing to go back taking the whole package...so all you could do was simply persevere and try to get better."[18]

The English Concert proactively sought a recording contract, and their first came in the form of English record label CRD, with whom the group recorded *Sons of Bach* harpsichord concertos in 1974. Maureen Garnham, of Basil Douglas Management, takes up the story: "Having got that one with CRD, then one of the people from Archiv got interested—Holschneider... he was responsible for getting Trevor for the five year contract."[19] Asked why Dr. Holschneider (manager of Deutsche Grammophon's Archiv label between 1970 and 1991) had taken him on, Pinnock notes, "they had a very successful time with the Schola Cantorum Basiliensis... and then they were looking for 'the new way'... whatever this might be."[20] Coincidentally, Holschneider (described as "a remarkable individual" by Sir John Eliot Gardiner) suggested the name "the English Baroque Soloists," and it was also very much with his support that Gardiner recorded Bach's *Mass in B Minor* (1985), the *Passions* (1986; 1989), and the *Christmas Oratorio* (1987) for DG Archiv.[21] Record companies are naturally on the lookout for fresh, exciting, and more often than not young, performers; their hope is, after all, that affordable talent today will develop into tomorrow's lucrative money earners.

THE TALLIS SCHOLARS (TTS)

The exclusive surroundings of Oxford and Cambridge can give the (false) impression of a world apart; of academics living in "ivory towers," and of the pragmatic concerns of the music industry little more than a distant irritation. In fact, as I shall be exploring in more detail in Chapter 7, universities (and particularly Oxbridge) provided a nurturing environment for the "spinning out" of early music, to say nothing of a vital entry-point to a career in music. Certainly, this was the case for Peter Phillips, whose early music vocal group The Tallis Scholars was set up whilst he was studying at Oxford. "I had no idea what I was doing and I was just 20 years old at the time." Phillips adds that he "was literally doing what young people do: I identified something that I enjoyed doing and wanted to do more of it."[22] Crucially, he was surrounded by good singers, and by his own admission, he "made the most of that." Like Trevor Pinnock, Phillips never entertained the idea that it would sustain his career for the next 40 years.

Whereas Pinnock had been performing professionally with the Galliard for six to seven years prior to setting up TEC, TTS was formed very much out of the familiar routine of university life. "At the start we were just an amateur undergraduate group of friends singing music we loved."[23] Oxbridge offered a tailor-made framework for ensemble singing, with choral scholars taking part in weekly services, reproducing an unbroken English choral tradition over many hundreds of years. The chapel choirs play a central role in college life, and places are much sought after. It is hard to imagine more conducive surroundings for spawning new choral groups, comprised, as they are, of young and highly trained singers, often under expert guidance from experienced choral directors, partnered by enthusiastic and talented conductors manqué—i.e., organ scholars, many of whom have gone on to have influential careers in Early Music and classical music more widely (some familiar names include Harry Bicket, Harry Bramma,

David Briggs, John Butt, Nicholas Cleobury, Stephen Cleobury, Stephen Darlington, Andrew Davis, Christopher Dearnley, Richard Egarr, Richard Farnes, Stephen Farr, William Glock, George Guest, Richard Hickox, Edward Higginbottom, David Hill, Andrew Lawrence-King, Stephen Layton, Andrew Lumsden, David Lumsden, Richard Marlow, Martin Neary, James O'Donnell, Simon Preston, Christopher Robinson, Alastair Ross, John Scott, Thomas Trotter, and David Willcocks).

The important transition to becoming a fully professional group took rather longer for TTS than was the case for the other members of the class of '73. As Phillips notes, "To turn that kind of thing into a professional touring ensemble requires some very hard decisions."[24] One of the group's hardest decisions must surely have been *not* to pursue a recording contract with one of the major labels, but establish their own label instead. "Gimell," the first of the single-artist labels (that are now commonplace) was set up by Phillips and Steve Smith (recording engineer, and general manager) in 1980, solely to record The Tallis Scholars.

THE TAVERNER CHOIR, CONSORT & PLAYERS (TCCP)

Whilst also at Oxford, The TCCP's founder, Andrew Parrott, had put together various groups and played and sang as a member of the Oxford Early Music Group, with Bernard Thomas (who later set up London Pro Musica) and Emma Kirkby (Parrott's first wife). His first professional early music engagement was actually for the Open University, assembling incidental music for a radio production of *Everyman*, in which he played rebec and recorder. But it was in the context of some Bath Festival programs (juxtaposing Ives, Bach, Liszt, and Tallis) under the characteristically inventive artistic directorship of composer Michael Tippett that the Taverner Choir was formed (demonstrating a market pull).

For Andrew Parrott, the new ensemble wasn't about creating a living or work for himself: "it was just one of many things I was doing—a vehicle for certain ideas, for putting those ideas into practice in repertories that interested me; that's what led me to start my own group."[25] This ethos is very much in line with that of Michael Morrow, founder of Musica Reservata, with whom Parrott worked as conductor between 1973 and 1975. One can detect something of a difference here between the motivations of Morrow and Parrott on the one side, and David Munrow and Christopher Hogwood on the other. Both Munrow and Hogwood might be regarded as more career performers. This distinction is explored in more detail in Chapter 8.

The TCCP recorded predominantly with EMI, who were also Munrow's Early Music Consort of London's recording company. After David Munrow's death in 1976, the market (and EMI) was left with something of a hole in the catalogue. Munrow's absence was influential on what happened next as Parrott recalls about his being taken on by EMI in the early 1980s: "it is indirectly connected with David Munrow's death. He was seen as the figure who could sell this new thing to the public in an attractive way— which he undoubtedly did; and he was making records for EMI. I'm not suggesting that

I was meant to be a replacement for him—I wasn't; nor did it happen that quickly, but I think EMI were on the lookout. They were aware that there was a market there."[26]

THE ACADEMY OF ANCIENT MUSIC (AAM)

Munrow's death was also influential in terms of the development of the AAM. Felix Warnock, bassoonist and later manager of TEC and the Orchestra of the Age of Enlightenment, remembers Munrow talking with him about moving out of very early Renaissance music. His next big project was supposed to have been the formation of a Baroque orchestra.[27] In the event, of course, this was not to be. Instead, Munrow's friend and colleague Christopher Hogwood went on to develop just such a project, which became the Academy of Ancient Music.

The perceived wisdom on the relationship between new period instrument ensembles and record companies holds that the record companies only waded in once things were already in place, so as to minimize risk on their investment. As author and music critic Helen Wallace remarks with reference to Decca's L'Oiseau-Lyre backing of Christopher Hogwood's AAM, "No sooner was an ensemble created, than record labels fell over each other to initiate comprehensive recording projects."[28] In fact, this is not quite an accurate depiction of what happened. At least in the case of AAM, the relationship between the new orchestra and the record company was much closer than this right from the outset.

Christopher Hogwood explains how the idea for AAM actually came from Peter Wadland, who was responsible for repackaging the L'Oiseau-Lyre label at Decca. "I met Peter Wadland at an Alan Hacker concert in London. We exchanged names...he then came to a Neville Marriner recording session (because it was Decca). He came to that and after we went for a drink...and he said, 'since you play with that group, would it be possible to conceive of a period group of about the same size playing to anything like that standard?' Rather foolishly, I said 'Yes!' Not so much because I knew the English players could, but I could see that the Viennese and the Dutch had—I could see no reason why we couldn't."[29] The first recording project was a record of Thomas Arne overtures. As John Dunkerley (senior balance engineer at Decca 1968-1997) recalls, "It required a very small string section, was fairly cheap to put together—there weren't very many period instrument players at that time. It seemed a very good way of putting one's toe in the original instrument waters, which were then basically very small beer."[30]

This sequence of events brings out the catalytic role of personal relations between individuals, over and above the positions that these individuals hold for their respective legally bounded entities (AAM and Decca). In emphasizing the market's relentless grip on the exchanges, transactions, and relationships discussed here, we have to be very careful not to lose sight of the human beings (the "music-makers") who are the chief protagonists of this unfolding story. Hogwood and Wadland got on very well with each other and "saw eye to eye." As Paul Hughes (general manager of the

BBC Symphony Orchestra) notes, "Peter had the same pioneering spirit that Chris did."[31] James Jolly (editor-in-chief of *Gramophone*) adds "Chris and Peter did enjoy this extraordinarily creative relationship. Peter was an enormously enthusiastic producer, and he was incredibly passionate about everything, from the sleeve design to who wrote the booklet, to who wrote the notes...It was a fantastic meeting of two very creative individuals."[32]

LABOR MARKET PROCESSES—KEY ISSUES

It is one thing to launch a new period performance ensemble or orchestra, but quite another to sustain its activities such that those involved are employed on a regular basis at a level that satisfies demand. In this next section attention is turned to the key labor market processes of hiring, training, rewarding, and promoting,[33] each of which has an important bearing on the ongoing exchange of the early musician's labor power.

HIRING

One of the defining features of the cultural and creative industries (especially in the arts) is over-supply.[34] In short, there are simply many more aspiring musicians, artists, writers, film-makers, and so on, than there are opportunities in the marketplace. Although this state of affairs characterizes the classical music profession in general, the early days of the early music revival were distinguished rather by a lack of skilled period performance musicians, or by *under*-supply.

Heather Jarman (formerly general manager of AAM) suggests that even into the mid-1980s there was a surprising lack of performers to choose from: "there simply weren't enough appropriately trained players around. I don't know how players finally learnt that there was this big job market...because certainly in my day they didn't seem aware of it."[35] Trevor Pinnock recalls, "Of course, yes, for our very first recording there weren't specialists. But as we went along there got more and more. I think the field started to get quite crowded by the end of the '70s."[36] In the early days, the groups rarely held auditions: "we were often scraping the bottom of the barrel to get players...there just wasn't the pool of players" says Jarman.[37] From time to time, leaders of each section (i.e., strings, woodwind, brass) would suggest musicians to come on trial with their respective orchestra.

Christopher Hogwood is candid about the very pragmatic approach that he needed to take in the early days of the AAM: "If we couldn't fill in the gaps, we persuaded good professionals like Alan Civil[38] to drop the modern horn and pick up an ancient horn. They didn't always do it on the same basis as we did. They were doing it more as a joke—to show that the old instrument didn't work—whereas we were doing it to show that the old instrument did it better. So there was a little bit of 'ho, ho, listen to this funny noise on the horn.' And I might say 'Alan, couldn't you use your lip to make it slightly more in tune, or put your hand in [to the bell of the instrument, to change the pitch or timbre of the note played],' and we got some very interesting results, because they were total professionals in another field, whereas we were total amateurs in this field."[39]

From the outset, professional period instrument ensembles sought to book players further ahead than most traditional classical music ensembles at the time. "It was necessary in order to get the players you wanted," says orchestra fixer Colin Kitching.[40] Another distinctive feature of hiring early musicians was that the leading groups (class of '73 together with EBS and LCP) ran an "anti-clash diary." With early musicians working for several of the top orchestras at the same time, it was imperative to ensure that the best players could be present. Colin Kitching recalls how "there was a lot of haggling with other groups to try and fit in recordings and other engagements. We did a Prom for Roger [Norrington] and AAM had a *Creation* at the Lucerne Festival, which was essentially a day in the middle of the rehearsal period for the LCP Prom; but we agreed to let the performers concerned do the Lucerne Festival engagement, because there were so many mutual players. But this sort of thing could have landed us in the soup on several occasions."[41] In the late 1990s the anti-clash diary developed into Period Instrument Managers Meetings (known affectionately as "PIMMs"), which were held twice a year between the early music "premier league" (AAM, TEC, Monteverdi, King's Consort, Hanover Band and Gabrieli Consort).[42]

Some kind of cooperative policy was essential, but problematic for younger players wishing to break through. Ensuring your name was on the fixer lists was absolutely vital so that when chances did arise (typically, older players with families might prefer not to go on long tours, for example), the new talent could be called upon. Of course, these fledgling early music ensembles did not always work harmoniously together. There were inevitable tensions born out of the passion and commitment of those involved. Trevor Pinnock, for example, admits "there was a rivalry" but adds "I think that was a good sporting rivalry. Of course, each of us wanted to get on."[43]

During the 1970s the power of the unions became a particularly thorny issue, especially for the choral groups. The actors' and singers' union Equity went as far as banning amateurs and professionals from working together in the late 1970s. A letter from Hugh Keyte's office at the BBC to Michael Morrow's Musica Reservata, dated April 25, 1979, notes that a planned series for the following Christmas was "impossible under the present Equity amateurs-and-professionals ban: let us hope that good sense prevails in the forthcoming talks."[44] The series sought to offer an "Octave of the Nativity" Christmas "reconstruction," featuring the Clerkes of Oxenford, Hilliard Ensemble, Taverner Consort, London Cornett and Sackbut Ensemble, Schütz Choir, and the William Byrd Choir, as well as nonspecialist early music groups such as the BBC Singers, the choir of Brompton Oratory, and Westminster Cathedral Choir. In fact, a degree of good sense did prevail, and in the following year Hugh Keyte launched a very successful series for Radio 3 under the title of "Octave of the Nativity." This included the first ever recording in the Sistine Chapel by an outside choir (the William Byrd Choir).

Writing in the editorial to *The Early Music Gazette* in April 1978 Nicholas Kenyon warned of Equity's involvement having "far-reaching consequences for the performance of choral repertoire."[45] Kenyon notes how Norrington preferred to work with a very small number of professionals, whilst Gardiner's Monteverdi Choir "has always existed on a half-and-half basis." For his part, Andrew Parrott regarded most professional choirs of the time as sounding "unacceptably fuzzy and wobbly" for earlier repertories. The Taverner Choir was in its early days a mixture of professionals and amateurs "primarily because I wanted a specific sound or type of voice...I knew some very good amateur singers but only a handful of professionals who could do what I wanted at that stage," Parrott recalls.[46] The professionals were paid but not the amateurs, "which Equity members objected to because it was seen to be subverting the professional market." To help solve the legitimate worry on the part of Equity, a conductor's meeting with Gardiner, Hickox, and others was called. After much wrangling, including over whether a "housewife" (a term used by one of those present) should be paid as much as a "professional singer," Parrott proposed the principle that full fees be allocated for the total number of singers but that the amateurs' fees be paid into a fund to be used to generate further work for the choir. As Parrott put it, "a bit of lateral thinking meant that I could keep control over the musical element without undercutting anybody...and at the same time generate extra resources."[47]

Union troubles were not confined to singers, though. In 1980, a year with significant Early Music Prom performances and recordings, Christopher Hogwood found himself in dispute with the Musicians' Union over his conducting the AAM from the keyboard. According to the MU's rules, only union members could do this. Hogwood out of "conscience and dislike of coercion"[48] refused to join the union. Over 200 musicians attended a consultative branch meeting in London and overwhelmingly backed the idea of permitting a musician to conduct from the keyboard according to "a flexible interpretation of rules never framed originally to cover the conditions on which they have been imposed."

TRAINING

Such was the novelty of performing early music on original instruments that those involved had to learn "on the job." In the early 1970s there were virtually no formal didactic channels in Britain for learning historically informed performance, to say nothing of mastering the technical difficulties of playing old instruments themselves. Looking back, what is most telling is that professional early musicians somehow managed to carve out the space to play and experiment, and the time they needed to teach themselves. It is no surprise that this sometimes came across to those professional musicians who "loathed the whole period-instrument movement"[49] as a mix of arrogance and incompetence. As a professional musician playing for a chamber orchestra such as the ECO in the late 1970s, one would have expected to perform early music repertoire as part of the regular performance diet (notably the works of Bach, Handel, and Mozart). With Early Music's rise, not only did these players begin to find this repertoire being taken over by other period instrument ensembles (therefore losing out on paid work), but unquestionably in the initial years, it was also being performed less competently. As Kenyon[50] observed, it would be "naïve to assume that a supposedly historical faithful approach to performance guaranteed anything at all about the artistry of the end result." In their defense, of course, "original" instruments demanded wholly different techniques, and early musicians could not be expected to master these overnight. Those involved were usually fully committed to early music, spending a great deal of their own time learning to play the instruments to a high standard and developing their understanding of performance practice. As Trevor Pinnock notes, "You see, the thing is, there are no excuses in music, so if you are playing on period instruments that is not an excuse to play less well than your modern instrument colleagues."[51] On the one hand, "the market" has been blamed for overcommercializing early music, such that the spread of repertoire was increasingly restricted to a popular core; but, on the other hand, one can also see that the market imperative forced the pace of change and with it, professionalization. Heather Jarman observes, for example, that when the AAM were recording the Mozart symphonies, "the wind tuning took hours. Parts of sessions would be spent on wind tuning (that was late 1970s into early '80s). By the time we had finished that project, the next generation of wind players were coming in, and they could just do it."[52]

With the benefit of hindsight, it is fascinating to consider here Sir John Eliot Gardiner's views on the importance of "musical excellence." For him, this can be broken down into three constituent parts: "technical security, a degree of commitment from singers and players so that there is nothing distancing or regurgitant about the way in which they do things, and passion in performance."[53] The acquisition and practice of technical proficiency and professionalism has been foundational to Gardiner throughout his career. For example, he still laments the "error-proneness" of the Baroque oboes and natural trumpets whilst performing some Bach Suites and secular cantatas in the early 1980s, adding it was "something I found hard to accept." He reflects, "while I could understand *why* it was so—these instruments are incredibly treacherous to play—I felt playing them in public before they were technically really secure was to some extent short-changing the audience and in the end insulting to the music." A contributory factor in Gardiner's approach is surely the time he spent as a pupil of Nadia Boulanger in the 1960s in Paris. "Nadia Boulanger was absolutely pitiless in her standards of aural training and preparation." He recalls: "I have never forgotten the homily that she gave to us students: When you get up in the morning you look in the mirror and you ask yourself 'What right do I have to call myself a professional musician?' Because if you can't answer that with full confidence, knowing that you've done your utmost to acquire a solid technique...then you're skating on thin ice, and to some extent you're open to the charge of being seen as a charlatan."[54]

REWARDING

Accessing the funding required to put on a musical performance, let alone promoting a concert tour or a recording project, has long presented a sizeable challenge to those managing early music orchestras and ensembles (the absence of public sector support for Early Music is explored further in Chapter 7). In the early days it was often a case of everyone mucking in together to make ends meet (and this, of course, remains the practical reality for many freelance professional musicians today). Maureen Garnham recalls how on one occasion she arranged a tour for TEC in Scotland: "the fares were not by any means covered by the fee they were getting, and one of the girls came to me and said 'I've just discovered that if you collect so many tops of Lux (soap) boxes, you can get a free train ticket.' So they all began like mad collecting tops of boxes, and we got most of our travel expenses like that!"[55]

It was not long, however, before early musicians from the class of '73 were demanding, and being offered, higher performance fees than were musicians in other parts of the classical music profession. Despite the inherent risks of putting off prospective venues and promoters, the rationale behind these higher fees was very simple—it was difficult to get sufficiently skilled players (especially wind and brass), so specialists had to be lured in instead.[56] Early musicians were not to be treated as faceless performers, merely providing the backing for superstar soloists, but were to be celebrated as musicians in their own right.

With the benefit of hindsight, it is clear that the Early Music ethos left little room for the development of its own "superstar" performers, with fees to match. At one level, this has been an attractive feature of the movement for many performers, dissatisfied with the classical music status quo (though, of course, they would have gladly welcomed remuneration more in line with the music profession's elite). As Laurence Dreyfus wrote in a postscript (1997) to his article "Early Music Defended Against Its Devotees" in 1983, "The balance of power has shifted in some important ways away from an omnipotent Mainstream culture casting its huge shadow over an impoverished but dedicated cadre of early-music revivalists, though the institutional hegemony of the Mainstream has never really been in any doubt: one need look no further than the fee schedules for Mainstream artists vis-à-vis their Early Music counterparts, where recitalists, concerto soloists, and opera singers—even conductors—receive easily two to three times more for their performances and recording dates."[57]

PROMOTING

Formal opportunities for promotion across the classical music profession are few and far between. Typically, there is little scope for progression within an ensemble or orchestra. Talented performers are appointed to top jobs often at a young age, perhaps in their mid-20s, and this results in a relatively static job market as compared with other industries. The classical music profession suffers from a chronic rigidity in job structure, where the opportunity for growing dissatisfaction represents a darker side of the industry. The relatively antisocial and non-family-friendly lifestyle of the freelance musician, with many late nights, tours away from home, high-pressure performances, a competitive labor market, and limited income, understandably lead some to look for alternative career paths as they get older.

As much as one can explain Early Music as a critical response to the status quo, it is also true that those involved were not immune themselves from seeking to develop further the very thing they had created. To the extent that there ever had been a "honeymoon period," it was quickly over. Indeed, running parallel with the movement's professionalization in the early 1980s, we can point to an increasing level of self-reflection within the early musician labor market. This manifested itself in three ways: Firstly, there was a gradual shift in the style of the musical works being performed, with an ever-greater emphasis on repertoire from the Classical and Romantic periods. Here again, British performers were learning from their continental European counterparts. By the mid-1970s the practice of performing small-scale works by Mozart, Haydn, and Beethoven on period instruments, for example, was no longer so unusual at some of the leading continental music conservatoires (notably the Vienna Academy of Music, where Eduard Melkus taught violin). Secondly, as discussed in Chapter 3, Early Music's ideological position with respect to authentic performance was increasingly the subject of intense and probing critique. Thirdly, for some of those early musicians who had been founder members of the class of '73, there was an uncomfortable feeling that they were losing control of their own careers. Something needed to be done about it.

CLASSICAL MOVES

Elizabeth Roche, writing in 1979, considered "early music" to refer to anything written before 1640. The market (comprising record companies, promoters, and audiences), by contrast, was seemingly very happy to shift the early music goalposts by as much as two centuries in only a matter of years. "Early music" now embraced Mozart, Haydn, and Beethoven, soon to be followed by Berlioz, Weber, and then Brahms and Wagner. Returning to the matter of "push or pull," a fair question to ask is whether this move to later repertoires was more the outcome of musicians' curiosity and interest (i.e., push) or a response to market demand (i.e., pull).

Reflecting on the circumstances surrounding the launch of the London Classical Players (LCP), Roger Norrington comments, "The name was an accident in a way. We had been playing as the London Baroque Players and, moving forward historically, we got to Haydn's *Creation*. Now what do you call the band? Maybe, the London Classical Players? A few years later we got to Berlioz, and someone sent us a birthday card saying 'Congratulations on the London Romantic Players.' By then we were too well known to change our name again. It was with a mixture of research and instinct that we gradually moved forward—feeling our way. You don't know what it is going to be like playing a Haydn symphony on historic instruments until you do it. But you know, it's incredibly exciting *not* to know in advance. The gradual rediscovery of one style after another has been the most extraordinary adventure—for 30, 40 years now."[58] For Norrington, one has the sense of a deep passion for music-making, no more tangible perhaps than in the series of sell-out "experience" weekends he devised and presented at the South Bank (notably focusing on the works of Beethoven in 1987). In my interview with the conductor, Norrington repeatedly referred to a "childlike" enthusiasm and curiosity, which he felt motivated his 40-year musical journey. Though Norrington's playful approach is certainly distinctive, one can't help feeling that this sense of curiosity and interest (push), is shared by many of those working in early music, and it has been this, first and foremost, which has fuelled the movement's growing interest in later repertoire.

THE LIMITS OF AUTHENTICITY

Though Early Music was moving "forwards," eagerly embracing Classical and Romantic repertoires, it would be misleading to characterize the movement as only advancing in one direction. A key event of 1980 was the formation of the vocal ensemble Gothic Voices by musicologist and performer Christopher Page. The group, which specializes in 11th- through 15th-century music, was launched at the specific request of the BBC, to broadcast 12th-century plainchant by Hildegard of Bingen (i.e., market pull). What followed has now become something of a legend: Ted Perry, who in the same year had founded a small independent record company (Hyperion), but who continued to work as a minicab driver in the evenings, heard the Gothic Voices recording whilst in his cab, and was so moved by it that he approached the musicians to set up a recording for the fledgling label. *A Feather on the Breath of God*, released in March 1985, not only made a name for Gothic Voices and established Hyperion in the marketplace, but proved to be one of the best-selling recordings of pre-classical music ever made.

Given the successes achieved by and for Early Music by the 1980s, it is easy to see how those involved were sometimes over-ambitious. As Peter Holman, founder of the Renaissance and Baroque string consort, the Parley of Instruments (1979), recalls: "like a lot of period instrument groups at that time, we tried to do far too much, everything from a medieval programme one day, to eighteenth century music the next."[59] Recognizing the need for a degree of circumspection, in 1984 Nicholas Kenyon put together a collection of essays under the title "The limits of authenticity" for the journal *Early Music*. In his opening editorial, Kenyon described the essays as an "attempt to redraw the boundaries of what is possible and what is desirable"[60] in Early Music at the time. Although musicologists, scholars, and critics were increasingly preoccupied with the merits (or otherwise) of "authenticity" (as discussed in Chapter 3), some of the performers themselves were about to challenge the boundaries of what was "possible and desirable" in an altogether different way. Things came to a head in 1985 when, in "one of the absolutely decisive moments in British musical life,"[61] the opportunity to break away from the hierarchical control of the music directors (notably Gardiner, Hogwood, Norrington, and Pinnock) presented itself.[62]

THE AGE OF ENLIGHTENMENT

"A most interesting new chapter in England's period-instrument revival was opened by the debut in London at the end of June of a new orchestra called The Age of

Enlightenment."⁶³ The Orchestra of the Age of Enlightenment (OAE), as it was soon to become known, had its origins in the near-cancellation of an AAM concert on November 30, 1985, at St. Margaret's Westminster. Very unusually, Christopher Hogwood was double-booked, but the players wanted to continue with the concert anyway and, unbeknownst to Hogwood, engaged the Belgian violinist and conductor Sigiswald Kuijken to direct instead. Having negotiated initial funding concerns, a small sum of money was found to make the concert work. Chris Sayers (Decca and BBC) remembers the concert well: "the orchestra was seething at the time...a lot was going on."⁶⁴ Discussions quickly followed as to how to start a player-run orchestra. Catherine Mackintosh, who was to lead the orchestra for many years, reflects, "I think it was one of those collective moments in all of our lives, where the nucleus of OAE people knew that something new needed to happen. We'd all been attached to Trevor or Chris or John Eliot, and sort of 'owned' as it were."⁶⁵

At the time, Christopher Hogwood was furious, referring to the orchestra as "The Age of Embezzlement."⁶⁶ "As far as he could see, a potentially important sponsor for the AAM had been hijacked...at a concert he had bankrolled."⁶⁷ The particular events of November 1985 aside, however, the launch of OAE had wider significance in terms of Early Music's professionalization. To explain the OAE phenomenon, we need to look at several factors that account for the level of discontent with what had, rather ironically, become the early music status quo.

Firstly, the OAE's core group of players, including Tim Mason, Marshall Marcus, Felix Warnock, Catherine Mackintosh, Annette Isserlis, and Antony Pay, were mostly in their mid- to late 30s at this time, and they had all played pioneering roles in the earlier HIP developments at the beginning of the 1970s. Looking back, some sort of structural change relating to their role in how period instrument ensembles and orchestras were run was inevitable. Marshall Marcus, violinist, notes: "As the 1980s progressed, the period instrument movement was becoming a victim of its own success—more quick recordings, more long haul tours, more success, less endeavour."⁶⁸ There was clearly a developing appetite for something different.⁶⁹

Secondly, despite the ostensibly "democratic" principles of the early music movement, the class of '73 and other leading professional ensembles had not in fact been set up as democratically controlled entities where the views of early musicians were paramount. Rather, they had been constituted in a form that was entirely consistent with the dominant organizational structure of modernity, which saw capitalistic control vested in the ownership of an individual or individuals. Felix Warnock takes up the story: "So, all the orchestras that existed were the property of their one artistic director—Roger Norrington had his orchestra, Chris Hogwood had his, John Eliot Gardiner had his group...I think a lot of it was a feeling that what we, the players, were doing, was making the careers of the people who ran them...By the time we got to the late '80s, the situation in London for people like myself who were working musicians, had got rather stuck. Nothing was really changing; and yet, if we looked forward 5 or 10 years, we could also see that the employment prospects for ourselves could actually be diminishing as the individual directors of these ensembles pursued their careers around the world, leaving us, the pool of players who made it all happen, without any focus for our activity. We had become marginalized."[70]

The mission statement of the OAE is very telling in its reactionary positioning (to say nothing of the fact that the orchestra had one at all!), and what it reveals about the state of play in the early musician labor market at the time. Musicians should "Avoid the dangers implicit in playing as a matter of routine; pursuing exclusively commercial creative options; under-rehearsal; undue emphasis as imposed by a single music director; recording objectives being more important than creative objectives."[71] Quite clearly the implication is that groups such as the AAM, TEC, EBS, and LCP had succumbed to just these "dangers," and, in part at least, this was what was being reacted against.

On the surface, the new orchestra fully embraced a democratic approach, very much in line with enlightenment principles. A democratically elected board—the Artistic Direction Committee (ADC)—decided on key programming and management decisions on the orchestra's behalf. The theory was that any professional early musicians who wanted could join this new "society," and at its inception there was a pool of around 100 performers to call upon. However, as Marshal Marcus recalls, the ideal was not necessarily something that translated well into practice: "In fact it was the maddest form of orchestral membership you can imagine, and it took a lot of unpicking at a later date."[72] Warnock adds, "How do you run a partnership of 100 partners if each one is able to veto everything? That was a problem that we thought we would have to solve later. Most important was to get people to sign up to the idea."[73]

Thirdly, perhaps the most compelling reason for the OAE's existence from the performers' point of view concerned a much longed-for freedom to perform work with "others" (non-British conductors and leading musicians in the mainstream classical music arena). Whilst early musicians had worked very closely with Hogwood, Pinnock, Gardiner, and Norrington, often becoming close friends, their passion for making music only made the opportunity to perform with the likes of Leonhardt and Kuijken or Harnoncourt, Rattle, Mackerras, and Fischer, all the more attractive. Of course, this was very much consistent with the Early Music ethos. Arguably it had only been curtailed by (i) the surprising success of the movement; and (ii) the largely unrecognized dominance of the capitalistic hierarchical organizational form.

SHAKING AND ROLLING WITH RATTLE

The first performances given by the Orchestra of the Age of Enlightenment were held in June 1986 at Oxford's Town Hall and London's Queen Elizabeth Hall (QEH). Robert Henderson of *The Daily Telegraph* summed up their importance, writing "the signs are that the performance of classical music on period instruments has finally come of age." Concerts with Norrington, Leonhardt, and Mackerras followed soon after, and a record deal with Richard Branson's Virgin Classics was agreed in 1987. The orchestra's big break also came that year, when they contracted Simon Rattle to conduct them in Mozart's opera *Idomeneo* at the QEH. Simon Rattle comments, "We needed a colossal number of rehearsals—about 20, I think,"[74] adding, "It was an unforgettable time. In many ways it changed my life."

Certainly it changed the outlook for the OAE, and arguably for the professionalization of Early Music in Britain. Rattle, who had been invited to conduct all the Da Ponte Mozart operas at Glyndebourne, insisted that he would need the OAE to accompany them (starting with *Figaro* in 1989). Glyndebourne agreed. To all intents and purposes, the OAE were now part of Britain's professional classical musical establishment. "We were on the map" says Warnock.[75] "For me, the OAE's entry into the rarefied world of Glyndebourne was the moment when the Orchestra really arrived" says Anthony Robson (OAE's principal oboe).[76] As Nicholas Kenyon observes, "The epoch-making Mozart *Idomeneo* of 1987 with Simon Rattle, so nearly cancelled for lack of money, turned out to be the way into Glyndebourne and Mozart, and thence to the currently dazzling Handel operas there: a central relationship."[77]

This was indeed a central relationship, and as is evident throughout much of this book, very much supported by the close and personal connections and networks between those involved. Rattle himself suggests, "For me it starts with David Munrow, at the Royal Academy. Obviously a lot of us worked with him during the little time we had him."[78] "He was unbelievably inspirational, but I didn't immediately go in that direction." Tim Mason, Antony Pay, and Marshall Marcus had played in the National Youth Orchestra (NYO) with Rattle, and Felix Warnock was a family friend. But at a broader level it is very apparent that the OAE, itself a "new kid on the block," needed the legitimacy of someone like Rattle—and his establishment connections to Glyndebourne, in order to secure the orchestra's future.

Arguably the Orchestra of The Age of Enlightenment has proved itself to be the most high profile of the period instrument orchestras. This is not just down to the musical abilities of its players, exceptional though these are, but also the way in which the orchestra embraced a progressive approach to marketing, fund-raising, and promotion right from the word "go." No time was wasted in developing a distinctive and cutting edge logo and brand image (contemporary images of players with their "old" instruments in a variety of striking poses have lost little of their impact, even now). Looking back, one has the feeling that the OAE marked a decisive shift from a "cottage industry" to a serious business proposition. The orchestra's seed funding, after all, came not from grant-giving bodies or endowments, but from hard-nosed City bankers (contacted initially through performers' personal and family connections) used to evaluating ventures on the basis of return on investment. The OAE is probably the professional period instrument orchestra that modern players most relate to—perhaps because it has been so fully embedded into the fabric of the musical establishment. Today, the orchestra's revolutionary Early Music origins seem something of a distant memory (there is no mention of "early music" on the orchestra's website, and none of its four "Principal Artists" (Sir Mark Elder, Ivan Fischer, Vladimir Jurowski, and Sir Simon Rattle) are early music specialists, as such. With the OAE, Early Music went mainstream. With success came other problems and issues, and these are discussed in the final part of the book. In the next chapter the focus shifts to the other "professionals" who have worked alongside early musicians, and without whom the early music revival would not have taken place—musicologists, editors, publishers, and instrument-makers.

Musical notation is a wonderful invention, but it is not as wonderful as all that.

ROBERT DONINGTON[1]

Live music-making must not be subordinated to a purely scholarly treatment of the existing problems, for we arrive at decisive insights only by active musical realization of a work.

JOSEF MERTIN[2]

6

Holding History in Their Hands

INTRODUCTION

Bringing early music to the concert platform requires a whole lot more than just musical talent. The following fictitious scenario illustrates just some of the numerous practical challenges encountered along the way: Our story begins with the composition of a musical work by a lesser-known Italian composer of the early-18th century; the now long-forgotten details of its first performance(s) at a provincial court outside Florence, and its subsequent fall into obscurity. Whilst looking through an archive in a library in Naples in 1972, the catalogue card for the score is "discovered" by an early music scholar. His excitement grows as he reads through the manuscript for the first time. Over the next few weeks and months, he diligently sets about working up a performing edition. One page has several staves blotted with ink; several others are missing altogether. It is not clear what the intended instrumentation is in the middle section, and the vocal line for the main "arioso" could be sung by either a soprano or a tenor. There are markings that suggest some later revisions to the original score—but they do not appear to be in the same hand as that of the original.

Fourteen months later, the new edition is ready for copying. Xerox parts are distributed to the performers of a recently established period instrument ensemble. Only a handful of the group's musicians actually own early-18th-century instruments in a playable condition (modest freelance incomes have prevented them from being able to make such an investment, and buying a reproduction instrument remains beyond most budgets). Most of the string players would make do using period bows with their later 19th-century instruments; the ensemble's wind-section was comprised of a somewhat eclectic mix of late 17th and early 18th-century French, German and Italian instruments. Acquiring an "authentic" instrument was one thing, being able to play it to the professional standard the concert-going public demanded, something quite other. All the performers had already spent months learning completely new fingerings and bowings, which in turn had required further detective work, and much trial and error (all time spent not earning).

After a short period of rehearsal (money was tight), the day of the performance arrived. Just getting to the venue threw up yet more challenges. It is not unheard of for woodwind and string instruments to develop splits, especially in the course of long international flights. Less dramatically, keeping fragile and temperamental old instruments in tune is always an on-going battle for their owners. Arriving at the concert hall, issues of style and performance practice now took center-stage. Under the watchful eye of the music director seated at his copy of a late-18th-century harpsichord, the ensemble had but a matter of hours to agree final tempi, dynamic range, ornamentation and much more besides. In keeping with the practice of the day, their standard set-up on stage had been re-adjusted (the modern orchestral arrangement is very much a post-1800 convention); they had agreed on the tuning and temperament to be used in earlier correspondence and rehearsals, but now needed to experiment with the group's sound in situ such that it could be adapted to the particular acoustical features of the hall, and how this might change once the audience was in. They had also to consider how the ambient conditions of the concert hall would affect the tuning of the instruments (it was a bitterly cold day and the central heating had only been turned on that morning). Finally, given that the "modern premiere" was to be recorded for a delayed radio broadcast, yet more decisions were rushed through concerning how best to capture the "authentic" sounds on tape.

Whilst the early music revival seemingly focused attention on the "old," the day-to-day reality of performing early music in the modern age has necessitated a host of "new" practices being undertaken. Understanding more about these practices is the aim of this chapter. To this end, we look in more detail at the practical domains of musicology, organology, and performance practice, beginning with a discussion of the musicological issues involved in preparing, editing and interpreting scores for period performance.

MUSICOLOGICAL ISSUES—SETTLING OLD SCORES

In his introduction to *The Directory of British Early Music Groups*, published by the Early Music Centre in 1981, Denis Arnold begins by noting that early music differs from other music "only in one or two ways; but they are important and demand specialized skills."[3] According to Arnold, the first major point of difference concerns the use of old instruments that are not in common usage today. There is much we take for granted when listening to classical music, but as Thurston Dart, "the Sherlock Holmes of period performance,"[4] points out in relation to one of its most canonised works—Beethoven's *Ninth Symphony*: "the only [instruments] whose sounds have not changed since the symphony was first performed in 1824 are the kettle-drum, the triangle, and the trombone."[5] The second difference stems from the fact that the notation of much early music "does not represent the composer's intentions." As a consequence, the early musician must also be something of a musicologist. For Arnold, "the mixture of these diverse skills has frequently resulted in the amateurism in which quasi musicologists play badly and otherwise good players have little appreciation of style."[6] Many early musicians taught themselves musicology. There were few opportunities of formal learning, after all (though in the early 1970s Arnold himself, together with his colleague Stanley Boorman, devised an MA in the Interpretation and Editing of Renaissance and Baroque Music at Nottingham University; and Dart's post-graduate course at King's College London (1964) had introduced courses on printing and diplomatics—the study of old documents in order to determine their age and authenticity).

When it comes to early music's "interpretation," we can do no better than draw on the ideas of Thurston Dart and Robert Donington, both giants of British historical musicology. For Dart, the subject was "vast, fascinating, and little understood, and its pitfalls are numerous, large and uncommonly deep."[7] He explains that "the musical notation in use today is the logical development of that used in earlier times, but the present-day significance of the symbols may be, and very often is, utterly different from their significance in eighteenth-century France or sixteenth-century England or fourteenth-century Italy."[8] Thus, while a breve used to mean "brief," it is used today to represent a long sustained note; or, while today a Sarabande denotes a slow dance, in the first half of the seventeenth century it was the name of a fast one. In dealing with the "problem" of notation, Dart provides "hints to editors"[9] which include such helpful advice as making certain that the contribution to the edition can be distinguished from the composer's; keeping the scholar "happy"; locating and identifying the sources used; warning the reader of any substantial changes made; distinguishing between the words "transcribe," "edit," "arrange," "orchestrate," and "realise"; and providing the performer "with a line or two about the music he is going to buy and play." Dart adds somewhat tongue-in-cheek: "make your preface short and readable; you are neither delivering a lecture nor applying for the Degree of Doctor of Philosophy."[10]

For his part, Robert Donington (who had studied with Arnold Dolmetsch) held that questions of interpretation reflected the intimate relationship between the "innate musicianship of the interpreters" and "questions of fact."[11] There was no such thing as an exact interpretation, and "not even the composer, plays a passage in exactly the same way twice running."[12] At the heart of Donington's work, however, was the belief that "music will ordinarily sound more effective and more moving when we make every reasonable attempt to present it under its original conditions of performance."[13] This is nothing less than the case "for" Early Music. Here we find no slavish or dogmatic commitment to restore history unchanged, but rather the view that music "sounded" better, was more musical, if you like, as a result of period performance. But of course, the devil is in the detail. Just what is it that constitutes a "reasonable" attempt to re-create an original performance? As Donington concedes: "We need a vast amount of traditional working-knowledge in order to bring even the most cunning and thorough of these notated marks on paper into living performance."[14] He explains that it is the musicologist's job to find out "the kind of detail which did not and should not depend on mood at all."[15] This was why Donington recommended reading what contemporaries of the music had to say about performance. Even the most serious of scholar-practitioners, however, can hedge their bets when it comes to deciding what does or does not count as evidence. Take the case of BBC producer, musicologist, and conductor, Denis Stevens. His strongly held views on early music, recorded in a review-piece for *Early Music* in August 1989,[16] nonetheless leave ample scope for interpretation: "my main prerequisites for a convincing resuscitation were the preparation of a musical text as close to the original sources and yet as imaginative as possible; the introduction of appropriate ornaments in keeping with good taste; the encouragement of a lively and audible continuo realization." One is compelled to ask—what exactly constitutes "imaginative" or "good taste?" Taste, after all, is something that changes over time, and is always subject to the particular background and social capital of the beholder.[17] However tempting it is to seek the "truth" of a musical work as the "Grail" of any given composition, the clear trajectory of performance scholarship over the last 40 years has been to challenge the "whole notion of what constitutes the musical work,"[18] as discussed in Chapter 3. At issue here is just how to strike the balance between a quasi-scientific approach to music-making ("evidence-based music-making"), on the one hand, and the Early Music practitioners' intuitive search for musical enchantment, on the other.

The discipline of historical musicology had been established well before the modern revival of early music, of course. We can trace a direct line of scholarship through the writings of Hawkins (1776), Gerbert (1784), Burney (1789) in the 18th century; Forkel (1788-1801), Fétis (1827), Kiesewetter (1834), Coussemaker (1852; 1865) in the 19th century; the likes of Ludwig (1902-3), Riemann (1905; 1908), Wolf (1913), Schering (1914), Adler (1924), Ficker (1924-5) and his pupil Josef Mertin (1986), who taught Harnoncourt and Leonhardt amongst others; so, too, in Britain, Terry (1907), Dolmetsch (1915), Fellowes (1941), Westrup (1941; 1967), Harrison (1952; 1963), Dart (1954), Donington (1963) and their pupils.[19] However, the modern early music revival represents an extraordinary confluence of theory and practice, in which musicologists found themselves, sometimes for the first time, in the thick of it, their views taken seriously and directly acted upon. As Leech-Wilkinson (2002) argues, in the 1970s and '80s there were in fact a very small group of like-minded scholars who were highly influential in terms both of how early music (particularly what I have termed Authenticity$_1$) was performed, and how it was critically received (frequently this core group also reviewed recordings). The essential role of the musicologist is considered further in Chapter 7; for now, it is the joined up nature of their activities—their scholarship, linking directly to what gets performed under what circumstances and by whom—which must be emphasized. However good the scholarship was, and as Leech-Wilkinson shows, on occasion it was far from "good", the fact that it was now taken seriously was to have very real implications for the working lives of classical musicians, and, indeed, everyone involved in the performance of early music.

EARLY MUSIC PUBLISHERS—UNSUNG HEROES

Early Music has been dependent upon the practices of many individuals. To better explain how such practices interact in this context, we can draw on Keith Negus's concept of "mediation," which takes three forms. The first is the idea that all objects, including works of art, are mediated by social relationships. This is very much in keeping with the view set out in Chapter 3 that musical works are reproduced and/or transformed through human practice. The second is the notion of coming in-between, or "of intermediary action."[20] This forms the focus of Part III of the book, where the entrepreneur's mediating role in Early Music is considered. The third is as "a means of transmission, an agency that comes in between reality and social knowledge."[21] This is about the distribution of sounds and words. Whereas Negus's concern is with the communication media that play a central role in the transmission of (popular) music, and whereas others have focused on the mediating role of the record or CD, in particular,[22] I would argue that the primary mediator of early music is, in fact, the (scholar-)performer. But, of course, without the music "in their hands" as it were, there would be no music to perform (this not being a genre of music where "the notes" are passed down from teacher to pupil, or performer to performer, directly by ear). With regards to this point it is notable that in the Sawkins vs. Hyperion case (introduced in Chapter 3), Mr. Justice Patten stressed that "the process of editing was also designed to produce a playable edition of the works which would not waste time in rehearsal or during the recording session and which would resolve any ambiguities in the original source material."[23] This very pragmatic mediating role of the editor/publisher is clearly also germane to the Early Music story, though easily overlooked.

Within the British Early Music scene from the late 1960s onward one figure stands out as having offered tireless service in regards to the dissemination and publishing of facsimile or Urtext performing editions of early music in Britain. That man is Clifford Bartlett, formerly of King's Music, now The Early Music Company. Bartlett ran the photocopying department at the Senate House library, University of London, for some years. At the time (the 1960s), photocopiers were seen as useful purely for their administrative function; Bartlett recognized the crucial role they could also play in making noncopyright music more widely available. After a three-year stint at the Royal Academy of Music, he moved to the BBC as Deputy Music Librarian. "Then I was in the position to give help to the burgeoning early music world," Bartlett recalls modestly.[24] Whilst in theory the BBC could only provide music for "BBC events," Bartlett was happy to interpret this "extremely broadly," and in so doing, enabled a significant number of pioneering Early Music events to happen.

Over and above distributing music for performance, Bartlett wrote reviews of new editions, books, and recordings, and published *Early Music News*, started in 1976 by Michael Procter, and taken over by the Early Music Centre in 1979. He launched his own magazine, *Early Music Review*, in 1994. Bartlett's work has also involved editing scores and cutting parts—a particularly time-consuming and laborious job prior to effective music-setting programs. A laser printer was only affordable thanks to a £4,500 fee for preparing by hand a *Messiah* edition for Andrew Parrott in the late 1980s. It survived for nearly 20 years.[25] Such was the variable demand for obscure early music repertoire that it became obvious that the way forward was through short runs on a photocopier. This way one could avoid tying up capital in stock. Speaking at the Early Music Exhibition in November 2003, Clifford Bartlett noted, "we don't have stock, so we are not dependent on borrowing—except photocopiers—which we get on short-term leases anyway."[26] With the benefit of hindsight, this now reads somewhat poignantly given what was to befall Bartlett several years later—for "he became the victim of a callous fraud by two unscrupulous and dishonest photocopier salesmen that forced him into bankruptcy, [and] relinquishing the business."[27] It is a measure of the extent to which Bartlett's back-room work for the early music revival has played such a vital role to so many that the appeal set up for him by friends and colleagues and led by luminaries such as Dame Emma Kirkby, Sir Peter Maxwell Davies, Sir John Eliot Gardiner, Sir Roger Norrington, Harry Christophers, Christopher Hogwood, Andrew Parrott, and John Rutter, has raised over £75,000 through concerts and events featuring many other early music performers.

Alongside Clifford Bartlett, another key figure, of the Andrew Parrott and Hugh Keyte (BBC) generation at Oxford, is Bernard Thomas, who founded London Pro Musica Edition. Writing in the second edition of *Early Music* in April 1973, Howard Mayer Brown comments, "the [Pro Musica] series promises to be a superior one, that will furnish professional as well as amateur groups with interesting music from the renaissance, not otherwise available, in reliable performing editions at reasonable prices."[28] The article goes on to explain that the publishers will keep their costs down, as "they are facing the challenge of the ubiquitous Xerox machine," through dealing whenever possible directly with their customers by mail order.[29] We are reminded that one of the biggest outlays for performing early music throughout the 1970s and '80s was actually the rather prosaic process of photocopying music (no doubt contributing, however unfairly, to the "amateur" status of those involved). The Chairman's Report from Musica Reservata's AGM, held on June 22, 1975, sheds further light: "Music copying was expensive and wasteful and Mr Morrow should be asked whether some of this could not be recouped with commercial publication."[30] But this was a problem that refused to go away, and in 1977 the Minutes of the group's Council Meeting (January 30) report that their manager had left Musica Reservata because "she had seemed to lose her enthusiasm when she found that there were not sufficient funds to get such jobs as duplicating done as easily or as quickly as she had expected." Furthermore, "it was probably the main reason that we had lost other managers who had felt that it was not worth the effort because of the lack of finance."[31] Given these difficulties, it is hard to imagine that parts were never inaccurately copied or distributed with pages missing, all of which would have clearly impacted the "authenticity" of performance, in practice.

ORGANOLOGICAL ISSUES—(RE-)MAKING HISTORY

The activities of a handful of British enthusiasts in the mid-20th century contributed significantly to the "science of musical instruments and their classification" (organology), which, in turn, has played a vital role in the early music revival. Amongst these, Philip Bate, musicologist, broadcaster, and collector of musical instruments, stands out on two fronts. Firstly, together with a group of ten friends, he founded and then chaired The Galpin Society[32] in 1946. This was the first group to specialize in the history and study of musical instruments. The Society's Journal has provided an unbroken forum for the communication of ideas and news about musical instruments since its launch in 1948. Secondly, though these scholarly activities were very important in raising the level of instrument-making in later years, there remained something of a gulf between the theoretical knowledge imparted and the actual performance of early music at a professional level in Britain. Through donating his extensive collection of woodwind instruments to Oxford University in 1968, on condition that it was to be used for teaching, Bate was able to reduce this gulf, at least to some extent.[33] Many generations of performers and scholars have had the opportunity to benefit from "hands on" experience with these instruments over the years.

One might reasonably expect the increased supply of, and demand for, early music repertoire to be a central factor in the rise in interest in instrument-making in the 1960s and '70s, and at one level this is indeed the case. The early music revival began with the unearthing of early music repertoire, and as Clifford Bartlett observes, this came "about a decade before the instruments."[34] However, as we shall see, the craft of instrument-making was itself a trailblazer when it came to authentic performance. For its part, the focus on making "authentic" instruments reached prominence in the early 1970s, about ten years before authenticity in performance was all the rage, and just as $Authenticity_1$ was giving way in the professional sphere to $Authenticity_2$. One marker of the importance of instrument-making was the formation of the Fellowship of Makers and Restorers of Historical Instruments (FoMRHI) in 1975. FoMRHI publishes a Quarterly with regular bulletins that have continued up to the present day. The archive of FoMRHI *Communications* provide an enlightening commentary on the range of interests enjoyed by its Fellows. Amongst the issues one can read about are such practical concerns as: The polishing of metal surfaces; Some notes on the use of benzotriazole as a preservative for copper and alloys of high copper content; Burning as an alternative to boring; Why are lute pegboxes bent back?; Felling your own timber; About old music wire; Clean edges on gold leaf; Nuts, bolts, and plugs; and, my personal favorite, Plane scraping for profit and pleasure. Or for those of a more philosophical bent: On the dangers of becoming an established scholar; A hypothesis on the symphony; What is a musical instrument?; The words authentic and original; Some ways with means; Is looking seeing?; and even, Enigmatic bars.[35]

This relationship between early music repertoire, original instruments, and period performance, also mirrors the more immediate "seamless process...faithfully to realize someone's edition."[36] As Andrew Pinnock notes, "there was an assumption that the moment you discovered a manuscript, then everything else would fall into place; the BBC would grasp its importance; musical collaborators would be paid...nobody asked 'was it worth performing?' or 'did he write it?' By the time of the CD he better have written it!"[37] An interesting case in point is the "re-discovery" of Handel's *Gloria* in 2001 by Dr. Hans Joachim Marx, from the Royal Academy of Music archive. With an enthusiastic musical press suggesting that this "lost work" might be something to rival Handel's *Messiah* (a somewhat sensationalist claim, as it turned out), there was no delay in making the work widely available. By May of that year, a BIS recording had been pressed, featuring Emma Kirkby and the Academy of Music Baroque Orchestra, performing on period instruments, conducted by Laurence Cummings. The idea that "if it exists, it should be made available for performance" is one that has its critics. The conductor Raymond Leppard, for example, is scathing about this line of thinking, and is particularly critical of the *Musica Britannica* series—an edition founded in 1951 by scholars including Fellowes, Dent, Howes, and Westrup, as an authoritative national collection of British music, whose "chief purpose [was] an accurate and scholarly presentation of the original texts," and which was "also intended to provide a basis for practical performance."[38] Leppard believes it has singularly failed in this latter regard, noting that out of 86 Volumes, "you can perform probably two!"[39]

THE DEMAND FOR ORIGINAL INSTRUMENTS

As discussed in Chapter 4, a distinction needs to be drawn between the "unfamiliar" musical instruments associated with Authenticity$_1$, and the Baroque and Classical versions of instruments that we are more familiar with in their role in the modern chamber or symphony orchestra (Authenticity$_2$). The modern-day early music revival began with just a handful of orders for Medieval and Renaissance instruments, largely on behalf of amateur musicians. Richard Wood, the founder of the Early Music Shop (1968), recalls that it was actually a tender from the local authority, including an order for a shawm (a Medieval wind instrument), that kicked things off. On the strength of this order he visited two makers of "posh recorders" in Frankfurt, where he bought two sets on spec.[40] Wood takes up the story: "Then fairly shortly after...I came across David Munrow; there was no one selling instruments world-wide at that point, and he said 'why don't you form a shop?' We even sat down and talked about a name—because early music was not a generic term at that stage—and I can well remember the conversation we had. 'Shall we call it *Old Music* or *Olde Music*?' and '*Early Music* surely implies youngsters.' So we actually invented the name, and the shop only had a handful of instruments at that stage. And we registered the name—and people like the *Early Music* magazine and even the *Early Music Centre* had to write to us for permission to use it."[41]

Demand for new "old" instruments grew rapidly. "What we took got eaten up by local recorder players," recalls Wood. "It became sensible to buy 10, 100—and it got to the stage that we couldn't cope. I was going to Germany and filling a car and trailer—5 or 6 times a year. The record I think was 95 [Viola da] Gambas on one load. We had the world to ourselves at that stage." Instrument-making in Germany was ahead of Britain. In the 1950s companies like Moëck were already busy selling a wide range of historical wind instruments, including krummhorns, cornamuses, racketts, shawms, dulcians, serpents, Baroque, and Classical instruments.[42] However, by 1973, Christopher Monk reported in his first column for *Early Music* "Where the wind blows": "Richard Wood of... Bradford, whose Early Music Shop has helped so many enthusiasts since it opened, now has a rapidly growing manufacturing side. He reports that they are turning out soprano and bass dulzians in batches of thirty at a time, which are consumed almost before the polish is dry."[43]

We can see the rapid rise in demand for old instruments in the figures recorded for the *Register of Early Music*. The first *Register* in 1971 listed 62 instrument-makers. This had grown in 1973 to 95, then in 1976 to 597, many of whom were "DIY enthusiasts." This boom in demand was happening around the shift from Authenticity$_1$ to Authenticity$_2$. The shape of demand for period instruments (originals and copies) relating to Authenticity$_2$ looks a little different. As we have seen, Baroque and Classical instruments tended to be more the province of newly-formed professional groups, and then soon after, aspiring young students who wished to emulate this first generation of professional early musicians. It became important for up-and-coming makers to establish contact with the leading professional performers. "Perhaps the most important thing for a young maker is to have his instruments played in public and by the best professionals," notes harpsichord-maker Mark Stevenson.[44] The teacher-pupil relationship was important in this chain of acquisition. Robert Deegan recalls his time working with the harpsichord-maker Bob Davies (1971-1978): "There are people like Virginia Black, Ruth Dyson, Virginia Pleasants, Francis Monkman, who were all Geraint [Jones]'s students... they all bought instruments."[45] Of course, they had to have money to buy these, but as Monkman notes, the kits were cheaper and still good quality.[46]

THE SUPPLY OF INSTRUMENT-MAKERS

One might surmise that instrument-makers and early musicians represent two quite separate groups of people with distinct motivations, passions, backgrounds, and skills. The great instrument-makers and the great performers have generally been specialists in their respective fields, rather than managing to bridge both successfully in a professional context (such specialist division of labor is a characteristic of the professional field, after all). However, the point of intersection between their different activities is worth a closer look. For Early Music, I would suggest, is the product of an unusually high level of integrated practice(s).

The "father" of Early Music, Arnold Dolmetsch, for example, has been variously described as "pioneer," "craftsman," "instrument-maker," "performer," "musicologist," and "scholar." Joel Cohen writes, "Dolmetsch was the first of a new kind of workman: the artisan-scholar."[47] In many ways, his practical involvement cut across the processes of "musicing,"[48] and in this regard he represents something hugely important within Early Music. In today's language, this notion of Dolmetsch as an "artisan" is problematic, however. For as Shiner (2001) has observed, whereas the pre-Enlightenment conception of the "artisan/artist" allowed for the *necessary* integration of art, craft, and enterprise (an integration that Dolmetsch himself would surely have recognized in his day), today's "artisan" is considered as somehow lacking the particular (higher) skills of the "artist."[49] Recalling Shakespeare's friendly mocking of the "rude mechanicals" in *A Midsummer Night's Dream*, it is as if the transcendental ideals of "true" art are destined to remain out of reach for Dolmetsch, the "artisan," as they are for Bottom. We are bound then to rethink this division between artisan and artist, and this is a task I take up in the final Part of the book.

There is no doubting, however, that Dolmetsch inspired many instrument-makers who followed in his wake. Cohen describes the Hubbards, the Dowds, the von Huenes, and many other contemporary craftsmen as "the spiritual descendants of Arnold Dolmetsch."[50] Dolmetsch first developed his skills in instrument-making whilst under apprenticeship at his own family's piano-making business. Later, he was to train his own sons and daughters, and it is important to observe how strong family ties represent a recurring theme in the craft business (several leading instrument-makers have passed their businesses down to the next generation). For all that Early Music, as so many other areas of life, has relied heavily on the work of women (often unrecognized and unpaid), professional instrument-making has largely remained a man's terrain.[51] There is no single career path or entry into the profession, as many makers have been keen to stress. However, such is the time and effort, aptitude and skill required, it almost certainly has to develop into an obsession. Whilst for some it was the lure of woodwork and cabinet-making that came first, for others, it was the sound of the music that drew them in. The eminent harpsichord-maker Robert Goble, born in 1903, "was brought up in an atmosphere of country craftsmanship where knowledge of timber and good workmanship were of prime importance."[52] Goble met Dolmetsch as a boy, and later apprenticed in his workshop, mostly on recorders. Instrument-maker Robert Davies provides a compelling insight as to the motivation for his own interest in music and the harpsichord in particular: "During this time (1948-50) I first heard Wanda Landowska and, just as when I first heard Bach as a small boy, I needed no explanation or further knowledge, I simply liked it...I still remember the emotional impact of my first Toccata and Fugue and first harpsichord more than almost anything since."[53]

Many instrument-makers took up their profession more or less "by chance." The highly influential harpsichord-maker Frank Hubbard began his study of the historic harpsichord "due to the fortunate location of his library reading stall [at Harvard] near the stacks holding books on musical instruments," as well as his amateur interest in violin-making, and "the interest of a boyhood friend, William Dowd, in the harpsichord."[54] Elsewhere, John Rawson muses, "I do not know whether I would ever have started to make harpsichords if I had not met Tom Goff."[55] Tom (Thomas) Goff (1898-1975) was wealthy by independent means, distantly related to the British Royal family, and lived in a big house on Pont Street, complete with a butler in the basement. The "Thomas Goff Circus" at the Royal Festival Hall in the 1960s featured Thurston Dart, George Malcolm, Valda Aveling, Geoffrey Parsons, and Simon Preston, playing Goff harpsichords. These highly-crafted instruments often had complex pedals and stops, giving them more flexibility of sound and timbre than any "authentic" instrument.

As in most walks of life, having money could prove distinctly helpful. Some "men of means," like Tom Goff and Michael Morrow, were freer than most to pursue their love of instruments and music. Whilst they personally did not need to "make a living," their projects and practices were deeply embedded in a network of individuals and organizations that did. Having sufficient resources to make quality instruments was always a concern. Harpsichord-maker Dennis Woolley, for example, remembers, "One of the problems in those early days was that hardwoods were obtainable only on licence, so that I was compelled to scrounge from whatever source I came across."[56] He used wood salvaged from old pianos for his first soundboards. All the same, making money wasn't a primary motivation for most of those involved in making instruments. Robert Bailey alludes to the maker's motivations: "most workshops are messy, dirty untidy places, but out of it comes these beautiful things—and you look at it and think 'oh my god, did I make this'?"[57]

Here we come to the central and unifying attribute of the *professional* instrument-maker, which is an unswerving commitment to quality (in contrast perhaps to the "enthusiastic ineptitude that so frequently is to be encountered among those persons infatuated with old instruments"[58]). As Richard Wood commented in 1979, "if you are an independent, you have got to produce instruments of superb quality to survive—'alpha minus' just isn't good enough."[59] Luthier Norman Myall further emphasizes the importance of quality: "My aim is always to provide the highest levels of craftsmanship and attention to detail."[60] Such a mind-set was no doubt shared by the early musicians who were keen to get their hands on the instruments. And yet, the difficult question remains: beyond a finely made instrument what exactly constitutes "quality?" Writing in 1979, for example, the violin-maker William Samson laments, "I have been disturbed by recent trends in the philosophy of makers and players of early instruments. It would seem that authentic appearance is far more important than authentic sound."[61] He goes on to suggest that the early instrument business would be much "healthier" if makers "spent rather less time on appearance and decoration, and rather more on acoustical considerations." Samson contrasts what he terms "a new living tradition of early instrument making on a businesslike basis" with "making expensive pieces of reproduction furniture, copied down to the last worm hole."[62]

TO COPY OR TO IMPROVE? THAT IS THE QUESTION

Although the troublesome question of authenticity has probably been discussed most extensively in respect of early music performance practice, it is arguably in the context of instrument-making that we find its roots. As Stan Godlovitch says, "the successes of the pursuit of authenticity are intrinsically, if not exclusively, *knowledge-* and *skill-laden*."[63] Craft traditions and practices were all but lost in the 18th and 19th centuries. As Hubbard observes, "makers as a whole were neither inclined nor able to write accurately of their trade and those who did attempt to deal with it were chiefly amateurs, cranks, or dilettantes."[64] As a result, instrument-makers have had to rediscover skills that are no longer part of an oral tradition passed down from master to apprentice. This has led to generations of instrument-makers who were largely self-taught (and in this respect there are again similarities here with performers, such as Morrow, Greenberg, and Munrow).

The much-revered luthier David Rubio (1934–2000), who grew up in London, was another self-taught man. His biography reads like something out of a Romantic novel—whilst a student at medical school, he ran away to join the gypsies, where he acquired the name "rubio" after his red beard, and started earning a living as a flamenco guitarist, first in Spain and later in New York. Whilst here, recalling time he spent "shooting the breeze" in Spanish guitar-makers' shops, and based solely on his memory, he made his first instrument. Returning to England in 1967, he quickly established himself as a leading luthier, also making harpsichords "to satisfy the demands of the 'period instrument' movement then burgeoning in European musical circles."[65] What the performers of the time wanted, of course, were instruments that "worked." The natural tendency was for makers not just to copy or restore fine old instruments, but to surpass them. As Carl Dolmetsch writes about his father, "his devotion to authenticity was neither blind nor pedantic and he saw no merit in the perpetuation of faults or limitations in many of the early instruments from which he learnt his craft, much as he admired their undoubted good qualities."[66] Carl goes on to explain how his father designed and built his own models very much "in the same spirit as a Stradivarius learning from an Amati."

Whilst the "nineteenth-century concept of perfectibility"[67] was very evident in much of the 20th-century revival of early music—one thinks in particular of the skillfully crafted harpsichords by the likes of Goff (so-called "Goffechords") and Goble that were intended to cope with the modern-day hazards of central heating and large concert halls, and offer a rival to the piano—something of a watershed moment happened around the publication of Frank Hubbard's *Three Centuries of Harpsichord Making* in 1965. Hubbard declared his intention "to give enough information to make it possible for builders of harpsichords to base their work on certain knowledge of the designs and methods of earlier makers."[68] By 1970 there was a demonstrable shift in approach, which now favored the "copy" as opposed to the "improvement." Writing about Goble in 1991, Mary Bennett notes, "In about 1970 it seemed that a change of direction would be necessary. The spread of the early music movement had led to many more people making early instruments, and it had also led to a return to much smaller ensembles. 'Authenticity' of sound was now demanded, and this meant relinquishing the search for improvement and returning to the exact baroque models."[69] For his part, Frank Hubbard expresses his views on "authenticity" in a forthright interview for *Harpsichord* in 1972: "this composer from the past, had a talent greater than anything

I will ever have. He used the means at his disposal in an imaginative way that staggers my imagination. Therefore, the only word I can apply is arrogance to the people who feel they can devise a harpsichord more suitable to his music than the instrument he had, because he wrote his music for that harpsichord. That's why I feel so strongly that one should attempt to return to the original instruments."[70] It is hard to find a clearer rationale for authentic performance, or indeed dispositional (historical) authenticity, than this.

The fashion for copies took off quickly, though even then it is worth noting that many such copies were reproduced in kit form—a modern-day innovation that already rendered the "authentic" label compromised. Hubbard's first DIY kit was modeled after a Pascal Taskin instrument of 1769. By 1975 nearly 1,000 of these had been produced. As John Rawson notes, however, "Unfortunately[,] copying an old design of known worth does not automatically produce a good instrument."[71] Mark Stevenson adds that the term "copy" is itself misleading, and many copies of the same instrument in fact sound completely different. In his view, "it is arguable that an exact copy cannot be made."[72] As another harpsichord-maker famously remarked "I can't even copy one I made myself!"[73]

The question of whether to copy or to improve was by no means limited to the making of harpsichords. Ian Harwood, who studied lute with Diana Poulton, one-time student of Arnold Dolmetsch, and who went on to teach many of today's musical instrument-makers either in his own workshop or at the London College of Furniture, where he was a lecturer in the 1970s, was fascinated by the difference between "historical instruments and the heavy German lutes then being built."[74] One can get some sense of the lightness of his instruments from Anthony Rooley's description that "they floated, almost, as one picked them up to play."[75] Harwood's interest in historical accuracy also spurred him, with Poulton, to set up The Lute Society in 1956. It would be misleading, however, to suggest that there was a wholesale renaissance of "authentic" lute building in the 1950s. Even by the time Julian Bream was performing in the 1960s, "much of the spirit of the lute was awaiting further recovery."[76] Bream's first instrument was "heavily constructed, fitted with fixed frets, nylon strings, a single second course, a saddle bridge, and an inset rose." According to Godlovitch, Hugh Gough the maker "got much of it wrong." Whilst Bream, "using right-hand fingernails and post-Tarrega guitar technique," also got much of it wrong, he was very influential in inspiring a new generation of luthiers and professional players, including the likes of Lundberg, Elder, O'Dette, and Smith.

HOLDING HISTORY IN THEIR HANDS—PERFORMANCE ISSUES

So familiar are we today with performances on old instruments that it is difficult to appreciate the scale of the challenges facing early musicians in the 1960s and '70s. Back then, adopting a somewhat laid back approach was often the best (if not, only) strategy. As Bernard Thomas, founder of London Pro Musica Edition and a much respected performer on recorder and other early wind instruments (including with Musica Reservata and his London Pro Musica ensemble), recalls, "in those days you just bought the instruments, learned them yourself, and hoped for the best."[77]

Getting Hands on Old Instruments

As we have seen, the first challenge was to get one's hands on an instrument at all. They were by no means widely available, and though instrument-making grew exponentially in a very short period of time, we are still talking about a relatively small "cottage industry," not mass production. Historical instrument collections such as the Bate offered a direct "way in" for the lucky few who had access to them, sometimes being able to hire instruments on semi-permanent loan. Historical instrument collections were established at the Royal Academy of Music; Royal College of Music, including a set of viols and bows made by Dietrich Kessler donated by Marco Pallis (The English Consort of Viols), which violinist Catherine Mackintosh played with early in her career; Edinburgh University Reid Concert Hall Museum of Instruments and St. Cecilia's Hall Museum of Instruments; and the Royal Northern College of Music Collection of Historic Musical Instruments (an amalgamation of Dr. Henry Watson's and Josiah Thomas Chapman's collections). Many of these have been extended as performers retire and bequeath their instruments for use by others. The Oxford University Bate Collection has grown significantly over the years, for example, and now also includes the Reginald Morley-Pegge Memorial Collection of Horns and other brass and woodwind; the Anthony Baines Collection; the Edgar Hunt collection of recorders and other instruments; the Jean Henry Collection; the Taphouse keyboard loans; the Roger Warner Keyboard Collection; the Michael Thomas Keyboard Collection; and instruments from the Jeremy Montagu Collection. Other important collections include the Mobbs Keyboard Collection in Bristol, the Finchcocks Musical Museum, the Cobbe Collection at Hatchlands, and the Dolmetsch Collection, which was purchased by The Horniman Museum in the early 1980s. Birmingham University's early music center has taken things one step further by setting up "The Conservatoire Collection" of digital copies of great 16th- through 18th-century instruments.[78] Instrument collections are not just valuable for performers. The collection at the Victoria & Albert Museum in London, for example, was influential in providing British instrument-makers with examples to work from. The museum's stated aim "was to acquire the best objects from every country and every period in history so as to help British manufacturers improve their designs and compete more successfully with their commercial rivals overseas."[79] Regrettably, the museum closed its instrument collection housed in Gallery 40a, in 2010.

The principal route to purchasing antique instruments was (and remains) through the major sales-rooms, dealers, and auction houses, e.g., Bonhams, Christie's, Phillips, and Sotheby's, as well as the many regional auction houses. Gaining knowledge about what is available often required extensive networking, i.e., making it widely known that you were interested in buying an instrument. The journal *Early Music* and its companion *Gazette* have regularly published "sales-room" facts and figures, and this has been an important source of information on instrument prices over the years.

Modern reproductions or "copies" tended to have been produced on demand, following direct commissions. Some of the best makers, particularly in the boom years of the late 1970s, '80s, and early '90s,[80] were working to capacity, and had long waiting lists as a result. Elsewhere, companies like the Early Music Shop worked more like a modern retail business. Richard Wood recalls, "one of the first calculated things I did was to produce a catalogue—it was a very good move because it immediately attracted attention."[81] An interesting characteristic of the market for Authenticity$_2$, and one that publishers found particularly galling, was the disparity between the limited amount amateur musicians were willing to outlay on printed music as compared with purchasing old or reproduction instruments: "Well, for the Renaissance people the instruments come first," observes Clifford Bartlett. "It amazes me—especially in the early exhibitions, they'd spend hundreds and hundreds of pounds on instruments and be reluctant to spend a fiver on music to play."[82]

Getting to Grips with Old Instruments

Many books, each with a specialist slant, have been published to address the breadth and depth of the practical challenges facing early musicians. Notable amongst these is the series *Cambridge Handbooks to the Historical Performance of Music,* which includes titles on the early clarinet, the early horn, early keyboard instruments, early violin and viola, and early flute.[83] Several general points can be made, however. Firstly, it is worth emphasizing that the challenges of playing old musical instruments were anything but new. Musical instruments have always been difficult to play. Colin Lawson comments, "It may come as something of a relief to learn that, even in the eighteenth century, clarinetists had reason to complain about their reeds," for example.[84] Secondly, although much of the discussion concerning period performance focuses on matters of style and performance practice, it is first and foremost a matter of overcoming distinctly mechanical changes to instrument design that presents the biggest challenges to the performer. For string players this involves going back to a time before the use of wire strings, chin-rests, or spikes. For brass players it involved mastering valve-less instruments (the valve instrument was invented around 1814).[85] Even the early music singer is concerned with the "mechanics" of producing a sound with much less vibrato than had become the norm, from the 19th century onward. Early musicians would often adapt modern instruments to make their own versions of old instruments—as Christopher Hogwood puts it, "it was slightly 'serve oneself.'"[86] Thirdly, for the professional period performer the problem (but also, of course, the opportunity) of playing music from a very broad repertoire, encompassing many different styles and genres, required access to a bewildering variety of instruments, each bringing with it its own particular technical demands. Anthony Rooley notes, "The alert, aware, sensitive lutenist today must own 8 or 9 different instruments (I have upward of 12 at last count) in order to cover the repertoire encountered in an average week's rehearsing—in anything like an appropriate manner."[87] The list of Baroque and Classical period clarinets that a professional period performer would be expected to play is daunting, to say the least, including but not limited to, four sizes of chalumeaux, two-keyed clarinets in C and D, Viennese clarinets in A, B flat, B, and C, basset clarinets in B flat and A, and basset horn in F. Finally, rather than concentrating solely on the inherent challenges—of concern primarily to the players of particular instruments—it is important to stress that the very difficulties involved in mastering old instruments have also been a catalyst for creativity and learning. As Catherine Mackintosh says in respect of her early career, "I started off with a really good bow...and that, the bow, was my teacher."[88] Equally, for the clarinetist Colin Lawson, "I believe that engagement with original conditions has the capacity radically to expand one's musical horizons."[89] So it is precisely through physical, natural, and embodied engagement with these old instruments that performers have been able to gain a much deeper and felt understanding of early music.

Having now considered the professionalization of early musicians and the many practical challenges they faced along the way, the next three chapters (constituting Part III) examine how, sometimes against considerable odds, those involved went about making early music *pay*. The emerging picture highlights the entrepreneurial spirit that was present not just within individual pioneering early musicians, but also in varying measures across ensembles, orchestras, cultural organizations, record companies, universities, and the BBC.

These advertisements appeared in *Early Music* in the years 1973-80. They provide an evocative reminder of this key phase in Early Music's development.

Instrumental in early music's revival (1973, 1(1):48).
Credits: The Early Music Shop; OUP

AUTHENTICITY

In 1969 Wolfgang Joachim Zuckermann published a book called *The Modern Harpsichord*, in which he surveyed the building practices of all the modern harpsichord builders he could find, and proposed that we could make progress in harpsichords in the twentieth century by going back to the eighteenth. Zuckermann's book was not a work of scholarship. It was timely journalism coupled with a powerful polemic against the massive structures, the hideous designs, the complicated gadgetry and 'improvements' and the weak, puling tone that resulted from trying to cross the harpsichord with the modern piano; there was also praise for those builders and their instruments who were trying to rediscover the methods and the sound of the great builders of the sixteenth, seventeenth, and eighteenth centuries.

The book caused a good deal of controversy—the German plucking piano manufacturers threatened law suits, and finally did succeed in having the book banned in Germany. But the times were right for Zuckermann's message, and scarcely anyone admits to building the 'improved' harpsichord today. At the Bruges exhibition in 1974 every instrument pretended at least to be based on the classic harpsichord. A wave of 'authenticity' has now swept through the small world of harpsichords.

In general, this has been a very good thing for the instrument. Builders have stopped inventing the harpsichord, and gadgets for it, and are now studying those preserved for us in museums and collections. Phonograph records featuring the distant tinkle of plucking pianos can no longer be sold, and the record companies are forced to tell us on the package what harpsichord is being used. We are beginning to hear harpsichord music as it was intended to sound.

Of course, the new-found taste for 'authenticity' has its absurd side. Builders who have pioneered in the return to the authentic instrument are being asked scornfully, "But what is your model; what instrument did you copy?" And one manufacturer of harpsichord kits, unable or unwilling to abandon his design with all of its 'improvements', advertises his instrument variously as a 'replica', a 'copy', and finally, as just plain 'by Pascal Taskin 1769'. The Russell Collection, St Cecilia's Hall, Edinburgh, publishes a drawing and a specification sheet of the noble instrument that is genuinely by Pascal Taskin and dated 1769. It is amusing to try to find some dimension or characteristic shared by the genuine instrument in Edinburgh and the kit that is advertised as 'by Pascal Taskin 1769'.

If you build a Zuckermann harpsichord, you do not build a 'copy' of some old instrument. Without compromising things essential to the tone, our instruments are engineered for amateur construction, without the jigs and costly equipment that a professional builder (ancient or modern) would have in his shop. We make things as easy as possible for you, but where something is essential to the tone of the instrument, we tell you what to do, why it is important, and how to do it.

Nor do we build a 'replica'—only Taskin could build a replica of a Taskin. We tell you who designed your instrument, and that it is manufactured 'by' Zuckermann Harpsichords, Inc.

But no one involved with harpsichords has been more influenced by Wolfgang Joachim Zuckermann's book than those who work in his own company. The instruments we offer are the result of continuing research into the methods and techniques of the old builders, and profound respect for the sound of their instruments. We were by several years the first among manufacturers of harpsichord kits to offer our customers the light case construction, correct bracing, correct scalings, light keyboards, soft iron wire, tapered tuning pins, and many other features that were standard on the old instruments.

The result is that when you build a Zuckermann instrument you do not build a fake anything. You build a genuine harpsichord, derived from the great tradition of harpsichord building. I have said that you cannot build for yourself a better harpsichord than a Zuckermann. Nor can you build one more authentic—in construction or in the sound it produces.

David J. Way, President

ZUCKERMANN HARPSICHORDS, INC.
Box 121, Stonington, Connecticut 06378, U.S.A.

Concerts . courses . festivals etc . AN EARLY MUSIC DIRECTORY

THE EARLY MUSIC CENTRE

We now invite applications for a second ONE-YEAR COURSE FOR LUTENISTS under the direction of Anthony Rooley

and a new ONE-YEAR COURSE FOR VIOL PLAYERS under the direction of Trevor Jones

These will be one-year performers' courses for advanced students of the Renaissance lute and viol. The courses will run from September 1978 to July 1979 at the Early Music Centre, London.

CONCERTS AND LECTURES

Autumn 'Mediaeval' Term

All lectures at the Early Music Centre's new lecture hall at 97 Wilsham St., W11, and concerts at St. James's Norlands, St. James's Gardens, W11. Both a short walk from the Centre.

Sunday 2nd October 1977: a lecture/recital by Christopher Page and Lewis Jones from the department of Mediaeval Studies at the University of York.
'The Instruments and Music of the Time of the Cantigas de Sancta Maria Paintings'.

Sunday 16th October 1977: Lecture: Philip Pickett, director of the New London Consort. Concert: The New London Consort; with Philip Pickett, William Hunt, Nigel North, Catherine Bott and John Potter.
'English Music Before 1380'

Sunday 13th November 1977: Lecture: Michael Morrow, director of Musica Reservata. Concert: Musica Reservata; with Margaret Philpot, Bernard Thomas, Roderick Skeaping, Daphne Webb and Tom Finucane.
'Music from the Court of Burgundy c 1450'

This year the Early Music Centre will be offering the following new classes: Lute-making, loud wind instruments, seventeenth-century workshop, lute song, cittern and bandora, Baroque plucked instruments, trio sonata group and Baroque orchestra and further children's classes.

For all details and further information contact:

The Early Music Centre
Director: Anthony Rooley
62 Princedale Road,
London W11 4NL, England
Telephone: 01-229 5568

A knowledge-base for British Early Music (1977, 5(4):602).
Credits: Anthony Rooley; OUP

YORK EARLY MUSIC WEEK

16–24 April 1977

A course for singers and players of medieval, renaissance and baroque instruments.
Directed by Anthony Rooley and John Bryan.
At the College of Ripon and York St. John.
With the support of Yorkshire Arts Association.

Featured composers:	Concerts by:	Lectures by:
MACHAUT (d 1377)	LANDINI CONSORT	DAVID FALLOWS
DOWLAND	CONSORT OF MUSICKE	ANTHONY ROOLEY
LOCKE (d 1677)	THE KING'S MUSICK	MICHAEL TILMOUTH
BACH	YORKSHIRE BAROQUE SOLOISTS	WILFRID MELLERS
	with ALAN HACKER (baroque clarinet)	

Tuition in consort playing and singing by members of the resident ensembles including:

John Bryan	Emma Kirkby	Peter Syrus
Ian Gammie	Andrew Parrott	Anthony Rooley
Trevor Jones	Jane Ryan	Polly Waterfield

Fee: £60 (reductions for non-residents and non-players; YAA scholarships for Yorkshire residents.)

Fringe events: lunchtime concerts
 exhibitions
 music shops
 instrument craftsmen at work
 renaissance dancing

For further details and application forms contact:

 John Bryan
 128 Micklegate
 YORK
 YO1 1JX.

The forerunner to the York Early Music Festival (1977, 5(1):110).
Credits: John Bryan; National Centre for Early Music/York Early Music Festival; OUP

Musical Instruments

On 29th October, 1976, Sotheby's held their first sale of Musical Instruments in New York. Included was this double virginals by Hans Ruckers the Younger, Antwerp, 1623, which was sold for $65,000 (£41,139)—a world auction record for a keyboard instrument and indeed for any instrument other than those of the violin family.

A second sale in New York has been arranged for March 1977.

In London the next Musical Instruments sale will be on Thursday, 10th February at 11 am.

Further information may be obtained from Graham Wells in London and from Joseph Kuntz or Wathena Slaughter,
Sotheby Parke Bernet Inc.,
980 Madison Avenue, New York, N.Y. 10021.
Telephone: (212) 472 3400
Telex: New York 23264.

Sotheby's
FOUNDED 1744

Sotheby Parke Bernet & Co., 34-35 New Bond Street, London W1A 2AA
Telephone: 01-493 8080   *Telex:* London 24454   *Telegrams:* Abinitio, London

Original instruments now big business (1977, 5(1):66).
Credits: Sotheby's; OUP

BLACK BOOKS ARE GOING ROUND IN PACKS

The reason for this curious but indisputable fact is that our black books, in these days of rocketing prices, are remarkably good value for money: so much so that many of our customers buy several copies of a particular score that they require—it is some indication of the philosophy behind our activities that four copies of one of our dance collections often cost about the same as a single copy of an imported publication of similar size. One reason for this apparent anomaly is that all our publications that are in score form only are available at a special price for a complete set, typically four copies for the price of three. But even single copies of our editions are much less expensive than those of conventional publishers of comparable material.

Enlightened pricing isn't our only preoccupation, of course. Regular customers find our editions highly practical, but informative at the same time. Perhaps the secret of our success is that we have bridged the gap that normally exists between music publisher and consumer: we are our own consumers, and understand the requirements of professional and amateur musicians.

Publications in preparation include madrigals by Jacques Arcadelt and Philippe Verdelot, chansons by Lassus and Thomas Crecquillon, canzonas by Banchieri, Bonelli and others, and dances by Erasmus Widmann, Michael Praetorius and others.

London Pro Musica Edition
61 North Street London SW4 0HQ

Performance editions prove essential (1977, 5(4):554).
Credits: London Pro Musica; OUP

Promoting early music performance in the 1970s (1979, 7(1):62).
Credits: Anthony Rooley; OUP

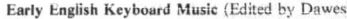

Early music's revival beyond doubt (1979, 7(1):72).
Credits: Schott Music Ltd; MDS (Hire & Copyright) Ltd; OUP

Not so *early* music (1979, 7(2):228).
Credits: Sony Classical International (Deutsche Harmonia Mundi); OUP

PROMS 80

Sunday 27 July, 3 p.m.
Bach: St. John Passion
The Taverner Choir
The Taverner Players
Andrew Parrott

Wednesday 30 July, 7.30 p.m.
Tallis, Lassus, the Gabrielis, Striggio, Schütz
Schütz Choir of London. London Baroque Players
Roger Norrington

Sunday 3 August, 7.30 p.m.
Dufay and his contemporaries
New London Consort
Philip Pickett

Friday 8 August, 7.30 p.m.
Handel and Cererols
London Oratory Choir. The English Concert
John Hoban. Trevor Pinnock

Sunday 7 September, 7 p.m.
Handel: Semele
London Bach Society. Steinitz Bach Players
Paul Steinitz

Prospectus now on sale
from the Royal Albert Hall, booksellers, newsagents,
or BBC Publications, PO Box 234, London SE1 3TH. Price (by post £1)

Early Music enjoyed by the mainstream (1980, 8(3):328).
Credits: BBC Proms Publications; OUP

PART THREE

Making Early Music *Pay*

> A university, it may be said, is a protected space in which various forms of useful preparation for life are undertaken in a setting and manner which encourages the students to understand the contingency of any particular packet of knowledge and its interrelations with other different forms of knowledge.
>
> JOHN HENRY NEWMAN[1]

> People do not indeed make history in circumstances of their own choosing, but they do make it.
>
> MERVYN HARTWIG[2]

7

Spinning Out Early Music

INTRODUCTION

Knowledge, whether of a musicological, historical, creative, entrepreneurial, artful, or performance-related kind, is fundamental to early music. The early music revival has taken place conterminously with a shift in the developed world's economic base—from a postindustrial economy, largely driven by the service sector, toward a knowledge(-based) economy. Knowledge and related aspects of education, often referred to in terms of human or cultural capital, are now treated both as productive assets and as products themselves. Knowledge of all kinds has become increasingly commodified. Some see this as characteristic of modernity's inexorable drive to rationalize and industrialize everything it can lay its hands on. Such was the pessimistic viewpoint underlying Adorno and Horkheimer's (1972) critique of the "culture industry," where the commoditization of art as mass-produced entertainment leads to the "alienation" and disenchantment of those involved. So whilst the innovative product "early music" is indeed brought into being through the intrinsically motivated knowledge producing labor of scholars, musicologists, instrument-makers, and performers, it is also a particular form of knowledge outcome sold in a commodified form as a packaged product—the LP, CD, or live concert. The aim of this chapter is to unpick this potentially alienating process of knowledge production, with a particular emphasis on explaining the motivating, enabling, and constraining role of key institutions, notably universities, music colleges, and the Arts Council.

SEVEN KNOWLEDGE CLAIMS

We can usefully refer to seven "knowledge claims" (see Table 7.1) to emphasize the pluralistic nature of knowledge within early music production. My aim here is to

TABLE 7.1.

Seven knowledge claims of Early Music

No.	Knowledge claim	Type of knowledge
1	Art-science	Heterogeneous; boundary-spanning
2	Mode 2	Interdisciplinary; problem-focused
3	Authenticity	Dispositional; personal
4	Creativity	Discovery; enactment
5	Art(ful)	Practical; embodied; aesthetic
6	Dialectic	Absent (not knowing); enchanted
7	Innovation	Recognizing; resourcing; communicating

demonstrate how much more there is to historical performance practice than simply translating the "evidence" from treatises and other contemporary accounts into musical performance.

First, the production of various kinds of knowledge is a central feature of the early music value chain. Writing in 1976, Nicholas Kenyon suggested that "concert giving, research, study of instruments, editorial work, instrument construction, all have to be carried out in an atmosphere of continuous development, rather than in a situation of isolated and erratic happenings."[3] This observation is pertinent not just for drawing attention to the sense in which knowledge is very much a productive asset in the continuous development of early music, but also in emphasising the *heterogeneous* nature of the practices involved. The process of getting early music performed in a professional context is based on a mix of quasi-scientific historical and musicological knowledge, on the one hand, and experiential, artistic, musical, and performer knowledge, on the other. As Sherman observes, "the historical-performance movement is the child of an unlikely union—that of scholarship and art."[4] Early music is a hybrid activity, a kind of "*art-science*."[5] It is certainly no coincidence that much of the pioneering activity of this art-science was first undertaken in the specialist knowledge-producing environment of university music departments.

Second, the production of knowledge is of a particular collective and co-creative kind, where early musicians necessarily engage with a "motley crew" of "others."[6] The early music project requires a mix of knowledge specialists, in what looks like a single and purposeful but interdisciplinary response to the problem of performing old music in an authentic style. This approach to knowledge production stands in stark contrast to the traditional, discipline-based "Mode 1" model of university-led knowledge, in which the lone researcher "makes" knowledge that may or may not have an application in the wider world. It is much more in keeping with "Mode 2" knowledge production, which is "socially distributed, application-oriented, trans-disciplinary, and subject to multiple accountabilities."[7] Interestingly, Etzkowitz and Leydesdorff[8] suggest that Mode 2 is not in fact a "modern" development at all, but harkens back to a pre-Enlightenment approach to doing research, science, and indeed, art. To some extent at least, the early music movement appears to have reclaimed not just the music itself, but the way of bringing music to an audience, through collective engagement of all those involved (in the process blurring the boundaries between the subsystems of modernity—State, Market, Culture, and Knowledge production).

Third, given the particular interest in historical performance, knowledge production in early music is characterized by its search for *authenticity*. As highlighted in Chapter 3, this involves working with a mix of knowledge. To begin with, historical performance seeks to perform early music according to what I have termed dispositional (historical) authenticity. This necessitates a (dispositional) concern for what must have been possible at the time the music was written and first performed. HIP's particular knowledge claims are made in relation to the specific types of instruments being used, the stylistic and practical limitations of notation and scoring, and the physical and sociocultural context under which the music was performed. The important distinction between dispositional (historical) and other, more widely discussed approaches to historical authenticity is that the former approach conceptually embraces these latter ones, but is not focused on repeating or reproducing any specific performance. A related type of knowledge claim concerns the presence (or otherwise) of personal authenticity. This is about being the person and musician you are without artifice; without "fabrication."[9] Clearly, this is a slippery form of knowledge, since to be aware of oneself as performing "authentically" would itself appear to be inherently inauthentic.[10] But it is nonetheless crucial to making early music in the modern age and more widely, to living with "real" authenticity. I return to these ideas in the final Part of the book.

Fourth, early music has required and given rise to *creativity*, generally defined as "the ability to produce work that is both novel (i.e., original, unexpected) and appropriate (i.e., useful, adaptive concerning task constraints)."[11] There are clearly problems with this widely cited definition. For example, what is (or isn't) "novel?" This would seem to be a very pertinent question in the particular context of performing "old music" in an authentic manner. Furthermore, who or what determines whether something is "appropriate" or valuable? The implication is that something is only deemed to be creative when value is recognized; but who is doing the valuing (this has practical implications in the case of public sector support, for example)? A critical realist definition of creativity asserts that it is "the human potential, power or capacity to make discoveries about the pre-existing potentials and powers of the world and to bring those discoveries into being."[12] This definition is helpful for drawing attention to the latent creativity of human beings, and the fact that it is also a particular kind of knowledge, involving both *discovery* and *enactment*. This would seem to characterize early music knowledge production rather well.

Fifth, early music is distinctive, inter alia, for being a form of *art*, requiring a certain kind of knowledge for its production, and giving rise to particular knowledge outcomes. "Art" involves the transformation of raw materials with ability and intelligence.[13] As Ibbotson says, "Art is entirely about doing and making, and if it isn't, you are not doing art, you are doing something else."[14] Thus, *practical* and *embodied* knowledge is, of course, central to the activities of the early musician and instrument-maker.

In addition, as Eisner suggests, the arts are "typically crafted to make aesthetic forms of experience possible."[15] Making early music involves the production of *aesthetic knowledge*, or "knowing on the basis of sensible perceptions."[16] Crucially, this moves us beyond the scope of the purely (social) scientific, in which knowledge is taken as a primarily cognitive and rational human response to the world.

Sixth, one of the major emerging themes of this book is that early music production is enabled by a form of knowledge that due to its paradoxical and transcendent nature has been largely overlooked in any causal explanatory account of cultural production, to say nothing of this context of Early Music. At its simplest, this is *not* knowing. The apparent absence of knowledge, I suggest, is itself a dialectical form of knowledge. On the surface this just looks like a statement about known unknowns, or worse, a confusion between knowledge and belief (knowledge, according to Plato, has to be a "justified true belief"). However, "not knowing" is indeed a transcendent form of knowledge that can take the form of a sense or awareness, or a cognitive feeling.[17] It is crucial as a motivational force in all areas of social change—including the apparently rational world of the market. For example, experts in social transformation, be they teachers, entrepreneurs, performers, or therapists, have developed strategies and approaches to fostering and sustaining just this form of "knowledge" in their chosen field (without it there would be no hope or prospect of change). In the case of early music practitioners this motivational dynamic has been key at a variety of levels. Indeed, the very fact that we don't know how early music was performed in 1721, nor what the second movement of Bach's Brandenburg Concerto No. 2 "means," provides a motivational starting point for intellectual and musical inquiry. To the extent that it is motivating—we are curious to find out—it is a form of knowledge that has an effect, and is therefore real. As I shall discuss in more detail in Part IV, this dialectical form of knowledge is also central to the performer's re-enchanting of music.

Finally, bringing all of the above together, we need to account for how knowledge in all its forms has been used (wittingly and unwittingly) to bring about Early Music as innovation. Innovation (from the Latin *innovare*, meaning "to make something new") is the process of turning ideas into new opportunities for value creation and putting these into practice. This requires accounting for the move from the musicologist's excitement over a long-lost manuscript through to live performances, broadcasts, recordings, and revenue generation via the sale of tickets, records, CDs, sheet-music, instruments, and so on. Innovation is in effect the post hoc recognition of creativity, involving a new and valuable discovery of some kind. The process of commercialization that saw Early Music become a significant market-driven innovation in the field of classical music was crucially dependent upon creativity (itself a particular form of knowledge) being recognized, resourced, and communicated.

EARLY MUSIC AND KNOWLEDGE-PRODUCING INSTITUTIONS

"Spinning out" early music involves a journey from within the cloistered courts and hallowed libraries of academia, moving out onto the glamorous world-stages of professional performance, passing through the "heterotopic" recording studio,[18] and, after the applause has faded, to the filing of expense claims and self-assessment tax forms. At each stage knowledge is being created and mediated by human beings operating under conditions that are not wholly of their making. Who these individuals are, and what characteristics they possess in terms of entrepreneurial skills, attributes, behaviors, and practices, will form the basis of Chapter 9. Over the next two chapters, however, the focus is on explaining the pre-existing structures and institutions,[19] which have conditioned early musicians' knowledge-producing practices. Industrial innovation is stimulated at the intersection with state and academia.[20] Our starting point in this chapter, therefore, is to explore further how publicly funded knowledge-producing institutions have contributed to Early Music's innovations, particularly in respect of their distinctive role in *recognizing* creativity (universities and music colleges), *resourcing* creativity (the Arts Council), and *communicating* creativity (the BBC). We look in detail at the BBC's publicly funded broadcasting of early music and its dissemination through privately funded recordings in the following chapter, but for now the analysis takes us back to university.

UNIVERSITY AND EARLY MUSIC

The university is the quintessential knowledge-producing institution, providing the environment for history's "great" men and women to generate groundbreaking ideas and innovations. In the words of Stefan Collini, universities are "perhaps the single most important institutional medium for conserving, understanding, extending and handing on to subsequent generations the intellectual, scientific and artistic heritage of mankind."[21] He adds (with obvious resonance to the subject of this book) that "we are merely custodians for the present generation of a complex intellectual inheritance which we did not create—and which is not ours to destroy." Many of those pioneering individuals who feature in the story of early music's revival began as students, undertook research, and/or taught in British universities. It appears, therefore, that the university represents a primary context for recognizing creativity. But the university's role in supporting the classical music profession is perhaps not as direct as one might think.

For virtually all of its history the university has had no interest in *teaching* the performance of classical music.[22] This has been left primarily to the music colleges (and before that to individual musicians). To read music at university in the early 1970s generally involved the study of musicology, musical analysis, history, and composition, with music technology, ethnomusicology, and performance (practice) only more recent additions. Most of the classical music-making that took place in university (of which there was much) was organized around the edges of the formal curricula, and often instigated by students themselves in their "free time." To this extent, the university was both central to, and yet also somewhat at the margins of, the music profession.

A fair question to ask, then, would be: did the university (as a knowledge-producing institution) recognize Early Music's potential in the late 1960s and early 1970s? The answer appears to be a mixed "yes" and "no." The actions and practices of particular individuals need to be distinguished from the support for early music at an institutional level. Whilst many early musicians have recorded a debt of gratitude to their teachers, colleagues, and mentors at university for inspiring them in the early days of the HIP revival, historical performance practice did not become a legitimized subject in its own right until much later.[23] That said, the launch of the academic journal *Early Music* in 1973 demonstrates a critical mass of interest by this time. Elsewhere, academic conferences focused their attention on Authenticity$_1$ (e.g., The Medieval and Renaissance Music Conference, "Med-Ren," first held at Nottingham University in 1972, and still going strong), and later, Authenticity$_2$ (e.g., the Biennial International Conference on Baroque Music, first organized by Jerome Roche in 1984). It is interesting to note that the first early music conference, *The Future of Early Music in Britain*, held in May 1977 in London, was in fact proposed by John Cruft, the then music director of the Arts Council of Great Britain, rather than from within the academic fold.[24]

Various commentators have highlighted the significance of the "collegium musicum" model (first introduced in Germany and Switzerland during the Reformation), in which the performance of music for pleasure is linked to academic or philosophical discussion.[25] During the 20th century, this model developed to become largely associated with the performance of early music by university ensembles, under the direction of paid faculty members. For example, cornettist and cofounder of His Majestys Sagbutts and Cornetts, Jeremy West, describes being at Durham University in the 1970s, when Jerome Roche was "bringing home the likes of Alessandro Grandi, fresh from the archives in Italy...When he put the baton down for the downbeat, the music jumped off the page, maybe for the first time in 400 years."[26] West now marvels at his being very much "in the right place at the right time." University students have not always been so lucky; as Nicholas Kenyon observes, "because of the dominance of academics rather than primarily practical musicians, performances can become indifferent."[27] Then again, West points out that support for young students to play Authenticity$_1$ repertoire on original instruments is virtually nonexistent in many university departments today (one can, of course, debate the relative advantages of an "indifferent" performance as against a "nonexistent" one).

There were virtually no formal didactic channels for learning about historical performance practice in the mid-1960s (honorable exceptions include Dart's (1964) MMus course in editing and interpretation of Renaissance and Baroque music at King's College London, and specialist early music courses at Nottingham and York, which started a little later), so anyone interested was very much forced to find his own way. Christopher Hogwood recalls, "we were in a period when reading music didn't have much to do with practical music," adding, "it still doesn't."[28] Jeremy West's description of his first university performance on the cornetto is a telling reminder of the way in which youthful enthusiasm can often engender life-changing experiences: "I'd been playing far less time than it takes to get to know the fingering chart when word got out that there was a cornetto player around...the noise came out through the practice room door and went round like a bush fire! They said 'right, we've got this group and you've got to come and play in it', to which I said 'thank you, I'd love to, but I need about 6 months.' They replied 'right, we'll be rehearsing on Thursday, see you there!, So I turned up, sat in front of this dance music, not knowing the fingerings and they said 'now play,' which I did. I'm still at it now."[29]

Early music knowledge production and practice have generally been cultivated at the edges of institutionalized learning, rather than through a centralized or top-down approach, such as in the collegium musicum. Of course, much of the very best performance, music, and comedy takes place at fringe festivals (in Edinburgh as elsewhere). There is something about these spaces that enables performers and comics to "play" with a degree of freedom. That said, opportunities at the fringe remain codependent upon the center in important ways.[30] Universities provide key resources to those working at their periphery. Early musicians have benefitted from a ready supply of talented performers, the loan of old instruments, the free or heavily discounted use of concert venues, an existing marketing machine through music societies and the like, and perhaps most importantly of all, a ready-made captive audience of students and university friends.

EARLY MUSIC AS "ART-SCIENCE"

Although often carried out by one and the same person, the practices involved in musicology and performance throw up competing demands in respect of knowledge production. As already mentioned, universities have traditionally been geared to provide support for historical musicology, but they are rather less well equipped when it comes to supporting historically informed performance in practice. Historical musicology, by its very nature, is conservative in approach (yet often carried out by progressives). It is a (social) scientific discipline, where "evidence" is contested primarily on the basis of rational inquiry. Applied music-making, on the other hand, requires being open to other types of embodied knowledge, as the performer dances (literally and metaphorically) to a different tune. The scope for conflict is sizeable. The editor of the academic journal *Early Music,* John Thomson, noted in 1981 how "Several readers have recently chastised us for becoming too academic."[31] With the shoe on the other foot, as it were, Leech-Wilkinson suggests that "the public influence of a scholar's work has a rather double-edged correlation with her power within the profession."[32] He further states, "the more abstruse the research, the greater the power it generates." The upshot, according to Leech-Wilkinson, is that the more public interest the knowledge has, the weaker it will be received by one's academic peers. This looks like a particularly significant observation in light of Richard Taruskin's assertion that musicology was "a Johnny-come-lately to the authentic performance movement."[33] Despite the opportunities for musicology to make its mark within the problem-centered context of early music performance, Mode 1 thinking appears to have been reluctant to release its positivistic grip on university-based knowledge production. This reluctance was surely one of the factors that Joseph Kerman was referring to when in the mid-1980s he suggested that historical performance was the field of musicology "possibly in the greatest turmoil of them all."[34]

Turning now to the institutional support for performance per se, it is striking to read the following interview extract from the founder of The Tallis Scholars, Peter Phillips, in which he sums up in just three words the role of the university as a knowledge-producing institution:[35]

> INTERVIEWER: I've met a number of you English conductors who have come out of Oxford and Cambridge: Roger Norrington, John Eliot Gardiner, you and Harry Christophers, Andrew Carwood and Edward Wickham from the younger generation. You're all quite alike in not apparently having had much formal training in what you do. Was there any particular magic formula in what you experienced at Oxford?
>
> PHILLIPS: Nobody stopped me.

Back in the 1970s at least, it seems that universities just let people "get on with it."[36] This was a kind of benign disinterest, where there existed a practical and characteristically British pragmatic tolerance to novelty. Writers in organizational management have used the term "absorptive capacity"[37] to describe the ability of organizations to take in new knowledge, and this seems appropriate here. Universities are (or rather should be) like sponges—full of spaces that can absorb new learning. Like the sponge, if the spaces are too large, e.g., there is too much freedom for unsupported behavior, or too small, e.g., there is not enough space in the timetable, the university will not be able to do its job so well. Sadly, some universities are now "stopping" such performers as Peter Phillips by closing their music departments or no longer offering music degrees (e.g., Exeter, Reading, University of East Anglia). With music also very much in the firing line at the level of secondary education (STEM subjects (science, technology, engineering, and mathematics) deemed to be of a higher status and value), there must be real concern not only about the future training and education of musicologists, but the vital role played by universities in promoting professional performance.

MUSIC COLLEGES AND EARLY MUSIC

Music, compared with most other skilled occupations, offers few natural barriers of age, physique, sex, or language. Children can learn to play most instruments from an early age, and generally speaking, professionals start young. As Francis Galton remarked in his study of hereditary genius: "There is no career in which eminence is achieved so early in life."[38] Since the early 19th century, many young aspiring musicians have studied at the country's music colleges or "conservatories."[39] By 1900 there were thirty-three "colleges of music" in London and few towns lacked a "conservatoire," although "many were merely family businesses or loose associations of teachers dignified by a label."[40] Music colleges are concerned first and foremost with training toward a career in performance, which contrasts markedly with universities. Godlovitch notes that in the context of classical music, this is a "professional practice governed by inherently conservative standards of manual skill and expertise."[41] Furthermore, "These standards are staunchly sustained and applied by a performance practice community which emulates many of the regulatory powers and obligations of the Guild tradition." Within the bigger story of early music's revival, this point is crucial, for two reasons. First, it meant that affecting change of any sort from within this type of establishment—such as that advocated by early musicians—was extremely difficult to achieve, and likely to encounter institutional resistance. As Andrew Pinnock suggests, "Well, they wouldn't let you in to study lots of early instruments, and they'd fail you enthusiastically if you dared to play your unaccompanied Bach on a baroque fiddle, or whatever."[42] A number of leading early musicians had personal battles with music colleges over the right to study their preferred instrument. Trevor Pinnock remembers being told by the RCM that "you'll never make a living as a harpsichord player, so you ought to become an organist and do the harpsichord on the side ... and if you do give up the organ we'll have to take away your scholarship money." He adds, "That decided me. I had to give up then. It was a silly thing to say to a teenager!"[43] Bruce Haynes similarly struggled to study harpsichord as keyboard minor instead of piano as a student in Amsterdam.[44] Second, we are reminded once again of the craft-like nature of performance practice that underpins the teleological project of making early music *pay*. The extensive nature of this craft-work challenges preconceived (enduringly Romantic) notions of the "artist."

In fact, one of the first early music departments in Europe had been established in 1938 by Edgar Hunt at Trinity College of Music (at Old Devonshire House, Bloomsbury). From its inception, Trinity's teaching program has focused strongly on the recorder and viola da gamba (instruments largely associated with Authenticity$_2$). It was not until the 1970s that the other London colleges followed suit. The Royal Academy of Music now held a modest number of workshops, including regular weekly sessions with Peter Holman, founder of the Parley of Instruments. The Guildhall founded its historical performance department in 1973, and the Royal College of Music started its postgraduate program, directed by Nicholas McGegan, in September 1978. The college's baroque orchestra, which students from the Guildhall were invited to join, benefitted from the expert instruction of violinist Catherine Mackintosh. In an informative review of early music training in 1978, Deborah Roberts (formerly of The Tallis Scholars, and cofounder of the Brighton Early Music Festival in 2002), appears less than overwhelmed about the overall provision at the time: "Clearly at present there is no satisfactory system."[45] This view is one echoed by Andrew Parrott, talking to me 25 years later: "we have not produced anything comparable to Basle, or as vigorous as the Hague ... despite having been in the forefront."[46] It is worth observing here that in the absence of home-grown early music tuition, many early musicians of the 1960s and '70s went abroad to study, where courses had generally started earlier, before returning to put their newly won knowledge into practice. Viola da gamba player Alison Crum, for instance, studied briefly at Basle "because Jordi Savall [Catalan viol player and conductor] taught there. Basle had a large department devoted to early music, which, unusually for that time, included specialists in 15th- and 16th-century music, some of whom (for example) taught how to play divisions by rote."[47] Andrew Parrott laments the fact that the Early Music Centre (EMC) was unable to develop into a serious teaching institution in the late 1970s in Britain.[48] The EMC's teaching provision was effectively unregulated and their hands were tied when it came to vetting who would and who would not be allowed onto their program. Parrott recalls, "when I discovered that they had to accept almost everybody for my singing course, and therefore that the standard was inevitably going to be unduly mixed—I felt I had to withdraw."[49] The Centre's teaching activities folded soon afterward.

Writing in 1988, Haskell states, "In the long run, the historical performance movement's most significant impact may well be in the area of musical education."[50] Noting that most music schools and colleges in Europe and the United States now had specialist courses in performance practice, Haskell suggests that "Early musicians in this increasingly competitive environment are learning what professionals in other fields have long understood: that specialized knowledge and abilities can be valuable assets." Twenty-five years after Haskell wrote these words, one has the strong impression that the British music colleges, overall, were far slower in putting their institutional support behind Early Music than they could (or should) have been. Indeed, it was only really when the market evidence was incontrovertible (HIP was here to stay) that they began seriously to embrace early music in their program. This market-led view finds support in Dawn Bennett's (2008) study of the classical music profession. Bennett notes that "competition between conservatories—particularly in Europe—led to the development of specialist courses in areas such as early music and ethnomusicology."[51] By the early 1980s the view of mainstream educational establishments that early music had no real place in the professional world must itself have seemed to belong to a bygone age. Margaret Thatcher's famous quip—"why train for unemployment?"[52]—was easily refuted by the evidence of copious and handsomely paid work for early music specialists. All the same, there was clearly a time lag between the first generation of professional early musicians and serious backing from music colleges (involving tuition from this very generation of players). It is interesting to speculate as to whether Early Music would have developed faster (still) if there had been more of a determination on behalf of the colleges to join the movement sooner.

THE ARTS COUNCIL AND EARLY MUSIC

The third knowledge-producing institution to come under the spotlight is the Arts Council (of Great Britain). The Arts Council's charter of 1967 (an auspicious date for Early Music) redefined its objectives as: "to develop and improve the *knowledge,*[53] understanding and practice of the arts; to increase the accessibility of the arts to the public throughout Great Britain and to advise and co-operate with departments of Government, local authorities and other bodies on any matters concerned, whether directly or indirectly, with the foregoing objects."⁵⁴ The Arts Council's credentials as a knowledge-producing institution need to be understood in the broader historical context of its own "golden age" between 1964 and 1970 under the Harold Wilson government, and then an increasingly difficult period in the 1970s, when it came under attack for being elitist and politically biased. The headline story is that despite the almost complete absence of core funding for early music, this most "legitimate" of art forms nonetheless managed to deliver innovation on a very significant level within the classical music field. So how was this possible, and what are the implications with respect to the arguments for (and against) subsidizing the arts?

SURVEYING THE EVIDENCE

There is precious little evidence of direct public sector funding for early music in the initial years of its revival. Modest levels of funding were, however, channeled through Regional Arts Associations (RAAs),⁵⁵ in consultation with the third "corner" of public financing, i.e., the local authorities. Amongst the most important sources was The London Orchestral Concert Board Ltd (LOCB), which represented the Arts Council of Great Britain and the Greater London Council. The LOCB typically provided funding in the form of guarantees against loss. Michael Morrow's Musica Reservata, for example, was able to appear at the Queen Elizabeth Hall on May 22, 1978, because it was the recipient of £700 of such funding.⁵⁶ We get a vivid portrayal of the harsh financial climate for early music groups in the 1970s in the 1973 *Recorder & Music* article titled "Research into early music": "After Musica Reservata's very first concert this journal hoped that 'encouraged by such phenomenal success, Musica Reservata will find ways and means of becoming a regular concert giving group'. Since then it has established an international reputation but this depends more than ever on the quality and extent of its research. Musica Reservata has never had enough money left over from its concert activities to create a research fund and it has now launched an appeal for this very purpose."⁵⁷ Here we find the kernel of the dilemma facing early music professionals—namely that the very nature of their enterprise required more up-front knowledge work to be done than other nonspecialist classical music groups. To the extent that such "work" was invisible, at least when it came to the performance itself, persuading someone to pay for it was by no means a straightforward negotiating position.

The biggest recipient of public sector funding was the Early Music Network,⁵⁸ which was established by the Early Music Centre soon after its launch in 1976. Arts Council grants, though still modest, grew steadily, from £8,300 in 1978–79, £14,000 in 1979–80, to £16,000 in 1980–81.⁵⁹ In addition, the Regional Arts Associations offered grants of 20 to 30 percent of the artists' fees to promoters in their region booking a concert on the Network. However, it remained difficult for promoters to pay the sorts of fees that early music groups were demanding. Speaking at the Early Music conference in 1977, Richard Phillips, the music officer for the Yorkshire Arts Association, appealed to early music practitioners: "all I ask is this; please, don't press us to get such big fees that the result would be we can get no concerts for you. It's a matter of dialogue between us, it's a matter of faith."[60] Such faith was often in short supply. A letter to Michael Morrow from Jennifer Eastwood of the Early Music Centre about the Early Music Network in February 1979 explains it was difficult to get bookings "at lower fee," and suggested trying again the next year, offering a smaller program "such as those you suggested at a fee of £300–£500."[61] In passing, it is necessary to note the contribution of the British Council in liaising and funding concerts abroad. This is particularly important in the initial years of the historical performance revival, because much of the income for fledgling early music ensembles and orchestras came from concerts and tours made abroad.

By the mid-1980s a higher level of subsidy looked to be forthcoming. In his *Early Music* editorial in 1984, Nicholas Kenyon comments on the Arts Council's recognition of the growth of early music (described here as "pre-Romantic music in an authentic style"), noting that the Council "intends to enhance its support in this area."[62] A more decisive milestone was reached in 1991 when the Arts Council convened a Period Instrument Orchestra Enquiry, chaired by Kenyon. "The reason why the enquiry was set up was that there was a feeling that the Council, which subsidized modern-instrument symphony and chamber orchestras, ought to be doing something for what were different but by then very well-established organizations on the musical scene."[63] A number of recommendations emerged from this enquiry that centered on the apparent need to subsidize touring performances and the administration of then leading ensembles. A small group of ensembles was named as being particularly worthy recipients of funding (the Monteverdi Choir and Orchestra, The English Concert, the Taverner Choir, Consort and Players, and Raglan Baroque Players, with London Classical Players as a "fallback").

At this time, the Network operated on a similar kind of model to the Contemporary Music Network, where, according to Andrew Pinnock (Arts Council early music officer from 1992 to 1999), an artistic panel "chose the programmes they believed in, leaving a hamstrung fixer to try to persuade promoters to buy them."[64] Nicholas Kenyon suggests that "what really should have happened, which would have been the best thing, was if the Symphony Orchestras who were resident in a city e.g., the Hallé or CBSO, took them in and promoted them regularly as part of their own seasons; but that never quite happened."[65] In fact, as Pinnock explains, the Arts Council moved to a promoter subsidy model, where "those ensembles who were prepared to negotiate repertoire with promoters were the ones that got the money."[66] In the view of Andrew Pinnock, "the Arts Council woke up to the sector about 20 years after the public had, and took a well-intentioned interest in it too late. We'll never know what could have been achieved had Arts Council investment happened in the '70s and '80s." However, he also remains somewhat sanguine about whether or not it would have been a good idea to fund the named orchestras as the Kenyon Enquiry had suggested: "had we invested heavily in the London Classical Players we would have prevented or delayed the dissolution of an orchestra over which waters rapidly closed when it did shut down. LCP members still play in the Orchestra of the Age of Enlightenment, and Norrington still conducts them."

Norrington, for his part, is adamant about the potential impact of Arts Council funding: "It would have made a hell of a difference. We had subsidy for just one tour of three concerts in the 20 years that LCP existed."[67] His response is closely echoed by John Eliot Gardiner upon being asked whether it would have made a difference: "Of course it would have done!... We've never had any regular state funding, we've had to subsist through any small profit margins that there might have been gained from foreign tours in the past, and through commercial recordings, but that's all gone now. To cover our overheads the rest has had to come through corporate sponsorship or individual patronage... and to win that requires incredible tenacity, persistence and a bit of charm or luck."[68]

Public sector funding has not only been a central issue for the larger Authenticity₂ groups. Jeremy West, who recently celebrated the 30th anniversary of His Majestys Sagbutts and Cornetts, refers to the "depressing draining of funding from the arts in general, and early music in particular, that just makes everything harder all the time."[69] He notes: "to stay where you are you have to keep pedalling even harder, even though you're getting older. It doesn't get easier." West argues that just a modest grant of £5,000 would make an enormous difference if it could be used to pay for an extra hotel room, cheap flight, or rail ticket there, or an additional rehearsal or performer here. Despite some theoretical support for this more inclusive and contingent funding position, cultural policy makers have generally avoided such an approach, no doubt mindful that it might be interpreted as nonstrategic piecemeal support of arts organizations.[70]

REVIEWING THE RATIONALE

While the scope, scale, and value of arts funding continues to provoke heated discussion, the underlying premise that the arts should be funded at all remains broadly accepted. As the cultural economist Mark Blaug observed in 2001, "what is striking about this entire and somewhat hoary topic of debate is the virtually universal consensus among economists in favour of public subsidies to the arts."[71] So what, then, is the economist's case for funding the "high" arts (as epitomized by early music)? The short answer is to be found under the label of "market failure" arguments.[72] In their book on *The Economics of Art and Culture*, Heilbrun and Gray explain that "the principal causes of market failure are monopoly, externalities, public goods, declining cost industries, and lack of information."[73] Of these, it is in respect of an art form's ability to produce collective benefits (understood here in the language of "externalities" and "public goods") that holds most sway as far as the case of Early Music is concerned. Six alleged public benefits are put forward:[74] (i) legacy to future generations; (ii) national identity and prestige; (iii) benefits to the local economy; (iv) contributions to a liberal education; (v) social improvement of arts participants, and; (vi) encouraging artistic innovation.

With the benefit of hindsight, there is a pretty strong case that the majority (if not all) of these alleged benefits accrued from professional Early Music activities.

Early Music was both building upon and preserving a "legacy" for future generations; unquestionably the leading period performance orchestras and choirs have contributed to national identity and prestige; local economic benefits as well as "multiplier" and "spill-over" effects are evident in London, York, Brighton, Oxford, and elsewhere; the teaching of performance practice has blossomed in both universities and music colleges; the National Early Music Association (NEMA) and its regional early music fora, alongside many educational outreach programs, have encouraged and widened participation in the performance of early music; and many of the movement's innovations have effectively been appropriated in professional classical music performance more generally (as discussed further in Chapter 10). The challenge, however, is to think back to the late 1960s and early 1970s and ask what kind of evidence would have been needed at that time to validate the meeting of such criteria. There is clearly a very important distinction between evidence of these benefits having been (already) achieved, and evidence of the possibility of their being fulfilled at some point in the future. Here, then, is the rub. On the one hand, scarce public funds must be allocated on a transparent and accountable basis. On the other hand, given that the rationale of public sector support is to provide backing that is not otherwise available (most commonly at the beginning of an organization or art form's life), it is at best counterintuitive to wait until benefits are "proven" to exist. Those with the unenviable task of deciding to which "good cause" public funding should be directed no doubt find themselves between a rock and a hard place.

Of the criteria just discussed, it is the last (encouraging artistic innovation) that is the most central insofar as this is the most distinctive, albeit controversial, feature of the early music revival in its initial days. As Nicholas Kenyon notes, "everybody who was involved in early music felt it was very innovative . . . and in fact several contemporary composers, much to their annoyance, realized it was at the innovative end of the spectrum!"[75] One problem for early musicians is that at the time, their achievement of all the other criteria must have looked like just "more of the same." The Arts Council was already funding many classical music events, organizations, and initiatives, and these would have looked and felt broadly similar to those relating specifically to Early Music's interests. John Cruft, music director of the Arts Council in 1976, is reported to have considered that "it was not the function of the Council or the LOCB to commit themselves to supporting the livelihood of any groups of artists, and that they preferred to keep as many as possible just alive than to make life comfortable for the few."[76] It might have been hard to see why early music was particularly deserving as a special case. Its distinctive quality ought to have been that it was indeed offering something novel and different from the mainstream. After all, it *was* innovative in artistic terms. But, of course, early music was ostensibly concerned with the performance of "old," not new music. In those days, early music was *more* classical music than "classical music" itself (as I discuss in more detail in the next chapter). Unlike contemporary music, which was easy to identify as "new" (and therefore purportedly innovative), early music was tarred with an all-very-familiar brush, and its innovative qualities overlooked.

Interestingly, the Arts Council and the LOCB accepted "that different principles must apply in subsidizing new music groups."[77] The problem seems to have been in determining when a group performing "old" music was in fact "new." In short, early music was new but it couldn't say that it was. If it did, it would appear to be undermining its own claims to authenticity.

In summary, reasons for not funding early music included the difficulty of determining what amounted to a promise of collective future benefits rather than a clear track record of achievement; the problem of assessing opportunity costs; and the singular challenge of recognizing innovation.[78] Compounding these issues was the fact that the Arts Council tended to support "organizations as organizations," whereas the early music orchestras were "essentially freelance...in which performers got paid for the work they did."[79] Whilst it is the nature of art to be risk-taking and to challenge the status quo, it is the nature of arts funding to be conservative in nature, and to lean toward the support of established arts organizations. It is really quite striking, for example, that it has taken 39 years for The English Concert and the Academy of Ancient Music to become regularly funded organizations—and this under the publicity of fourteen "outstanding *new* organisations" in the Arts Council's "National Portfolio of organisations" (NPOs), which replaced regularly funded organizations in April 2012.[80] The Orchestra of the Age of Enlightenment is also an NPO, as is the National Centre for Early Music (launched in 2000 following a National Lottery grant of £1.5 million). Funding between 2012 and 2013 amounted to TEC (£78k); AAM (£170k); OAE (£227k); NCEM (£270k).[81]

A further issue relates to the compartmentalization of funding sources for the arts and, by implication, the boundaries of what Arts Council money can and cannot be spent on. In his talk on education at the 1977 Early Music Conference, Anthony Rooley warned that "early music cannot be compartmentalized as are the various funding bodies set up at present. This must change because the present system is going to cripple the development of early music."[82] For Rooley the central question was determining when something was "creative" as opposed to "educational." This issue had been raised a couple of years earlier by Nicholas Kenyon in his article on "The economics of early music" in *Early Music* (1976). Firstly, the Arts Council could not fund purely or even "quasi-educational"[83] initiatives (despite a Charter laid out to support "knowledge" and "understanding"). Learning to play instruments in the "right" style remained outside the council's remit for support. Secondly, whereas the rationale for funding contemporary music was in part the fact that the concerts couldn't be sustained on the basis of box office income, Early Music found itself "penalized for having such large box-office receipts!" In addition, the very nature of early music performance (and recording) necessitated a different format to the otherwise dominant two rehearsals and concert scenario. Early musicians, as we have seen, needed the development time to experiment and to learn "new tricks on old instruments." One has the feeling that in the absence of sufficient funding (the reality faced by most early musicians) there was always pressure to cut corners. It was inevitable that from time to time this impacted both on the concert stage and in the recording studio.

SPINNING OUT EARLY MUSIC

Money had to be found from somewhere else and it was. Record companies and individual investors/sponsors became absolutely central to making early music pay. This part of the story unfolds in the course of the next two chapters. For now, however, it is tempting to ask whether the early music movement, contrary to conventional wisdom, was actually an example of a market for high culture working rather well—since the record companies came in and did the job that otherwise we might have expected the state to perform (the sort of argument that free marketeers might want to leap on with more than a degree of enthusiasm). Or, was there in fact market failure, in the sense that public benefits could or should have been supported, according to the criteria above?

Certainly, the evidence suggests that over time the market adjusted and, to some extent compensated for its own "failures." A more radical explanation would point out that the market's attraction to "authentic performance" in the first place was itself influenced by the very externalities and public good benefits, which theory tells us lie beyond the maket's scope or interest. Whilst on the one hand an interest in "authenticity" conjures up precisely the sort of societal level "public benefits" discussed in terms of cultural heritage, legacy, and artistic innovation, on the other hand it also helps to make Early Music products (bought and sold in the market) as distinctive and valuable as they are. It could then be argued that it was in the best interests of the market to play up the nature of just such externalities. This, in turn, would explain why record companies were not overly critical when it came to adopting "authenticity" and "heritage" as alluring labels with which to sell their wares. After all, the early music audience appeared more than happy to be taken along for the ride.

Given the commercial trajectory of Early Music, it is worth asking what lessons we can draw from this case of "spinning out" knowledge from a university context. Many of the groups featured in this book started life as student projects, drawing on ideas from research and teaching (the "vital R&D function" of the period instrument movement, as Nicholas Kenyon refers to it[84]) and have gone on to be successful in commercial as well as artistic terms. While not exaggerating this point unduly, the early music revival took place within a cultural environment where there was a general absence of funding for early music at a professional level, and an absence of taught historical performance practice.[85] These absences are important, for as I have argued in terms of a dialectical knowledge (see Table 7.1), absence can be causally generative, i.e., motivating and enabling those involved to seek "other" forms of finance and to learn for themselves. When it comes to asking what lessons we can learn from all this, it would seem a somewhat counterintuitive proposition to claim that the absence of funding and teaching was a good thing, pure and simple. All the same, there are implications for how we might think of the wider process of "spinning out" knowledge from a university context.[86] It may appear incongruous to refer to Early Music in terms of the commercialization of knowledge. This is certainly not the image presented by journals and books relating to early music performance. Nor was it the explicit intention or emphasis of those involved. But at one level this is exactly what has taken place. During much of the 20th century there was a clear demarcation between the activities of performers and scholars. As Pearson suggests, "Persons able to function to a high level across both practice and theory were only able to survive...by doing one at a time."[87] However, the success of Early Music highlights the sense in which historical performers have been able to travel along the theory/practice continuum "with an ease and fluency impossible for previous generations."[88] The role of "performer-scholars" (as opposed to "scholar-performers") has been especially influential in this respect. Whereas scholars remain relatively free to keep all their options up in the air, the performer does not have the freedom to equivocate. In the end, "they must say 'this is the way to perform it,' and perform it thus with total conviction."[89] It is ideas actually taken up in the practice of performance, after all, that become tomorrow's norms. The absence of funding and formal learning gave rise to an "other" space of "not knowing," which offered those involved a degree of freedom from the conventions and norms of the classical music profession. Early Music developed as a cultural movement out of a "play" space; a motivated and motivating space, found only at the edges of university, music college, and the music profession. Here, then, was the real engine room of cultural production, home to musicians and cultural entrepreneurs alike.

He who prides himself on giving what he thinks the public wants is often creating a fictitious demand for lower standards which he himself will then satisfy.

LORD REITH[1]

Hildegard pays for my mistakes.

TED PERRY[2]

8

Jumping on the Old Band Wagon?

INTRODUCTION

Was it simply a question of the record companies being in the right place at the right time? Should we see them as somehow poised on the sidelines, waiting to pounce when Early Music had proved itself viable? This is certainly how the relationship between record companies and Early Music is often portrayed. Leaving aside the music industry's apparent lack of speed in responding to both the opportunities and the threats of digitization in the 1990s, it had previously wasted little time in taking up the latest recording technology. Unquestionably, this proved hugely beneficial to Early Music's cause. First there was the LP (introduced in 1948), offering unprecedented access at an affordable price to a rapidly expanding catalogue of early music and period instrument performance from home and abroad. Later, during the early 1980s, record companies could hardly move fast enough to re-record the complete classical music canon on Compact Disc. As "early adopters," record companies have, of course, been central to Early Music's success. But unraveling cause and effect is trickier than it might first appear. In singling out the record companies, we must be careful not to overlook the BBC's decisive role in propagating an interest in early music (as part of its public service broadcasting agenda). In this chapter I cast a critical eye over the commercialization of early music, considering the integral relationship between public and private sectors, and highlighting distinctive ways in which their respective institutions and organizations provided a much-needed lifeline to the new cultural movement. Above all else, the analysis highlights the challenges of making Early Music *pay*, given conflicting beliefs concerning the "value" of music.

Making music in the modern age, enabled as it is by industrialized capitalist production, requires professional performers (of any genre) to negotiate embedded and competing discourses of value. Simon Frith discusses these in terms of three "world views" in music—art, folk, and commercial. The bourgeois discourse of *art* (in Bourdieu's language the "dominant culture") is most closely associated with Early Music's home field of classical music. The value of this discourse is in its "provision of a transcendent experience that is, on the one hand, ineffable and uplifting but, on the other, only available to those with the right sort of knowledge."[3] Charges of elitism and musical snobbery are never far away. Art music is constructed according to a set of largely 19th-century performance conventions and rituals, which can place rigorous demands on those involved, such as listening silently and only applauding at the end of a musical work. On one level, HIP's focus on historical performance practice demanded a thorough re-examination of the relationship between musical performance and "art"-based knowledge (as discussed in the previous chapter). The second discourse is associated with *folk* music ("popular culture"). Here the emphasis is on authenticity, understood as the preservation of tradition and its associated ideals. By all accounts, this looks like it ought to be the primary discourse of the early music movement. However, whereas folk music is typically presented as being allied to an "anti-modernist" ideology, therefore finding its natural home in studies of non-Western and non-capitalist cultures, Early Music is a cultural force that has been deeply embedded in both an advanced Western and a capitalist context (one of the reasons that makes it such a fascinating subject to study). And so we come to the third of the value discourses—the *commercial* music world ("majority culture"). This discourse is concerned with values created and organized around the music industry, i.e., the possibilities of turning sounds into commodities.[4] While Frith's own work is very much focused on popular music, he is careful to argue that musical genres should not be understood according to just one of these distinctive world views, but rather in terms of their characteristic response to how all three are negotiated by its players. It is just such a viewpoint that motivates the analytical approach taken here.

PUTTING VALUE DISCOURSES INTO PRACTICE

Figure 8.1 presents a visual take on how the three art-worlds just discussed coexist in the context of Early Music. Of course, the institutions and organizations featured are by no means homogenous in nature. In accepting that the BBC is indeed a large, even "monolithic" structure, for example, we also need to bear in mind its being comprised of many parts (covering interests relating to all three art-worlds), as the influence of key individuals operating within it pull in different directions. Similarly, the record companies involved in classical music recording range from the independent micro-firm operated by sole traders, to the "majors" with their classical music divisions, international reach, and power-based distribution deals. The early music movement, as we have seen, is comprised of a diverse range of individuals and organizations, bringing distinctively different ideas, skills, and interests. The artistic ecology represented in Figure 8.1 needs to be understood primarily in terms of the fluidity and flux that takes place *between* different stakeholders, both at the level of

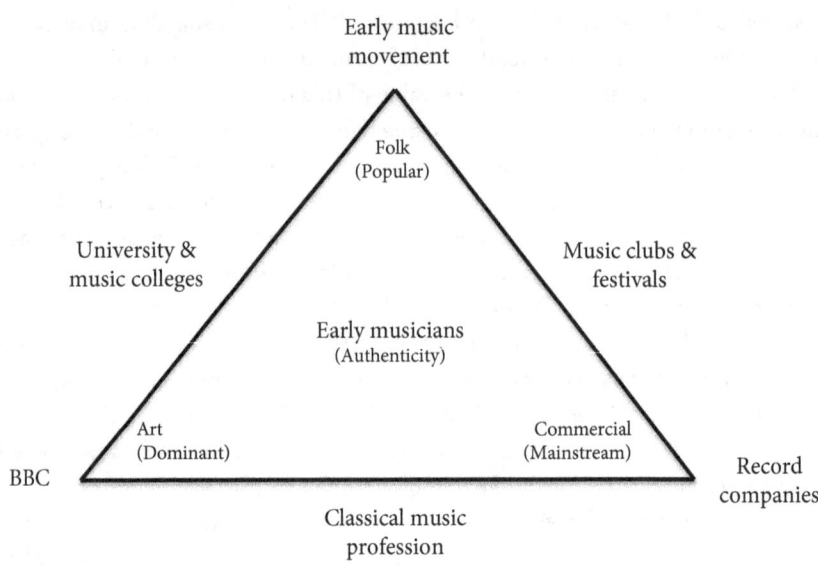

FIGURE 8.1 The Ecology of Early Music

organizations and individuals. Those involved are constantly shifting their position with regard to each other (knowingly and unknowingly). For example, producers in the BBC's music department in the 1950s through the 1970s (e.g., Arnold, Beckett, Bennett, Lam, Stevens, Wearing) were also actively involved in editing and performing early music themselves.

The analysis begins within the "art" world context of the British Broadcasting Company (BBC), its music department, and The Third Programme (later Radio 3).

"ART" AND THE BBC

Lord John Reith, the first general manager and director general of the BBC, has become synonymous with a set of values targeted toward the betterment and refinement (more controversially "civilization") of the British public. The BBC's espoused aims were "to educate, inform and entertain." Though now largely scorned for their high-brow stance, Reithian values continue to underpin much that is championed in the BBC's Charter.[5] As Georgina Born notes in her contemporary study of the Corporation, "Despite its paternalist origins, Reith's definition of public service broadcasting repays scrutiny and still has power."[6] In the years after World War II, the discourse of "art" found no more receptive a home than in the performance of classical music. Classical (art) music, after all, was considered to be "good for you" both intellectually and spiritually, if, that is, you were prepared to invest the serious effort required to engage with it (for which the BBC were happy to provide music appreciation classes). The home of classical music at the BBC was the Third Programme, launched on September 29, 1946 (becoming Radio 3 in 1967). Functioning at first only in the evenings, often with repeated programs, the Third "could be seen as a sort of intellectual ladder [with the lower rungs being the Light and Home programs, respectively] which listeners should be encouraged to climb."[7] We get a strong sense of the BBC's appetite for early music repertoire in the early 1950s from this extract from a letter written by the then controller of the Third Programme (1948-52), Harman Grisewood, praising a recent broadcast of a Vivaldi oratorio: "This sort of music...is ideal for us since it is delightful to listen to at first hearing and hard to come by from any other source...We are doing a real work for music, I am sure, in giving currency to music of this date."[8]

By the mid-1950s, however, there were rumblings of discontent concerning the BBC Music Department's rather conservative attitude toward less familiar repertoire, including early music.[9] Edward Sackville-West's leading article in the *Listener* in the week of the Third Programme's 10th anniversary (1956) comments: "it is hard to resist the conclusion that, where music is concerned, the planners succumb with too great alacrity to the lure of *musica antiqua*. I would not for a moment suggest that it was a mistake to explore the pre-classical periods, but for every one such programme that has held a high content of beautiful and interesting stuff, there have been at least two that resembled a monastic diet of pumpkin soup and lentils."[10] A general view was also emerging that the BBC's musical showcase, the annual Proms Festival (founded in 1895 but taken over by the BBC in 1927), needed to become more broadminded. In the appointment of William Glock as the Corporation's new controller of music in 1960 (a post he would hold until 1973), Early Music found something of an unlikely advocate. Glock, who otherwise sustained Reithian values, was seen as a champion of modernist (especially European avant-garde) music. He was also a lifelong supporter of musical education, and was director of the Dartington Summer School (affectionately known as the "annexe" by those in the BBC, on account of its close connections with the Corporation) for 30 years. His arrival at the BBC Proms brought "a radical shake-up" of the institution's otherwise "cosy culture" and "undemanding audience expectations."[11] He modernized the Proms by bringing in what he termed "novelties," i.e., pieces given their debut at the festival.[12] Glock explained to The Pilkington Committee, convened by the government in 1960 to consider the future of broadcasting, that he sought to give audiences "what they will like tomorrow."[13] He also wrote in his music policy about "creative unbalance" being essential, which no doubt accounted for "unexpected, sometimes astonishing juxtapositions," including performances of less well-known early music.[14]

The opportunity to hear more early music at the Proms (and elsewhere on the radio, of course) was vital in broadening its audience base and developing a potential record-buying public. Glock's support of the work of David Munrow, Roger Norrington, John Eliot Gardiner (who performed Monteverdi's *Vespers* in 1968, becoming the youngest conductor thus far to have appeared at the Proms), amongst many others, is indicative of the newly enabling conditions that allowed young performers and instrument-makers to specialize in the area. As David Wright puts it, "the Proms played a part in contributing to the process that has made historical performance very much part of the warp and weft of today's musical environment."[15] In an interesting development, the director of the Proms between 1996 and 2007 was to be early music critic and former editor of *Early Music,* Nicholas Kenyon. By Kenyon's time, of course, early music had become firmly established in the mainstream repertoire. Glock had remained influential throughout the 1980s, and in fact it was he who originally proposed to Kenyon the idea of a book on "the whole nature of authenticity," which became *Authenticity and Early Music* (1988). He was even consulted on the season of late Haydn *Masses* planned by the South Bank in 1989, and it was Glock who suggested employing the OAE for this project.

William Glock was by no means the only individual to play a part in the BBC's incubation of early music, however. Though he deserves recognition on account of his overall control of radio and Proms output, it is the producers working within the Music Department who warrant our particular attention. From its inception, the tie-up between university (especially Oxford) and the BBC Music Department colored the Corporation's coverage and support of classical music. Here was a group of highly-educated and skilled musicologists and musicians who were open to the kind of Mode 2 knowledge production process discussed in the previous chapter—where academic scholarship was positively encouraged to mix with application through performance. Denis Stevens was one such figure, giving Early Music an early "tactical advantage"[16] upon his appointment to the BBC in 1949. Stevens's work on early Italian Baroque music, and especially that of Claudio Monteverdi with his group Accademia Monteverdiana (which included Nadia Boulanger amongst its first trustees), was particularly influential. Known for his "wry and penetrating sense of humor," Stevens saw it as his mission to demonstrate both the validity and the accessibility of musicology as a discipline. But he also had "absolutely no time for a misguided veneration of the past."[17] Other producers who also managed to straddle the scholarship-performance divide have included the likes of Basil Lam (Stevens's predecessor in charge of "pre-classical" programs, who had "gone off to make harpsichords" in 1949 but returned in 1960, becoming editor of Pre-Classical Music);[18] Hugh Keyte (noted for his editing of choral works, including an anthology of carols with Andrew Parrott); Denis Arnold (editor of the *New Oxford Companion to Music*); John Beckett (composer, musician, and conductor of Musica Reservata); Clive Wearing (director of the Lassus Ensemble); and Clive Bennett, who later worked for Philips Records.

The majority of producers in the BBC's Music Department, however, were first and foremost university-trained musicologists—"scholar-performers" as opposed to "performer-scholars." They acted as gate-keepers for the industry as a whole. Their role in recognizing creativity becomes quite evident when we look at how up-and-coming musicians in the 1960s and early 1970s went about making a broadcast. First off, they had to apply for an audition, which rather like a job interview required submitting a decent set of references on a pro-forma. Michael Morrow, for example, supplied the names of references alongside his invitation to the BBC's Music Department to attend Musica Reservata's debut concert at London's Fenton House in 1960. On the official BBC form he was instructed to name "at least TWO well-known people in the musical world" who were acquainted with his work and "to whom reference can be made."[19]

That two of the three names given by Morrow were well-known Oxford University academics (F. L. Harrison and Roger Fiske), might come as no surprise. The majority of the men (and they were mostly men) working in the BBC's Music Department were themselves Oxford graduates or had links to the university's music department. However, the fact that references were required *at all* serves to highlight a distinctive (and undesirable) feature of the field. All too often, the classical music business seems to necessitate the "provenance" of its musicians to be demonstrated through biographies (or references) that identify where and with whom they studied. The danger of this is that talent (like creativity) becomes a quality that only gets recognized by a select group allegedly possessing sufficient qualifications to "allow" them (and only them) to pass judgment.[20] The onus shifts from the talented and creative musician to the institutional framework that legitimizes their activities.

Without a doubt, the BBC's Third Programme represented a hugely influential pillar in the building of Early Music in Britain. It provided a foundation for the likes of Thurston Dart, Arnold Goldsbrough, Alfred Deller, and Walter Bergmann in the late 1940s and '50s. Thurston Dart, in particular, was (in the words of Neville Marriner) "just what they needed."[21] But it was far from one-way traffic: the BBC was just what Early Music needed to help it reach a wider audience. Here we can draw attention to the decidedly empowering structure of the BBC for producers (up to the mid-1970s, at least), and notably the freedom afforded them to follow through their own creative decisions regarding programming. Whilst Glock's hierarchical control stamped his authority on the types of music being heard (including much early music repertoire), it was also flexible enough to give autonomy to individual producers in the Music Department. This combination of top-down and bottom-up control proved a powerful pairing. As Clifford Bartlett comments (referring to the 1960s), "the great advantage of the BBC then is that it wasn't management dominated. You appointed someone to a job and then let them get on with it."[22] In addition, as Denis Stevens explains, there was often a flexible budget: "Nobody asked any questions. Producers were responsible; if I went wild and spent a lot one week, people would say 'Be careful—only do chamber music for the next two weeks.'"[23] This was just the sort of editorial freedom needed to give early music exposure. Of course, early music was "new" and so it needed advocates to plead its cause. Furthermore, the project of performing early music in a period style necessitated a deeper engagement with the "facts" (so far as they were available) concerning the circumstances surrounding the music's composition and first performance(s). In turn, this encouraged some ambitious ideas for the kinds of early music projects to be broadcast and how they should be packaged. None came larger than the epic 70-episode *History in Sound of European Music*, commissioned in 1948. More than 20 years later it was a similar commitment to historical musical context that informed David Munrow's memorable sound-tracks for the successful TV programs *The Six Wives of Henry VIII* (1970) and *Elizabeth R* (1971), which certainly helped to establish his reputation.[24] Record companies, too, were attracted by something of an academic approach to large-scale programming (such as HMV's *History of Music in Sound* (1953-59), which was released as a companion to Gerald Abraham's *New*

Oxford History of Music).²⁵ Records were increasingly accompanied by lengthy explanatory booklets (see the AAM's (1979-81) recordings of the complete Mozart symphonies with detailed liner notes by Neil Zaslaw).

Throughout the 1970s and well into the early 1980s, Early Music enjoyed the enlightened support of a team of dedicated music producers at the BBC, including amongst others Basil Lam, Nicholas Anderson, and Hugh Keyte. It is important to add here that the presenting skills of performer-scholars of the likes of David Munrow (*Pied Piper*) and Christopher Hogwood (*The Young Idea*) were also crucial in bringing early music to a much wider (and younger) audience. As Humphrey Carpenter observes, "It soon became clear that [in David Munrow] Radio 3 had acquired one of the most brilliant and appealing broadcasters in the BBC's history."²⁶ Nicholas Kenyon suggests, "there was an enormous freedom at that point for commissioning and recording special projects in the studio ... It wasn't just a matter of relaying live concerts."²⁷

All the same, early music continued to be treated as a specialist field, to some extent ghettoized within the BBC under the label of preclassical repertoire. By 1981, feeling that early music was underrepresented, a group of producers (including Anthony Burton and Chris Sayers, backed up by public opinion and the support of some articles written by Elizabeth Roche), went to head of music Ernest Warburton to put this to him. Speaking in 2003, Chris Sayers recalls, "Eventually he gave us a slot ... and the slot was Saturday lunch-time at 1pm—we called it *The Early Music Forum* ... and the precise thing, in a sense, has just happened all over again!"²⁸ Sayers was referring to Radio 3's programming of *The Early Music Show* to include both Saturday and Sunday lunchtime slots. This was the successor to the weekly program *Music Restored* (1998-2003), which in turn followed the very successful *Spirit of the Age*, hosted by Christopher Page from 1992 to 1997. Understandably, perhaps, given his background as editor of *Early Music* journal prior to joining the BBC (and later also being one of the presenters of *The Early Music Show*), Nicholas Kenyon remembers how he "bent over backwards *not* to over-emphasize early music"²⁹ while controller of Radio 3 (between 1992 and 1998).

A feature of the BBC's output going all the way back to its launch in the early 1920s was broadcast transmissions featuring its own ensembles (initially a dance band, military band, and light orchestra). The BBC Symphony Orchestra (the first permanent salaried orchestra in London) was set up in 1930 in a response to international peer pressure. Having looked on enviously at the Berlin Philharmonic under Wilhelm Furtwängler, the Concertgebouw Orchestra under Willem Mengelberg, and the Philharmonic-Symphony Orchestra of New York under Arturo Toscanini, the time came to establish a home-grown orchestra that could emulate such artistic prowess. By the mid-1970s the BBC Symphony Orchestra, the BBC Philharmonic, National Orchestras of Wales and Scotland, and the BBC Concert Orchestra (formerly the "plain man's symphony orchestra") had all become firmly established at the heart of British cultural life. Perhaps it wasn't so unexpected, therefore, to begin to hear talk of a dedicated BBC early music orchestra.

In 1976 Nicholas Kenyon prophesied "Soon the problem of a permanent, subsidized baroque orchestra will arise,"³⁰ adding, with a note of caution, that "the climate must be created in which its existence will be an attractive proposition to bodies whose present idea of an 18th-century orchestra is a group playing Haydn and Mozart badly to a sold-out Festival Hall." In the same year, the editor of *Early Music*, J. M. Thomson, made explicit reference to a BBC orchestra, suggesting that this would be "no more improbable than a BBC Training Orchestra."[31] Further momentum appears to have been given to the idea at *The Future of Early Music* Conference in 1977. What is interesting about these articles and discussions is that they give the impression that any resistance to the idea would be most likely to come from the BBC's side of the table, rather than from early musicians themselves. In reality it seems that the opposite was the case. Christopher Hogwood, who was instrumental in the idea being mooted by the BBC, takes up the story. "One opportunity that came up and was turned down by the players interestingly, was the BBC, years ago... I got them to sit down and discuss having a house period orchestra, that would give us proper rehearsals and stability (players from more than AAM). But they [the players] voted overwhelmingly against it. They didn't want to have to commit themselves for so many weeks. They wanted to do a week's recording with the Academy, and then go home to their families or their teaching, or their string quartet. Nobody wanted to be in the pay of an institution. Nobody wanted to sink their existing groups, like The English Concert, or AAM, for something called The BBC Baroque Orchestra... They turned it down."[32] Perhaps unsurprisingly, Hogwood adds, "the BBC have never quite forgiven us for getting them to that pitch and then saying they didn't want it." This is perhaps most interesting in terms of what it reveals about the motivations of early musicians at the time, as well as their strong allegiances to the class of '73.[33] But it also cautions against trotting out the standard line about freelance workers lacking power in their relations with employers.[34] Bringing things more up-to-date, Kenyon recalls that "the nearest we came to a successor to that Baroque orchestra conversation was to establish [from 1995] a residency for the OAE at St. George's Brandon Hill, in Bristol, and having them broadcast regularly from there." In fact "it didn't go as far as creating a resident orchestra, but it was a firm commitment—put it that way."[35]

"FOLK" AND EARLY MUSIC PROMOTERS

In Chapter 4 the "folk" vantage point was introduced under the label of "Sense and Sensibility." My purpose was to put the *sound* of early music, and musicians' felt response to it, first. The folk discourse referred to in this chapter encourages consideration of some further characteristics present in the genre of folk music. The British folk revival first got under way in the early years of the 20th century, and was characterized by a heightened interest in traditional music and its preservation in and through performance. The overlap with the pioneering work of Arnold Dolmetsch, motivated as he was by the restoration of music traditions, is striking (although perhaps the strongest link with folk is to be found in the guise of period dance, which Arnold's wife, Mabel, pioneered).[36] The "second folk revival," or "contemporary folk music," coincided with the modern-day revival of early music, amidst the broader social, cultural, and political stirrings of the mid- to late 1960s, or the so-called "long 1968." The actual coming together of folk and early musicians in live performance was (and remains) relatively rare. A notable exception is the early music band City Waites, who "managed to get into the world of the Maddy Priors and The Albion Band early on in the 1970s."[37] Lucie Skeaping (founder-singer and instrumentalist with the band, and now presenter of *The Early Music Show* for BBC Radio 3) recalls: "we performed easily 50 percent of the time in folk clubs...and there was a good living to be made out of the whole burgeoning of medieval banquets." The Scottish Early Music Consort (which performed from 1973 to 1998) also gained a particular reputation for being able to cross boundaries between early and folk music (including medieval and Gaelic traditional music and dance). Beyond performing live, early and folk musicians were able to market themselves more extensively through the recorded medium. The wider availability of recordings in the 1960s and '70s proved influential in shaping performers' and listeners' tastes and expectations, whilst also enabling musical styles to move across traditional boundaries. As Elizabeth Upton (2012) argues, "Classical music and 'low art' pop music were not so absolute or impermeable as they were perceived to be at the time."[38]

Further common ground between Early Music and folk can be found in their shared ideological and practical concern with authenticity. Frith suggests that the folk world seeks to solve the problem of musical authenticity through offering an experience of the "folk ideal, the experience of collective, participatory music making, the chance to judge music by its direct contribution to sociability."[39] According to this view, authenticity is not so much concerned with origins as the process of musical transmission itself. Folk clubs attempt to minimize the distance between performer and audience, so as to provide a "different form of socializing in which active performance and participation [are] integrated."[40] We can see how this socializing agenda has pervaded Early Music in respect of its "audience" of amateur players who were keen for the widening gap between professional performers and themselves to be narrowed.

Performing early music, like folk music, is very much a collective pursuit (the majority of the discussion in this book concerns chamber music, ensembles, orchestras, and choirs rather than solo performance and soloists). There is much more of a commitment to the participatory nature of performance than the "star," "diva," or "maestro" culture of 19th-century classical music-making. Furthermore, early musicians, like folk artists, generally go about their business "with no special flourish which says 'we are performers.'"[41] The Dutch conductor, recorder player, and baroque flautist Frans Brüggen, for example, cofounded the Orchestra of the 18th Century in 1981, not just as a vehicle for period performance, but also as a protest for equal fees. It was set up as a collective, with all orchestra members receiving equal shares of concert earnings. Though Early Music has indeed portrayed a strong sense of revolutionary and collective protest, a yearning to offer an alternative, which mitigated against the "cult of the artist" (seen as getting in the way of the direct, unmediated relationship between music and audience), we should also recognize that this was never a movement running in full opposition to the classical music establishment. Most early musicians had begun their musical training by taking lessons from classically trained teachers, playing with county-level youth orchestras (in many cases also the National Youth Orchestra), and enrolling on mainstream performance courses at the music colleges. Quite a number (David Munrow (Birmingham) and Trevor Pinnock (Canterbury) among them) sang as choristers in local cathedrals or Oxbridge chapels, giving them a rigorous musical training early on in life. At one level, therefore, early musicians were dependent on the very educational and training institutions that they sought to transform.

The folk discourse is often understood as a critical reaction against the everyday reality of doing commerce.[42] Performance spaces for folk music frequently reflect this liminal feel, whether this is in a room off to the side of a sleepy country pub, or amidst tented fields over a "long weekend" (the folk festival is gently subversive in defying the normal rhythm of the working week). In Early Music's case there is perhaps rather more of a blurring of the economic interests and motivations of those involved. It was only through the passion, drive, and philanthropic cash injection of those running them that many local music clubs, operating largely on subscription income, were able to keep going at all. All the same, music clubs and the university performance circuit represented a vital first port of call for early musicians in the 1960s and '70s. David Munrow and Christopher Hogwood, for example, cut their musical teeth at local music clubs, such as the Hinckley Music Club in Leicestershire—which incidentally held its earliest meetings in an upstairs room at a pub (Munrow later became the club's first president).

Whilst the logistics of running and promoting a music club can be relatively low-key, the organization of an early music festival usually requires a much greater level of planning and resourcing. Typically, a festival's financial model is built around its "big earners" who cross-subsidize other, less well-known acts. The hardest part of funding any festival is to cover core operating expenditure, including fixed costs that nobody sees upfront, such as festival administration, PR, and marketing. Sponsors like to bask in the reflected glory of big box-office names, so by turning its back on the "star" system, Early Music was also making life difficult for itself.[43] In teaming up with an airline as its principal sponsor, the Lufthansa Festival of Baroque Music was able to leverage more from the deal than most, flying over many internationally acclaimed ensembles and artists to Britain, often for the first time.

Over the last 40 years, a handful of UK early music festivals have established themselves as landmark events in the classical music calendar. In addition to the Lufthansa Festival, the York Early Music Festival, the London Handel Festival, the Greenwich Early Music Festival (encompassing the Early Music Exhibition), and festivals in Birmingham, Leicester, Nottingham, and Brighton have gained the most prominence in Britain (the Oxford Early Music Festival held its inaugural concerts in May 2013, indicating a continuing attraction for such events). In the early days of the revival, however, opportunities to perform at such tailor-made umbrella-series remained relatively few and far between. In fact, it quickly became apparent that the only way to make a living in early music was to take up (or create) opportunities abroad. John Bickley, formerly director of the music agency Magenta Music, recalls "it was all export led—70 percent of our work was outside the UK very early on—within two or three years of starting [in 1977]. There would be almost no other sector in the country where that was the case at that stage... but how could you ever make a living traipsing around the early music clubs in the UK, relying on the fairly fuddy-duddy music festivals in this country... when there were interested people in other countries? The only way to develop yourself fast enough was to talk to them."[44] Bickley and others were highly proactive in setting up early music festivals abroad. He notes, in this respect, that "we didn't start Utrecht [the world's largest early music festival, established in 1981], but we got called in because we could supply artists." These observations point to the fact that from a purely economic point of view, size matters. In other words, the ability to reach an audience of sufficient scale to "make early music pay" at a commercial level, was essential. The role of the recording medium was absolutely vital in this respect.

"COMMERCIAL" AND THE RECORD COMPANIES

We turn now to consider the third of the three discourses of value (the *commercial*) and in particular the "double-edged sword" that is the record company. To extend the swashbuckling metaphor a little further, record companies have been considered variously as knights in shining armor, charging in on white stallions to save the maiden music from an otherwise ignominious end; or they are cast as ruthless villains, out only to exploit innocent (naïve) early musicians in the pursuit of bounteous profit. The truth, as so often, lies somewhere between these extremes. Record companies by necessity aim to make a return on their investment, but, nonetheless, invest they do. As Colin Kitching (librarian and violist with OAE) notes, a deal with a record company acted like "a forcing house."[45] Early musicians were "overtaken in a flood of activity generated by this strange phenomenon which is the recording industry." A key advantage for the British scene was the fact that so many of the leading recording companies worked in London (the majority of professional early music groups have been based in London and the South East).

It goes without saying that record companies' motivations are not solely musical. However, making music pay is just as much a requirement for the professional performer. Pursuing a career in music entails being paid for doing musical "work" as a job. As Laurence Cummings, conductor and professor of Historical Performance at the Royal Academy of Music, observes, "as soon as you've agreed to do the job, in a sense, you've perhaps compromised something."[46] The crude distinction between "intrinsic" and "extrinsic" motivation,[47] so often written about to distinguish the cultural worker from other "normal" workers, should be replaced with something more realistic (and more human). The history of Early Music's association with record companies bears this out. For what is most striking about Early Music's commercial relationships is that they are so often forged between like-minded and similarly impassioned individuals, not between faceless organizations. There are many examples, which serve to reinforce the point: the impact David Munrow made on Christopher Bishop, which led to

EMI's contracting of the Early Music Consort of London; Decca's Peter Wadland and Christopher Hogwood of the Academy of Ancient Music, who together formed one of the most successful recording partnerships of the post-war years; Michel Garcin of the French record label Erato, who despite considering the move toward period instruments something of an "aberration," nonetheless backed John Eliot Gardiner in various seminal recordings of Purcell, Handel, and Rameau; John Shuttleworth, cofounder of Meridian Records, whose ear for great music made him "that sure, that keen"[48] that in 1982 he signed up His Majestys Sagbutts and Cornetts for a record deal during the interval of their first-ever concert, at London's St. Martin in the Fields; or Peter Phillips and student recording engineer, Steve Smith, who in 1980 cofounded Gimell, the first of the single-artist labels in classical music, devoted to the output of The Tallis Scholars.

Amongst the most influential British independent record companies in the field of Early Music is Hyperion. Its founder Ted Perry is said to have "made repertoire decisions rapidly, by apparent instinct, sometimes even on impulse, but always because he truly loved recordings."[49] It was just such an impulsive response to hearing a BBC broadcast of music by Hildegard of Bingen in 1980 that led to his making *A feather on the breath of God*, one of the best-selling and most influential recordings of pre-classical music ever made. Simon Perry, Ted's son and successor as director of the company, remarks, "Ted never operated on the principle that money should be a main objective—he purely made a record because it needed to be made, that the music should be heard." He goes on: "It was a winning formula back in the 1980s and '90s but the record industry has changed hugely over the last ten years and one can no longer ignore the tough commercial realities of the business."[50] The background to the Hildegard broadcast is further revealing of the richness of close personal connections. For the program had been commissioned by the BBC following a conversation between Andrew Parrott and Hugh Keyte. At Parrott's suggestion, the group assembled (in which he sang tenor) was under the musical direction and musicological guidance of Christopher Page. This specialist vocal group subsequently became Gothic Voices, albeit with a lineup that no longer included Parrott on the tenor line.

Elsewhere, it was Peter Wadland's "remarkable natural musicianship," his "love and knowledge of records," as well as his involvement "in every aspect of the recordings he made"[51] that contributed so enormously to the commercial and cultural success of Decca's L'Oiseau-Lyre label, where he was chief producer. To this it must be added that it was the ability of Decca to operate their early music label more or less as an independent—with an extraordinary freedom on repertoire and artist choice, coupled with a basic trust in Wadland's decision-making—that made his contribution so powerful. As Chris Sayers, who took over from Wadland at Decca after his death in 1992, remembers, "we were allowed to dream something up, cost it out and have a go, put it forward...and often as not, to our surprise, it got accepted."[52] A producer at the BBC for much of his career before joining Decca Records, Sayers was himself steeped in early music, and had previously studied harpsichord with Ruth Dyson at the Royal College of Music. He recalls his excitement on hearing Harnoncourt at the

Stour Music Festival in Kent organized by Alfred Deller: "I heard Concentus Musicus[53] in about 1965. Looking back the standard was probably not very high, but you were so convinced. There was enough about it to really transport you; and this is an emotional response, nothing to do with arguing the case, nothing to do with the theory—the thing appeared to be revealed."[54]

In assessing the contribution of the record companies to Early Music's commercial success, we need to be very careful to distinguish between the lived experience of those individuals involved (with their varied motivations and interests), and the underlying organizational-level drive of always chasing after more money. For John Eliot Gardiner the "overall culture" of record companies in the 1980s, with certain important exceptions, was "predominantly cynical."[55] "They realized that there was a market there...but I don't think there was much serious commitment to the underlying philosophy of HIP...it was just that there was an opportunity to record, re-record or 're-enchant' an audience that was used to standard modern instrument interpretations." Gardiner's viewpoint might suggest that the "early stage innocent creativity" of early musicians was just as susceptible to "co-optation, commercialism and commodification" as any other area of cultural production.[56]

No single (or widely mentioned) case better exemplifies the perils of early music's commodification than the American release of the AAM's recording of Pachelbel's *Canon* (1983) in an "Authentic Edition," which offered "the famous Kanon as Pachelbel heard it."[57] It is easy to ridicule the ontological naïveté of such a claim. But to dismiss this as mere "commercial propaganda" pedaled by "press agents and promoters" (as Early Music's critics have been quick to do[58]) misrepresents a more complex reality. For one thing, as has been discussed in Chapter 3, Early Music's pleading for "authenticity" was based on a legitimate argument for one performance approach being more authentic than another (implicitly, at least, on the grounds of dispositional (historical) authenticity). But, over and above the definitional issues, the claim being presented was very much in tune with audience demand for just this break with "traditional" (i.e., modern) approaches to the performance of early music. Furthermore, the audience in question was much more knowledgeable than is usually given credit for (indeed, music audiences in general are far from passive dopes when it comes to decisions about consumption). What has gone unnoticed with respect to the opprobrium directed at marketing departments is that behind the criticism there continues a patrician (Reithian) view of the capacities of Early Music's audience to discern the value of what they are buying. It is easy to miss the fact, first and foremost, audiences liked what they heard. There is more to the discourse of "authenticity" than just its promotional value, as we will now explore further.

THE LEGITIMIZING AND MEDIATING DISCOURSE OF AUTHENTICITY

Just how early musicians and those managing their choirs, period instrument ensembles, and orchestras have managed to navigate their way between the different discourses (art, folk, and commerce) and their value propositions, without compromising their distinctive position on "authenticity," remains a point of contention. Peterson's (1997) work on the country music business in the United States between 1923 and 1953 concludes that those working in that particular industry were involved in "fabricating authenticity." He shows how the authentic nature of the country business in the US was "continuously negotiated in an ongoing interplay between performers, diverse commercial interests, fans, and the evolving image,"[59] but that this involved images of the "old-timer," the "hillbilly," or the "cowboy" being knowingly fabricated in the "creation" of country music. The related issue for Early Music is whether its explicit adherence to authenticity was similarly "fabricated" in the context of commercial gain (a line implied in Taruskin's critique of the "authenticity movement"). To better understand the importance of the discourse of authenticity in the context of Early Music's efforts to "break in" to the classical music establishment, we can usefully draw on Bourdieu's (1993) ideas on *The Field of Cultural Production*:

> The dominated producers [i.e., Early Music], for their part, in order to gain a foothold in the market, have to resort to subversive strategies which will eventually bring them the disavowed profits only if they succeed in overturning the hierarchy of the field without disturbing the principles on which the field is based. Thus their revolutions are only ever partial ones, which displace the censorships and transgress the conventions but do so in the name of the same underlying principles. This is why the strategy *par excellence* is the 'return to the sources' which is the basis of all heretical subversion and all aesthetic revolutions, because it enables the insurgents to turn against the establishment the arms which they use to justify their domination, in particular asceticism, daring, ardour, rigour and disinterestedness. The strategy of beating the dominant groups at their own game by demanding that they respect the fundamental law of the field, a denial of the 'economy', can only work if it manifests exemplary sincerity in its own denial.[60]

Early Music's "authenticity" represents a subversive strategy of a "return to the sources," a means of "beating the dominant groups [of the existing classical music profession] at their own game." Authenticity in this context might be thought of as doing what the classical music establishment was doing, only more so. The argument runs along the following lines: effectively historically informed performances of Bach, Handel, or Haydn were *more* Bach, Handel, and Haydn than "traditional" or "modern" performances. The discourse of authenticity took the spotlight off the performer and back on to the artistic and aesthetic credentials of the composer—from whence springs the legitimacy of the cultural field. But here we need to throw into the mix a further and distinctive feature both of the classical music establishment and the emerging early music movement (characteristic of both *art* and *folk* discourses already discussed). For such is the unspoken nature of classical music's disavowal of the economy, i.e., its unwillingness to talk of music in terms of sheer popularity or commercial value, that it cannot explicitly draw attention to its own legitimacy in this context. It must be just taken for granted. We might then ask—how did proponents of Early Music "manifest exemplary sincerity" in their own denial of the "economy?" The answer is—by appealing to the very legitimacy underpinning the classical music establishment and by "going back to the sources," i.e., including the intentions of the composers themselves. In other words, in applying the discourse of authenticity, early musicians were effectively arguing that they were more legitimate than the mainstream, and therefore needed to be taken seriously by the field of classical music production. At a discursive level, this was a form of argument to which the existing classical music establishment had no answer, since to respond would effectively bring with it the danger of undermining their own position (which was above and beyond discussion on account of their disavowal of the economy). This is not to say that there haven't been fierce debates over the nature of historical performance practice and the role of authenticity (as has been touched on in earlier chapters); however, where these have emerged, they have largely been confined to the pages of learned journals and academic books, some way removed from the everyday realities of the cultural field of production. Indeed, the debate among classical musicians *themselves* has tended to gravitate toward a critique of practice rather than theory: the view that HIP players are essentially "failed" modern players is one that continues to resonate within the profession, despite the many individual examples demonstrating this to be palpably untrue.

For the record companies, promoters, and other representatives of the field of large-scale cultural production, Early Music's legitimizing ideology of authenticity (both as it was argued between scholars and written up in program and sleeve notes) was crucial to its being treated seriously at a commercial level. Those involved in the financial backing of historically informed performances wanted to be sure about their investment—that claims to authenticity were legitimate. They needed to know that (i) they weren't just dealing with a cultural fad, dreamt up by a bunch of enthusiastic amateurs; and (ii) that those involved in pursuing authentic performance weren't just "making it up." The double irony of this position is that at the level of artistic and aesthetic practice (as Leech-Wilkinson (2002) has argued in relation to musicological "evidence" and as many early musicians would readily now acknowledge), many of those involved *were* indeed making it up, and it was this very creativity, inter alia, that proved hugely attractive to Early Music's burgeoning audience.

JUMPING ON THE OLD BAND WAGON—CONCLUDING REMARKS

Was it simply a question of being in the right place at the right time? To answer the question posed at the beginning of this chapter, it could certainly be argued that they (record companies as much as early musicians) were. But there is a good deal more to it than that. For one thing, the early music movement benefitted enormously from the timely support it received from the BBC. As Andrew Pinnock suggests, "The economic base on which the whole of English early music rested was the recording industry, with Radio 3"[61] (or The Third Programme pre-1967). The BBC's role in incubating early music through its "infancy" and "growth" was absolutely crucial (though it didn't generally see itself as undertaking this role at the time). It set the stage for the commercialization of early music, with the record companies stepping in when the developing brands (e.g., AAM, TEC, EBS, LCP) were becoming well known both at home and abroad. The BBC's approach was itself underpinned by deep links forged with academia, exemplified by the Music Department's reliance on a clutch of musicologists who were open to the possibilities of turning scholarship into musical sound. Record companies, for their part, were often represented by equally excited and passionate advocates of early music. As such, early music recording projects were largely collaborative affairs. Important as musical direction is, it was clearly in the nature of the relationships between early musicians and recording producers that great results were achieved (or indeed to begin with any results at all). We get a strong sense of this in John Dunkerley's (Decca) comment about the Academy of Ancient Music's first recording in 1974 of Thomas Arne Overtures: "Had it not been for the sheer tenacity of both Christopher [Hogwood] and Peter [Wadland], in persuading a much larger group of artists and repertoire producers that this could grow into something important, serious, and commercially viable, I doubt if Christopher would be as well known as he is now."[62]

As more and more early music was aired on the BBC or at the Proms, it gained further legitimacy in the eyes of the wider music profession and industry. More straightforwardly, it allowed early music to be heard, offering the real possibility of an audience being built up around it. It was only then, in the light of the BBC's initial support, that record companies boarded "the old band wagon." By analogy, we might liken the support of the BBC and the record companies, respectively, to the kind of investment behavior characteristic of business angels and venture capitalists. The BBC and some other early adopters (including the likes of Wadland at L'Oiseau-Lyre and Holschneider at DG in the early 1970s) acted like business angels. They invested in Early Music in part, at least, out of a passion and personal connection with individual performers. Though concerned in achieving a reasonable return on their investment, this did not primarily motivate them. Over the course of the 1980s and '90s, however, many record companies (though not all) operated according to a venture capital model. In an increasingly difficult economic climate, this necessitated both high returns on investment and also a more hands-on role at board level. For early music groups this involved less autonomy when it came to deciding repertoire choices, as well as more pressure to rely on superstar soloists (for further discussion, see Chapter 10). Inevitably, there were to be casualties, as can be seen, for example, in Deutsche Grammophon's withdrawal from the Bach Cantata pilgrimage recording project with Gardiner's Monteverdi Choir and the English Baroque Soloists in 2000.

The discussion of different discourses of value within this chapter reminds us that the very practical challenges of making early music pay has involved some complex position-taking. The ideology of authenticity has played a vital mediating role, allowing early musicians to navigate their way between competing art, folk, and commercial values. As we shall see in the next chapter, a further decisive factor in early music's successful commercialization was the ability of its music directors to perform multiple roles, acting as musicians, cultural entrepreneurs, and communicators, whilst holding the play-space open, so that ideas could be turned into practice.

There is no clear dividing line between this play and life.

MIKHAIL BAKHTIN[1]

Today the conductor, more than any one musical figure, shapes our musical life and thought. That may not be how things should be, but it is the way they are.

HAROLD C. SCHONBERG[2]

9

Everything to Play for

INTRODUCTION

It is remarkable how *small* the field of professional historical performance in Britain has actually been, given Early Music's credentials as "one of the most important developments in our intellectual and musical life during the last 50 years."[3] In fact, the movement itself has been dominated by just a handful of pioneering individuals, who founded, and in several cases, continue to manage and direct their respective HIP ensembles, choirs, and orchestras.[4] In this chapter we look in more detail at these cultural entrepreneurs, and their "off-stage" leadership and organizational practices in particular.

Whilst one could be forgiven for thinking that Early Music's leading exponents in the 1960s and '70s shared much in common, drawn as they were to this countercultural movement at a time when HIP was anything but fashionable, the evidence points to something much more interesting. As we shall see, Early Music's founder-directors have brought many distinctive qualities to their work, and on occasion this has meant they did not always see eye-to-eye with each other. The youthful David Munrow occasionally performed with Michael Morrow's Musica Reservata, for example, but the two men's approaches toward Early Music were colored by quite different outlooks and a somewhat "icy" personal relationship. Morrow made clear his views concerning Munrow's distinctive approach to performance in a newspaper article written by music critic Phillip Sommerich: "He said recently that his aim is to popularise old music, which I think he does very successfully. My aim is *not* that."[5] Elsewhere, a letter in the archive at King's College London reveals Morrow to be not averse to expressing candid opinions about other leading early music groups. He somewhat mischievously describes Anthony Rooley's Consort of Musicke, for example, as "mouse music for vegetarians," sounding like "squeaking in the wainscoting."[6]

There were inevitable tensions and disagreements, too, between the leaders of the class of '73, though this must be set against a broadly supportive and collaborative working relationship borne of the logistical need to avoid clashes in the diary. Maureen Garnham (formerly manager of The English Concert) recalls that "Christopher Hogwood's Academy of Ancient Music was really a bitter rival," but adds, "we didn't shout and hate each other!"[7] For his part, Trevor Pinnock talks of friendly rivalry: "In the early days too, just occasionally I remember Christopher Hogwood coming and staying at my house and having nice exchanges; we were quite good colleagues."[8] It was indeed Christopher Hogwood who first introduced Simon Standage (who went on to lead TEC) to Pinnock. Later, when John Eliot Gardiner made the transition to period instruments, he asked all of TEC's principals (including Standage, whom he knew from university days) to work for him. Pinnock notes: "I managed to negotiate that Simon would only lead for me. From that point we started a different way of looking at The English Concert...we started making a more fixed way of having regular members in a hierarchical system and then extra players beyond that."[9]

Rather than Early Music presenting a standardized offering to the performance mainstream, it has comprised a much more varied alternative. Its multifaceted nature comes through clearly in Bernard Sherman's book *Inside Early Music* (1997). Noting that his "interviewees' motives, creeds, and methods vary"[10] somewhat, the author concludes that "historical performance has never been stronger—or harder to define," adding that it "wouldn't surprise me if in the future historical performance becomes even harder to define and, not coincidentally, even stronger."[11] Early Music, after all, with its "spirit of discovery—whether reviving forgotten repertory or finding new ways to play familiar pieces"[12]—attracts nonconformist types, and individuals who know their own minds. Over and above the shared pursuit of HIP that unites this group, therefore, we can usefully explore their individual and characteristic entrepreneurial behaviors in organizing and managing ensembles, choirs, and orchestras.

CULTURAL ENTREPRENEURSHIP AND EARLY MUSIC

At first sight, reference to entrepreneurship in the context of early music (to say nothing of a book with "re-enchantment" in the title) might appear misplaced. Entrepreneurship is generally thought of as the domain of profit-seeking capitalists, not historically minded musicians. However, while the history books will rightly focus on the musical prowess of Early Music's pioneers, their "main act" would never have arrived on the concert platform without lower profile but critically important "off-stage" work. As Bennett (2008) stresses, performing music is only one practice the professional classical musician must be proficient in. When it comes to explaining the entrepreneurial role of Early Music's "artists," we are faced with a choice between "Freedom (*Play*)" and "Trade (*Pay*)."[13] Either we continue to follow the deeply idealized and Romanticized view of the artist as being above and beyond the quotidian reality of work (leaving "trade" to the managers, agents, producers, and record company executives), or we rethink the artist in terms of the more holistic conception of the "artisan," where "the old union of facility and inspiration, genius and rule, innovation and imitation, freedom and service"[14] is put back together. In fact, this distinction doesn't just dictate our perception of who does what in the context of the classical music profession; the assumed disciplinary divide (to say nothing of practical division of labor) continues to structure the context of higher education and academia, including how professional performers, musicologists, and arts managers are trained.

Nowhere is the choice just outlined more clearly evident than in respect of emerging debates concerning "cultural entrepreneurship." This term was introduced by Paul DiMaggio (1982) in "Cultural Entrepreneurship in Nineteenth-Century Boston," in which he explored the creation of an organizational base for high culture, notably the Boston Symphony Orchestra, in America. DiMaggio's "cultural entrepreneur" relied on high levels of social and economic capital. He was a collector of "cultural capital," and thus had "knowledge and familiarity with styles and genres that are socially valued and that confer prestige upon those who have mastered them."[15] Whereas the "cultural capitalist" was successful in business, interested in the arts, willing to invest, and a collector of social capital, the "cultural entrepreneur" had the organizational power to actually realize a (shared) vision. Most crucially, therefore, cultural entrepreneurship requires a practitioner to have a practical engagement with the whole of the value chain, necessitating him to act very much as an intermediary or broker between people, positions, and perspectives. Such "culturepreneurs"[16] are able to see beyond the immediate concerns of producing art (for art's sake), engaged as they are not only in the production of art and culture (performing early music), but in its distribution or circulation (negotiating engagements, tours, and record deals) up to the point of consumption (presenting informative radio broadcasts, hosting pre-concert talks, meeting sponsors).

Although Bilton (2006) has argued that *all* artists are cultural entrepreneurs (suggesting that those "vindicated and supported in the discourse of the cultural industries and cultural policy...recognise their work's potential as a commercial commodity"[17]), the reality must surely be that most musicians are brought up so as *not* to think of themselves as entrepreneurs. Weatherston, for example, notes that staff and students in a university music department show a "natural disinclination to be seen as entrepreneurs."[18] What, then, does this thing called entrepreneurship actually entail? My own perspective holds that "entrepreneurship is the emergent process of recognizing and communicating creativity such that the resulting (economic) value can be appropriated by those involved."[19] The likes of Munrow, Hogwood, Pinnock, and Gardiner behaved entrepreneurially in respect of their ability to "recognize" and "communicate" such creativity. From this definition it is also clear how important knowledge-producing institutions, such as those discussed in Chapter 7, are in respect of the entrepreneurship process. Wennekers and Thurik's (1999) more applied definition of entrepreneurship puts some further flesh on the bones. They define entrepreneurship as "the manifest ability and willingness of individuals, on their own, in teams, within and outside existing organisations, to perceive and create new economic opportunities (new products, new production methods, new organizational schemes and new product-market combinations) and to introduce their ideas in the market, in the face of uncertainty and other obstacles, by making decisions on location, form and the use of resources and institutions."[20] This provides several helpful pointers about the nature of entrepreneurial practice, which form the basis of discussion in the next section. First, attention is drawn to the willingness of those involved to engage in this process. Not everyone can play the role of the entrepreneur, even if they are indeed willing to do so in the first place. Second, entrepreneurship is not restricted to the individual. Indeed, the implication is that it is through the relational qualities of those involved (i.e., through social networks) that entrepreneurship is brought about. Third, the perception of opportunities, and how these are manifest in the market context, needs looking at in some detail. How good were Early Music's pioneers, for example, in spotting opportunities, such as concert engagements and record deals? Fourth, there is an emphasis on the importance of being able to make decisions in the absence of detailed knowledge, i.e., the capability to deal with ambiguity and uncertainty. The entrepreneurial decision-making process is distinctive in this respect. Finally, entrepreneurs don't just have a vision for what might work; they put it into practice through the active recombination of resources. Being able to leverage scarce resources is a key quality of the entrepreneur. In a context such as the early 1970s, when specialist early musicians were in chronic short supply, such an entrepreneurial quality would have been vital.

Entrepreneurship in Practice

Labels, of course, can be off-putting. Not surprisingly, perhaps, very few of the musicians interviewed in the course of compiling this book thought of themselves as (cultural) entrepreneurs, until prompted to ponder further about what this entails in practice. Nor, for that matter, did they spend much time reflecting on their undisputed role as employers. It is revealing to see their range of views on this particular point when questioned. Roger Norrington (London Classical Players) wore the "employer's hat" without any evident difficulty:

INTERVIEWER: Did you ever think of yourself as an employer?
NORRINGTON: Yes! When we had the orchestra—very much so. I was an employer, we had a board, we had a staff. We had a manager, and a fixer and a librarian, so yes.[21]

To the same question, John Eliot Gardiner replied:

GARDINER: I see myself more as a facilitator...to some extent an entrepreneur, yes, but I don't actually pay the fees. I try to distance myself from the direct administrative management, which is a skill of its own. Where I am very hands-on is in the choice of players and singers via audition, and the choice of soloists, and above all in the choice of repertoire and projects.[22]

For his part, Trevor Pinnock (The English Concert) draws attention to a significant change in his perspective over the years:

PINNOCK: In the early days I didn't think anything like that at all. But much later on...during that last 10 years I would say that I was very aware that because we had fixed places and we'd had this tremendous loyalty, them to me and me to them, and no job security, it was my job to provide enough work; and by this time people had mortgages, families, all sorts of things, and were relying on The English Concert to give them work. So I did in that sense feel like an employer.[23]

Andrew Parrott (Taverner Choir, Consort & Players), on the other hand, appeared far less comfortable with this leadership role, stating, "If an 'employer' is what I was supposed to be, I have clearly been an abysmal failure...but no, I don't think I ever did see myself that way."[24] Interestingly, Christopher Hogwood (Academy of Ancient Music) was perhaps the most emphatic of those interviewed about not thinking of himself as an employer:

INTERVIEWER: Did you feel or have you ever felt of yourself as an employer?
HOGWOOD: I don't—though I should, having run it for so long. A lot of people depend on it. I think now [2003] a lot of people regard it as their employment...but I'm very 'off centre'. While we were doing it then, it was much more of a commune; I happened to organize it, but anybody else could have run (and did run) similar groups.[25]

SOCIAL CAPITAL

Hogwood's concluding remark is telling, not least because the reality must surely have been that *not* "anybody else could have run...similar groups." Within a small field (the number of professional early music performers in Britain cannot have been more than several hundred, even at its peak of commercial success during the 1980s and '90s), the leaders were mostly drawn from a very particular stratum of society. DiMaggio refers to the "Boston Brahmin" in his paper on the cultural entrepreneur. In this context of Early Music I have referred similarly to an "Oxbridge Oligarchy," responsible for founding and directing the majority of early music ensembles and orchestras established from the mid-1960s onward. Commenting on the social origins of some of the pioneers of the movement, the former early music officer for the Arts Council of Great Britain notes: "The social origins of supposed mold-breakers are interesting to track. To get to the top they needed a whole lot of things: talent undeniably, an Oxbridge or equivalently high-prestige musical education, parents or other supporters willing and able to fund small-ensemble start-ups. Competitors without these advantages made very little headway."[26] Being able to draw on family wealth, connections, and benefactors certainly was advantageous when it came to pursuing a professional interest in early music. One thinks of Michael Morrow's independent means, for example, relieving him of the need to forge a career as a paid musician. Released from the pressures of "making a living," Morrow was able to pursue on a practical level a distinctive (arguably more dogmatic) approach toward historical performance practice as compared with, for example, David Munrow.

It goes without saying that along with social capital, most of the music directors of early music ensembles, choirs, and orchestras were themselves highly talented and experienced musicians and performers in their own right (ill-health prevented Michael Morrow from performing regularly, though he had taught himself to play the lute, recorder, crumhorn, and rauschpfiefe). It was as professional performers that many of them gained the cultural capital and its associated legitimacy to be taken seriously by colleagues and peers (John Eliot Gardiner is unusual amongst Early Music's pioneers, in respect of his taking to conducting at an early age (15), and training as an apprentice conductor with the BBC Northern Orchestra—but he also played the violin as a student, backing the great Lebanese singer Fairuz at the casino outside Beirut during his gap year in the Middle East). This point reminds us not to treat music directors as operating solely on the "demand" side, i.e., as employers, but to be aware of their origins in terms of the "supply" of musical performance. After all, today's employer was most probably yesterday's employed. Labor economics has generally failed to take this into account, therefore overlooking the sociocultural significance of early bonds between performers (workers), which come to shape organizations and even industries in the years to come.[27]

Ultimately, regardless of social and cultural capital accumulated, it is important to recognize that it takes a certain kind of person to "step up to the mark" when the opportunity presents itself. David Munrow was clearly that sort of person. As Oliver Brookes (a member of the Early Music Consort of London) reflects, "In mentioning his team management and ability to produce a successful concert under difficult circumstances, I often thought that he would have been equally capable of planning an ascent of Everest or sailing an ocean."[28] A quality of more everyday pragmatism underpins other early music directors' approaches. Peter Phillips (The Tallis Scholars), for example, writes, "This was the simple truth. If we wanted to put on concerts, we just did it. Nobody cared if we did, nobody cared if we didn't."[29] Turning to Peter Wadland's (Decca) discussions with Christopher Hogwood concerning the setting up of the AAM, Hogwood could well have come up with a list of reasons as to why a "larger period instrument group" would *not* have worked at that time; but he didn't. It seems likely that many professional musicians working at the cutting edge of the early music revival would have toyed with the idea of setting up their own chamber groups, ensembles, choirs, or orchestras. The fact remains, however, that only a handful did so. It is also worth stressing here that Authenticity$_1$, with its emphasis on consort music, collegiality, and roots in amateur music-making, "attracts people who are...less dictatorial";[30] this may well have a bearing on the difficulties many such groups experienced in raising their professional profile through self-promotion.

NETWORKING

The capacity of the cultural entrepreneur to foster relations, friendships, professional ties—in short to network—is absolutely central to any subsequent success. Having the necessary "flexibility" in their social networks required early music's pioneers to operate between worlds, in a sense maneuvering such that they could work both at the margins and at the center, i.e., they could converse with colleagues and fellow performers on an equal footing, whilst also being able to enter the worlds of recording executives, management, and organization wherever and whenever necessary. Given this, perhaps, it is all the more intriguing to see that HIP's musical directors frequently allude to themselves as being "outsiders" at some point in their careers. Trevor Pinnock, for example, saw himself as an outsider with respect to the early music network: "of course I always felt...slightly separate...because I didn't come from the university background."[31] It is particularly interesting here to reflect on Pinnock's hierarchical and fixed approach to the make-up of The English Concert, which demanded "strong ties" and considerable loyalty from its players: "we actually made fixed seating places because although people had to accept where they were sitting, this gave a sort of stability, which was a welcome contrast to the general 'pool of players' mentality."[32]

Elsewhere, Roger Norrington discusses "belonging" in terms of his contrasting involvement with modern classical music orchestras: "I'm rather different from others, because I've always been in touch with modern instruments. Although for several years I was extremely involved with early instruments, I'm nearer to an outsider; more like Charles Mackerras—who came from the edge but became very interested. But the other thing that stands out immediately, of course, is that now I hardly do any early music. I'm a regular modern conductor. I felt relatively 'inside' in the sense that I had successful groups and also Kent Opera for 15 years. We were busy...LCP was an exciting ship to be aboard."[33]

Andrew Parrott, for his part, now feels that he may have suffered from being an outsider to the classical music mainstream on the grounds of class. Educated at a local grammar school, from an "ordinary middle class background," and a first-generation university student, Parrott comments: "I didn't place myself on the outside. It is a realization that in our class-ridden British society and in this compartmentalized world most people are expected to stay in their pigeon-holes—and that's understandable, a very human thing."[34] The distinction between real and perceived "compartmentalization" is blurred here, to say the least. After all, Oxford graduate Parrott appears really rather adept at making connections within the classical music mainstream, e.g., he enjoyed a close working association with Sir Michael Tippett and the Bath Festival, secured a recording contract with EMI in the late 1970s, and worked closely with Hugh Keyte and other producers at the BBC. It is tempting, rather, to explain Parrott's apparent uneasiness with the classical music profession in terms of his uncompromising musicological position (very much in the Morrow mold), as this frank reflection reveals:

Insights into music are what it is all about for me. Of course I quite understand the financial argument that if people don't share my interests then they are not going to subsidize me to indulge my fantasies; but at the same time it is not my mission to entertain. I'm not using that word in a pejorative sense, but we *can* separate entertainment from art—even if it seems terribly pompous to do so. It grieves me that currently there is a greater emphasis on the need to entertain than there was when I was exploring these things for the first time. Back then we were exploring them for their intrinsic merit, and Radio 3 was putting money into studio recordings and making whole programmes of Lassus because that music had never been heard before, and there was a curiosity to see what it was all about... Those days are long gone.[35]

Although Sir John Eliot Gardiner is today very much part of the classical music establishment (a fact corroborated by his being awarded a knighthood for services to music in 1998, presented with several honorary fellowships, and voted into the "Gramophone Hall of Fame" in 2012), this was not always the case: "I was a late starter: most of my contemporaries had much more technical know-how and experience than I had at that stage—but I soon realized how much music mattered to me! Cambridge was bursting with talented musicians just then, but divided into opposing cliques. I didn't feel I belonged in any of them."[36] It is tempting to apply this label of a "late starter" to his adoption of period instruments within early music, waiting until 1978 before forming the English Baroque Soloists (EBS), and 1989 for the Orchestre Révolutionnaire et Romantique. However, this would be to overlook that formative performance of Monteverdi's *Vespers of 1610* in Cambridge back in 1964, which amongst other period instruments included cornetts and sackbuts, despite Thurston Dart's advice to use oboes and clarinets in unison instead.

SPOTTING OPPORTUNITIES

Gardiner's apparent circumspection before setting up his own period instrument orchestra (the EBS had formerly been the Monteverdi Orchestra who played on modern instruments, but with gut strings and outward curved bows) could be interpreted as a cautious and considered approach, as well as one focused on achieving a rigorous standard and quality of performance. Clifford Bartlett remembers a conversation with Gardiner in the queue at one of the BBC's canteens in the mid-1970s, during which he explained that he wasn't going to have early music "until the players are technically good enough."[37] In his own words, Gardiner recalls, "I was right in there at that time... but then the transition was a bit of a culture shock to me."[38] Having gone on to forge a close relationship with the players of the Monteverdi Orchestra, Gardiner adds, "by 1978 we had developed as far as I think it's possible to go without actually taking the plunge of adopting period instruments, and we'd now hit a brick wall stylistically. I'm very loyal to my players... and it was a heart-breaking moment to have to disband the Monteverdi Orchestra, while persuading as many of them as possible to 'come over' to playing period instruments in the EBS." Gardiner was alert to the "opportunity" that early music performance presented, but was also calculating in terms of how such an opportunity should be developed over time. There is a fascinating parallel here to the research of David Galenson (2007) on the nature of artists' creative life cycles (his focus includes painters, sculptors, poets, novelists, and movie directors). Galenson draws a distinction between so-called "experimental innovators," who arrive at their major contributions later in life, and the young "conceptual innovators" who make breakthroughs earlier on. Perhaps one might then contrast David Munrow's ("Young Genius") *finding* innovation, early on in his career, with Gardiner's ("Old Master") *seeking* innovation, over a much longer time span. Over the long term, of course, both approaches appear vital to the success of any art form (although, interestingly, Galenson has suggested that the conceptual innovator role of the young genius has been particularly important in the development of contemporary modern art).

The classic entrepreneurial trait of "being alert to opportunity" assumes a set of antecedent conditions already touched on, notably that one has sufficient social and cultural capital and networks to allow "playing the game" in the first place. But more than anything else, spotting the early music "opportunity" involved keeping ears open to the sounds that were emerging from the continent. As we have seen, the likes of Nikolaus Harnoncourt and Gustav Leonhardt, through teaching, live performance, and most of all through their recordings, represent much more than simply an aural backdrop to British early music performance in the early 1970s. They offered a precedent that could be actively drawn upon by those contemplating their own early music projects. For record companies making decisions about whether or not to engage fresh new early music groups in the UK, this precedent was significant. Trevor Pinnock recalls the cautious manner in which Dr. Andreas Holschneider (head of DG Archiv) decided to contract The English Concert. Holschneider, whom John Eliot Gardiner described as "a very cautious, circumspect man,"[39] attended TEC's London debut at the English Bach Festival in 1973, and as Pinnock notes, "He let us know of his interest and waited five years before offering us a significant contract."[40] The "opportunity" in early music terms, i.e., the possibility of both commercial and cultural success, emerged very much as a co-creative and relational outcome of negotiated positioning and practices of commercial record companies, promoters, venue managers, and agents, working alongside Early Music's cultural entrepreneurs.

ENTREPRENEURIAL DECISION-MAKING

Co-creative and collective behaviors aside, in the final analysis decisions are generally taken by individuals (even those decisions that are ostensibly made "by committee" are often the product of a single dominant voice). There has, understandably, been a good deal of research undertaken to study the decision-making processes of entrepreneurs. Of this, one of the most interesting strands is Sarasvathy's (2001; 2008) work on the "logic of effectuation." Sarasvathy shows how our usual mode of decision-making is based on causation. This is founded on the premise, "To the extent that we can predict the future, we can control it." She contrasts this causal logic with effectual logic's premise, "To the extent we can control the future, we do not need to predict it."[41] Sarasvathy explains that entrepreneurs (who are typically effectuators) "rarely see opportunities as given or outside of their control...they work to *fabricate,* as well as recognize and discover opportunities."[42] It is revealing here to pick up on Sarasvathy's emphasis on the word "fabricate" (i.e., making), just as Peterson (1997) does in the context of the "creation" of country music (as discussed in Chapter 8). For Sarasvathy, entrepreneurs "begin with who they are, what they know and whom they know, and immediately start taking action and interacting with other people."[43] At a pragmatic level, entrepreneurs "focus on what they can do and do it, without worrying much about what they ought to do." The personal authenticity of the entrepreneur, therefore, is very much at the core of their operations.

Looking now at Early Music's cultural entrepreneurs, we can point to something of a division between those who tend to operate with a causal logic (e.g., Morrow, Parrott, and Gardiner) and those who appear to favor an effectual logic (e.g., Munrow, Hogwood, Pinnock, and Norrington)—even if, as Sarasvathy herself stresses, entrepreneurs typically engage both logics to some degree. For example, as Clifford Bartlett notes, Michael Morrow's (causal) approach can be contrasted with the (effectual) approach of David Munrow: "there was a tension between Musica Reservata and David Munrow, because David was obviously sorted out commercially. He had a group of six players or something, which was ideal for nothing, but was wide enough to do a broad range of music more or less plausibly. I don't know how cleverly he worked that out."[44] Several years later, we can see how Andrew Parrott's Taverner Choir, Consort & Players looks like it should have been as successful as the Early Music Consort of London model, but in fact it may have suffered from applying a causal logic. Parrott explains that he "wasn't creating as defined a group as TEC or The Tallis Scholars; there was no fixed personnel; everybody was engaged on an entirely ad hoc basis." He goes on to note that his policy was to "choose horses for courses"; and if none of his three first choices was available, then "forget it!"[45] This can be contrasted, for example, with Christopher Hogwood's pragmatic approach in the face of Early Music's chronic under-supply of specialist performers in the early years of the AAM (see Chapter 5). Being prepared to engage brass players who were not historical performance specialists (there was no such thing at the time) was clearly effectual in nature.

RESOURCE LEVERAGE

The final aspect of entrepreneurship under consideration here is the entrepreneur's ability to recombine and leverage resources. Entrepreneurs are principally recognized on the basis of what they do (i.e., their ideas + actions), not what they plan to do (i.e., ideas alone). A good example of such behavior comes from Robert King, founder of The

King's Consort: "I had all these wonderful people around me: tenor Charles Daniels just down the road at King's College, Angus Smith, now of the Orlando Consort, about two rooms away from me, and many other good singers. So I thought we'd get out and do a concert."[46] The Oxbridge "sub-college" system is particularly suited to encouraging an "entrepreneurial culture," as students "put on small-scale things all the time."[47] King continues, "The standard of poster advertising in Cambridge was very poor, so we designed the most eye-catching posters imaginable. Final proof that we were doing something worthwhile came with a concert in which we put on the Monteverdi *Vespers*. Come the night, the queue to get in stretched out of St. John's College chapel, down the road past Trinity College and at one point got as far as Caius College. There were about 2,000 people trying to get into the concert, for which there were only 1,100 seats." King goes on to outline the sense in which his job was very much about recombining resources (a key feature of entrepreneurship first outlined by Austrian economist Joseph Schumpeter): "So that proved to me that if you did good music, got good performers, and a buzz going, the momentum would carry things along. Along with the quality of the performers, the marketing is all-important. The whole thing of being slick on stage, looking good on stage, and communication with the audience is all part of the attention to detail that is just as important as playing in tune."[48] Of course, such entrepreneurial behavior can carry with it a significant level of personal risk—as we can see in this no-nonsense comment by Trevor Pinnock concerning the risk/return profile of the standard royalty arrangement between a record company and group's conductor: "if it didn't sell, then I wouldn't make any money at all... and if it sold a lot, then I'd make a lot."[49]

Reflecting on Early Music from this cultural entrepreneurship perspective highlights the practical need for a level of compromise, i.e., willingness to concede ground in favor of an alternative view, on behalf of all those involved. Without this, Early Music would not have been made to "pay" in the modern age. But, this is not to say that compromise necessarily involves a lowering of artistic standards or any loss of authenticity (in fact, compromise well executed can be a tactic that leads to exceptional results, precisely because it is constructive, co-creative, and relational in nature). It is important to remember that music-making in any ritual context, whether this is pre-Enlightenment, in a church, a theatrical performance, or indeed in today's market context, has always involved compromise of some kind; after all, the act of performance itself is a form of negotiated agreement, both enabled and constrained by the genius and the frailty of its principle mediator—the human being. It is the very fact that music is *not* mechanically reproduced by turning a handle on a black box (save in the case of the organ-grinder's monkey), which makes live performance such an exciting and important conduit for human interaction.

Taking stock, the really interesting question here is not so much *who* was a cultural entrepreneur, or who was *more* entrepreneurial than the others, but rather in what distinctive ways were all of these individuals "entrepreneurial" (for whether they admit it or not, they were, on occasion)? One rather novel way of looking at this question is through the particular lens of "play."

PLAYING WITH CULTURAL ENTREPRENEURSHIP

The etymology of the word "entrepreneurship" harks back to the Old French verb *entre-prendre*, meaning to begin something, or to undertake. Taken literally, "entre-prendre" means to take between, and it is in this between-ness that we can begin to see the close association with play. Turner describes a liminality within play, a "temporal interface" through which meaning can be generated "between established cultural subsystems, though meanings are then institutionalized and consolidated at the centers of such systems."[50] Novelty emerges from "unprecedented combinations of familiar elements"[51] such as that perhaps between the performer, scholar, record company executive and audience. Within the context of early music performance, of course, play assumes a greater significance in that we "play" music, and its chief exponents are "players."

Play is indeed a slippery concept. "Like a rabbit in a briar patch, just as one closes in, the concept eludes categorization."[52] There are many different types of play, many different ways of playing. Schoolyard games, competitive sports, the Olympic games, video games, gamesmanship, theatrical play, play fighting, playing the fool, playing music, idle play, serious play. There is a vagueness to play;[53] it is "double edged, ambiguous, moving in several directions simultaneously";[54] but at its core, some common themes emerge. For example, play usually involves a "stepping out of 'real' life into a temporary sphere of activity with a disposition all of its own."[55] This is surely as true of playing music as it is playing with a new idea for a business. For Richard Schechner, play "has a quality of not being entirely 'real' or 'serious.'" It is "a mood, an activity, a spontaneous eruption."[56] Whilst we must be careful not to reify or privilege play here (a key criticism of play theorists is that they don't take sufficient account of class bias; many people in the world do not have the leisure time "to play"), this is important for bringing our attention to a "play-space," and the necessity of being prepared (emotionally, culturally, politically, financially) to keep that space open. In sports it is the job of the referee, umpire, or match official to do this, and therefore to keep the movement going (when the ball goes "out of play" everyone stops). In therapy it is the therapist; teaching, the teacher; and in entrepreneurship, it is the entrepreneur (who has had the temperament to "step up to the mark" in the first place) who holds the play-space open. It is this ability of entrepreneurs to maintain the possibility of delivering some new and innovative product or service (in the face of uncertainty, opposition, etc.) that characterizes their role in the introduction of new economic activity. The cultural entrepreneur similarly holds the play-space open in the context of the cultural field—itself defined as "a space of *play* and competition."[57] A further feature concerns the potential of play to facilitate communication with others, often in the absence of any linguistic content (play is a pre-linguistic mode of communication). Through play we emphasize our relational nature—even when playing on one's own there is usually an imaginary "other," whether this is a character in a child's fantasy game, or the endurance athlete's positive visualization of herself.

All play is, or has the potential to be, transformational. Through play we take the opportunity to be someone (else), or do something (different) that can transform both ourselves, and those around us.[58] Just as I introduced seven rhetorics of early music in the opening

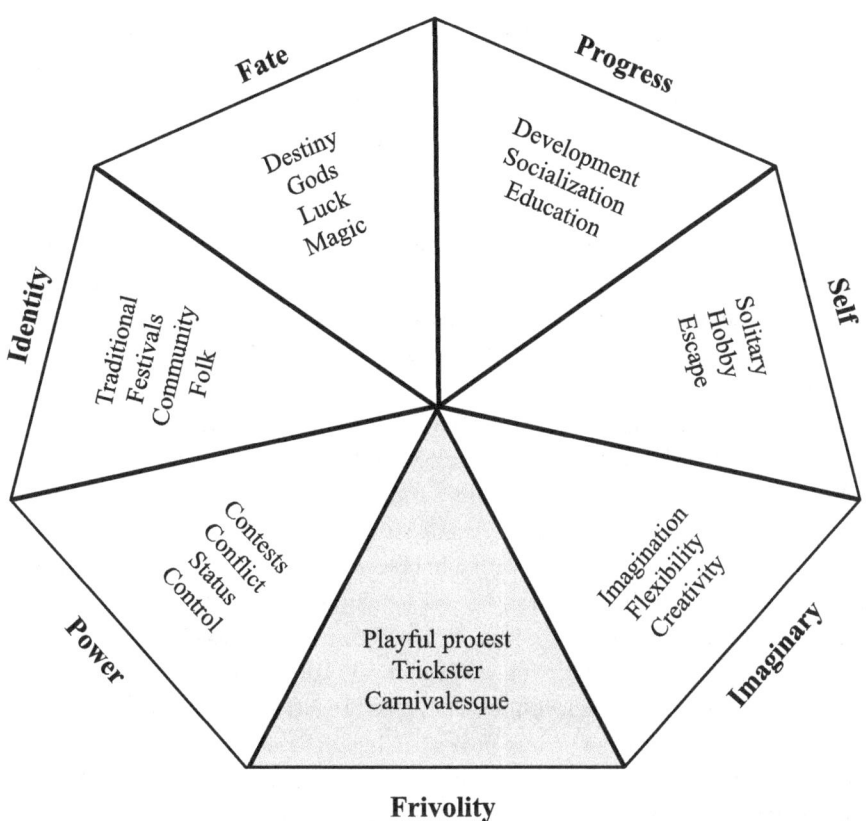

FIGURE 9.1 Seven Rhetorics of Play
(Adapted from Sutton-Smith 1997.)

chapter, Brian Sutton-Smith (1997) has discussed seven rhetorics of play. These provide a flavor of the plurality of play (and its players) and the various different approaches that there might be to bringing about transformation through play (see Figure 9.1).

The first rhetoric is labelled "progress" and captures the sense in which play, especially that of children, is often understood as a form of developmental behavior essential to socialization and growth (Chapter 2's Early Music life course strongly implies such a developmental strand in human beings). Associated with this rhetorical position is a form of play that prioritizes curiosity and learning, as well as an important source of knowledge production. Play of this kind underpins much of the scholar-performer/performer-scholar's fascination with music of a bygone age. The "fate" rhetoric, by contrast, emphasizes the kinds of play that involve chance. Any view that considers life to be controlled by destiny, some higher order, or luck would conform to this second rhetoric of play as fate. We roll the dice but cannot predetermine on which number it will land (unless by "magic"). The rhetoric of play as "power" is most evident in the context of sports, competitions, and contests. Sutton-Smith suggests that this rhetoric "is about the use of play as the representation of conflict and as a way to fortify the status of those who control the play or are its heroes."[59]

Of all the play rhetorics, "identity" is perhaps the most obviously associated with the early music movement in its collective sense. Play as identity is usually applied to traditional and community festivals and celebrations; it "occurs when the play tradition is seen as a means of confirming, maintaining, or advancing the power and identity of the community of players."[60] "Playing" early music with its distinctive approach to authentic historical performance looks like just such a case in point. Under the "imaginary" rhetoric of play we find an interest with improvisation, imagination, and "creativity of the animal and human play worlds."[61] There is clearly a particular connection here to my earlier definition of entrepreneurship in terms of recognizing and communicating creativity. This said, there is also a tension (as discussed by Taruskin) in terms of the lack of improvisatory performance when early music is approached too dogmatically. Of course, play can also be something we do for our own pleasure and gratification. The rhetoric of the "self" is described by Sutton-Smith as involving "forms of play in which play is idealized by attention to the desirable experiences of the players—their fun, their relaxation, their escape—and the intrinsic or the aesthetic satisfactions of the play performances."[62] Often this sort of play is associated with a hobby or interest, which in turn characterizes the amateur rather than the professional. Finally, we come to the "frivolous." This rhetoric involves an inversion of the "classic 'work ethic' view of play";[63] in other words, this rhetoric captures best the very playfulness of play. Although applied to the "idle or the foolish," it is also associated with "enacted playful protest against the orders of the ordained world."[64] Max Weber, whose own work highlighted the disenchanted nature of life in bureaucratized society,[65] readily acknowledged the appeal of play, frivolity, and game activity.[66] So, frivolous play has repercussions; indeed, as much as (and may be more than) any of the other rhetorics, it holds the capacity for transformation.

Each of us gets involved in different forms of play depending upon our particular personalities and the circumstances of our lives at any given time. We do not act rigidly according to just one rhetorical position, but some forms of play appear to be favored above others. So, too, Early Music's founder-directors can be contrasted in terms of their most readily observable play-perspective, which when taken together comprise a set of distinctive approaches to both cultural entrepreneurship and music-making. For example, the notion of "progress" (understood in terms of individuals' development and enculturation, rather than the modernist notion of societal progress) ties in closely to Christopher Hogwood's characteristically scholarly and thoughtful journey through the historical performance of early music, where critical understanding as well as stylistic feeling for the compositions and performances of the time have always been central to his work. For his part, Trevor Pinnock's approach is very much founded on the view that "Whatever one does...one's got to do in the spirit of discovery, of learning; there has to be a freshness to it."[67] Early music and education go together closely, and Anthony Rooley's educational work—notably as director of the Early Music Centre—appears characteristic, too, of the progress rhetoric. For Rooley (whom Dame Emma Kirkby describes as "a real Renaissance thinker"),[68] "fate" also plays its hand in life in general. In his book *Performance: Revealing the Orpheus Within* (1990), Rooley writes "Each of us plays a part, or a series of parts, more or less willingly, more or less consciously, more or less capably," adding, "Every action, interplay of relationships, pursuits of all kinds can be seen as 'performance.'"⁶⁹ The part is written for us, and as such there is a pre-determinist streak, which sees life as "nothing other than a play..."

Keeping the idea of contrasting positions firmly in mind, we can point to the organizational approaches of Michael Morrow (Musica Reservata) and Andrew Parrott (The Taverner Choir, Consort & Players) as being of an appreciably different character to that of many of the quintessentially English vocal groups (e.g., The Tallis Scholars, The Sixteen, Gothic Voices, The Hilliard Ensemble, The Cardinall's Musick), other Authenticity₁ groups (e.g., Musica Antiqua of London, the Rose Consort of Viols, His Majestys Sagbutts and Cornetts), and perhaps even the player-led Orchestra of the Age of Enlightenment. On the one hand, Morrow and Parrott personify that deeply committed lone musician and scholar, whose profound passion, knowledge, and love of early music (here very much in the *ama-bo* sense of amateur) drives a sometimes uncompromising agenda; whilst on the other hand, such vocal groups and period instrument ensembles epitomize (on the outside at least) a sense of ensemble, blend, togetherness, or in musical terms—homophony and harmonious polyphony. Of course, this is in no way to imply that such qualities haven't also been important to the likes of Morrow or Parrott (nor that the individual drive and commitment of such figures as Peter Phillips, Harry Christophers, or Philip Thorby have been anything other than crucial to their respective group's success), but merely to emphasize a different and, I believe, distinctive underlying quality to their work.

Both these playful approaches of "self" and "identity" are powerful in their own right. But the rhetoric of "power" speaks to us of a more overt position in which conflict is tackled directly. By his own admission, Sir John Eliot Gardiner has been "difficult and temperamental" in the past.⁷⁰ He is widely recognized as being a powerful figure not just in Early Music circles but the classical music profession more generally. There is no question that Gardiner's qualities as a cultural entrepreneur have tested others as much as they themselves have been tested—most notably perhaps in the course of putting together the Bach Pilgrimage project in 2000. It is a testament to Gardiner's resilience that he continued to see this epic performance and recording project through, despite many setbacks. Gardiner himself sums it up this way: "I think the entrepreneurship of running a freelance orchestra or running a choir is no easier nor any less challenging today than it was in '64...it's bloody hard work and in financial terms very discouraging sometimes. But I only carry on with it because I believe in the value of these projects so strongly, and because the artistic rewards are so immense."⁷¹

Naturally, there is much more to Gardiner (as, indeed, there is to anyone else) than the partial rhetoric of "power" implies. For example, whilst Gardiner holds that orchestras are "intrinsically undemocratic in their internal mechanical functions as a musical organism" and therefore "although collaboration is an absolute prerequisite, someone needs to take overall responsibility and be in charge,"⁷² he also considers "an element of exuberance and elation as essential to good music-making and that is something that can't be dictated or imposed from the conductor's podium: it can only be encouraged, elicited, stimulated, pleaded for!" This nod toward power's shadow-rhetoric "fate" is also evident in a remark he gave in an interview in 2005, when he referred to "the ineffable mystery of the whole process of musical transmission" being "so potent" and of that being "the reason why all musicians [he respects] are in music in the first place."[73] For Gardiner, being a musician requires a capacity for "engagement between different realms of existence" and what Keats in a letter to his brothers described as "negative capability," i.e., "when man is capable of being in uncertainties, mysteries, doubts, without any irritable reaching after fact or reason." As I shall be exploring in the final part of the book, the ability to reconcile the apparently irreconcilable is a key component of authenticity for each and every one of us, not just those we label "artists."

The idea of play constituting the context for novelty and value production (i.e., creativity) underpins much of the discussion in this chapter. Again, all of the early music pioneers discussed could readily be listed here; however, I would highlight Sir Roger Norrington for one particular feature of the "imaginary" rhetoric—which is its association with a kind of childlike fun. "When I forget about any form and harmony I ever knew and just conduct a Beethoven symphony—it's for the children in the back row that have never been to a concert before. I really want them to be excited by it. It's not 'early music.' It's not 'elitist' professorial activity. It is for fun."[74] In this comment, Norrington personifies the creative, imaginative approach, and this must surely have positively influenced those senior staff at National Westminster Bank (as much as anyone else) who took the decision to sponsor Norrington's successful Beethoven and Berlioz "weekends" in London in the late 1980s.

And so we come to the final rhetoric of "frivolity." This holds something of a special place amongst the seven rhetorics. Although a key concern of my study of Early Music has been to avoid conflationary theorizing—in which either the importance of individuals or of societal institutions is overstated at the expense of the other—I have found myself returning time after time to the catalytic figure of David Munrow. As Howard Mayer Brown wrote in his obituary piece in *Early Music*, "David Munrow's great gift, and the reason why we should honour him now, is that he was successful—he persuaded people to listen to his music—without patronizing his audiences, without offering them cheap thrills or bland pap, and without distorting the character of the music he performed."[75] There is no single factor to explain his powers of persuasion. As a musician he was a "dazzling virtuoso" performer; he was a serious scholar (his book on *Instruments of the Middle Ages and Renaissance* was published shortly before his death); he was a great organizer; but above all these perhaps he was also a great communicator.[76]

The rhetoric of frivolity is associated amongst other things with the "trickster." This has unfortunate connotations—particularly in the context of this discussion of the "authenticity movement." All the same, there is an uncanny connection here given the title of Munrow's long-running radio program for the BBC—*Pied Piper*.[77] It is very tempting to follow Lewis Hyde's thesis in recasting the trickster as anything but a shallow or discredited figure, and rather as representative of change—the "creative destructor" of entrepreneurship theory, perhaps. As Hyde discusses in his book *Trickster Makes This World* (2008), the trickster functions as a kind of catalyst within traditional societies: "The trickster is a boundary-crosser"..."the mythic embodiment of ambiguity and ambivalence, doubleness and duplicity, contradiction and paradox,"[78] instigating change by breaking rules and violating taboos. Munrow didn't just break rules, but played a vital role in making new ones up. John Potter suggests, for example, that the "small-scale, refined, straight, disciplined early music singing that we [are] used to" may not have come "out of nowhere," but "perhaps the head of David Munrow!"[79] Be that as it may, Hyde also notes that the trickster is usually "caught in the act." One can't help wondering whether our relationship with Early Music would have been any different had he not ended his life in 1976.

Overall, Munrow stands out for the way in which his characteristic brand of early music-making was able to cross boundaries, bringing together otherwise separate contributions (and people) relating to performance, scholarship, cultural entrepreneurship, and communication. What I term as this "Munrow effect" is particularly important when it comes to explaining the macro-level development and commercialization of the early music movement into a "blossoming industry." But, as I hope to have conveyed in this chapter, such a transformation wasn't achieved single-handedly, and each of Early Music's cultural entrepreneurs *played* a distinctive role, "revealing" their own "Orpheus within" (as Anthony Rooley would have it) in the process.

PART FOUR

Making Early Music *in the Modern Age*

It was noted in *The Daily Telegraph* that the OAE's 'invariably capacity audiences' were making it an attractive prospect for City benefactors.

HELEN WALLACE[1]

And Jacob said to Rebekah his mother, Behold, Esau my brother is a hairy man, and I am a smooth man.

BOOK OF GENESIS[2]

10

The Thief Who Came to Dinner

INTRODUCTION

The achievements of the early music movement in Britain over the last 40 years are cause for celebration. More early music repertoire than ever before now gets performed at the highest level, much to the delight of appreciative, knowledgeable, and still-growing audiences. HIP has become the default approach for performing the Baroque and Classical canon, and modern orchestras all over the world are embracing in their own work many of Early Music's core tenets and practices. Most music colleges offer specialist instruction as a matter of course, and university music departments actively encourage students to bridge the musicology–performance divide. The rancorous debates over the authenticity of "authenticity" have largely subsided. Once an unwelcome intruder, Early Music is now an altogether familiar component of making classical music *in the modern age*. It is "the thief who came to dinner."[3]

A rather more mixed picture emerges, however, once we start to explore the detail of Early Music's apparent successes, especially the extent of its so-called "mainstreaming," for its achievements have certainly *not* been all encompassing. It is the purpose of this chapter to provide a balanced view of the early music movement, and in so doing bring our story up to date. The primary focus will be on the central relationship between Early Music and the classical music mainstream. At issue is how far the movement has transformed the way we perform classical music; or, alternatively, how far has the way we perform classical music transformed Early Music?

The sociologist Margaret Archer[4] has persuasively argued that people are inescapably shaped by the culture in which they live, while at the same time culture itself is made and remade by people. This theoretical foundation provides the basis for the analysis that follows. To work through Archer's ideas in relation to the early music movement, consider first Early Music's ideological beliefs and practices regarding performance in the late 1960s and early 1970s as (A), and the prevailing classical music profession's ideas, beliefs, and practices as (B). A and B, it might be suggested, were logically inconsistent. You could not ascribe to both an Early Music and a "modern" approach to performance without some form of "constraining contradiction." Of course, early musicians had no choice but to live and work within the prevailing views, beliefs, and practices of the classical music mainstream (B), what Archer terms a particular "situational logic." Under this situational logic, in which early musicians remained deeply committed to realizing A, some kind of "correction" of the relationship with B was inevitable. In analytical terms, the result of this correction is "ideational syncretism," i.e., "the attempt to sink differences and effect union between the contradictory elements concerned."[5]

According to Archer, the nature of this sinking of differences can take the form of three different paths or options, each giving rise to a varying form of syncretism. The first option is correcting B so that it becomes consistent with A. Under this approach the classical music mainstream would be seen to take on all the precepts of HIP, integrating these "new" ideas into its own practices such that they become synonymous with Early Music's. To all extents and purposes, there would no longer be any difference between the mainstream approach to performance (in its now modified form) and the Early Music approach. Contradiction is, in effect, done away with. The second option would be to correct both A and B such that they become mutually consistent. This form of "symmetrical syncretism" is clearly less desirable to advocates of A than the first option above, as it would involve compromise. Nonetheless, it would be more attractive than the third option, which would involve correcting A so that it becomes consistent with B. Under this last approach, Early Music would be required to fall into line with the traditional classical music mainstream in order to survive. This would clearly be for the early musician an option of last resort—and in the case of Early Music it is hard to see how this would in fact represent anything other than a caving in to the status quo.

The question for this chapter then is—which of the three paths just outlined best represents Early Music's "mainstreaming?" My approach to answering this question, whilst seeking to avoid a purely arbitrary division between Early Music and the classical music mainstream (in practice the boundaries between these two identities are much more fluid than separate labels suggest), takes the form of a balance sheet of Early Music's achievements.

A BALANCE SHEET OF THE EARLY MUSIC MOVEMENT

The launch of the Orchestra of the Age of Enlightenment in 1986 heralded Early Music's "coming of age." A new spirit of independence permeated early music-making in Britain. During the 1980s and '90s this gradually matured and was further consolidated as early musicians found themselves increasingly in demand on the concert stage and in the recording studio. Nicholas Kenyon (1990) was full of optimism: "Without sounding triumphant about the matter, it is difficult to avoid the conclusion that the 1980s have seen the early music movement sweep all before it with remarkable vigour."⁶ Despite seeds of self-doubt first planted by the likes of Taruskin, Dreyfus, and Leech-Wilkinson in the early 1980s, consolidated in publications in the mid-1990s,⁷ the movement's "restlessness" could not apparently deviate the "juggernaut" or "steamroller"⁸ of Early Music from its course. All the same, things *were* changing, and not always for the better. Already by 1992, for example, Neil Zaslaw was warning of "the dangers of increased professionalism and commercialism that have accompanied the parallel successes of 'early music' and *Early Music*," referring here not just to the practices involved in bringing early music to the market, but also to the (academic) discourse that surrounded it.⁹

Assessing such a broad sweep of British Early Music activity as has taken place between the mid-1980s and today is a daunting task, to say the least. It is impossible to do justice to the scale and scope of performances, recordings, exhibitions, and other events that early musicians and instrument-makers, both professional and amateur, have been involved in. I have drawn attention to some of the key landmarks in previous chapters (refer to Figure 2.1 for a list of professional groups formed in this period). Forty years on from the class of '73, now is as good a time as any to look back and reflect on the positives and the negatives of the early music movement (see Table 10.1). The "Positive" column is associated with the ideas, beliefs, and practices in line with Early Music's (A) ideological interests and aims; the "Negative," those of the classical music establishment (B) more generally.

LEGITIMACY

Positive, i.e., toward (A)	*Negative, i.e., toward (B)*
Widespread familiarity with Early Music and HIP practices considered the norm.	"There Is No Alternative," as Early Music becomes the "new orthodoxy" for performance of earlier repertoire.

My assessment of the general profile and coverage of Early Music begins with the notion of *artistic legitimation*: "how cultural productions are repositioned—both institutionally and intellectually, so as to allow them to be redefined—from merely entertainment, commerce, fad, or cultural experimentation to legitimately artistic."¹⁰ At issue here is the cultural transformation from the enthusiastic amateur's faddish pursuit of early music to its being taken seriously as an alternative to the establishment norm.

Legitimation theory has focused primarily on a triad of factors—opportunity space, mobilization of resources, and legitimating ideology—as constituting the "necessary mechanisms by which an object achieves its status as legitimate art."¹¹ Some discussion of the central importance of being "alert to opportunity" and "leveraging resources" was presented in the previous chapter. Early Music's legitimating ideology (as discussed in

TABLE 10.1.

	Early music movement's balance sheet in 2013	
Theme	Positive, i.e., toward (A)	Negative, i.e., toward (B)
Legitimacy	Widespread familiarity with Early Music and HIP practices considered the norm.	"There Is No Alternative" as Early Music becomes the "new orthodoxy" for performance of earlier repertoire.
Repertoire	Huge expansion of repertoire (i.e., embracing both earlier and later musical works).	Commercial logic drives choice; ghettoization of Authenticity$_1$; progressive tendency.
Training	Specialist early music/HIP training now commonplace.	Bottleneck supply issues (esp. for 19th-century and later repertoires); limited time for artist development.
Recording	Extensive early music catalogue, industry awards, and so on.	"Early music sound" characterized by default synchronicity; no rough edges.
Authenticity	HIP principles taken up by both period instrument and modern orchestras and ensembles.	"Authenticity" per se no longer considered a viable (or desirable) performance ideal.
Leadership	Independence; professionalization of management and support.	Market-driven appetite for "big name" conductors and "star" soloists.
Integration	Knowledgeable global audiences; great access to instruments, editions, players.	Increasing separation of amateurs and professionals (and performers and instrument-makers).

Chapters 3 and 8) has been that of authenticity. Over and above these proposed mechanisms, however, attention must also be drawn to the aesthetic nature of art, since it is through shared sensory "experience" (Dewey, 1934) of cultural products, rather than mere intellectual understanding of related arguments per se, that those involved are actually "moved" to action. Explanation of artistic legitimacy, whether at the level of "legitimate," "middle-brow," or "popular taste,"[12] must take into account whether the art is actually enjoyed in the first place.

Fortunately for Early Music, of course, people liked what they heard. As Kenyon states, "As the movement gathered steam, audiences and record buyers...responded instinctively to performances they enjoyed, and did not argue the finer points of faithfulness to the past."[13] Kenyon's personal views (expressed at a lecture he gave in 2009 marking the 25th anniversary of the Lufthansa Festival of Baroque Music) put the case very well: "for me as a listener it wasn't because of the historical evidence that I liked these performances, it was because—to adapt Thomas Beecham—I loved the noise they made."[14] This enjoyment was a product of getting several things right in terms of the aesthetic experience of early music performance. There is no one feature we can point to as being more important than all the others in this respect, but contributory factors include the distinctive sound of the original instruments; the less self-indulgent, bouncier, faster speeds with which familiar repertoire is performed; the historical project itself, which captures audiences' attention in a new way; and, of course, the musicality, passion, and enthusiasm of those involved.

Over the years, Early Music's orchestras have changed the way in which they market themselves. Whilst there remain some explicit references to "historical performance practice" and even "authenticity" on websites and press materials, it is fascinating to see how the top-flight instrumental groups have increasingly identified themselves as chamber orchestras rather than as period instrument orchestras. Christopher Lawrence (manager of the AAM in the late 1990s) explains that period instrument orchestras had to respond to the way in which big promoters such as the BBC Proms or Symphony Hall, Birmingham, worked. In what amounted to quite a shift from how they promoted themselves when appearing at specialist early music festivals (such as York and Utrecht), these groups now had to compete more generally with other "great orchestras." Lawrence very much regarded the AAM as a chamber orchestra "specializing in a certain repertoire."[15] Violinist Margaret Faultless expressed similar views about the OAE: "we should be judged against any orchestra, we don't need special pleading, nor is there a sense that we are on the moral high ground any more. There are good orchestras and bad orchestras, good conductors and bad conductors."[16] This perspective is similarly evident in the Association of British Orchestra's (ABO) report "A 2020 vision for chamber orchestras,"[17] for example, which includes both the AAM and OAE as exemplar chamber orchestras, but with no mention at all of early music, historical performance, or the like.

In reviewing the ways in which Early Music has introduced the legitimized norm for professional performance of "early" repertoire, we can also point to something of a loss of what it originally offered. Early music performances no longer always surprise, their radical and revolutionary credentials being asserted in program notes rather than on the concert platform. It is as if HIP has become just what classical music "does" with old music. More worryingly, musicologist and cultural historian David Irving points to "the institutionalization of a new orthodoxy of 'historical performance practice,'"[18] adding that this is "passed down—often uncritically, as 'received wisdom'—from teacher to student." As Bernard Thomas puts it, "there is a problem in Britain in that there is too much consensus about what they think early music is. There shouldn't be a consensus; we don't know enough for there to be a consensus."[19] Nowhere is this observation more apparent than in respect of the repertoire choices that get made under the label of "early music."

REPERTOIRE

Positive, i.e., toward (A)	Negative, i.e., toward (B)
Huge expansion of repertoire (i.e., embracing both earlier and later musical works).	Commercial logic drives choice; ghettoization of Authenticity$_1$; progressive tendency.

As we have seen, "It is something of a problem to know where 'early music'... actually ends."[20] For Elizabeth Roche, "early music" denoted music written up to 1640.[21] According to Arnold Dolmetsch, the study of performance practice ended with J. S. Bach (who died in 1750).[22] Robbins Landon suggested that early music ended "with the death of Joseph Haydn, who brought music out of the Baroque into the Classical."[23] Haydn died in 1809. Landon added, "It is questionable whether even Beethoven should be excluded from 'early music.'" For its part, the BBC's *Early Music Show* continues to treat Haydn as an unspoken cutoff for early music,[24] and in its 2009 survey report, The National Early Music Association limits its interests to music written pre-1830.[25] However, Early Music appears stubbornly resistant to any kind of temporal boxing in. Over the last few years, Berlioz, Brahms, and Wagner (notably his opera *Das Rheingold* with the OAE and Rattle in 2004) have all been given the period instrument "makeover," barely raising an eyebrow in the process. Even Elgar can now be heard again, with what were previously considered "tasteless" portamenti and rubatos fully restored to their rightful places (contemporary recordings providing proof of their "authenticity"). The influence of HIP extends to what gets published, too, of course, and over the last 40 years the market has been flooded with countless new editions and series devoted to "old" music. The apparent trend in publishing new and undiscovered "partially completed" or "deleted" versions of otherwise well-known more recent musical works (e.g., Britten's *Serenade for Tenor, Horn and Strings* or *Winter Words*) might also be taken as evidence of an extended HIP phenomenon. Is it stretching things too far, I wonder, to suggest that even attempts to "complete" works (e.g., Mozart's *Requiem*; Elgar's *Third Symphony*; or Mahler's *Symphony No. 10*), have in some way been influenced by Early Music's repositioning of musicology as an activity that can (and very much should) be put into practice?

The move toward later repertoire has apparently captured the public imagination, but it is also the case that "there is not so much 'early' early music in concert programmes as there used to be."[26] Authenticity$_1$ (i.e., Medieval, Renaissance, and early Baroque music) has fared less well than later repertoire. One reason for this, perhaps, is that at least in the early 1960s and '70s, performers were not able to improvise and build upon what were otherwise very short pieces when played "as written." Bernard Thomas recalls taking part in a Musica Reservata concert, for example, comprised of 65 short dance pieces. As he notes: "unless you were very skilled at constructing a programme, that was very exciting at first, but then quite tiring to listen to!"[27] An important distinction between vocal and instrumental music should be made here.

Whilst the instrumental Renaissance dance enjoyed something of a short-lived revival in the 1970s, early vocal music has continued to flourish. Britain can boast an array of specialist chamber choirs, often supported by their "in-house" musicologists (performer-scholars), who consistently push at the boundaries of early music repertoire. Alamire, The Cardinall's Musick, The Clerks, the Dufay Collective, the Gabrieli Consort & Players, Gothic Voices, the Hilliard Ensemble, I Fagiolini, Polyphony, The Scholars, The Sixteen, Stile Antico, The Tallis Scholars—these are just some of the groups that have performed and recorded "new" (i.e., neglected) repertoire from early Baroque, Renaissance, and Medieval periods. It is interesting to note that quite a number of these groups have also experimented both with contemporary music (The Tallis Scholars' premiering of works by John Tavener, or their collaboration with the National Centre for Early Music in running an annual competition for composers), and with more contemporary takes on "old" music (one thinks of the Hilliard's successful collaboration with saxophonist Jan Garbarek, or I Fagiolini's *Tallis in Wonderland*).

On the face of it, such an expansion of repertoire under the "early music" label is symptomatic of success for the movement. But it also points to some important implications for what is held to constitute period performance practice. Speaking at the April 1992 "Early Music in Europe" conference, organized by Christopher Kite (Guildhall) and the Early Music Centre, Christopher Hogwood talked of a "progressive tendency" and the "forward march from the High Baroque, where most early music specialists start out, on to the classics, on again to the early Romantics and conducting stardom if all goes well."[28] One can't help but read into this something of an autobiographical slant, given Hogwood's own career trajectory (his website biography describes him as "equally passionate about music of the 19th and 20th centuries: with a particular focus on the Early Romantics and the neo-classical school (Martinů, Stravinsky, Britten, Copland, Tippett and Honegger)."[29]

For critics and devotees alike, Early Music's developing repertoire choices have been problematic for two main reasons. First, there is the concern that the music performed is increasingly chosen on the basis of what sells. Writing in 1991, the historical performing practice scholar Clive Brown, for example, described the period instrument "push" into the 19th century as "commercially motivated."[30] Claire Holden (OAE violinist and Arts & Humanities Research Council (AHRC) Fellow) argues more strongly that such market-focused decision-making is entrenching "a new 'period' canon."[31] For his part, Nicholas Kenyon talks of Early Music now being characterized by "dizzying diversity," adding that there is "no shortage of exploration of the most obscure repertory on disc." However, he concedes, "the economics of concert-giving have changed to make performance of these rarities more challenging."[32]

The second problem arising from Early Music's ever-wider "embrace" is neatly summed up in this comment by Michelle Dulak (1993): "Historical performance has painted itself into an ideological corner. For decades, its announced purpose has been to wipe the distortions of Romanticism from the face of the pre-Romantic repertory...Yet the underlying aesthetic assumptions of the musicians venturing into this territory appear to have changed not at all: the goal is still to lighten, quicken, clarify."[33]

As observed, such light touch and quicker tempos are integral to Early Music's legitimacy, so one can understand a reluctance to forgo them. In the absence of definitive and concrete examples (which would take us beyond the boundaries of this study), it is difficult to comment further on the specific charges leveled. Individual cases in point can no doubt be found, but then historical performance practice has also moved on from the mid-1990s. Unquestionably, 19th-century performance practice has been on its own learning curve, very much mirroring that of the Early Music pioneers of the late 1960s and early 1970s.

TRAINING

Positive, i.e., toward (A)	Negative, i.e., toward (B)
Specialist early music/HIP training now commonplace.	Bottleneck supply issues (esp. for 19th-century and later repertoires); limited time for artist development.

In Chapter 7 it was suggested that music colleges were generally slow to put their support behind Early Music; but in more recent years training provision has improved substantially. Specialist early music and HIP tuition is offered as standard in most leading British, European, and American conservatoires, even if in some cases, as Nicholas Kenyon suggests, "they are not integrated enough with the day-to-day provision." "I firmly believe that every student at every conservatory ought now to be exposed to early music performance practice, even if they don't pursue it professionally."[34]

My 2003 survey of British Early Musicians and Instrument-makers, which remains the most comprehensive survey of early musicians in Britain,[35] provides some further data to draw upon. It reaffirmed that early musicians (like "classical" musicians) generally come from a particular middle class stratum of society—whether their involvement is at an amateur or professional level. As shown in Table 10.2, the majority of

TABLE 10.2.

Occupational status of early music performers' parents Occupation[a]	Mother %	Father %
Managerial and professional	47.1	78.1
Administrative and skilled	11.0	14.0
Other occupations	2.9	5.0
Housewife/househusband	30.4	–
No response	8.5	2.9

n=480 (includes amateur and professional early musicians)

a = categories re-code listed occupations according to the Standard Occupational Classification 2000 (SOC 2000) early music performers are born into families where one or both parents undertake managerial or professional occupations.

This profile was even more marked for professional early music performers, with 59.7 percent having managerial or professional mothers and 81.6 percent, managerial or professional fathers. There is little here to dispute prevailing sociological views on "legitimate taste," access to educational capital, and the centrality of "life chances" in becoming involved in early music (at any level).[36] One area where this has perhaps had most bearing on the early music movement is in respect to the restricted access to Oxbridge-style vocal training. Joel Cohen (director of the Boston Camerata) provides an interesting take on this issue from his trans-Atlantic vantage point. "One of the most striking developments in the early music field has indeed been the appearance on the scene of so many fine, well-trained English singers."[37] Cohen makes the point that English singers can perform madrigals and chansons without the audience having to put up with "five or six frustrated soloists each straining to outdo the other."[38] Commenting on the "phenomenally high level of sight-reading skills" of the English singers, he also comes to the plausible conclusion that English singers release many new recordings because they can "churn them out so fast."[39] As one of these singers myself in the late 1980s and early 1990s, I know where Cohen is coming from, as most engagements in Britain were underpinned by minimal rehearsal time. I recall my sense of good fortune on being booked to perform (and record) a program of Palestrina *Masses* with Phillipe Herreweghe's Ensemble Vocal Européen De La Chapelle Royale, comprising singers from across Europe and (very unusually) an extended period of rehearsal time ahead of us to be spent in Paris and the beautiful Abbaye in Saintes. Whilst there is no question that learning the music ("note-bashing") would have been more speedily accomplished by a professional English choir, here there was the space to explore the music (and its text) at a depth that many British choirs simply did not have the time to get near. Of course, it is important to emphasize that this was not just a case of cultural preferences and style, but very much an issue of money (with generous subsidies available to support such continental European initiatives not similarly available in Britain). Interestingly, despite the lack of public sector funding for Early Music throughout the 1970s, 1980s, and 1990s (see Chapter 7), some of the movement's pioneers were adept at carving out development ("play") time and space in ways that would surely be impossible in today's more rigorous economic climate. Trevor Pinnock recalls, for example, how in the early 1990s he was able to persuade his record company (DG Archiv) to give The English Concert generous session time when they came to record the Mozart symphonies. He notes: "they also paid a huge amount of money for us to have 'music days'...preparing the symphonies, because I said 'we can't do this unless you give us time'...No one would do that nowadays."[40] Having the time to try things out is vital for all musicians. As Bernard Thomas observes, "all the best forms of music are the result of experimenting...of having the luxury to fail."[41]

Trend data on the profile of early music performers by age (Table 10.3) provides some further insights on the state of early music training in Britain.

TABLE 10.3.

Early music performer profile (% per cent)		Age of respondent	
Early music performer profile	Under 40 (n=87)	Between 40-60 (n=242)	Over 60 (n=141)
Professionals	81.6	46.0	10.1
Studied early music (F-T)	59.8	19.0	5.7
Not studied early music	12.6	34.3	47.5
Studied at music college	74.7	35.1	14.2
Intended to have career in classical music	60.9	34.7	11.3
Intended to have career in early music	27.6	11.6	2.8
Been paid for performing early music	93.1	76.0	35.5
Hold regular position with early music ensemble	56.3	36.4	4.3
Undertake paid work on or with modern instruments	73.6	42.6	11.3
Play a Medieval or Renaissance instrument	11.5	16.5	22.7
Play a stringed instrument	29.9	17.4	9.2
Male	37.9	50.4	55.3

n=480

Reading between the lines, there have become many more options to specialize in early music performance both in terms of cultural acceptance as a career option, and in relation to the increased opportunities that exist for dedicated study at music college. There is also further evidence of the move from Authenticity$_1$ to Authenticity$_2$. This has involved an increasing polarization between the professional Baroque or Classical performer (notably, young string players in this survey) and the amateur or semi-professional Medieval or Renaissance specialist (the proportion of over-60-year-olds playing a Medieval or Renaissance instrument was double that of the under 40s). Elsewhere, two thirds (66.3 percent) of today's professional early musicians have attended university, with over one third of these (38.8 percent) having studied at either Oxford or Cambridge.[42]

We get a helpful snapshot of the distinctiveness of British courses as compared with their European counterparts in the record of the "Early Music in Europe" conference, held in April 1992.[43] Andrew Pinnock contrasts "British pragmatism" in bolting early music onto conventional courses of study, with the Swiss/Germanic "rigor"—in which "the whole early musical personality" is trained "in figured bass playing, improvisation, choral singing, analysis and so on";[44] the "uninhibited medievalism" of the French; and "flourishing Dutch enterprise." However, despite the laudable appetite for really getting behind early music training in British music colleges in the 1990s and beyond, a key problem remained—how to make the meaningful transition into employment.

Two main issues need to be addressed here. First, there has always been a lack of "churn" in the early musician labor market. A very small group of professionals came to dominate the scene, and then remained in place for many years. On this point it is worth highlighting a particular feature of the labor market, which this letter in 1978 from the music officer of the British Council to Michael Morrow articulates:[45]

> As I have stated in my letter... German organisers are often unaware of the trouble they cause to British ensembles of such high quality as MUSICA RESERVATA by expecting them to recruit the players again for a concert that they had previously cancelled. For, the situation is rather different about comparable groups in Germany (though there are very few if any at all who compare with MUSICA RESERVATA) in that they mostly work as a team of unchanged members on a permanent contract basis, which gives the individual player very little chance to perform in any other ensemble than his own. The cases where an instrumentalist of the soloist category appears as a more or less regular performer in more than one ensemble are in fact very rare in Germany. I dare say that Britain's fame for having so many outstanding chamber ensembles of all categories is largely due to that far more flexible system that has been developed in Britain to give the musicians a free choice to join as many groups as they like and are able to manage. In my view an admirable system because of giving a large number of first-class ensembles the chance of participating in the very elite of specialists, but obviously not without problems for musicians and managers if it comes to the question of coordination.

As we have seen, the "flexibile system" discussed here was, in part at least, born out of necessity. There remained a chronic *under*-supply of specialist early music performers throughout the 1970s. Today, the situation is rather different. In terms of professional viol players (representative of Authenticity$_1$), "there used to be just ten of us, or perhaps up to 20. Now there's probably 40 or 50."[46] Alison Crum adds, "I don't know if there is less work than there used to be, but certainly it is spread much thinner." The situation is equally competitive in relation to Authentcity$_2$, which although offering a much greater frequency of performance opportunities, also attracts many more young players (coming through the music college system). However, it remains the case that many of the top jobs are shared amongst just a handful of performers. One reads on the AAM's website, for example, that their principal viola is also principal with the Dunedin Consort, Brecon Baroque, the English Baroque Soloists, and the Amsterdam Baroque Orchestra; whilst their principal horn also leads the horn section in The Hanover Band, the English Baroque Soloists, the Orchestre Révolutionnaire et Romantique, and the Orchestra of the Age of Enlightenment. Competition for jobs is further exacerbated by the increasing trend for modern players to rub shoulders with early music specialists. As John Eliot Gardiner puts it with reference to his Orchestre Révolutionnaire et Romantique, "there have always been some refugees from the standard London orchestras who come over and do a bit of 'learning as you earn.'"[47] For the performers who do make it into these higher echelons of early music performance, keeping a foot in the door of various ensembles is an economic necessity (to say nothing of a welcome artistic challenge). However, for the young early musician emerging out of music college, it must be galling to see so few opportunities for furthering their career in their chosen specialism. This is all the more concerning when the cost of tuition (subject to a marked rise in 2012 after parliamentary approval for the raising of the cap on higher education tuition fees), equipment, and indeed, just living (especially in London and the South East), is becoming prohibitive for many.[48] Much to their credit, early music ensembles themselves have been keen to try to deal with this bottle-neck in various ways. The OAE's Jerwood/OAE Experience, and more recently the Ann and Peter Law OAE Experience, have given up-and-coming students a chance to perform with the orchestra, and there have been discussions over setting up a training orchestra.[49] The English Concert has organized a series of master-classes (including some with its conductor Harry Bicket); and the Monteverdi Choir and Orchestra run an "Apprenticeship scheme," first set up in 2007 "to address the problems faced by young singers attempting to embark on a professional career."[50]

The second issue concerns the extent to which those being trained are in fact "fit for purpose." This is more a question of the content of training itself, rather than the potential of those involved. For period performers have largely been trained in the performance of Baroque and Classical repertoire, whereas their first taste of professional work is more likely than not with larger orchestras performing 19th-century repertoire, "for which they are unprepared and unskilled."[51] Such a "hugely ironic" situation is compounded by the "slightly uncomfortable mix of period instrument baroque specialists and modern players who drift in for an occasional break from their regular work."[52] Claire Holden suggests that "In order to make the ensemble 'work' in limited rehearsal time, the solution is the development of a default style with which both groups can cope," adding that this "prioritises the elements which seem to matter most to conductors, audiences and critics, namely tight ensemble, good intonation and pleasing tone quality."[53] Of course, this raises some difficult questions concerning the nature of "authentic performance," as well as the issue of "synchronicity" in musical performance, and particularly in recordings—the area to which we now turn.

RECORDINGS

Positive, i.e., toward (A)	Negative, i.e., toward (B)
Extensive early music catalogue, industry awards, and so on.	"Early music sound" characterized by default synchronicity; no rough edges.

It is widely documented that the opportunity to make recordings presented a crucial lifeline for the early music movement (particularly in its infancy). A cursory glance through any compendium of classical music recordings reveals an extensive early music catalogue, to say nothing of a long list of industry accolades and awards.[54] As we have seen, recordings have proven hugely influential to performers and listeners alike. For many professional groups, the sale of LPs, later tapes and CDs, also provided essential income to keep them afloat.[55] Cultural sociologist Antoine Hennion goes as far as arguing that "the general recourse to once forgotten instruments owes much to the silence of its principal actual mediator: the disc. Only the extensive use of modern recording techniques has allowed Baroque music to speak out again."[56] Crucially, of course, recording technology offered Early Music a means of sidestepping the vexed question of how any given work might actually be "authentic" in terms of its performance setting and location. Many of HIP's instruments were not designed to be played in big spaces, or indeed concert halls of any description (yet often with success came the invitation to perform in large venues). The recording offered an expedient way round this particular problem—a proposition that was simply too good to be ignored. Surely, it is worth reflecting here that *none* of Early Music's leading performers ever refused to record on the basis of such a process being de facto *in*-authentic.

Whilst it seems that the "balance sheet of achievement" is firmly tipped to one side (in a positive direction), there is a more complex story to emerge here. We can draw on the biblical account of Esau's selling of his birthright to his twin brother Jacob as an insightful (however unlikely) allegorical tale from which to reflect further on Early Music's relationship with recordings:

> One day, Esau returned to his brother Jacob, being famished after a day in the fields. He begged his brother for some food that he was preparing. Jacob offered to give his brother a bowl of stew in exchange for his birthright (the right to be recognized as firstborn). Esau agreed. In so doing, his (transcendent) birthright is given away in respect of his (immanent) hunger. Later, when their father Isaac is dying, Jacob pretends to be Esau so that he can gain his father's blessing. Jacob covers his arm in the hide (for Esau was "a hairy man" and Jacob a "smooth man"). Upon Isaac's death, Jacob becomes the spiritual leader of the family and "the heir of the promises of Abraham."[57]

By analogy, Esau here represents Early Music's Authenticity$_1$—the rekindling of interest in unfamiliar Medieval and Renaissance music, associated with old instruments, pageants, rituals, dance, and oftentimes, outdoor events; the "hairy" rough-edged traditional (folk) world of a decidedly fallible and altogether human approach to music-making, caught on record. One thinks particularly of the tremendous energy and vitality that comes across in many of the recordings by Munrow's Early Music Consort of London, or Morrow's Musica Reservata, here with the unmistakable vocal sound of Jantina Noorman—described by one critic as "the Ethel Merman of early music." Such raw performances offered something distinctively new. It is fascinating in this respect to read Thurston Dart's advice to Michael Morrow on the occasion of his 1960 debut performance of Musica Reservata, written in a short letter: "Make the music sound robust now & then—so often one hears it as though everyone were wearing kidgloves."[58]

What, then, of Jacob—the smooth man? We can find him (taking his brother's place) in the guise of Authenticity$_2$, and the particular "smooth" sonority that became a feature of HIP recordings of both early vocal and orchestral music during the 1980s and '90s.[59] This smooth sound is epitomized in the voice of Dame Emma Kirkby, whose "pure" melismatic singing on the 1981 Gothic Voices recording of Hildegard of Bingen is even now considered a game-changer. It is also present in the ethereal voices of English vocal ensembles (The Tallis Scholars, The Sixteen, etc.), their floating (disembodied) quality owing much to the resonant acoustics of the chapels, churches, and cathedrals in which they record. But we can also point to a third type of "smooth" sound that typifies many orchestral and choral recordings of Baroque and Classical repertoire, where a clear, light, and synchronous approach suits the "rhetorical" style of the music, i.e., music that aims "to evoke and provoke emotions—the Affections, or Passions—that were shared by everyone, audience and performers alike."[60] Though it is invidious to pick upon just one example of such a widespread phenomenon, Christopher Hogwood's 1980 recording of Handel's *Messiah*, with the Academy of Ancient Music and the Choir of Christ Church Cathedral, Oxford (with Kirkby amongst the soloists) is a compelling example of what I have in mind here.

Just as Jacob's success came at Esau's expense, so it would seem that Authenticity$_1$ was destined to lose out to Authenticity$_2$. Over and above reasons already given, we can point to the recording process itself as being a key factor in this change. For it is in the very nature of recording that sounds get abstracted from their context, and "problems" (which, in HIP's case comprised "out of tune," "difficult to play," "strange-sounding" original instruments) get picked up and cleaned up, in order "to obtain a neat and tidy, easily assimilable product."[61] Thus begins an unstoppable journey to iron out rough edges. But it also has to be acknowledged that the sound and style of Authenticity$_2$ simply proved itself extraordinarily well-suited to the recording medium. As Kenyon puts it, "the glassy, transparent, rhythmic and exciting clarity of the period instruments perfectly suited the sound-world of the new CD."[62] Indeed, for many second-generation early musicians, it was precisely this bright, newly professionalized early music "sound" that captured their attention. The conductor Laurence Cummings, for example, remembers hearing Emma Kirkby with Simon Preston and the AAM at Christ Church in the early 1980s, and "being carried away by that sort of sound."[63]

There remains the big issue, of course, of whether Early Music (like Esau) ended up selling its "birthright" (understood here in terms of its commitment to authenticity) for the benefits that recordings could offer in the immediate term. Did this cultural movement "sell out" to the recording industry, or should we see it as remaining true to its transcendent ideal? These are questions taken up both in the next section and more extensively over the final two chapters.

AUTHENTICITY

Positive, i.e., toward (A)	Negative, i.e., toward (B)
HIP principles taken up by both period instrument and modern orchestras and ensembles.	"Authenticity" per se no longer considered a viable (or desirable) performance ideal.

On the plus side, there is no question that principles of historically informed performance have been taken up both by dedicated period instrument groups (as one would expect) and by modern orchestras and ensembles. Whether it is Roger Norrington's "pure tone" work with the Stuttgart Radio Symphony Orchestra,[64] Claudio Abbado's use of "original" instruments with his Orchestra Mozart, or the way in which Simon Rattle's regular engagements with the OAE rubs off on his performances with the Berlin Philharmonic Orchestra, HIP principles are now pretty much all-pervasive across the classical music profession.

Serious questions remain, however, as to just what such a level of acceptance actually entails. There is a difference between what people say about historically informed performance and what they do in practice. As Cohen notes, "Nowhere in the early music scene is the tug-of-war between the scientific and the intuitive more clearly delineated."[65] Indeed, "like politicians, early music practitioners often say one thing and do another; the ideology of the 'authentic' performance is constantly at odds with the concrete problems of making old music heard now." Speaking of contemporary viol players, Alison Crum points out that "even now, the great majority play Renaissance music on string types which they never had at that time, and yet they go on about their authentic instruments."[66] Writing in 2004, Clive Brown complained that "there is still, in most instances, a gaping chasm between the practice of those professional and amateur musicians who play on period instruments or sing, in a so-called period style, and the state of our knowledge about historical practices."[67] Recognizing that professional musicians "have to make compromises" on the basis of "earning a good living," he suggests that the best thing about the HIP movement is that it has "provided a powerful stimulus to make modern musicians reflect on the manner in which they perceive their musical heritage." This, of course, is something that Taruskin (1995) was very keen to see happen as a result of the "authenticity movement."

A further issue concerns the change in the early music discourse itself, and in particular a retreat away from the language of authenticity. For Hogwood the metamorphosis from "early music specialist" into "all-round musician" includes stopping "calling anything he does 'authentic.'"[68] The label "historically informed," or HIP, is considered "a good deal more relaxed." As I have begun to argue (in Chapter 3) and will take up again in the following chapters, this general position contains within it a characteristically postmodern response to the intellectual challenges of authenticity claims. The more "relaxed" position of HIP has much to commend it, if, that is, one is concerned about an overly dogmatic and militant tendency in the early music movement's "alternative" approach (a tendency that I suggest only ever had a fringe presence). However, it also appears as a dangerously relativist position that threatens to pull the rug from under its own feet. The paradoxical nature of this turn of events was highlighted by Kenyon in 2009 (quoting from Robert Philip's *Performing Music in the Age of Recording*), when he referred to the early music movement "rushing, as fast as its little messa di voce legs will take it, away from the idea that there was a single historical style,"[69] while "our most traditional musical institutions" are "wanting desperately to get up to speed with what is going on and to use the insights of the early music movement to rejuvenate themselves."

LEADERSHIP

Positive, i.e., toward (A)	*Negative, i.e., toward (B)*
Independence; professionalization of management and support.	Market-driven appetite for "big name" conductors and "star" soloists.

The story of the early music movement is also the story of individual early musicians, with those who founded period performance groups taking a prominent position (both literally and metaphorically) at the center of the stage. The setting up of the OAE has been discussed as a decisive shift away from the ego-dominated world of the maestro. As Roger Norrington memorably remarked, the OAE's appearance marked the "end of the era of the robber barons,"[70] including himself in this grouping. Musicians were escaping "the tyranny of conductors,"[71] as they wrenched back control of their own performance destinies. In fact, life without a key-man (and with only very few exceptions it has always been a man) at the top has not always proved easy. As the conductor Laurence Cummings has observed, "You can never have a truly democratic situation in music-making I think. Even in a string quartet you are going to have dominant players; you can't have four equally minded, dominant people."[72]

Artistic decisions are invariably influenced by commercial concerns. Concert goers and many performers, to say nothing of the nonmusicians (appointed for their business skills or their bank balance) who sit on orchestral boards, readily buy into the celebrity status of big-name conductors and soloists. There is a natural inclination, after all, to want to be seen working with "the best." So the decision to engage high-profile household names, can be readily defended on marketing and prestige grounds, regardless of how little (if any) experience they might have with period instruments and "historically faithful period style."[73] On occasion, no doubt, problems are exacerbated once the celebrity conductor is on the podium and actually working with the orchestra. Rather than being open to a generally shared dialogue, a melding of artistry between all players, there can be a tendency for conductors to consider their engagement as a sign that the orchestra wants them to deliver "their" interpretation.

In more recent years, leading groups such as the AAM and TEC have had to deal with the difficult reality of succession management, as their founding-directors stepped down from the podium through retirement or a desire for pastures new. Nicholas Kenyon has remarked on Christopher Hogwood's generosity in allowing others to develop the ensemble that he had nurtured so personally for so many years.[74] Succession is a notoriously difficult thing to manage for any small business[75] and it is clear that for many people, Hogwood has been synonymous with AAM, as much as Pinnock has been with TEC. Nevertheless, they do seem to have been able to move forward in what Kenyon describes as the ideal outcome, whereby "a great ensemble can re-invent itself."[76]

The behind-the-scenes management of early music groups has probably undergone as big a transformation as has happened on the platform. It is interesting to read through the Minutes of the AGM and Council meetings of Musica Reservata in the 1970s, for example, as this reveals a sometimes amateurish, even haphazard approach to management, which one imagines might have been more widespread during this period (and which was clearly a continuous source of stress to its founder). In 1973 Musica Reservata's financial advisor warned that it "may have to go into liquidation" on account of the money allocated to pay repeat fees for artists having been erroneously spent on "promotional tours."[77] There were calls to take the general manager to court. Altogether, there was a shortfall of £1,910 [circa £20,000 in today's money], which then led to several rounds of managerial appointments, as they fought to bring the situation under control. Similar such problems no doubt continue to befall management teams today (and not just for early musicians), but there is certainly a sense in which the administration and organization of early music has undergone its own process of professionalization over the years.

The case of early musicians taking on management roles within their own orchestras has not been infrequent (notably, Felix Warnock at TEC and later OAE, and Marshall Marcus at the OAE). This has had the benefit of seeing "insiders" involved on the management side of the organization. It is particularly striking to note how many who started off in the early music sector have gone on to head up classical music's leading institutions (e.g., Nicholas Kenyon at the BBC Proms and then Barbican; Marshall Marcus as head of music at the South Bank (2007); and David Pickard at Glyndebourne). There has also been movement in the other direction, with the Barbican Centre's classical music programmer Gijs Elsen, for example, taking over as chief executive of The English Concert in 2011. It is hard to imagine any clearer evidence of the now taken-for-granted legitimacy of Early Music within the classical music profession.

INTEGRATION

Positive, i.e., toward (A)	Negative, i.e., toward (B)
Knowledgeable global audiences; great access to instruments, editions, players.	Increasing separation of amateurs and professionals (and performers and instrument-makers).

The final theme on this balance sheet of Early Music's achievements concerns the extent to which it has managed to widen its appeal across as broad a set of people (performers and audience) as possible. In the late 1960s and early 1970s the movement clearly enabled a narrowing of the gap between amateurs and professionals—and this was one of its main attractions at the time. Enthusiastic amateurs could feel "on a par" with the professional performers, as they all did battle together with the technical demands of old and unfamiliar instruments, approaching historical musicology on a more or less equal footing. However, this rapprochement did not last long. By the end of the 1970s Authenticity$_1$ had all but given way to Authenticity$_2$, and early music was becoming much more of a specialist pursuit for highly trained early musicians. By 1992 Andrew Pinnock was commenting that it was a shame that summer schools and courses for amateurs were hardly mentioned under the context of early music "education," especially since "these gatherings do as much as anything to keep up the level of enthusiasm among early music's most devoted followers."[78] By 2009 the National Early Music Association was reporting on the "growing scarcity of young amateurs," whilst noting that "The professional scene is almost too healthy, with numerous professionals and groups competing for audiences and delivering many generally high quality concerts, broadcasts, recordings, summer schools and workshops."[79] As Alison Crum observes, "most viol and recorder players are 50 upwards, and there is a really big worry about who is going to carry on."[80] There are "No 'stars' like David Munrow to capture [the] imagination of [the] general public."[81] It would seem that the divide between amateur and professional has been pushed back to a level equal to or perhaps even wider than it had been when Morrow and Munrow were selling out the South Bank back in the late 1960s.

And yet it would be misleading to paint an overly gloomy picture for the amateur early musician. The 2009 Early Music Register listed more than 200 groups active in the UK, as compared with about 40 UK groups in 1972 (the second Early Music Register, edited by Christopher Monk and Eric Hedger).[82] By 2012 the Register included details of over 1,400 "practitioners of early music," 10 regional early music fora, 40 early music societies, more than 300 instrument-makers, 144 publishers, and 144 record companies focusing their activities on Early Music.[83] We have witnessed a huge improvement in the availability of musical editions, parts, books, and original and reproduction "old" instruments over the last 40 years or so. The success of the Greenwich International Early Music Festival (now in its twelfth year at that venue), incorporating extensive exhibition of instruments, sheet music, facsimiles, and all things early music, is a testament to this burgeoning contemporary interest from a wide range of individuals. As the festival's title suggests, such interest goes well beyond London, or indeed the British Isles. Whilst continental European (and especially German) instrument-makers were trailblazers well before the British got involved, their continuing presence at the festival has been swollen by producers and makers from the rest of the world. Today, Early Music is very much an international phenomenon, and there are strong currents of interest as far afield as Japan (e.g., Masaaki Suzuki's Bach Collegium Japan) and South America (e.g., the Chilean group Les Carillons; the Bolivian Coro y Orquesta Arakaendar, and Ensemble Barroco Chiquitano; the Argentine group La Barroca del Suquia; or Grupo Banza from Brazil).

THE EXTENT OF MAINSTREAMING—ON BALANCE?

Writing about the pop arts in Britain (1970), George Melly talked evocatively about "the decay of revolt into style," referring to those exciting years in music, fashion, film, and art, in which "everything changed." The question we return to at the end of this chapter is whether the revolutionary spirit of Early Music has "decayed" into little more than an appropriated style that now belongs to the classical music field, or whether in fact it has managed to retain any of its revolutionary zeal, albeit in a grown up professionalized form? The answer, it seems, is a bit of both. For many of Early Music's pioneers themselves, the journey is far from over. Sir John Eliot Gardiner comments: "I think there is a vast amount of pioneering work, research and experimentation still to be done...you cannot just sit back on your hunkers and think 'Es ist vollbracht!'"[84] Reading through the 34 essays that mark *Early Music*'s 40th anniversary edition in 2013, it seems that this is a view widely shared.[85] In Archer's terms, Early Music has undergone ideational unification involving movement on both sides, i.e., the second of her three paths—symmetrical syncretism. There have been winners and losers. There has been a good deal of compromise from all involved. The productive nature of this compromise is revealed in more depth in the next chapter, as the spotlight shifts from the early music movement to the early music performer, and then most tellingly, to our distinctive human capacity to live with authenticity.

> We are a Faustian age determined to meet the Lord or the Devil before we are done, and the ineluctable ore of the authentic is our only key to the lock.
>
> NORMAN MAILER[1]

> And above all, watch with glittering eyes the whole world around you because the greatest secrets are always hidden in the most unlikely places. Those who don't believe in magic will never find it.
>
> ROALD DAHL[2]

11

The Ineluctable Ore of the Authentic

INTRODUCTION

My purpose in this penultimate chapter is to commence a constructive reengagement with the concept of authenticity (a notion that has lost much of its appeal in these modern times, including, as I have suggested, within Early Music). In order to develop my argument, I shall have cause to engage with two even more unfashionable terms: enchantment and magic. Already, some readers will be feeling uneasy. Fairy tales and wizard adventures the likes of *The Lord of the Rings* and *Harry Potter* are written largely with children in mind. We feel uncomfortable using the "m" word. So before going on, two reassuring points need to be made. Firstly, in referring to enchantment and magic, I am not talking here about wizards, witches, the supernatural, paranormal, or the occult. This is territory well beyond my experience, and indeed interest. But secondly, nor am I using the discourse of magic and enchantment simply as a rhetorical device to weave a compelling narrative (magic, after all, is fun). Rather, my objective is to engage with the serious methodological approach of immanent critique.[3] My focus in this respect is on the distinctive context of "making early music *in the modern age*,"[4] for which I turn once again to the words of Max Weber:[5]

> The fate of our times is characterized by rationalization and intellectualization, and, above all, by the "disenchantment of the world." Precisely the ultimate and most sublime values have retreated from public life either into the transcendental realm of mystic life or into the brotherliness of direct and personal human relations.

According to this perspective, meaning and value are not so much qualities intrinsic to the world, but are constructed through heroic acts of human intellect. Human beings are no longer subject to mysterious forces, spirits, magic or the Gods,[6] but are firmly in charge. Behind this concept of disenchantment lies the inexorable rise of scientific knowledge and the power of logic as our primary means of understanding the world, and then of controlling it. The direct connection with the critique of Early Music, with its supposed reliance on "musical science" (historical musicological scholarship) over and above the performer's intuitive and transcendental "musical instinct" (musicianship) is striking.

As much as disenchantment points toward the rise of rational thought, manifest in the increasingly dominant role played by (social) science and technology in modern society, it is also intimately linked with the other key societal development that characterizes Weber's conception of the modern age, namely capitalism. The economic system of capitalism can best be thought of as "a process in which money is perpetually sent in search of more money."[7] The dominant form of capitalism since the mid-18th century has been that of the industrial capitalist. This *homo economicus* is motivated by a rational approach to wealth creation based on utility maximization. Through combining the requisite amount of labor power and means of production, he is able to produce commodities, which can be sold in the market for a profit. For Weber the nature of this work required what he called a "capitalist spirit," or the rational pursuit of economic gain and the rationalization of production, maximizing efficiency and productivity. Weber's capitalist spirit originated in the Protestant religion, and its distinctive work ethic. Disenchantment, according to Weber at least, is suggestive of a move away from a primarily spiritual (religious) context.

Over a century of modernity (and two world wars) later, Weber's words have lost little of their impact. The Enlightenment and associated philosophies of scientific explanation remain very much in the ascendant. Indeed, I find myself writing this on the morning after the opening ceremony of the 2012 London Paralympics, which took "The Enlightenment" as its theme. Of course, the huge advances in science and technology that we have seen over the last couple of centuries are to be celebrated. The motto "be curious" that was blazoned all over the athletic stadium's big screens is surely one with which we can wholeheartedly agree. In saying this, however, it is interesting that *understanding* humanity remains the preferred emancipatory goal, rather than *being* humanity. We will see that living with "real" authenticity is very much about managing the relationship between these two goals on an everyday basis.

To its detractors, Early Music bears all the hallmarks of a project born out of disenchantment. Here were classical musicians (i.e., those individuals that society designates "artists" on account of their autonomous skills and practice) apparently being told *how* they should perform old music on the basis of rational knowledge claims rather than musical intuition. It is hardly surprising that such a prescriptive position stirred up strong feelings. For Raymond Leppard, a staunch critic of the early music movement (though contiguously someone whose own work influenced others to examine music's scoring), scholarly fact was being used to trump musicality. "Just because you've got an authentic text doesn't mean you are going to give a good performance—and unless music is performed, it isn't anything!"[8] Describing authenticity as "the most magic of all the magic words," he goes on: "When the inhibitions and restrictions of false authenticity are felt; or even the self-indulgence of undisciplined compromise, then the wrong road has been taken."[9] Could it be that Early Music had indeed taken the wrong road? Was Early Music, in fact, nothing less than a modernist project born of an increasingly disenchanted and overly rational worldview? Is this Leppard's critique coming home to roost?

I don't believe so. Early musicians are still *musicians*, after all. In over a decade of researching the early music movement (to say nothing of my 25 years' involvement in performing early music) I have never met a musician who either professes to put knowledge and scholarship above musicality, or indeed whose music-making indicated that this was what they were intentionally doing (even if reviewers and critics have exhorted us to believe otherwise).[10] The relationship between modernity and cultural production is more complex than any simple dualism can convey. To give an intriguing angle on this, we can turn to someone with both a practical and scholarly interest in the practice of musical performance—the tenor Ian Bostridge. Bostridge is much respected as a professional musician, performer, and interpreter of songs, lieder, oratorio, and operatic roles. Coincidentally, he also has a doctorate on the subject of 17th-century witchcraft. He suggests that after rationalist materialism drove witchcraft off the map, music remained the magic realm where people could still encounter the ineffable. This, as will become clear, is a viewpoint with which I have a good deal of sympathy, even if we continue to encounter the ineffable in many (artistic) contexts, not just in music. Bostridge asks, "what place can there be for the ineffable in a world defined by an iron cage of rationality?"[11] This is a profoundly important question—and one I take up further now.

DISSING ENCHANTMENT

Whilst there has been a general acceptance of *dis*-enchantment by sociologists and critics of modernity, especially amongst those associated with Adorno and the Frankfurt School, it is much harder to find those who have ventured to ask, let alone explain, what *enchantment* actually entails. Over and above Weber's own writings with their particular religious connotations, it is taken more or less for granted that enchantment is a hang-over of now-outmoded (pre-modern) views about the world, which we have no need to take seriously. It is easy to see why this state of affairs has arisen. For one thing, prejudicial opinions about many of the contexts in which enchantment is supposed to exist—wizardry; animism; religion; spirituality; Eastern philosophy; meditation; and, of course, art—give it a bad name. We have all encountered this sort of "dissing" of enchantment in one place or another. It is particularly endemic in the very locations where (rational) knowledge production is most prized—our education system and especially universities. As we saw in Chapter 7, higher education is characterized by an alarmingly disenchanted approach to knowledge production, increasingly geared as it is toward preparing young people for employment, i.e., where their utility will be maximized in an industrial context.

Philosophy has had next to no interest in enchantment, since it falls under the category of the "nonrational." To some extent, any critical (i.e., rational) engagement with enchantment threatens to explain away the very thing we seek to understand. Applying a rational logic to the ineffable, which I readily admit is what I am doing in this book, throws up a paradox whereby my best efforts might be construed as little more than disenchanting enchantment. However, in my defense (a defense that could also be made of the early music movement), we can, and do, enchant the world through all forms of knowledge production. Indeed, there is plenty of evidence to suggest that the more we know about the world (or, indeed, early music) the more enchanted it can become. We should not be deterred from following Douglas Adams's suggestion, therefore, and "think the unthinkable... do the undoable... prepare to grapple with the ineffable itself, and see if we may not eff it after all."[12]

Very much in this spirit (and motivated by an interest in discovering what it is that so powerfully drew a generation of performer musicians away from the mainstream), I address the question—what *is* enchantment? It is helpful to distinguish between an experience of enchantment and the nature of enchantment itself (to the extent they are analytically separable, at least). Enchantment entails a state or mood, but it results from an (authentic) experience of life that defies simple explanation. For those whose starting point is the cause of enchantment, there is general agreement that it has its foundation in "truth." Tymieniecka,[13] for example, states that "Enchantment is above all the elevation of heart and mind toward the enigma of truth, truth beyond empirical and mental cognition, truth as the very meaning of reality, truth that fulfills our hearts' longings and expectations." It is surely this very "enigma of truth" that motivated many of Early Music's pioneers, as they sought to find the "true" musical work in and through their own performances.

For Patrick Curry, enchantment is a quintessentially human experience, concerning the interconnected nature of life "and a reminder of its truth"—a truth that is generally overlooked by the modernists. He writes, "In life as it is actually lived, we are embodied, embedded, and utterly interdependent beings, not only with each other but many, many nonhuman others... we are everything the modernists want to forget, destroy or 'transcend.' Strictly speaking, therefore, the contrary condition of modernity is not pre-, post-, counter-, or even non-modernity. It is humanity."[14] One of the pioneers of Early Music, Nikolaus Harnoncourt, has put forward a compelling personal take on this link between enchantment and humanity:[15]

> We as musicians—and indeed all artists—have to administer a powerful, a holy language. We have to do everything in our power to keep it from getting lost in the maelstrom of materialism. There is not much time left, if it is not already too late, because the exclusive focus on thought and the language of reason, of logic, and the fascination we experience with the progress in science and our civilisation, increasingly alienate us from the essence of human life. It is probably no coincidence that this alienation goes hand in hand with the obliteration of religiousness: Technocracy, materialism and prosperity do not need religion; they

don't know religion, not even morality. Art is not a nice extra—it is the umbilical cord which connects us to the Divine, it guarantees our being human.[16]

Harnoncourt acknowledges music's potential both to express and give rise to a connection with the world around us—a world that we cannot "know" in its entirety. For John Eliot Gardiner the capacity of music to enchant is a "gift": "You don't have to be Christian, Buddhist or Muslim to possess or transmit it; but you do need to have a deep awareness of music's capacity to enchant, and to lift people out of their quotidian struggles, their drudgery, or, if they are bereaved, out of their grief…and therefore, it is an incredible gift, one that has to be cherished, and it needs singleness of mind to realize its potential. It needs devotion and understanding on the part of everybody involved in the process—obviously the musicians you work with, but also staff, patrons, concert promoters and agents, and record company executives (as long as they are around) and not forgetting audiences."[17] For others, enchantment is first and foremost something that we experience. Jane Bennett notes, "enchantment entails a state of wonder, and one of the distinctions of this state is the temporary suspension of chronological time and bodily movement."[18] To be enchanted is to "be transfixed, spellbound." This, of course, is a state very often associated with a child's reading of a fairy-tale, and it comes close to the dictionary definition of "a feeling of great pleasure; delight—such as when we talk of 'the enchantment of the mountains'; or the state of being under a spell; magic: a world of mystery and enchantment."[19] Bennett refers to enchantment as a "mood" involving "a surprising encounter"; "a mood of fullness, plenitude, or liveliness, a sense of having had one's nerves or circulation or concentration powers turned up or recharged—a shot in the arm, a fleeting return to childlike excitement about life."[20] We can all identify with this mood—whether in the context of early music or something quite other.

There is a connection here to the idea of peak experience or "flow" which Mihaly Csikszentmihalyi has studied for many years (see especially his books on *Creativity* (1996) and *Flow* (2002)). Enchantment is associated with this sense of immersion in a feeling of energized focus, but it is not the same as flow; rather, it involves a heightened awareness of meaning and value, and the self's relational nature, albeit present often in the flow state. Furthermore, enchantment is not the same as remembering something wonderful or desiring something wonderful to happen in the future (though, of course, this might be enchantment). This is effectively a form of daydreaming, and it is like entertainment—a form of distraction from the present. The modern world offers us various solutions to boredom (a state whereby we have lost any meaning or value in the world). We can think of "art" as escaping *into* the present; being taken out of the rigors of daily life and into the "here and now"; understood as an inherently meaningful and valuable (enchanted) presence. The author and poet Thich Nhat Hanh, for example, suggests that the substance of art is complete awareness. "Entertainment," on the other hand, involves escaping *from* the present, i.e., a distraction away from the mundane reality of life but without (necessarily) any heightened awareness of its inherent meaning and value (enchantment). It does not (necessarily) follow that one is "better" than another, nor that any concrete example (such as a performance of early music) will be *either* one *or* the other. The value of art and entertainment can only be determined as a function of context. A great deal of "old" music was written specifically to entertain and divert rather than to enlighten, and, of course, this still very much has its place, too.

A third approach to explaining enchantment emphasizes the ambiguous nature of the relationship between enchantment's cause(s) and effect(s). As Jenkins states, "Enchantment conjures up, and is rooted in, understandings and experiences of the world in which there is more to life than the material, the visible or the explainable; in which the philosophies and principles of Reason or rationality cannot by definition dream of the totality of life."[21] Although it appears easy to dismiss Early Music's quest for authenticity as misguided dogma (see Chapter 3), the vast majority of early musicians were surely motivated by just this enchanted view of the world—a world of "other" possibilities. Jenkins goes on to say that the everyday "norms and routines of linear time and space are only part of the story." Importantly, he suggests that "the collective sum of sociability and belonging is elusively greater than its individual parts." This final observation draws attention to the characteristically *social* and *emergent* nature of enchantment. Firstly, enchantment is a participatory and social experience, such that even when we are on our own in a beautiful place or absorbed in a work of art, our awareness of enchantment is nonetheless a form of "relational consciousness"—with ourselves, with others, with the aesthetic, or with "the other" (i.e., God, the divine, the universe, or other (nonreligious) aspects of our larger context of existence).[22] Secondly, enchantment as a whole is greater than the sum of the parts. We can attempt to explain the parts—and we do this drawing on the tools of rational thought and logic at our disposal. However, the emergent whole, the totality of life, extends beyond the reach of our rational thought. This is important because enchantment refers to the part of life (as a totality) that is beyond reason. Indeed, one could say that enchantment is a consequence of our inability to *know* reality fully.[23] Our knowledge of the world is not the same thing as the world itself. Enchantment is therefore an emergent property of life, which, in turn, is both meaningful and valuable.

There are, of course, many implications arising from this core philosophical perspective, which take us well beyond the domain of early music. A little closer to home, it can help us to reevaluate Simon Frith's observation that classical music offers "a transcendent experience that is, on the one hand, ineffable and uplifting but, on the other, only available to those with the right sort of knowledge."[24] Adopting the emergentist view, the "transcendent experience" (enchantment) can be seen as an emergent property, dependent upon, *but not reducible,* to knowledge. So whilst Frith's observation stands as a generality (clearly the language of classical music is a barrier to many), it does not have to be accepted as a universal given (as I discuss further in the final chapter). Moreover, we can now make an important distinction between enchantment and magic. For whilst our experience of "enchantment" (on hearing an unfamiliar piece of music, or seeing a painting for the first time) can be enhanced by knowledge (such as details of its composition, technique, history, etc.), we find that "magic" (and its corollary, religion, understood in its traditional sense) is generally enhanced by a *lack* of knowledge (the unknown, unknowable, etc.).

According to what I have just described, both enchantment and magic are far from being peripheral or vestigial properties of human beings in the modern age. They are absolutely central to who we are, and have a bearing in all areas of our life—even those that modernity characterizes as alienating, such as the market. Furthermore, enchantment, in particular, is a characteristically human experience that we actively seek. Since enchantment is more likely to be present under some conditions than others, we can (and we do) foster experiences of it. One such natural home for enchantment is the arts—for it is here that we allow ourselves to imagine, to ask questions of "what if?" and, in turn, to explore life's meaning and value (implicitly, at least).

At a more general level, a life without enchantment (a disenchanted life) is surely not one anyone would want to (or perhaps even could) live. This brings us back to the Weberian conception of modernity and challenges us now to ask how we might square this view of enchantment (on a practical as well as theoretical level) with the inherently alienating world of capitalism that dominates so many of our practices and plans, including the performance of early music?

MONEY, MAGGIE, AND MAGIC

Whether we like it or not (and many people say they don't, but feel powerless to do anything about it), the forces of capitalism wield an extraordinarily pervasive power over what we do. This extends to all aspects of our music-making. For example, previously in the book I drew attention to the fact that Early Music's pioneers founded groups that were constituted as legal entities, of which they were the "owners." Private ownership constitutes one of the major cornerstones of capitalism. The separation between capital and labor—commented on in earlier chapters—represents another such cornerstone. The fact that capitalists (whether ensemble founder-directors, record company executives, venue managers, promoters, agents, or instrument-makers) employ others to work for them for wages, is often overlooked; and yet it is clearly central to any full understanding we might acquire of the competing motivations and demands that lie behind making Early Music in the modern age.

The writer and historian Hilaire Belloc, famous for his cautionary tales, warned of the problems of capitalism when stating that "wealth obtained indirectly as profit out of other men's work, or by process of exchange, becomes a thing abstracted from the process of production. As the interest of a man in things diminishes, his interest in abstract wealth—money—increases."[25] For the likes of Marx, Hegel, and later, Adorno and his colleagues at the Frankfurt School, this is the source of "alienation" that so characterizes the modern world. Coupled with the capital/labor divide it gives rise to an asymmetrical power relationship that perpetuates division, inequality, exploitation, and injustice. But Belloc's cautionary tale also turns our attention to the "marvelous specificity"[26] of "things" as a potential source of enchantment and, by implication, the illusory (i.e., "magical") lure of finding enchantment in abstract wealth (money).[27] Although history has yet to cast its final definitive judgment on Marx's belief that capitalism carries the seed of its own destruction (the collapse of actually existing "socialism" notwithstanding), we have more than enough evidence of the instability of capitalism, run through as it is with theory-practice inconsistencies. These inconsistencies come about as a result of the process of money being sent in search of yet more money. Crucially, they also represent a deeply embedded challenge to our authenticity.

One of the most discussed of these theory–practice inconsistencies concerns the view that "there is no alternative"—to the free market, free trade, and economic liberalism. The Conservative Prime Minister Margaret (Maggie) Thatcher used this phrase so often that one of her Cabinet ministers nicknamed her "Tina." In fact, the acronym TINA *There Is No Alternative* had been used by a range of philosophers and sociologists (Freud, Marx, and Derrida amongst them) well before Britain's Iron Lady. "A TINA formation in its simplest form just specifies any complex totality in which a false structure or level or belief co-exists with a true one."[28] For Alan Norrie, "Tina means trouble."[29] We will find a TINA formation wherever there is a split between our theory and practice, or more proverbially between our "talk and our walk." As we shall see, TINA formations are a particularly pervasive feature of capitalism, and it should come as no real surprise that they are to be found in the context of Early Music, just as they are across cultural production in general. Adorno's writing on "the jargon of authenticity," for example, was premised on what he saw as the mismatch between what existentialists such as Martin Heidegger said about "authenticity" as a source of freedom, and the fundamental lack of freedom, which the capitalist context allowed. Elsewhere, his critique of jazz as a commodified cultural form was based on the premise that "what appears as spontaneity is in fact carefully planned out in advance with machinelike precision."[30]

Having put forward the broad assertion that people are driven to behave *in*-authentically on account of their false beliefs, and that this impacts (early) music-making as much as the wider affairs of capitalistic production, we now need to return once more to the subject of "magic." For capitalism is as dependent upon the particular skills and practices of the "magician" as it is upon the "rational man." The dictionary explains that magic is the power of apparently influencing events by using mysterious or supernatural forces. However, it also tells us that the magician is a performer of illusions and conjuring tricks. As any conjurer will know, such tricks have their effect on the audience not so much through the application of "mysterious or supernatural forces," but by the following-through of practiced, planned, and most importantly, *rational* behaviors. Here it seems that the distinction already alluded to between magic and enchantment is crucially important. For the author J. R. R. Tolkien, whereas "Enchantment...in its purity...is artistic in desire and purpose," "Magic produces, or pretends to produce...it is not an art but a technique; its desire is power in this world, domination of things and wills."[31] Aleister Crowley describes magic as "the art of bringing about changes in conformity with will."[32] Whilst it is clearly the case that the term "magic" embraces a wide range of phenomena, from the wholly mysterious to the purposefully concealing, the consistent theme to arise here is that magic involves practices of *power,* albeit power of a particular kind.

Power is central to capitalism, as it is to art. But the primary form it takes in each case, I suggest, is quite different. To account for the difference, it is helpful to draw on Bhaskar's[33] conceptualization of power$_1$ and power$_2$. Power$_1$ refers to "the general causal powers of human agency whose characteristics entail the possibility of human emancipation."[34] This includes our capacity to "investigate, communicate, plan, construct moral and ethical systems, feel and care for others, and come to agreement based on judgementally rational argument." Power$_2$, on the other hand, refers to "negative characteristics such as domination, subjugation, exploitation and control that can be identified in given social structures." At stake, therefore, is a conception of power firstly as "power *to,*" and secondly, "power *over.*" To some extent at least, art and capitalism involve a mix of both types of power, but we can readily see that power$_1$ is the basis of art, whereas power$_2$ (the master-slave relation, as Marx referred to it) is the basis of capitalism. Furthermore, the power of the magician wielding his magic wand in front of a confounded audience is very much of the "power over" (power$_2$) variety. Capitalism and magic (which, of course, remains mysterious to all but the magician) have much more in common than we might think.

It is here that the distinctiveness of making early music *in the modern age* (under the dominant capitalist mode of production) should start to become clear. For whilst early musicians have been pursuing an artistic "enchanting" agenda motivated by the desire to perform classical music in an alternative uplifting and ultimately transformational way (drawing on the principle of dispositional (historical) authenticity in the process), they have also had to perform the "magical" act of turning art into commercial activity, jobs, employment, and personal wealth. Doing this has required a mix of power$_1$ and power$_2$ relations. These, in turn, have given rise to a set of TINA formations that account for many of the contradictions, compromises, and apparent inauthenticity discussed in earlier chapters. We can now look again at some of these, in this fresh light.

AMATEURS VS. PROFESSIONALS

Weber's conception of the modern world suggested that enchantment had not been done away with altogether, but rather had retreated into the "brotherliness of direct and personal human relations." Such a phrase is telling in the context of Early Music, where amateur music-making has played such a central role. We have seen how Authenticity$_1$ (entailing an interest in Medieval, Renaissance, and early Baroque music) was founded on the strong amateur interest in performing, researching, and making instruments. Such interest found its natural place in the home, with amateurs coming together to play through consort music, discuss research, or enjoy the pleasures of constructing a new instrument kit, in surroundings wholly conducive of fostering "direct and personal human relations." Whilst it would be wrong to suggest that the world of the amateur musician has been immune from the influence of capitalism (one only need think of the requirement to purchase music, recordings, instruments, etc.), the extent of its reach is certainly limited when compared with the context of the professional.

There is no doubt that the early music revival owes much of its initial success to its ability to better embrace the amateur musician. (As discussed in Chapters 4 and 5, by the early 1970s the field of professional classical music had become largely separated from that of the amateur enthusiast.) However, this very success necessitated the gradual professionalization of Early Music—and with it, the estrangement of the amateur once more. This constitutes our first TINA formation. Early Music's increasingly specialist and professionalized approach to performance (notably in respect of Authenticity$_2$) becomes ever more difficult to square with the underlying democratic and embracing principles that set it on the road in the first place.

A second TINA formation around the relationship between work and play can be highlighted. On the one hand, (cultural) work depends upon play. This is particularly evident in the context of the arts, where the job of the artist is not readily confined to the hours between 9am and 5pm.[35] Professional early musicians typically devoted many hours of their "free time" to learning old instruments and researching performance techniques. They were not paid for this, but their waged labor very much depended on this kind of "nonwork" activity (of course, all wage labor is dependent upon (often unacknowledged) domestic support, and it is referred to as a "quasi-commodity" for this reason). On the other hand, the increasing professionalization of Early Music demanded the "work" of early musicians be taken seriously; those involved could not be seen anymore to be just "playing" at it. The lingering view of the enthusiastic amateur dabbling with old music was one that had to be done away with in order to stand any chance of commercial success.

THE REVOLUTIONARY LURE OF TECHNOLOGY

As we have seen, the opportunity to broadcast and produce recordings has been an absolutely central determinant in Early Music's success. If not the "primary mediator" (unlike Hennion (1997), I argue the performer should take this credit), the record or disc nonetheless offered a means of diffusing early music to a much larger audience than would otherwise have been possible.[36] To explain the conflicting forces at work, and a number of further TINA formations that arise in this context, it is helpful to highlight capitalism's underlying interest in technology. As Marx and Engels famously wrote in *The Communist Manifesto*, "the bourgeoisie cannot exist without constantly revolutionizing the instruments of production [c.f., the gradual modernization of *musical* instruments], and thereby the relations of production, and with them the whole relations of society."[37] A bunch of amateurs getting together to perform pieces from "the music of the crusades," very much inspired by their hearing Munrow's 1970 recording with the Early Music Consort, might seem far removed from such world-changing counter-cultural ideals; but as Daniel Barenboim reminds us "Everything is connected."[38] Indeed, the technological advances of the LP, and later the

CD in particular, have had a marked impact on the success (and timing) of the Early Music project. In recognizing capitalism's "fetishization" of technology—as a means of fixing any potential problem or crisis—we can better understand the source of that relentless pressure to adopt new technology, including new musical recording formats. As Harvey notes, "Machines cannot produce profits by themselves. But those capitalists with superior technologies and organisational forms typically gain a higher rate of profit than their competitors and eventually drive them out of business."[39] The development of the CD and the novel appearance of young, affordable, professional early musicians, it seems, were made for each other.

At least three TINA formations emanate from this relationship between technology and capitalism's insatiable desire for accumulation. First, there is the widely noted observation (explored in the previous chapter) that the authentic performance movement's success was only possible because of its reliance upon that most in-authentic of practices—recording. As Early Music's critics have enjoyed pointing out, there is nothing more inauthentic than recording, both in terms of the process involved for its performers (filling an otherwise empty performance space with microphones, screens, and other recording paraphernalia, or the editing of numerous performances (takes) into a "unified" whole), and the product that results for the consumer (the packaged and commoditized recording). Second, attention has been drawn to the rise of synchronicity (the need to get tuning, timing, and ensemble all perfectly in order) as a distinctive feature of early music recordings over the years. On the one hand, it was the "rough edges" of early music that were integral in attracting an audience in the first place (making the "familiar unfamiliar").[40] On the other hand, the process of commercialization effectively rubbed off these rough edges to leave a smooth-sounding "professional" product that could be enjoyed by more and more people. Third, as much as the involvement of the record companies was vital in enabling a dramatically expanded repertoire to be heard, it was also this very success that in turn led to the increasing prevalence of commercially motivated repertoire choices being made, seeing the popular (e.g., Vivaldi's *The Four Seasons*; Handel's *Music for the Royal Fireworks*; Pachelbel's *Canon*) win out over the unusual.

The relationship between live and recorded music continues to evolve.[41] It is interesting to note, for example, that across the music industry as a whole, it is live performances, and associated merchandising (much less prevalent in the classical music sector)—not recordings—that represent the main money earner. It is tempting here to invoke Walter Benjamin's famous argument about the "aura" of works of art (though he was not writing about music *per se*)[42] and the idea that something is lost from the original through the act of reproduction. Clearly there are parallels with the nature of enchantment as an emergent property of our relationship with things, though we should be careful not to imply that a recording is in some way incapable of enchanting.

Taking this point a little further, it might be argued that we tend to listen to (especially familiar) recordings in a different way to live performances. Part of the reason for this, of course, is that technology enables us to enjoy music whenever (and wherever) we want. Recordings often induce moods, perhaps of nostalgia, or remind us of a particular association with something or somebody; we put them on whilst we are in a certain mood, so as to intensify and sustain it, often allowing us to reflect on something and/or call it up in our memory. Live performance, on the other hand, bucks the technological trend, requiring us to be in a particular place at a particular time (regardless of our mood). This, one might suggest, can lead to a different experience in a live concert, where enchantment generally grabs us unawares.

BETWEEN MAGIC AND ENCHANTMENT

The "culture vs. commerce" debate can be (re)cast in terms of managing the distinction between magic and enchantment. Here, too, three TINA formations can be highlighted. The first and most acute of these theory–practice inconsistencies reveals itself in the daunting task facing cultural entrepreneurs (literally those who "take" (*prendre*) "between" (*entre*)) as they seek to bridge their own demands and those of their fellow musicians with the requirements of hard-nosed business. "Walking the talk" in this situation demands *both* magic and enchantment. Cultural entrepreneurs must give the impression that they know what the commercial outcome of their collective decision-making will be; but, of course, they don't. "Success" in market terms is only measurable after the event (once the concert has sold out, or recording sales meet or surpass expectations). Tolerating the inevitable risk and uncertainty of this "between space" is done not so much by a strategy of "muddling through," but rather as the result of many hours of practice, on the job experience, and rational calculation, very much as is the case, of course, for the (illusory) magic of the magician. The cultural entrepreneur's main job is to persuade others to go along with his ideas.[43] To do this, magicians must "enchant" others, which as Kimmel reminds us, includes amongst other things, a capacity "to bewitch, enthrall, mesmerize, captivate, enslave, fascinate, transport, enrapture, charm, enamor, hex, and beguile."[44] The very real challenge for the cultural entrepreneur, however, is that they must do this without losing their own sense of enchantment in the music itself. This, as we shall see shortly, also gets to the heart of why "authenticity" as a recurring leitmotiv of this study obstinately refuses to give up its significance.

Following on from the above, the second TINA formation concerns the early music movement's demonstrable reliance on charismatic individuals to lead its orchestras, ensembles, choirs, and consorts, despite an ideological commitment to a more democratic and collective approach to music-making. One of the reasons for this is surely the need for the cultural entrepreneur to wield his magic over others (especially audiences, promoters, festival organizers, and record companies). Early Music repudiated the "master-slave" relationship of the maestro and orchestra, but this has actually been the model it has reverted to—and which has seen it achieve success. Even the Orchestra of the Age of Enlightenment continues to market itself under the direction of an elite group of "Principal Artists." The lure of the star conductor or soloist has as much to do with our love of magic (being astounded by the capacity of an individual to perform the impossible) as it does with genuine enchantment.

The third area where there is theory-practice inconsistency concerns the early music movement's reliance on something new (so-called "creative destruction"[45]) in order to preserve the old. Early musicians have consistently relied on their musical and musicological creativity in "preserving" and "restoring" old musical works. Whilst for the purists such "making it up" is clearly inadmissible, from a market perspective "being creative" is fully justified as a necessary response to a competitive field. The only other available competitive strategy is to compete on costs. It could be argued that just as the capitalist system leads to an accumulation of *profits* in the hands of some individuals; *credit* in the hands of many nation states and individuals (a situation that we only belatedly are struggling to come to terms with); it has also led to an accumulation of *innovation*. The market craves novelty and difference, and this, albeit paradoxically, has underpinned the insatiable commercial interest in old music over the years, as well as a "new" approach to performing it.

REVISITING EARLY MUSIC'S COMING OF AGE

As I have suggested, it was the launch of the Orchestra of the Age of Enlightenment (OAE) in 1986 that signaled Early Music's coming of age. In the light of this chapter's discussions, however, there are strong grounds for rethinking this position. Rather than explaining the OAE in terms of a mature response to the classical music status quo, it could be argued that in fact it was a classic story of labor unrest under capitalism. Despite other signs of professionalization in the mid-1980s, there remained limited expansion of the early musician labor force. As we saw in Chapter 10, the music colleges had been relatively slow to get behind Early Music, with the consequence that the pool of professional players available remained small in number. An essential ingredient in capitalism is having what Marx referred to as "an industrial reserve army," a set of people who are "accessible, socialised, disciplined and of the requisite qualities (i.e., flexible, docile, manipulable and skilled when necessary)."[46] It is important for employers that there is such a "reserve" workforce standing by, lest labor get too powerful. The fact of the matter is that such a reserve army just wasn't yet there by the mid-1980s. The launch of OAE was organized by a highly powerful group of early music performers, who, in turn, presented Early Music's "robber barons" with a very real problem.

For all the rebelliousness of the OAE and its players, however, it could not have become so successful so quickly without the support of the musical establishment. As was discussed in Chapter 5, the relationship with the likes of Simon Rattle, Glyndebourne Festival, and later, a variety of highly regarded "modern" conductors and soloists, has been essential to the orchestra's commercial (and artistic) development. Here is another TINA formation. Before moving on, however, one final comment should be made concerning the orchestra's name. One might well ask why it was that "The Age of *Enlightenment*" was chosen, especially given what I have introduced in this chapter about the tension between modern enlightenment thinking and apparently pre-modern enchantment. In a fascinating historical footnote, it seems extraordinarily apt that it was the orchestra's principal investor, Michael Rose—a banker with the Bankers Trust Company—who chose the name in the first place.[47] The orchestra's launch came right in the middle of the boom years of Thatcher's neoliberal free-market experiment (memorably finding its satirized form in the guise of Harry Enfield's TV Loadsamoney character—also created in 1986). It was indeed "a coming of age," but more than anything else, a coming of age in terms of the early music movement's mature response to the challenges of modernity, i.e., making early music in the age of advanced capitalism. As I noted in Chapter 5, the OAE was ahead of the game when it came to its adoption of marketing, fund-raising, and promotional activities. Although the orchestra was indeed giving audiences what they wanted (and weren't getting elsewhere), one might say that the OAE's publicity materials "worked like magic." But lest we lose sight of this in any rush to condemn capitalistic cultural production, it was crucially the promise of enchantment that truly motivated the orchestra's founders, and no doubt its principal investor(s), too.

THAT OLD DEVIL CALLED AUTHENTICITY

As we have seen, there is something troublingly contradictory about a movement that purports to constrain classical musicians in their approach to performance on the basis of liberating them from a perceived lack of freedom. And yet this is a logical inference of pursuing (historical) authenticity, based as it is on a scholarly approach to the facts of historical performance rather than on the musician's innate musicianship. The philosophy of art holds that "authenticity" requires the artist to be faithful to their "self," rather than conforming to external values such as historical tradition. The early music movement, with its explicit ideology of historical authenticity, nonetheless promotes a practical approach toward tradition that on this basis at least, renders it *in*-authentic. So what are the possible explanations for this state of affairs?

The first is to throw up our hands and admit that Early Music simply got it wrong and was based on flawed ideological beliefs about the practices and virtues of authentic performance. This is not a position I agree with (as I have already argued). The second alternative is to highlight yet another TINA formation and put the blame at capitalism's door, suggesting that the enthusiastic promotion of authentic performance as an approach *all* performers of early music repertoire should adopt was essentially thrust upon early musicians by overzealous record company executives and their like, as they struggled to gain a foothold in the classical music market (see Chapter 8). If the impression given was that all performances of old music should be presented using period instruments and in a HIP style, and that historical accuracy effectively trumped all other performing values, well, so be it. Overstating the case was a necessary response simply in order to overcome the pre-existing opposition from the status quo. There *was* no alternative. Though I believe there is some truth to this explanation, and it is also consistent with John Eliot Gardiner's assertion that pioneers tend to "exaggerate—to push things to the extremities,"[48] this is by no means the whole story. This leaves the third alternative, which is to appeal to a more rounded, more human conception of authentic performance that relies upon our newfound understanding of enchantment and magic.

Authenticity remains a powerful quality that can distinguish those musicians we want to listen to from the rest. This is as true for HIP as it is for hip-hop. But what can "keeping it real" mean in an age in which ontology and enchantment are ostensibly denied, i.e., where there is no space for a meaningful reality beyond our knowledge? Amongst current sociological explanations of authenticity in the context of cultural production, Richard Peterson's work on the creation of the country music business in the US[49] is probably the most frequently cited. Peterson draws attention to the "authenticity work" and "authenticity claims" that performers and their managers construct to give the impression that they are what they say they are. Such fabrication of authenticity is reminiscent of the magician's illusory power, also crafted to influence others. Incidentally, the Greek ancestry of the word authentic, *authenteo,* has the meaning "to have full power," i.e., being "the master of his or her domain." According to this theoretical perspective, authenticity is primarily a discursive device, wielded as the magician wields his wand, to achieve particular ends in a particular context, i.e., the market. Authenticity is in a Foucauldian sense a source of power-knowledge, and the means of achieving "power *over*" others (power$_2$). Here is the master/slave relation, central to the business of cultural production, where a competitive context dictates how people must behave. This, it seems to me, is the primary form of authenticity referred to in debates concerning Early Music, as well as being very much the dominant voice in public discourse about authenticity more generally.

However, authenticity is never exhausted by discourse nor, indeed, by our ideas of what "being authentic" involves. As I have argued in Chapter 3, the world that we come to know is not the same as the world that exists. There is always an epistemological gap. Such an ontological commitment to the reality of the world and of our (fallibly understood) place within it clearly opens up another source of meaning and value, indeed another aspect of what it means to be authentic, where power is bestowed upon each and every individual by virtue of their (truly) being who they are, doing what they do (what philosophers have referred to as their "natural necessity" and "alethic truth"), independent of their knowledge of themselves. Behaving authentically, according to this way of looking at things, is always beyond (only) rational explanation. This type of knowledge cannot be sought; it emerges and is beyond the direct control of the individual, though it is always present in and of the individual and their relations with others (musicians learn this kind of insight when their teacher encourages them to let the music "speak for itself"). For, as Kimmel notes, "Like grace, enchantment is not the prerogative of the person, but one can be open to its reception, or not."[50] The state of being open to enchantment and subsequently being able to communicate this to an audience is a primary requisite of making music, indeed of performing in general—where performance is understood as "showing doing."[51] But I would go further here to suggest that *authentic* performance (over and above the constraints of dispositional (historical) authenticity already referred to) must also comprise a relationship between performer and musical work (constituting the musical work as it is performed) that is direct and unmediated, such that the inherent meaning and value of the musical work (its enchantment) can emerge and be communicated to the audience. An authentic performance occurs only when the performer and the musical work are "as one." As Barenboim states, "The task of the performing musician...is not to express or interpret the music as such, but to aim to become part of it."[52] For T. S. Eliot, "You are the music," at least "while the music lasts."[53] For Virginia Woolf, "We are the words; we are the music; we are the thing itself."[54] Where the performer is overly concerned with matters of historical accuracy or technical delivery (i.e., they are focused on the means-ends relationship), we would not consider the performance to be authentic, because the direct and unmediated conditions for communicating enchantment would be absent (criticisms referring to unnecessary "artifice" or indeed to the negative connotations of "fabrication" reflect this). In the spontaneous moment of performing, the early musician cannot "perform a treatise." Their accumulated knowledge of how the early music *should* be performed, based on study, practice, and the precepts of dispositional (historical) authenticity, is central to an authentic performance, but only if it does not prevent the performance of the musical work from enchanting both performer(s) and audience.

Rather than understanding "authenticity" (and authentic performance) in terms of an idealized and dogmatic goal that dictates how those involved strategically manage doing art, we should see authenticity as the human capacity (and for some a developed capability[55]) to reconcile the apparently irreconcilable on an ongoing everyday basis. Understood this way, authentic performance is not about the winning out of old over new, head over heart, text over act, or scholarship over performance, but rather the way in which these seemingly contradictory interests and approaches come together in and through the *lived* process of doing art. Furthermore, authenticity is not just about the "unimpeded operation of one's true- or core-self in one's daily enterprise,"[56] since the very inevitability of being "impeded" is, if you like, the starting point for living and behaving with authenticity. The dilemma facing the early musician was not choosing between historical (dispositional) authenticity and personal authenticity, but rather determining how to live with both of them. In short, "real" authenticity, i.e., as we live and practice it, is not so much to be found in the longed-for ideal, but in the ebb and flow of daily life.

The "ore of the authentic" referred to in the title of this chapter does indeed involve a "pact," but rather than this being with the Devil, it is (so to speak) between our rational and enchanted selves. As Daniel Barenboim has written, "What is, ultimately, perhaps the most difficult lesson for the human being—learning to live with discipline yet with passion, with freedom yet with order [with magic and yet with enchantment; with historical (dispositional) authenticity and yet with personal authenticity]—is evident in any single phrase of music."[57] Here is the key to "being authentic." So whilst Peter Kivy (1995) is surely right, on one level, to draw our attention to authentic*ies* (in the plural), the quality of authenticity that I am suggesting here is to be understood in terms of our overarching capacity to manage the tensions that inevitably arise between them (as in performance, so in life in general).[58] As we shall see in the final chapter, making early music in the modern age has required putting this "difficult lesson" into practice.

> We are awakened into enchantment—in the theatre as into life—and it is here that we learn the truth of our lives. This truth is not simple, not direct, not easy, but it is the human possibility and genius of great art.
>
> LAWRENCE KIMMEL[1]

> The world and man reveal themselves, by undertakings. And all the undertakings we might speak of reduce themselves to a single one, making history.
>
> JEAN-PAUL SARTRE[2]

12

The Art of Re-enchantment

INTRODUCTION

Over the several years that I have been working on this book, I have frequently been asked what it is about; more often than not, I'd end up saying "oh, it's about the *business* of early music." Actually, it isn't. It is about much more than that. But the tendency for disciplinary pigeonholing is difficult to avoid. I finish this book by contemplating the importance of overcoming separation; of moving toward a more joined up, more authentic approach to understanding and doing art in everyday life. For this is one of the main lessons to be drawn from this study of making early music in the modern age.

Under capitalism's "spell," early musicians have been forced to compromise. As we have seen, the Early Music story is riven with contradiction and theory-practice inconsistencies (TINA formations). Nevertheless, Early Music has been consistently motivated and sustained by a desire to reconnect—not just with the music of the past, but with the inherent meaning and value that such music can provide for us today. Making early music has required a collaborative coming together of people who otherwise operated independently within the classical music field. At the level of the individual, it has also required the playing of multiple roles and negotiating between internal positions and perspectives that otherwise appear quite at odds with each other.

Of course, much of Early Music's success is attributable to the musical and performance-related skills of the talented individuals the movement attracted. But this is by no means the whole story. Also underlying the success of Early Music has been the practical capacity of its principal cast of players to reconcile the apparently contradictory on a day-to-day basis—being a scholar *and* a performer; an artist *and* an artisan; a professional *and* an amateur; a musician *and* a cultural entrepreneur; a magician, enchanter, *and* the enchanted. The natural necessity for each one of us to be greater than the sum of our parts is both a reflection of our (emergent) individual authenticity and a commentary on the nature of the world as it is, rather than what we can know about it. In seeking to explain just what has been involved in making early music *in the modern age*, I have had course to highlight the mundane and the magical; the everyday and the enchanted. There is a natural tendency in the field of art to keep these apart. Trevor Pinnock's views on the responsibility of musicians to "lift people out of the mundane 'everyday' onto another level"[3] will strike a chord with musicians and their audience. As Pinnock further comments, "We don't have to question it too much...luckily we have the music and we know that it creates certain sorts of magic." My discussion of enchantment resonates strongly with this view; music does indeed "lift" us up out of ourselves. However, it is important to resist any simple dualistic explanation that reifies a part of our lives as if it only happens in the ritualistic context of a concert hall, distinctive though this is, and as if such experiences were not borne of a much wider set of practices that make the music possible.[4] John Dewey's quote from the beginning of Chapter 1 is worth repeating here: "Mountain peaks do not float unsupported; they do not even just rest upon the earth. They are the earth in one of its manifest operations."[5] My aim in this last chapter, therefore, is to explore the broader message that Early Music has to tell us about the often overlooked two-way relationship between art and everyday life, i.e., the role of everyday human practices in doing art, and the role of art in the doing of our everyday lives. This brings us now to "the art of re-enchantment."

THE ART OF RE-ENCHANTMENT

The art of re-enchantment is nothing short of the primary underlying mechanism for making early music in the modern age. It explains how early music can be both old and new. It is the artful practice we engage in to re-enchant art (specifically, in this case, music that was composed many years ago). It involves everything needed to "create that decisive moment, when the memory of tradition...a reaching beyond the musical text...the choice and technology of instruments...[performing] with powerful expression...accepting diverse cultural influences...using contemporary information...and deciding how to direct...all come together to be forged into a vivid communication to the listener."[6] More broadly, however, it is also our route to living life with greater authenticity (re-enchanting ourselves). The art of re-enchantment is, then, a corner-piece in the explanatory jigsaw of Early Music, but it is also part of a much bigger picture altogether.

Taking the concept of *re-enchantment* first, what I have in mind is the idea of restoring something that was lost or occluded. Early musicians, through playing on period instruments and performing in styles consistent with historical performance practice, have *re*-enchanted early (old) music, revealing and communicating something of its original inherent meaning and value. As argued in Chapter 3, each time a musician performs a precomposed musical work they (potentially) re-enchant it for us in the here and now. It becomes something fresh and new. But since musical works change over time, what makes the job of the early musician distinctive is that they have done this by paying particular attention to the conditions that made it possible for the musical work to be what it was when composed and first performed, i.e., broadly speaking following the principle of dispositional (historical) authenticity. Early musicians have not done this single-handed. Their "re-enchanting" has involved collaboration with historical musicologists, scholars, instrument-makers, editors, publishers, and so on. Incidentally, it might well be argued that instrument-makers have similarly *re*-enchanted old instruments (in part, at least, through the communication of detailed historical back-stories used to legitimate their provenance), such that they became meaningful and valuable objects of desire in their own right. Contrary to those who see HIP as a triumph of head over heart, this process of re-enchanting music has *not* been at the expense of art.

The art of re-enchantment is altogether an *artful* process; in other words—an aesthetic, poietic process of shaping, making, doing, not merely the product of logic, or subject to volitional control; an unfolding, emergent, and to some degree, spontaneous source of shared meaning and value. This process of doing art is practiced skillfully: it requires a mix of knowledge (such as of 17th-century performance practice) and doing (such as proficiency in playing a musical instrument). Crucially, it is also characterized by its aesthetic dimension, whereby we gain knowledge of the world through sensible perceptions that we "experience."[7] The scope of this aesthetic knowledge varies enormously. In the context of early music it might be associated with anything from the toe-tapping, thigh-slapping musical rhythms of a 16th-century dance devised principally to entertain; the sophisticated vocal polyphony of a Gesualdo motet carrying an esoteric devotional message; the inventive flair of a Biber violin sonata; or the extraordinary union of intellect and inspiration in Bach's *Art of Fugue*. As Goehr has argued convincingly, what we might now refer to as early music was not generally conceived of as being constituted by "works of art." Although this points to the fact that our views about early music have changed, the way in which music "works" has not. It remains the case that in our experiencing of the aesthetic qualities of (early) music we are made aware of, or get in touch with, those parts of our lives that are both inherently meaningful and valuable, but which cannot be readily expressed or explained through rational discourse. This is the root of music's uplifting, spiritual, and ineffable power.

All of us share the capacity for doing art, i.e., being artful. Whether or not this capacity is developed into a publicly recognized capability (for example, as a professional baroque violinist, singer, or harpsichord player) depends upon our individual makeup as well as a host of contingent life chances, including our family upbringing, our education, and of course, the amount of "work" we put in. Doing art is therefore something both ordinary and extraordinary. Indeed, we draw on this capacity for doing art in all sorts of ways, and in a wide range of contexts that otherwise go unacknowledged, including scholarship, craftsmanship, management, and cultural entrepreneurship. As we have seen with all those "off-stage" individuals who have been so central to Early Music—one thinks of the likes of Basil Lam, Hugh Keyte, David Fallows, Denis Stevens, Robert Donington, Frank Hubbard, Robert Goble, David Rubio, Clifford

Bartlett, William Glock, Ted Perry, Andreas Holschneider, Christopher Bishop, James Burnett, Michel Garcin, Peter Wadland, and Chris Sayers, but the list could go on and on—their diverse knowledge and skills would count for little were they not motivated by and imbued with something of the same artfulness as that of their performing colleagues. It is surely through their shared practical interest in early music on a primarily artistic level (their common capacity for doing art) that they were able to work together.[8] At a broader level, the way in which we listen to music also draws (more or less) on our capacity for doing art. Though "the audience" is generally considered in terms of being passive receivers of musical sound, we use our (aesthetic) knowledge and our artfulness to recreate meaning and value (enchantment) for ourselves. To this end, the active role of the audience for Early Music has also played a vital, though largely overlooked, role in its development.

As a *dialectical* process (i.e., constituting argument, change, freedom, and so on), the art of re-enchantment is fundamentally about absenting some current situation or bringing about some desired-for alternative. This is actually the very process that characterizes music (and is the job of the musician). After all, music is always changing as each note is absented into another or into silence.[9] The primary dialectic in Early Music (at least in terms of that which we can readily observe) has involved the absenting of constraints on our ability to perform music of earlier times with "historical authenticity." At a deeper level, however, this very process necessarily gives rise to an altogether more profound transformation of "personal authenticity," to borrow Kivy's phrase, as we ourselves are re-enchanted in the process. In the opening chapter I drew attention to the dialectical relationship between doing art and being authentic. I suggested that we need to absent the constraints that prevent us from doing art if we are to become fully ourselves; but equally, we need to absent those constraints that prevent us from being authentically ourselves, if we are properly to do art. Attention is cast on the disenchantment, alienation, separation, inauthenticity, and split (also discussed in terms of TINA formations), which we need to do away with if we are to become our joined-up, (re-)enchanted selves. The art of re-enchantment is, then, a lived process of negotiating this unfolding dialectic between art and authenticity. In the next section I work through an alternative reading of Early Music's emergence, deliberately highlighting the nature of this process of re-enchantment along the way. In so doing, my aim is *not* to make some grand claim for Early Music as being particularly good at the art of re-enchantment (though certainly some individuals have managed it extremely well), but rather to highlight the universal nature of a process that we all encounter.

RE-ENCHANTING EARLY MUSIC

By its very nature, enchantment is an aspect of human experience that does not lend itself readily to discourse. It is not surprising, perhaps, to find that the art-world has been altogether more receptive toward the concept of "enchantment" than elsewhere. Notably, following the horrors of World War I, a war-weary public sought escape through "a new and enchanted view of life"[10] that focused very much on the artistic portrayal of fantasy and fairy tale. Artists and illustrators of the caliber of Edmund Dulac, Kay Nielsen, and Arthur Rackham are now referred to collectively as belonging to a golden "age of enchantment" (1890-1930). Intriguingly, their activity coincided with that first flowering of British early music under the leadership of Arnold Dolmetsch. What we find here is a common interest in escaping the contemporary "modern" world, coupled with a Romantic reassessment of the pre-modern era. These are characteristics one might equally find in some 20th-century "heritage" projects, and certainly there are many commentators who would seek to explain Early Music in terms of an increasing interest in heritage and the preservation or "restoration" of old music.[11] By any measure, making Early Music in the modern age has been a remarkable restoration project (restoring instruments, old scores, performance practices, etc.). The precise nature of what has been restored, however, goes well beyond the general conception of restoration projects in museums, art history classes, or the grounds of country estates.

Central to all heritage projects is the idea of inheritance, such that valuable objects and qualities from the past are saved for present day, and tomorrow's society. Heritage is about taking the "best of the past" and "protecting" it so that it can "enrich our lives today."[12] As Butt (2002) outlines, the link between HIP and heritage is complex, and "different commentators can look at what is essentially the same cultural phenomenon and draw extraordinarily contradictory conclusions."[13] Though it is certainly tempting to group the rise of Early Music in the 1960s and '70s within a wider set of heritage projects (interest in restoring both domestic and national houses, for example, after the wholesale modernization that came after the Second World War),[14] the evidence does not readily support the view that Early Music and early musicians have been directly motivated by the principles of heritage. Generally speaking, early musicians have *not* seen it as their calling to restore or maintain our musical heritage for the future. Of course, many musicians have shown a commitment toward "discovering" the treasures of forgotten repertoire, but I would suggest that this has been largely directed toward the immediate pleasure of the living (and the benefit of themselves—both spiritually and financially), rather than any more altruistic longer-term interest.

The rise of Early Music as a distinctive cultural movement coincided with the much broader phenomenon of new social movements and the birth of "postmodernism" around 1967. Here it is insightful to read Zygmunt Bauman's thoughts on how postmodernity represented "a re-enchantment of the world that modernity had tried hard to disenchant."[15] Bauman refers to modernity's "war against mystery and magic," a "war of liberation leading to the declaration of reason's independence." For him, "[this modern] world had to be de-spiritualized, deanimated: denied the capacity of subject ... It is against such a disenchanted world that the postmodern re-enchantment is aimed." Though superficially this appears compelling, we should not uncritically accept the view that modernity has been successful in its aims, as implied.[16] A strong theme coming through this study is that enchantment was never "taken away" per se, but rather occluded, hidden from our awareness and experience. To this extent, Early Music was a "restoration" project with a difference. What needed restoring were not simply the instructions as to how to perform (as found in treatises—important though these are) but the lived experience of performing, such that it came alive once again both for performers and audiences. Catherine Mackintosh, for example, found playing early music with period instruments "like suddenly finding that you could speak another language that you thought you always knew."[17]

It is not difficult to see why the Romanticist desire to view the past as if it was "something far off, legendary, fictitious, fantastic, and marvellous, an imaginary or ideal world which was contrasted with the actual world of the present"[18] held increasing appeal during the first quarter of the 20th century. Such a view must have rubbed off on Dolmetsch, though clearly not to the same degree as it did for the likes of Dulac, Housman, Rackham, and their "enchanted" artist contemporaries. As Donald Jay Grout, author of *A History of Western Music*, observes, "romantic art aspires to transcend immediate times or occasions, to seize eternity, to reach back into the past and forward into the future, to range over the expanse of the world and outward through the cosmos."[19] Romanticism is characterized by a "boundlessness," which "cherishes freedom, movement, passion and endless pursuit of the unattainable" rather than working within "the classic ideals of order, equilibrium, control, and perfection." Above all else, Romanticism is "haunted by a spirit of longing, of yearning after an impossible fulfillment." For Early Music's critics (including Taruskin), the pursuit of authenticity in performance is a case in point of this "yearning after an impossible fulfillment."

For some other commentators, this search for Romanticism in modernity is itself a form of re-enchantment. Jenkins, for example, describes a "diverse portfolio of perspectives and practices that developed as a response to the rationalism of the Enlightenment, and which shelters—or lurks—under the broad umbrella of Romanticism" as a "definitively modern movement of (re)enchantment."[20] He refers to "Romanticism's imagining of, and yearning for, a mythical pre-modern, un-rationalized past," noting its continuing influence, even though this is largely "commoditized, routinized and organized, if not thoroughly rationalized. It is big business." But here there is an important distinction to be drawn (one that was introduced in Chapter 11) between enchantment and magic. For the "mythical pre-modern...past perfect" is the stuff of *magic*, not enchantment. As such, it is as illusory as the promise of capitalism—just as modern and just as disenchanted. Romanticism tacitly accepts the disenchanted logic of the rational world and calls for something "other"—which it can never reach, because underlying it is lurking the same unshakable belief in the rational world order. Early Music's re-enchantment, however, relies on a view of the world that accepts the enchanted as part of that order.

On a rather more immanent level, the early music movement of the 1960s and later demonstrated in a very practical sense that the way one performed early music actually mattered. For it was in and through the "art" (doing and making) of the early musicians, engaging practically with old instruments (and instrument-makers), old scores (and historical musicologists), and the practice of performance (with other players) in a professional context (supported by broadcasters, record companies, promoters, etc.) that early music's enchantment has been revealed. It is not incidental here that the etymology of enchantment is close to *en-chanter* or *incantare*—literally "to sing or chant a spell over." The root of enchantment is concretely situated embodied practice; it is projected into the physical space as a singer projects their voice in the concert hall. Enchantment does not come from keeping things to oneself. Equally, Early Music did not win its battles on the basis of an ideology of "authentic performance" alone.

On the face of it, Early Music was primarily a response to the existing state of classical music, which by the mid-20th century had (for some) become a "helpless situation." Rather than asking how or why the early music movement was successful, however, we might begin by asking a different question altogether: *Why* early music (at all)? This challenges us to think again about what motivated a small group of classically trained musicians to embrace early music (and all that it entails) as opposed to other possible musical developments in the context of the classical music field in the late 1960s. Part of the answer lies in its distinctive potential for re-enchanting classical music.

RE-ENCHANTING CLASSICAL MUSIC

Making early music in the modern age has required classical music to undergo a profound and sometimes painful program of change. But what was "wrong" with classical music as it was? What was missing—and why was there any need for its "re-enchantment?" By putting ourselves in the shoes of those classically trained musicians who first engaged with the Early Music project, we can begin to venture an answer. This might also help us to see why the early music movement happened when it did. Early Music can be understood as a contextualized response to the *situational restrictions* of classical music as experienced by its protagonists. For these performers working in the 1960s and early '70s, it was becoming a *helpless situation,* where they felt at *the limit or the edge*.[21] There was both a lack of applied knowledge and skills (historical musicology; knowledge of performance conventions, etc.) and a lack of resources (original instruments; motivated and trained musicians; development time) to perform early classical music repertoire as they believed it should be performed. These highly trained classical musicians experienced an "agitated immobility" or "lack of play range (Spielraum)."[22] Such was the "guild-like" reinforcement of classical music's rules of engagement (carefully preserved 19th-century performance practices designed for playing 19th-century instruments in 19th-century concert halls to an audience schooled in 19th-century ritualistic behaviors) that the question of how earlier musicians had performed music was not just a nonquestion, but any deviation from the established norm was positively discouraged.

One is reminded of the institutional pressures on the likes of Julian Bream, and later Trevor Pinnock, to conform by concentrating on their "proper" studies (guitar and organ, respectively) rather than wasting time strumming and plucking at the lute and harpsichord. The classical music profession worked to reproduce its own.[23] Musical training was geared toward individuals having a career in music; inevitably, this meant conforming to the standards expected, cherished, and upheld by those orchestras, choirs, and ensembles that were deemed to be "excellent."[24] But in addition, the classical music avant-garde of the late 1960s had become a deeply challenging performance terrain, for performers and audiences alike. The highly dissonant, atonal musical language of the modern serialists was just too unfamiliar (and too difficult) for many of classical music's audience to engage with. It is hard not to agree with Morgan (1988) that the "authenticity movement" was to some extent born out of a deepening sense of "cultural identity crisis."[25] Morgan indicates that such a state of affairs arose because "we [had] no purposes of our own, or at least [were] so unsure of the validity of those that we [did] have as to render them purposeless."[26] Here we find all the hallmarks of TINA (see Chapter 11), where the false belief that "there is no alternative" ends up supporting the very state of affairs it mistakenly believes in.

In thinking of Early Music as a therapeutic response to the state of classical music (its re-enchantment), we might turn once again to the idea of restoration. Here I borrow the phrase "rite of restoration" from expressive arts therapy[27]—a form of therapy that specifically adopts art as a central medium of its practice. Interventions in rites of restoration typically have the increase of the range of play as their primary goal. Other examples include psychotherapy, counseling, supervision, coaching, and various religious healing rituals. However, this can readily be extended to include musicians, performers,[28] artists, entrepreneurs, teachers—indeed, all those professionals involved in managing change (whether in learning, commerce, or art). What is being restored? In the case of Early Music it is not so much the stated aim of the "original" music or performance, but the space to play, to imagine possibilities of performance that might, in fact, bring us closer to the music as first conceived, composed, and performed. This kind of restoration is not like rebuilding a dilapidated old building, but rather is about restoring broken or separated cultural bindings, reconnecting with a sense of cultural identity, and most importantly, the possibility of becoming.

So what does this rite of restoration involve? We can point to three aspects, which relate directly to Early Music's development. First, a process of decentering; second, the provision of an expanded play space; and third, the process of holding the play space open. The first phase of decentering is specifically required to "move away from the narrow logic of thinking and acting that marks the helplessness around the 'dead end' situation in question."[29] As Levine notes, "in order for therapeutic change to occur, there must be a process of destructuring in which one's old identity comes into question and is taken apart."[30] We can readily see how this might have worked in the context of classical music, with its deeply entrenched institutionalized training and employment structure, coupled with a deepening crisis of identity. To the extent that early music repertoire is both "familiar" (in so much of its tonal language) and yet "unfamiliar" (in terms of its having been created in a world now gone), it represents an obvious focus of interest for such a project.

The second aspect of this rite of restoration was to provide an expanded play space where classical musicians could "play" with performing early classical music repertoire in ways that were not restricted by the institutional pressures just described.

Kimmel observes that play "is the subjective capacity of the human being to disengage from the pervasive presence of an existential and operational modality—the otherwise inseparable unity of time and space—which makes possible a re-presentation and projection of an 'objective world.'"[31] Central to the notion of play is "imagining what is not present."[32] "The phenomenon of play is experienced in the 'doing as if,' in the open-endedness, and in the circularity of the here and now that is usually connected to all alternative world experiences."[33] There is clearly a distinction to be drawn here between a play-space characterized by Romanticized boundlessness, where the "freedom" imagined is pure fantasy (Sartre refers to the "vertiginous" experience of absolute freedom), and a play-space where concretely situated (i.e., actually realized) performances of the music of the 16th or 17th centuries are being reimagined. At issue is the critical nature of the creative constraints that "hold" the play-space open; this brings us to the third and perhaps the most important of the three aspects of this rite of restoration.

Paolo Knill writes that individuals' or communities' situations of change usually have ritual containers within which they are framed in space and time."[34] Such "ritual containers" don't just exist, however, but are managed strategically. Again, there are several facets to this. First, the primary importance of the early music *movement* has been in respect of its acting as a "ritual container" for early musicians to expand their range of play. The movement as it emerged provided a community of support and of practice (CoP).[35] This was vital in nurturing the social fabric that could foster the sharing and encouragement of ideas, often against considerable opposition from the classical music mainstream. Though it is tempting to adopt something of a "soft" portrayal of Early Music's CoP, its activities were always subject to the hard forces of capitalistic production. So, for example, the closing of the Early Music Centre in the 1980s was not just a symbolic loss, but also resulted in the very tangible foreclosing of a physical "space to play," i.e., where musicians could rehearse, study, perform, hold meetings, and interact with like-minded performers, as well as with instrument-makers in their workshops.

Second, the very ideology of authentic performance can be understood as acting like a "ritual container." It is in the bounded nature of dispositional (historical) authenticity, i.e., the idea of being able to recreate the conditions of possibility for any performance of a musical work, and its apparently constraining influence upon how classical music should be performed, that we can account (albeit paradoxically) for the expanded play-range of early musicians, and their newfound freedom to perform early music in a novel way. What needs highlighting here is the crucial importance of setting creative constraints in the process of promoting change, learning, and, indeed, enchantment. As Patricia Stokes observes, "it is not boundary-less creative freedom that inspires new ideas, but self-imposed, well-considered constraints."[36]

Finally, classical music has been re-enchanted through the Early Music play-space being held open by a range of "ordained or graduated" individuals, otherwise referred to as cultural entrepreneurs or "change agents"[37] (notably the founder-directors of early music groups) working on behalf of and alongside colleagues and/or employees. Their ability to hold the play-space open has called upon a variety of "playful" approaches to cultural entrepreneurship (see Chapter 9), as well as a distinctive mix of magic and enchantment (see Chapter 11). Despite the initial decentering, it has also required early musicians to (re-)connect with the wider classical music profession. This analytical perspective challenges our preconceived notions of the (classical) musician as isolated artist, living on the fringes of society, and somehow aloof from the mundane reality of making a living. It also challenges us to look more broadly at just what is involved in making *art* (more generally) in the modern age. Specifically, how should we understand "doing art" and "being authentic" in contemporary capitalist society?

MAKING ART IN THE MODERN AGE

The way we talk about art is in need of re-enchantment. This is not so much a commentary on the abilities and interests of artists themselves, but more a reflection of art's position in society, where its intrinsic worth (its capacity for enchantment) is increasingly overlooked. Such a state of affairs has arisen, I believe, as a direct consequence of the power of the market. Public discourse has (understandably at one level) been appropriated by those who need to assert art's *economic* potential (whether as a prudent investment, a source of jobs and regional or national productivity, or in terms of the local multiplier effect). But this has resulted in there being little or no space to celebrate all that is so palpably present in the doing of art itself. This study of Early Music provides a chance to pause and reflect on not only what it takes to meet the challenges of making *art* in the modern age, but also what art is, or rather, can be, in the world we (want to) live in.

Re-connecting Art and Nature

For the ancients, the ultimate source of music's power was to be found in our natural relationship with the cosmos, e.g., the "harmony of the spheres," or Plato's Pythagorean view of music as the direct perception of the mathematical order underlying the world. By the 19th century, however, it was the miraculous power of individual human beings bestowed with "genius" that had become the focus of veneration. Historical performance practice has to some extent refocused our attention on classical music as a *natural* phenomenon. For example, whereas modern instruments require little more than being taken out of their cases, Early Music has often necessitated making instruments from scratch. An applied knowledge of instrument-making, organology, acoustics, tuning, and temperament (to say nothing of the historical background of those involved)—these all became part of the early musician's diverse new portfolio of skills. Beyond the tools of the trade, however, there are more profound implications of this development in terms of (re-)enchantment, which as Curry notes is the result of restoring a "right relationship with the Earth."[38] A helpful analogy here might be with an inner-city school trip to a country farm, where the children come face-to-face with the source of their food for the first time. They realize (in a moment of enchantment perhaps) that food doesn't come ready-prepared and prepackaged; rather, there is a raw[39] nature to what is put on their plates each day. For these children, this is a revelation. They will not look at food in the same way again. In the context of Early Music, it is art rather than food that has been reconnected with everyday life. This is really rather important, because it reminds us that classical music doesn't *have* to be written off as a source of spiritual transcendence for the privileged few. In fact, what is at stake (though still of a transcendent nature) emerges from something much more immanent, much more connected, and potentially (at least), much more widely available for everyone.

Reconnecting Art and Knowledge

The relationship between art and knowledge is complex, as the last point about privileged access indicates—N.B., the implied criticism of classical music and classical musicians is, in fact, much more a commentary on the priorities that capitalist society and its educational institutions hold. In reflecting on the "spinning out" of early music from university music departments, one could make an argument for Early Music as a remarkably successful story of "knowledge exchange." Here was a paradigmatic case of theory being adopted by practitioners and used to innovate their field. Early Music took historical musicology seriously. In return, some historical musicologists (though not all) sought to take Early Music seriously, and to work with performers, editors, publishers, instrument-makers, and others, to bring the music alive—to re-enchant art.

Whilst, of course, it would be grotesquely overstating the case to imply that early musicians were all capable of and actively engaged in extraordinary levels of musicianship, scholarship, historical musicology, organology, and cultural entrepreneurship, there has been nonetheless a heightened level of interaction that marks them out from the established classical musician (indeed artistic) norm. Early musicians' newfound interest in instrument-making was not mere scholarly curiosity—it was a necessity. Furthermore, although by no means all early musicians intensively studied historical treatises, bent on establishing the historical authenticity of their performance practice, they generally did get caught up in the kind of knowledge practices that involved reading books and treatises, visiting museums, and studying cultural history. Elsewhere, the founders of early music groups engaged with investors, sponsors, promoters, festival organizers, broadcasters, and record company executives, to say nothing of their fellow musicians and employees, and, of course, their audience, not as an alternative to music-making (though as we have seen, for some this did provide a route to promotion), but because it was a necessary part of making music. Just as Howard Gardner has brought attention to "multiple intelligences,"[40] perhaps we should become more aware of the plurality of knowledge-types that are required to make art work in the modern age. This necessitates thinking more carefully about the best educational environment for stimulating the required mix, rather than catering exclusively, say, for the promotion of musical intelligence, however central this might be.[41] This is surely all the more important in the light of the commercial success of this "high art" form, as discussed in Chapters 7 and 8.

Re-connecting Art and Cultural Entrepreneurship

The debt that Early Music owes to Arnold Dolmetsch and his "crusading" activities of the early 20th-century has been widely acknowledged. Cohen (1985) refers to Dolmetsch as an "artisan-scholar, able to blend learning with manual dexterity in the reproduction of old instruments."[42] He goes on to suggest that the "more industrialized shops, where recorders and harpsichord kits are turned out like cans of Campbell's soup, could not have come into being without the market for their wares that the Dolmetsch ethos helped to create." Such a view skirts round the fact that Dolmetsch himself found it difficult to overcome the divide between art and the market—indeed, if anything, his position reinforced the separation that existed already (his reputation as an eccentric amateur enthusiast lives on despite a sizeable business in historical performance and instrument-making). In earlier discussions (notably Chapter 9) I have drawn attention to the behaviors, skills, and practices of Early Music's cultural entrepreneurs in the 1960s, 1970s, and later. Their ability to bridge the art-market divide went beyond that of Dolmetsch, or anyone else who had gone before. Most notably, this depended on their ability to communicate with others, and to hold the play-space open, such that the commercial as well as artistic potential of early music (now available to a much wider audience through the recorded medium) could be fully developed.

The gradual divide that first emerged in the Renaissance between the craft-like practices of the "Artisan," where values of calculation, embodied skill, reproductive imagination, copying, and trade were central, and the inspired genius and spontaneity of the "Artist," whose work was characterized by creative imagination, originality, and freedom (play),[43] has been further entrenched over subsequent centuries, as capitalism has increasingly challenged the "value" of art in society. What is striking about the early music revival is that it required many of those involved to adopt a position much more in keeping with the pre-modern conception of the hybrid Artisan/Artist than with its modern counterparts (the Artist or Artisan, respectively). This "joined up" picture of the artist as someone for whom (the business of) making art both work and pay is part of their make-up, is extremely important; not least because it mitigates against the enduring (Romantic) stereotype of artists as either hopeless or hopelessly uninterested managers of art. Early Music's cultural entrepreneurs are, by necessity, highly networked and collaborative Artisan/Artists. Many of them have had to also learn how to be accountants, bankers, and businessmen, when the occasion called for it. As Jeremy West, cofounder of His Majestys Sagbutts and Cornetts, highlights, "nobody teaches you how to do this."[44] It is a lesson that has had to be learned "on the job."

Reconnecting Art and Capitalism

As I have suggested, most modern Western economies today prioritize art's economic value—its capacity to make money. Unfortunately, this has only further separated art from everyday life. Rather than seeing "art" as in some way characteristic of being human, "art is what *artists* do." Such a state of affairs is premised on a false belief (the most significant TINA formation uncovered in this study). For as much as the capitalist system is responsible for perpetuating an apparently disenchanted world where rational explanation and knowledge is valued above all else, it is nonetheless a system that depends upon enchantment for its survival. (I have been careful *not* to frame this as a science vs. art argument; scientific knowledge can be (and is often) enchanting.) Capitalism, after all, is devised and sustained by human beings' capacity to recognize and be motivated by meaning and value in their lives, even where this meaning is not rationalized in or through our shared discourse. There are many examples of where this "felt" truth can be seen to underpin the story of making early music in the modern age. One thinks of Christopher Bishop's signing up of David Munrow for EMI; or Decca's L'Oiseau-Lyre label taking on the Academy of Ancient Music, a decision very much motivated by the passion of its chief producer Peter Wadland; or Ted Perry's moment of enchantment on hearing Hildegard of Bingen performed by Gothic Voices on Radio 3; or National Westminster Bank's backing of Norrington's Beethoven "weekend" at the South Bank; or the bank-rolling of the OAE in its early days by investment bankers Michael Rose and Martin Smith; or, indeed, the decision by all those early musicians, instrument-makers, publishers, editors, and so on, to make their living from early music—to make early music "work."

It is in and through the process of art that we are made more aware of our totality, of our wholeness as human beings situated in time and space. Early music brings us in touch with our past, but it also connects us with the present. "Art is the living and concrete proof that man is capable of restoring consciously, and thus on the plane of meaning, the union of sense, need, impulse and action characteristic of the live creature."[45] Art therefore offers a singular perspective from which to better understand the alienating and separating tendencies of capitalism. The influential economist John Maynard Keynes, who was instrumental in setting up the Arts Council of Great Britain and was its founding chairman, lived a life surrounded by art and artists (belonging to the Bloomsbury Group). For Keynes, the pursuit of the arts and the value they gave was predicated upon there being a firm economic foundation for such activities. The story presented in this book highlights the intimate relationship between making early music in the modern age and the economic basis on which this could happen. But as I have indicated, this is anything but a one-way street. Capitalism itself is contingent on human beings' capacity to (re-)enchant and be (re-)enchanted. The irony of this, of course, is that it is usually arts funding that gets cut first, since this is seen as most expendable in times of austerity. Turning Keynes's world upside down, what we might think of as the economic foundation for life is itself dependent upon the very thing that the arts miraculously make us aware of—the inherent meaning and value that is experienced as enchantment.

Re-Connecting Art and Authenticity

Under normal circumstances, art takes the authenticity of the artist for granted. It is only when authenticity is doubted, when there is some experience of inauthenticity, or the art-work is considered to be a "fake," that it becomes an issue. Prior to the marketization and commodification of art in the late 18th and early 19th centuries, questions of authenticity were much less likely to arise. With its charge of inauthenticity, Early Music's discourse of authentic performance was always going to rock the boat, causing considerable resentment and mistrust from the classical music establishment. If we get behind the heat of the debate, however, we can see that the concept of authenticity focuses attention on two main issues central to the process of art: (i) the nature of the creative *constraints* that artists work within; and (ii) the degree of *freedom* artists enjoy. Intuitively we feel that these two exist in a dialectical relationship, where the absenting of one (constraint) leads to the presence of the other (artistic freedom), and vice versa. It is precisely for this reason that Early Music's detractors felt that its espoused views on authenticity, i.e., the apparently "dogmatic" focus on recreating the conditions of performance of an early musical work, deprived classical musicians of their artistic freedom, preventing them from being able to make great music.

In reality, of course, all artists, by necessity, work within or against a set of constraints. The sculptor begins with a block of marble; the painter, his brushes, paints, and a blank canvas; the composer with a commission, the request of a patron, a set of lyrics, a musical theme, a title. Even the contemporary modern artist, who ostensibly eschews the traditional constraints of "art," sets self-imposed limits (the admonition to be fully free to do whatever comes to mind is a constraint in itself). The same is true for all performers, of course, who are constrained by their knowledge of the musical work or play as it is codified in a score, a script, or libretto, as well as their contingent knowledge of the circumstances of the work's origins, their training, skills, talents, imagination, taste, and so forth. Artists do not escape these constraints but work with them to reveal, unfold, "bring forth" the artistic work. Seen in this light, the doing of art depends above all else upon the skillful setting of creative constraints. Too few, too many, too unrealistic, too easy, too obvious, too obtuse... and the art doesn't "work." Dispositional (historical) authenticity (the self-imposed goal of performing a musical work according to the possibilities of performance at the time of its having been created) can then be understood as a creative approach to such constraint-setting.

Authentic performance requires the asking of questions, prior to actual "performance". However, once the performance is under way, the artist must be "free" to enchant. This requires a mode of behavior that absents constraints on enchantment. First, in order for the performer to be "at one" with the musical work, they must rid themselves of thoughts of the past or future, be fully in the present, in the here and now (described by some performers and athletes as being "in the zone"). The greatest performing artists are especially good at this, of course, and it is worth observing that there is an increasing interest from Western society in the qualities of "presence"[46] and "mindfulness."[47] Entrepreneurs, teachers, therapists, a whole range of occupations, similarly from time to time require this skill in their own work. Second, in the moment of performing, musicians must abandon preconceived plans and schemas (these are for rehearsals only); the performing space, which has an "ontology of non-reproducibility,"[48] is characterized by a sense of spontaneity, rather than instrumental means-ends thinking. As the conductor Laurence Cummings observes, "If you are re-creating something, thinking that you're right...that's actually not so interesting. Whereas, if you feel like you're discovering it for the first time, you know, spontaneity is so important...for any music, but particularly for older music."[49] Third, whilst the performer relies on charisma to enchant, they must leave their ego in the green-room, lest it get in the way of the music.

Reconnecting art and authenticity requires moving beyond dualistic oppositions; as I have already inferred in relation to the properties of music, it is in the lived relationship and active tension between constraint and freedom that we find "real" authenticity. The philosophical concept of co-presence, understood as "the co-occurrence of the absence and presence of something" or "the co-existence of the existentially constitutive past and of the future as increasingly shaped possibility within the present"[50] brings further weight to the argument (and it is fascinating here to read Taruskin's reference to T. S. Eliot's views on performance as the "sense of the timeless as well as the temporal and of the timeless and the temporal together" that clearly point toward just this understanding of the world).[51] Constraint and freedom—apparently irreconcilable—are not mutually exclusive, but rather co-present. Dispositional (historical) authenticity is then both constraining—in the sense of limiting the possibility of what a musical work might be—and also freeing—in the sense of providing the necessary conditions for that work's inherent meaning and value (its enchantment) to be communicated. This enabling quality is true of all creative constraints, of course, and it is one of the most important (and difficult) tasks across art, science, entrepreneurship, therapy, and education to set the right sort of creative constraints to enable humans to flourish. A better understanding of the process of doing art might help us in all these contexts.

So despite many views to the contrary, authenticity still matters today, not least because it represents a vital response to the split and alienation of the modern condition. Being whole in terms of human "being" requires art and science, knowledge and not-knowing, enlightenment, magic and enchantment. Most crucially, it is through our transformational capability to reconcile the apparently contradictory, whether this is understood in terms of head vs. heart, scholarship vs. performance, culture vs. commerce, professional vs. amateur, or old vs. new, that our "real" (practiced; lived) authenticity emerges. The challenge facing all of us (including Early Music's next generation of performers), is to allow space for this transformational capability to flourish. In doing so, we will have found the art of re-enchantment.

CONCLUDING REMARKS

"And they all lived happily ever after..."

We will always have much to learn from the past. History is our greatest teacher, even if, as Aldous Huxley ruefully remarked, the most important of all the lessons that history has to teach is that men do not learn very much from the lessons of history. Judging by the barely concealed hostility amongst some classical musicians today toward the use of the word "authenticity" in the context of musical performance (the taste for "HIP" being now almost universal instead), it would seem that our willingness to learn from the history of the early music movement is itself under threat. Early Music's commitment to authentic performance is already subject to a form of revisionist history-making, written off and best forgotten. In the words of Frans Brüggen, however, "a musician's duty is sacred: to bring together *all* the information";[52] and though this book presents nothing like "all the information" it does, at least, begin to reveal some otherwise hidden aspects of the story. Looking beyond the rhetoric of "authentic performance," what we have found is an epistemologically humble position, where a group of classical musicians were prepared to admit that we might have got it wrong over how to perform early classical music repertoire. This is the first, albeit paradoxical, step in learning: to recognize and accept the state of things as they are. For only then is it possible to open up a genuine space for change. It is not a new lesson, of course. We will find it, albeit dressed up in period language, in the 17th- and 18th-century performance treatises that historical musicologists have gone back to for instruction. The composer and castrato singer Pier Francesco Tosi's *Observations on the Florid Song* (1743), for example, states: "He that studies, let him imitate the ingenious Bee, that sucks its Honey from the most grateful Flowers. From those called *Ancients*, and those supposed *Moderns*, (as I have said) much may be learn'd; it is enough to find out the Flower, and know how to distill, and draw the Essence from it."[53]

What, then, is Early Music's distilled "Essence" that will nourish tomorrow's generation of music-makers? Above all else, there *is* always an alternative. Although period instrument performances no longer shock the way they did forty years ago, and although hearing the London Symphony Orchestra, the Philadelphia Orchestra, the Leipzig Gewandhaus, or the Orchestre de Paris play with "historical awareness" no longer surprises, Early Music's journey is not yet done. The proverbial jug may be "beginning to be half full, instead of half empty,"[54] but there is still much to learn, much to put into practice.

This study of "making early music in the modern age" challenges us going forward to take authenticity off the page and to bring it into our lives as musicians, music-lovers, musicologists, instrument-makers, cultural entrepreneurs, and indeed as human beings. In so doing, our extraordinary and transformational capacity to reconcile the irreconcilable will be revealed for what it is. So, the early musician's achievement has not been to slavishly reconstruct, but to allow old music to sound fresh and new, heard as if for the first time. The professional early musician has striven to acquire technical mastery, such as that which Nadia Boulanger demanded of the young John Eliot

Gardiner; but equally, early music has been at its best when carrying with it something of the spontaneous music-making of the amateur (one think's of Gardiner's father's "lusty enthusiastic tenor" as he "sung when riding his horse or driving his tractor"[55]). The musical *Text* has been shown to be valuable and meaningful because when considered skillfully, it is often the best representation (however fallible) we have of the musical work; but then, it is also as nothing without the inspired and artful *Act* of performance that re-enchants.

Come what may, music will always find a way of bubbling up from its source. From time to time, however, it also needs the help of individuals (with or without a baton in their hand) to steer it in the right direction. Within the next decade or so, the vast majority of Early Music's pioneers will have retired, handing on their ensembles and their knowledge of HIP to the next generation. Early Music, too, is destined to grow old, of course. As it does so, our knowledge of the early music revival and those characters that have featured in its story will begin to recede from memory. I hope that this book, in its own small way, will inspire tomorrow's early music-makers to be even bolder in their vision, yet more charismatic in their communication to others, and just as playful in their "rule-breaking" as their illustrious predecessors have been.

Is this, then, a story with a happy ending? Ultimately, the future of early music, and indeed classical music in general, is dependent upon whether we choose to make a space for it in our lives. The embodied activity of music-making demands time and effort, concentration, and many hours of dedicated practice. To some extent, at least, these are things that can be learnt, providing there are the supportive social structures and institutions that can enable the "ritual containers" for such human activity. But as well as generations being brought up with little or no knowledge of classical music (let alone an experience of its enchantment), there is also less and less time both at school and in home-life for such learning to take place (as Alex Ross says, "All the rest is noise"[56]). Unless we find ways of keeping this play-space open, of joining up art and everyday life, classical music will once more be in a helpless situation. For some, this is just part of the natural evolution of things. Classical music has had its day. We move on. However, I can't help thinking that reports of "the end of classical music" (likewise the demise of early music and art) have so far proved greatly exaggerated. Perhaps this is because our special relationship with music, whether as performer or listener, is always changing, always becoming, just as we ourselves are.

NOTES

PREFACE

1. From *Ode* in O'Shaughnessy 1874.
2. This is not to say that Early Music hasn't attracted the attention of many leading commentators, including sociologists: Adorno 1967a; Bourdieu 1984; Hennion 1997; Hennion and Fauquet 2001; musicologists: Brown 1988; Butt 2002; Dart 1954; Donington 1963; Dreyfus 1983; Leech-Wilkinson 2002; Page 1993; Taruskin 1988; 1995. Harry Haskell's (1988) history of the early music revival is a key-text, but written before it was possible to capture the broader historical importance of the "modern" (British) early music movement.
3. Barone and Eisner 2012:1.
4. In its first edition, *Early Music* described its aims as offering an "international forum where diverse issues and interests can be debated and discussed" and providing a "link between the finest scholarship of our day and the amateur and professional listener and performer." (Thomson 1973:1). In celebration of its 40th anniversary, the February 2013 edition featured 34 "pieces" (short essays) "some looking back, some looking forward, and all with interesting and provocative perspectives" (Knights 2013:1), written by many of the "finest" scholars of historical performance practice today.
5. Donington 1963:26.
6. Mellers and Martin 1987:ix. Mellers provides a fascinating exploration of European music, using the classical myth of Orpheus as his starting point.

CHAPTER 1

1. Dewey 1934 [2005]:2.
2. Ruskin 1866: Lecture IV: The Future of England, section 151.
3. "The past is a foreign country: they do things differently there," is the opening line of L. P. Hartley's 1953 novel *The Go-Between*. See also Lowenthal (1985).

4. Blacking 1973:108–109.

5. See Roche 1979a–d; Roche and Roche 1981.

6. The Baroque period in music is defined as beginning in the early 1600s and continuing through to the time of J. S. Bach's death in 1750.

7. See Holschneider 1980.

8. Sometimes, HIP is instead referred to as "historically *influenced* performance" (see Haynes 2007).

9. See NEMA 2009 survey; Nwanoku quoted in Wallace 2006:29.

10. Geulen 2006:2.

11. Small 1987:19.

12. Lindholm 2008:28.

13. Ibid., 29.

14. Schumacher 1973:2.

15. See, for example, Adorno 1967a; Dreyfus 1983; Lindholm 2008; Taruskin 1982.

16. de Mille 1991:264.

17. The (first) Academy of Ancient Music was established in London in 1726.

18. See Butt 2002; Haskell 1988; Haynes 2007; Kenyon 1988; Kivy 1995; Lawson and Stowell 1999; Sherman 1997, amongst others.

19. Weber 1905.

20. Atkinson 2007:6.

21. Guillet de Monthoux 2000.

22. My position on the inherent value of art should not be confused with the "art for art's sake" movement from the early 19th century, which held that the only "true" art was devoid of any moral or utilitarian function. Nor should the broader focus of my argument be lost in the case for or against arts *funding* (see Pinnock, 2006 for a very helpful discussion of "Arts Keynesianism" and the public value vs. intrinsic value debate).

23. Poole 2013:28.

24. Sutton-Smith 1997:8.

25. Haynes 2007:41. Kailan Rubinoff (2013:254) suggests that the "status of HIP as an avant-garde or counterculture is relative, dependent on musicians' own experiences during the 1960s and their perceptions of that tumultuous decade."

26. Sir John Eliot Gardiner: interview with author, November 6, 2012.

27. Sir Nicholas Kenyon: interview with author, November 12, 2012.

28. Goehr 2007.

29. The premium-funding model (see Gaunt 2009) that lies at the heart of music college education is highly resistant to change.

30. David Munrow's *Instruments of the Middle Ages and Renaissance* (1976) distinguishes between the pre c.1400 instruments of the Middle Ages and the later ones of the Renaissance. Munrow very much enjoyed telling the story of how the BBC Pronunciation Department felt obliged to provide "Important Instruction" to announcers on the radio concerning how to pronounce *naker* (a Medieval percussion instrument), as this had caused offense to some outraged listeners (i.e., NAY-ker with a considerable stress on the first syllable).

31. This memorable phrase appeared in Munrow's publicity for the group, as recalled by Sir Nicholas Kenyon (in interview with the author, November 12, 2012). For Munrow, at least, such an apparently self-contradictory combination of qualities was indeed possible in performance.

32. Donington 1975a:x.

33. Campbell 1975.

34. Butt 2002:ix–x.

Notes

35. See Bourdieu 1993.

36. The "master-slave" relation was introduced by Hegel and Marx to describe the key power-relationship in capitalism. In 1993 this rhetoric was appealed to in the context of the popular music industry, when in a very public court case, George Michael famously described his relationship with his record company as "professional slavery."

37. DiMaggio 1982.

38. See Lounsbury and Glynn 2001 on the subject of cultural entrepreneurship as a form of persuasion.

39. See Fabian 2001 for discussion.

40. Author's transcript of Nicholas Kenyon being interviewed as part of the "Hogwood at 70" tribute, produced by *Gramophone*. Available at: http://www.gramophone.co.uk/classical-music-news/happy-birthday-christopher-hogwood, accessed May 4, 2012.

41. Paul Henry Lang in Kenyon 1988:5.

42. In fact, both positions appear to be held in some cases by the same critics.

43. Leech-Wilkinson 2002.

44. From an interview for *Opernwelt* (1984) available on Hogwood's website: http://www.hogwood.org/archive/interviews/opernwelt-interview-1984.html, accessed May 16, 2013.

45. Potter, John (no date) "Early music," from John Potter's website. Available at: http://www.john-potter.co.uk/blog/category/early-music, accessed February 22, 2011.

46. Sternberg and Lubart 2007:3.

47. Ibbotson 2008.

48. It is intriguing to note that "The magic circle," a club devoted to "the *art* of magic," was formed in 1905, the same year that Arnold Dolmetsch made his first harpsichord.

49. Jenkins 2000:12.

50. In Butt 2002:5.

51. Morgan 1988:57.

52. Taruskin 1995:5.

53. Butt 2002.

54. Lindholm 2008:29.

55. Leppard 1988:33.

56. Haynes 2007:10. It is fascinating to note here that Sir John Eliot Gardiner's musical upbringing was strongly influenced by his father, Rolf Gardiner—a pioneer of re-afforestation, conservation, and organic farming, and a founding member of the Soil Association. Also that he, too, has been actively involved in organic farming for the past 45 years.

57. Dulak 1993:36.

58. Leppard 1988:34.

59. Fabian 2001:153. See also Kivy 2002:129–130, who suggests that "authenticity...has taken on a somewhat negative connotation due to the dissatisfaction some people felt with the performances that went by that name."

60. Explanations based solely on what people believe are susceptible to the "epistemic fallacy...the analysis or definition of statements about being in terms of statements about our knowledge (of being)" (Bhaskar 1993:397).

61. For readers who want to find out more, I recommend Bhaskar and Hartwig 2010; or Archer et al. 1998 for a general overview; Ackroyd and Fleetwood 2000; or Fleetwood and Ackroyd 2004 in relation to organization and management studies; Carter and New 2004 on using critical realism in an applied empirical context.

62. Bhaskar 1989:11.

63. See Goehr 2007.

64. Bhaskar and Danermark 2006:11.

65. Susan McClary defines music as "a medium that participates in social formation by influencing the ways we perceive our feelings, our bodies, our desires, our very subjectivities—even if it does so surreptitiously, without most of us knowing how" (in Brett et al. 1994). Recent articles in the field of cultural sociology offer a further theoretical underpinning to my position here—see Born 2010; and Tia DeNora's *Music in Everyday Life* (2000).

66. Bhaskar 1993.

67. Bhaskar 2002a; 2002b.

68. Hartwig 2007:304.

69. The term "dispositional authenticity" has been used, notably by Kernis and Goldman—see especially their "multicomponent conceptualization of authenticity" (Kernis and Goldman 2006). However, my use of the term "dispositional" is quite different, and takes its meaning from dispositional realism (see Bhaskar 1997). It is for this reason that I refer to "dispositional (historical) authenticity," to distinguish clearly between the two.

CHAPTER 2

1. From *As You Like It*, Act 2, Scene VII.

2. See "What is early music?" on the Renaissance Workshop Company's website: http://www.renwks.com/knowledge/earlymusic/earlymusic.htm, accessed November 14, 2012.

3. Brown's review (1988:30) provides an excellent historical background to the early music movement.

4. Blume 1950.

5. Roche 1989:382.

6. Brown 1988:36.

7. The Classical period in music is held to have been between about 1730 and 1820, including works by the composers Haydn, Mozart, and Beethoven (his earlier works). The Romantic period followed.

8. Sacher married the heiress to the Hoffmann-LaRoche pharmaceutical company—an important source of funds for his projects, including the founding of the Schola Cantorum Basiliensis.

9. Landowska (1879–1959) began her musical training on a modern instrument (the piano), like most early music performers even up to the present day.

10. See Campbell 1975.

11. Brown 1988:39.

12. Donington in Campbell 1975:ix–x.

13. Brown 1988:46.

14. See Lawson and Stowell 1999.

15. Conductors Raymond Leppard and Sir Neville Marriner represent important exceptions—both well known for their historically informed performances of Baroque and Classical repertoire with modern chamber orchestras.

16. Butt 2002:ix–x.

17. By way of historical parallel, there were only a handful of active ideologues ("situationists") behind the student riots of 1968 in Paris.

18. Kenyon 1988:2.

19. I have sought to include the most active and well-known early music groups; however, I do not claim this to be fully comprehensive in its coverage, not least because the number of

groups performing early music on an irregular basis well exceeds the possibilities of presentation within one Figure.

20. There are exceptions. Gothic Voices, directed by Christopher Page, for example, was set up at the request of the BBC, to make studio recordings of Medieval and Renaissance vocal music.

21. Stage models of growth are familiar in research on small businesses (see Churchill and Lewis 1983; Greiner 1972; Scott and Bruce 1987). However, such growth models are applied to individual organizations rather than populations of new businesses, so any parallels should be treated with caution.

22. I am indebted to an anonymous reviewer of an early draft for this information. The reader will note that the number 7 features prominently in my own thinking in this book, with 7x7 models used to structure my analysis (this was not something I consciously planned at the outset).

> 23. His acts being seven ages. At first, the infant,
> Mewling and puking in the nurse's arms.
> Then the whining schoolboy, with his satchel
> And shining morning face, creeping like snail
> Unwillingly to school. And then the lover,
> Sighing like furnace, with a woeful ballad
> Made to his mistress' eyebrow. Then a soldier,
> Full of strange oaths and bearded like the pard,
> Jealous in honour, sudden and quick in quarrel,
> Seeking the bubble reputation
> Even in the canon's mouth. And then the justice,
> In fair round belly with good capon lined,
> With eyes severe and beard of formal cut,
> Full of wise saws and modern instances;
> And so he plays his part. The sixth age shifts
> Into the lean and slippered pantaloon
> With spectacles on nose and pouch on side;
> His youthful hose, well saved, a world too wide
> For his shrunk shank, and his big manly voice,
> Turning again toward childish treble, pipes
> And whistles in his sound. Last scene of all,
> That ends this strange eventful history,
> Is second childishness and mere oblivion,
> Sans teeth, sans eyes, sans taste, sans everything.
> (*As You Like It,* Act 2, Scene VII)

24. See Steiner 1973. My illustrative phase descriptions are loosely based on reading various popular treatments of Steiner's work available online; see, for example, Tony Crisp's article "Every Seven Years You Change," available at http://dreamhawk.com/body-and-mind/every-seven-years-you-change. Though I stop the cycle at 49, Steiner's own approach continues through 63 and beyond.

25. Couldry 2010:4.

26. Andrew Pinnock: interview with author, May 29, 2003.

27. Catherine Mackintosh: interview with author, April 29, 2004.

28. Thomson et al 1994:538.

29. Clifford Bartlett: interview with author, November 25, 2003.

30. The "spectacle" is highlighted as important here. Other notable early music spectacles include Munrow's "The Six Wives of Henry VIII" project for television; Norrington's "Experience" weekends; and John Eliot Gardiner's Bach Cantata Pilgrimage.

31. In Bruno 2007:15.

32. Thomson et al. 1994:537.

33. Ibid.

34. Thomson et al. 1994:538.

35. Ibid.

36. Sir John Eliot Gardiner: interview with author, November 6, 2012.

37. See Kernis and Goldman 2005; 2006.

38. Thomson et al. 1994:537.

39. From a podcast *David Munrow On The Record—On an overgrown path*, 2008. Available at: http://itunes.apple.com/podcast/on-an-overgrown-path/id269102376, accessed July 5, 2011.

40. Brown 1976:288.

41. See Bourdieu 2002.

42. Trevor Pinnock: interview with author, October 13, 2012.

43. Christopher Hogwood: interview with author, January 10, 2003. Sir John Eliot Gardiner cites a recording of Couperin performed by the Kuijken brothers in the late 1960s as particularly inspiring him in the direction of period performance (he launched his own period orchestra in 1978).

44. Christopher Hogwood: interview with author, January 10, 2003.

45. See discussion in Leech-Wilkinson 2002.

46. Establishment recognition of the early music movement came in 1997 in the form of Roger Norrington's knighthood; John Eliot Gardiner was similarly honored in the following year.

47. Cloonan 2007:36.

48. Hewison 1995:263.

49. Kenyon 2009.

50. Sir John Eliot Gardiner: interview with author, November 6, 2012.

51. Sir Roger Norrington: correspondence with author, November 8, 2012.

52. See Evidence-Based Medicine Working Group 1992; Packwood 2002; Wilson et al. 2008.

53. See Church 2013.

CHAPTER 3

1. Taruskin in Kenyon 1988:137.

2. Trilling 1972:100.

3. Trevor Pinnock: interview with author, October 13, 2012.

4. Morrow 1978:233.

5. Ibid., 244.

6. Ibid. See also Adorno 2003.

7. Berman 1970:325. See also Guignon (2004) for an interesting discussion "on being authentic"; Fleming 2009; Gilmore & Pine 2007; Goffman 1959; Vannini & Williams 2009.

8. Adorno 1967b, 1976.

9. Harker 1980.

10. Hirsch 1970, 1972.

11. Becker 1982.

12. Peterson 1976.

13. See Negus 1996:28; Adorno 1989.

14. Dutton 2004:1.

15. Negus 1996:38.

16. Adorno had little time for those seeking historically authentic performances of classical music, referring to their enterprise as "historical fetishism" (Adorno 1967a).

17. Godlovitch 1998; Kemal and Gaskell 1999; Lindholm, 2008; Thom 2011:91; Young 2005:501.

18. DeNora 2000; Lippman 1992; Scruton 1997.

19. Barker and Taylor 2007; Frith 1998; Moore 2002.

20. Harrison 2008, 2009; McLeod 1999; Wìllliams 2007.

21. Grazian 2003.

22. Peterson 1997; 2005.

23. See Donington 1963; Dreyfus 1983; Fabian 2000, 2001; Godlovitch 1999; Haynes 2007; Kelly 2011; Kenyon 1988; Leppard 1988; Thom 2011; Young 1988.

24. Haskell 1988:175; Rosen 1990.

25. Brown 1988:39.

26. Haskell 1988:175.

27. Morrow 1978:246.

28. See Taruskin 1982, 1984, 1988, 1995.

29. Taruskin 2007:vi.

30. Taruskin 1995:92.

31. Hennion and Fauquet 2001:87.

32. Rogers 1984:524.

33. Bartlett 1983:149.

34. Sir John Eliot Gardiner: interview with author, November 6, 2012. Trilling (1972:11) suggests that authenticity implies a "more strenuous moral experience than 'sincerity' does, a more exigent conception of the self and what being true to it consists in, a wider reference to the universe and man's place in it, and a less acceptant and genial view of the social circumstances of life."

35. Holden 2012.

36. See Austin 1964.

37. Dutton 2004:1.

38. From England and Wales High Court (Chancery Division) Decisions. Neutral Citation Number: [2004] EWHC 1530. Available at: http://www.bailii.org/ew/cases/EWHC/Ch/2004/1530.html, accessed October 25, 2012.

39. Davies 2001:3.

40. Ibid., 4.

41. Taruskin 1995:277.

42. Ibid., 24.

43. Goehr 2007:19.

44. Ibid., 13–17.

45. See Collingwood 1938; Croce 1922.

46. Explanation of the existence of the musical work has a seminal bearing on the controversy between those who believe music to be humanly meaningful and those who deny

this outright (see Reid 1969: Chapter VII). Key contributions in the study of musical meaning include Goehr 2007 [1991]; Higgins 1991; Langer 1957; Maconie 1990; Meyer 1956; Reid 1969; Robinson 1997. For a helpful overview and discussion of related issues see Gracyk and Kania 2011.

47. Goehr 2007:7.
48. Ibid., 111.
49. Ibid., 206.
50. Ibid., xlii.
51. For a discussion of the parallel shift towards "art-works" see Shiner 2001.
52. Kivy 2002:134.
53. Ibid.
54. Ibid.
55. Kivy 2002:135.
56. Haynes 2007:87. See also Butt 2002:74; Kivy 1995:45.
57. Koopman 1987:2 quoted in Davies 2001:207.
58. Taruskin holds that "We cannot know intentions, for many reasons—or rather, we cannot know we know them" (Taruskin 1995:97).
59. For Sir John Eliot Gardiner, "the act of making music always entails an act of interpretation." Interview with author, November 6, 2012.
60. Hoffmann 1919:69, cited in Goehr 2007:1.
61. Taruskin 1995:10.
62. Taruskin 1995:317. As Michael Morrow used to tell his performers, if you didn't know how a Viennese Waltz sounded, you'd have no idea from just looking at the music (it looks like it just has three beats in the bar).
63. Taruskin 1995:10.
64. See Kivy 1995; O'Dea 1994.
65. Taruskin's first contribution in this debate was the paper "On letting the music speak for itself," given at the national meeting of the American Musicological Society in Boston on November 13, 1981. This was published the following year in the *Journal of Musicology*.
66. Sir Nicholas Kenyon: interview with author, November 12, 2012.
67. Kenyon 1977.
68. Taruskin 1995:76 quoting Trilling (1972).
69. Taruskin 1995:8. My italics.
70. See Rosen 1990, for example.
71. See also Robert Donington 1989 for a similar critique in relation to Leppard's *Authenticity in Music*.
72. Taruskin 1995:5.
73. Ibid., 19.
74. This list is based on Shiner's (2001) thesis of "art divided"—see especially Table 3 From Artisan/Artist to Arts versus Artisan, p.115.
75. See, for example, Butt 2002; Haynes 2007; Kenyon 1988; Leech-Wilkinson 2002; Sherman 1997.
76. Butt (2002:xiii) makes "liberal use of...'theory'"; Leech-Wilkinson (2002:261) describes himself as an "ultra-positivist with liberal leanings."
77. See Taruskin 1995:10 & 74.
78. Cook 1999:256.
79. Goehr 2007:xliii.

80. Sayer 1992. It is worth noting that ontology gets a bad press even in books that are ostensibly about philosophy and music. Davies (2001:37), for example, describes ontological arguments as "dry and difficult." Elsewhere, R. A. Sharpe warns that "ontology is ideology" (1974). Apart from this being an ontological position (as well as an ideological one), it overlooks the fact that there are clearly better and worse grounds for our beliefs.

81. The melody is taken from *Good Morning to All*, written by the Hills sisters in 1893, and *Happy Birthday to You* only first appeared in print in 1912. I deliberately chose this everyday musical work to prove a point without appealing to a canonical piece from the classical music repertoire. The argument presented holds for purely instrumental or absolute music too.

82. Upton 2012:1.

83. See Bhaskar 1993:222-223.

84. Goehr 2007:2.

85. According to Peirce (1883), the semiotic triangle can be understood in relation to other triangles operating at different levels of analysis. Focusing on the musical score, for example, we can distinguish musical notes (signified) represented through accepted symbols on the page (signifiers), which individually and together relate to their referent subject—which is sound. A musical score, perhaps an Urtext edition, is composed of signs, but is also a sign itself—comprised of all three elements of the semiotic triangle.

86. See Archer 1996 [1988]; 1995, for detailed discussion of social and sociocultural systemic emergent properties.

87. Davies 2001.

88. Upton 2012:7.

89. Note that this is not to imply a musical work can come into existence just by people talking about it.

90. Dewey 1934 [2005]:113.

91. Bhaskar 1993:54.

92. Norrie 2010:32.

93. Bhaskar 1995:143. Note Taruskin's own reference to "The Pastness of the Present and the Presence of the Past;" this is a theme taken up further in the last Part of the book.

94. Schechner 2006:30.

95. Ibid., 28.

96. Davies 2001.

97. From England and Wales High Court (Chancery Division) Decisions. Neutral Citation Number: [2004] EWHC 1530.

98. In Vulliamy 2005.

99. Davies 2001:207.

100. See Bhaskar 1993; Bhaskar and Hartwig 2010; Hartwig 2007 for further explanation of these concepts.

101. Hartwig defines alethic truth as "the truth of things as distinct from propositions" (Hartwig 2007:24).

102. Sir Roger Norrington: correspondence with author, November 7, 2012.

CHAPTER 4

1. Dickens 1859:1.

2. Cohen and Snitzer 1985:99.

3. Kenyon 2011. The group was Juilliard415.

4. Kenyon 2011.
5. Catch 1999.
6. Haynes 2007:40–41.
7. Butt 2002:ix–x.
8. Bennett 2008:121.
9. See Gill and Pratt 2008; McKinlay and Smith 2009.
10. Perks 1993.
11. John Bickley: interview with author, August 5, 2003.
12. Brown 1978:xiv.
13. Neel 1950:93.

14. From "Mr Munrow, his study." The Archive Hour, Radio 4; July 21, 2007 8pm, with Jeremy Summerly. Leech-Wilkinson (2002:96) notes how a similar issue faced the Studio der frühen Musik, constrained as it was by the need to travel between concerts in a single car.

15. Sir Roger Norrington: interview with author, June 23, 2004.
16. Roche 1979b:216.
17. Lucie Skeaping: interview with author, November 10, 2012.
18. Roche 1979b:215.
19. Ibid., 216.

20. From I Fagiolini website: http://www.ifagiolini.com/about-us/the-name/, accessed February 27, 2012. The naming of *I Fagiolini,* founded in 1986, owes something to the New Age movement. As Robert Hollingworth, the group's founder, remarks, "It was just a student joke referring to the apparent connection in the 1980s of Early Music with vegetarianism. At New College, early music was generally referred to as 'Beany music'...so it just stuck." (From an Interview with Robert Hollingworth, May 2, 2011. Available at: http://www.earlymusicand-dance.co.uk/2011/05/02/interview-with-robert-hollingworth, accessed February 27, 2011.)

21. Andrew Pinnock: interview with author, May 29, 2003.

22. In *The New Spirit of Capitalism,* Boltanski and Chiapello (2007) discuss the rise of a new form of network-based organization that arose in the 1970s. Their "artistic critique" is motivated by (i) the demand for liberation; and (ii) a rejection of *in*authenticity. To the extent there has been a newfound "freedom" in the workplace, they argue that this came at the expense of material and psychological security. The parallels with Early Music are striking.

23. A view held by Andrew Pinnock, formerly early music officer at the Arts Council, amongst others.

24. Kenyon 1988:2.
25. Donington 1975b:238.
26. Catherine Mackintosh: interview with author, April 29, 2004.
27. Bennett 1991.
28. Lucie Skeaping: interview with author, November 10, 2012.
29. Kenyon 1988:8.
30. Sir John Eliot Gardiner: interview with author, November 6, 2012.
31. Colin Kitching: interview with author, May 4, 2004.
32. Quoted in Mather 1997.
33. Catherine Mackintosh: interview with author, April 29, 2004.
34. Ryan 1999:508.
35. In "Munrow, his study." See note 14 above.
36. Haskell 1988:108.
37. Catherine Mackintosh: interview with author, April 29, 2004.

38. The Camden Chamber Orchestra was founded in 1967 and became the Orchestra of St. John's in 1973.
39. Haskell 1988:127.
40. Roche 1979b:216.
41. Haskell 1988:110. See also Gollin 2001.
42. Fellows 1981. See Aoyama 2004 for a detailed review of Greenberg's career and influence.
43. Safford Cape retired in 1967 and died in 1973.
44. See Roche 1979b.
45. Kenyon 1988:49.
46. Fallows 1995.
47. Harker 1985:ix; back cover.
48. Upton 2012:1.
49. Ibid., 4–5.
50. Ibid., 1.
51. Ibid., 3.
52. Fellows 1981:1.
53. From press clipping of an interview with journalist Phillip Sommerich in 1974 (in an unnamed newspaper), in the Morrow Collection (ref:K/PP93), King's College, London.
54. Biography in the Morrow Collection, box 10, King's College London.
55. Haskell 1988:63.
56. Page 1993:457.
57. Ibid., 458.
58. Thomson 1974:1.
59. See Mackerness 1964, cited in Ehrlich 1985:224. Intriguingly, Palmer's (1947) biographical gazetteer of musicians and musical organizations in Britain (*British Music*) makes no mention of early music, or early musicians (such as Dolmetsch, Deller, Dent, Dart, Landowska, Ord, etc.)
60. Ehrlich 1985:224.
61. Marriner played baroque violin with Robert Donington in the 1950s, but decided not to pursue this (interview with Sir Nicholas Kenyon, November 12, 2012).
62. "Hogwood at 70", (2009) *Gramophone* podcast, transcribed by author. Available at: http://www.gramophone.co.uk/classical-music-news/happy-birthday-christopher-hogwood, accessed December 7, 2012.
63. Andrew Parrott: interview with author, December 3, 2003.
64. Maureen Garnham: interview with author, March 10, 2003.
65. See Kenyon 2009.
66. Goldsbrough and Goldsbrough 1992.
67. Sir Roger Norrington: interview with author, June 23, 2004.
68. See Lawson 2000.
69. See Duffin 2008 on *How Equal Temperament Ruined Harmony: And Why You Should Care*.
70. From "Harnoncourt": http://www.styriarte.com/harnoncourt/index_en.php/article/articleview/1404/1/35, accessed November 11, 2005.
71. See Upton 2012.
72. See Rooley 1990.
73. Trevor Pinnock: interview with author, October 13, 2012.
74. Sir John Eliot Gardiner: interview with author, November 6, 2012.
75. Catherine Mackintosh: interview with author, April 29, 2004.

76. Christopher Hogwood: interview with author, January 10, 2003.

77. Potter n.d.

78. *Opernwelt* interview (1984). Available at: http://www.hogwood.org/archive/interviews/opernwelt-interview-1984.html, accessed August 9, 2011.

79. "Hogwood at 70," (2009) *Gramophone* podcast.

80. Taruskin 1995:318.

81. Hogwood studied harpsichord with Gustav Leonhardt, who was criticized, especially early on in his career, for his "excessive sobriety" (Salter 2012).

82. Hogwood's interview for *Opernwelt* (1984) supports this viewpoint.

CHAPTER 5

1. *Shake, Rattle and Roll* was first recorded by Big Joe Turner (February 1954). Bill Haley & His Comets brought out a cover version soon after (July 1954). Both records sold well, and the two artists became close friends, performing together on tour in Australia in 1957.

2. Kenyon 2006:5.

3. Cohen and Snitzer 1985:47.

4. Kenyon 1988:7.

5. Wallace 2006:10.

6. See Wilson 2007a; 2007b for further discussion of labor market emergence.

7. Fine 1998:257.

8. Archer (2003:6) defines the agential project as "an end that is desired, however tentatively or nebulously, and also some notion, however imprecise, of the course of action through which to accomplish it."

9. Smith 1776:107.

10. Towse 1995:36. Amongst the research focusing explicitly on artists' labor markets, there has been informative analysis of the employment of singers (see Towse 1992; 1993), performing artists (Throsby 1996), dancers and actors (Freakley 2000; Jackson, Honey, Hillage and Stock 1994), visual artists (Brighton, Pearson and Parry 1985), and artists of all kinds (Abbing 2002; Alper and Wassall 2006; Freakley and Neelands 2003; Menger 1999, 2001, 2006; O'Brien and Feist 1995; Towse 1995, 2006; Wassall and Alper 1992).

11. Bennett 2008:36.

12. There is a very sizeable literature on the entrepreneurial "opportunity," which distinguishes between such "subjective" and "objective" positions. See Eckhardt and Shane 2003 for discussion.

13. See Stokes and Wilson 2010, Chapter 12 for discussion.

14. TEC first performed together in November 1972, but made their London debut in 1973.

15. Andrew Parrott: interview with author, December 3, 2003.

16. Pinnock 2013:18.

17. Trevor Pinnock: interview with author, October 13, 2012.

18. Ibid.

19. Maureen Garnham: interview with author, March 10, 2003.

20. Trevor Pinnock: interview with author, October 13, 2012.

21. Sir John Eliot Gardiner: interview with author, November 6, 2012.

22. *Goldberg* interview with Craig Zeichner in 1999, on the goldbergweb.com website, accessed June 20, 2003. This website is no longer available.

23. *Goldberg* interview with Craig Zeichner.

24. Ibid.
25. Andrew Parrott: interview with author, December 3, 2003.
26. Ibid.
27. Felix Warnock: interview with author, March 10, 2003.
28. Wallace 2006:10.
29. Christopher Hogwood: interview with author, January 10, 2003.
30. "Hogwood at 70", *Gramophone* podcast, transcribed by the author.
31. Ibid.
32. Ibid.
33. See Villa 1986.
34. See Bilton 2007; Caves 2000; Hesmondhalgh 2005.
35. Heather Jarman: interview with author, August 5, 2003.
36. Trevor Pinnock: interview with author, October 13, 2012.
37. Heather Jarman: interview with author, August 5, 2003.
38. Principal horn of the BBC Symphony Orchestra for many years.
39. Christopher Hogwood: interview with author, January 10, 2003.
40. Colin Kitching: interview with author, May 4, 2004.
41. Ibid.
42. This was introduced by the then manager of AAM, Christopher Lawrence: interview with author, August 5, 2003.
43. Trevor Pinnock: interview with author, October 13, 2012.
44. From the Morrow Collection, box 2, King's College London.
45. Kenyon 1978.
46. Andrew Parrott: interview with author, December 3, 2003.
47. Ibid.
48. *Early Music,* 8(2):147 (1980).
49. Kenyon 1988:7.
50. Ibid., 12.
51. Trevor Pinnock: interview with author, October 13, 2012.
52. Heather Jarman: interview with author, August 5, 2003.
53. Sir John Eliot Gardiner: interview with author, November 6, 2012.
54. Ibid.
55. Maureen Garnham: interview with author, March 10, 2003.
56. It is interesting to speculate on whether The English Baroque Soloists were named with this rationale explicitly in mind.
57. Dreyfus 1997:28.
58. Sir Roger Norrington: interview with author, June 23, 2004.
59. Interview with Brian Robins, *Goldberg* Magazine (2002). Website no longer available.
60. Kenyon 1984a:2.
61. Kenyon 2006:5.
62. There are several precedents for this. In 1904, musicians broke away from Henry Wood's "dictatorial baton" at the Queen's Hall Orchestra to form the London Symphony Orchestra. The London Philharmonic and Royal Philharmonic became self-governing after the outbreak of war in 1939. In 1964 Walter Legge suspended the Philharmonia and attempted to disband it. The Philharmonia players decided to become self-governing and re-form as the New Philharmonia.
63. Kenyon 1986:322.

64. Chris Sayers: interview with author, November 25, 2003.
65. Catherine Mackintosh: interview with author, April 29, 2004.
66. Wallace 2006:12.
67. Ibid.
68. Wallace 2006:10.
69. The OAE has been cheekily dubbed the "Orchestra of the Age of Retirement" by some, reflecting the difficulties young players find in gaining a foothold (despite laudable initiatives such as the Jerwood/OAE Experience).
70. Felix Warnock: interview with author, March 10, 2003.
71. Wallace 2006:19.
72. Ibid., 13.
73. Felix Warnock: interview with author, March 10, 2003.
74. Wallace 2006:19.
75. Felix Warnock: interview with author, March 10, 2003.
76. Wallace 2006:31.
77. Kenyon 2006:5.
78. Wallace 2006:19.

CHAPTER 6

1. Donington 1963:26.
2. Mertin 1986:xiii.
3. Arnold 1981:ii.
4. Sir John Eliot Gardiner: interview with author, November 6, 2012.
5. Dart 1954:34.
6. Arnold 1981:ii.
7. Dart 1954:16.
8. Ibid., 13.
9. Ibid., 21–28.
10. Dart 1954:28. Thomas (1977) discusses the problems of editing, and particularly "how much" to put in an edition, such as note values; barring; musica ficta; pitch; scoring/performing medium; underlay of text.
11. Donington 1963:25. See, for example, Bartlett and Holman 1975 on the "tentative rules" of performing music by Giovanni Gabrieli.
12. Donington 1963:27.
13. Ibid., 25.
14. Ibid., 26.
15. Ibid., 27.
16. Stevens 1989:416.
17. See Bourdieu 1993.
18. Faultless 2010:196.
19. See Leech-Wilkinson 2002 for a detailed review in relation to Medieval music.
20. See Negus 1996, Chapter 2:66-98.
21. Negus 1996:66.
22. See Hennion 1997.
23. From England and Wales High Court (Chancery Division) Decisions. Neutral Citation Number: [2004] EWHC 1530. Available at: http://www.bailii.org/ew/cases/EWHC/Ch/2004/1530.html, accessed October 25, 2012.

24. Clifford Bartlett: interview with author, November 25, 2003.
25. Ibid.
26. Ibid.
27. Clifford Bartlett Appeal flyer. Available at: http://www.eemf.org.uk/CB%20appeal%20flyer.pdf, accessed July 3, 2012.
28. Brown 1973:115.
29. Ibid. The most expensive was 90p for 50 dances in playing score, and the cheapest was 35p for the score and parts of a five-part fantasy.
30. Morrow Collection, box 4, King's College London.
31. Ibid.
32. Named after his friend Canon Francis Galpin, a priest with a lifelong practical interest in studying, collecting, and making musical instruments. A number of other early music societies were formed around this time. Amongst these, the Society of Recorder Players (founded in 1937 by Carl Dolmetsch and Edgar Hunt) has remained particularly active. Walter Bergmann (1902-1998) was musical director of the Society from 1946, and later collaborated with Michael Tippett at Morley College.
33. Dr. Horace Fitzpatrick (who set up a precursor to The Hanover Band) was the collection's initial honorary curator. Anthony Baines held the position between 1970 and his retirement in 1980.
34. Clifford Bartlett: interview with author, November 25, 2003.
35. From FoMRHI website: http://stremen.home.xs4all.nl/fomrhi_i.html, accessed October 26, 2012.
36. Andrew Pinnock: interview with author, May 29, 2003. Denis Stevens notes how the BBC's Music Department could turn to its "army" of copyists in the case of works for which no performing edition existed: "We had a top floor with about ten men sitting there scribbling away frantically. It was all done by hand." (In Carpenter 1997:104.)
37. Andrew Pinnock: interview with author, May 29, 2003.
38. Musica Britannica website: http://www.musicabritannica.org.uk, accessed July 4, 2012. Thurston Dart was Musica Britannica's first secretary.
39. Raymond Leppard: interview with author, January 5, 2012. As of December 2012 there were 93 Volumes with a further 15 in preparation.
40. Richard Wood: interview with author, November 25, 2003.
41. Ibid.
42. The company was founded in Celle in 1925. In 1964 it took over the designs and rights of instruments made by Otto Steinkopf, one of the 20th-century pioneers of instrument-making, and a former bassoon player with RIAS Berlin.
43. Monk 1973:35.
44. Stevenson in Paul 1981:139.
45. Robert Deegan: interview with author, November 25, 2003.
46. Source: http://www.progressor.net/interview/francis_monkman.html, accessed March 1, 2012.
47. Cohen & Snitzer 1985:21.
48. See Elliott 1995; and Small 1998 on the process of "musicing," or "musicking."
49. Shiner 2001.
50. Cohen & Snitzer 1985:21.
51. Five of the eleven students on the harpsichord-making course at the London College of Furniture in 1981 were "girls," according to David Law, in Paul 1981:114.

52. Robert Goble's son, Andrea, joined the family business; he was named after his godfather Andrea Pallis—brother of Marco, who founded the English Consort of Viols (in Paul 1981:99).

53. Davies in Paul 1981:197.

54. McGeary 1975.

55. Rawson in Paul 1981:120.

56. Woolley in Paul 1981:150.

57. Robert Bailey: interview with author, November 25, 2003.

58. Kirkpatrick 1965:v.

59. In Morrison 1979:7. At this time, the EMS workshop employed 17 workers in all. The majority were trained from scratch (i.e., school), since as Wood explains, "Most of those coming out of the London College of Furniture, for example, usually want to set up on their own" (Morrison 1979:7).

60. From http://www.normanmyall.co.uk, accessed March 1, 2012.

61. Samson 1979:34.

62. Ibid. In 2012 Claudia Fritz and colleagues undertook a double-blind experiment to test whether performers preferred "Strads vs. Modern Violins." For discussion of the intriguing results see http://en.wikipedia.org/wiki/Player_preferences_among_new_and_old_violins, accessed May 19, 2013; or Claudia Fritz's website: http://www.lam.jussieu.fr/Membres/Fritz/HomePage/Indianapolis_paper.html, accessed May 19, 2013.

63. Godlovitch 1999:156.

64. Hubbard 1965:x.

65. From the website of David Rubio Luthier: http://www.rubioviolins.com, accessed July 4, 2012.

66. Dolmetsch in Paul 1981:60.

67. Stevenson in Paul 1981:140.

68. Hubbard 1965:xi.

69. Bennett 1991.

70. From Haney 1972.

71. Rawson in Paul 1981:128.

72. Stevenson in Paul 1981:142.

73. Comment attributed to William Dowd.

74. Godlovitch 1999:162.

75. In *Guardian* obituary by Thea Abbott, September 7, 2011.

76. Godlovitch 1999:162.

77. Bernard Thomas: interview with author, November 9, 2012.

78. See http://www.soniccouture.com/en/products/28-ancient-rare-and-experimental/g30-the-conservatoire-collection, accessed March 1, 2012.

79. From http://www.vam.ac.uk/content/articles/t/musical-instruments-collection-history, accessed March 1, 2012.

80. It is a sign of the rapid growth of the musical instrument industry in the early 1970s that *Early Music* 3(2) considered it worth including an article on "Buying a harpsichord," penned by Trevor Pinnock (1975). It must also be observed, however, that not all instruments were so well catered for. Jeremy Montagu on "Choosing brass instruments" in *Early Music* (1976) 4(1):35 notes, "There are as yet no sources of supply of medieval brass instruments"; although, "Once we arrive at the late renaissance and early baroque things become different and there are a fair number of instruments available."

81. In Morrison 1979:7.

82. Clifford Bartlett: interview with author, November 25, 2003.

83. See Lawson and Stowell 1999; Lawson 2000; Humphries 2000; Rowland 2001; Stowell 2001; Brown 2003. See also Montagu 2007 on the origins and development of musical instruments; Montagu 1976 on making early percussion instruments; Moeck 1971 on crumhorns and cornamuses; and Boydell 1982 on crumhorns and other windcap instruments. Lawson and Stowell 2012 also provide comprehensive coverage of performance issues.

84. Lawson 2000:36.

85. See Humphries 2000 for discussion of the valve's (contested) invention.

86. Christopher Hogwood: interview with author, January 10, 2003.

87. Rooley 2009.

88. Catherine Mackintosh: interview with author, April 29, 2004.

89. Lawson 2000:xii.

CHAPTER 7

1. From John Henry Newman's *The Idea of a University* (1852), quoted in Seabright 2012.

2. Hartwig 2011:508.

3. Kenyon 1976:447. It was most probably as a consequence of writing this piece for *Early Music* that Nicholas Kenyon was asked to join the Arts Council's Music Panel, which otherwise did not have any representation for Early Music at the time.

4. Sherman 1997:400.

5. See Born and Barry, 2010 for discussion of "art-science" more generally.

6. Townley et al. 2009.

7. Nowotny et al. 2003:179.

8. Etzkowitz and Leydesdorff 2000:116.

9. See Peterson 1997. Kernis and Goldman's (2006) discussion of "dispositional authenticity" as "the unimpeded operation of one's core or true self in one's daily enterprise" (p. 344) provides more commentary on this form of personal authenticity.

10. See Ansdell 2005 for discussion in the context of music therapy.

11. Sternberg and Lubart 2007.

12. Martin 2008:6.

13. Strati 2000:18.

14. Ibbotson 2008; also discussed in Darsø 2004.

15. Eisner 2002:10.

16. Strati 2000:18.

17. See Schubert 2009.

18. Heterotopias are "spaces of otherness"; neither here nor there. See Foucault 1967.

19. Social structures are comprised of "a latticework of internal relations between entities that may enable and constrain (but cannot transform) the intentions and actions of agents who draw upon, reproduce and/or transform these relations," whilst Institutions are "systems of established rules, conventions, norms, values and customs" (Fleetwood 2008:247 and 259).

20. See Leydesdorff and Etzkowitz 1998.

21. Quoted from Collini's book *What are Universities for?* in Reisz 2012. Available at: http://www.timeshighereducation.co.uk/story.asp?storycode=419068, accessed July 16, 2012. See also Clark 1998.

22. Philip Shirtcliff's discussion of "early training of instrument makers" at the department of musical instrument technology, the London College of Furniture (in Thomson

1978), provides further background to some of the key issues in this related area of early music-making.

23. As an undergraduate at Cambridge in 1985, I took a module in performance practice tutored by the Bach scholar John Butt. With the benefit of hindsight, it is interesting to read Butt (2002:ix) suggesting that "historical performance was fundamentally anathema to the modernist regime" at Cambridge, in the early 1980s. As I recall, the group Cambridge Musick (comprising Richard Egarr, Andrew Manze, and Robert Ehrlich) represented a high-point of student period instrument performance at the time.

24. In Anthony Rooley's "Foreword" to Thomson 1978:ix. Margaret Bent (2013:8) suggests there has been a "squeezing of early music in academic departments throughout the Western world" since the 1970s. However, commenting on Med-Ren's 40th anniversary in 2012, she also reports on how "Attendance has blossomed from 30 to 40 at the earliest meetings to nearly 200 in recent years, with papers of high quality."

25. See Haskell 1988.

26. Jeremy West: interview with author, November 10, 2012.

27. Kenyon 1976:447.

28. Christopher Hogwood: interview with author, January 10, 2003. It is worth noting that Cambridge University's Music Faculty introduced the new role of director of performance studies (OAE violinist Margaret Faultless) only in October 2010.

29. Jeremy West: interview with author, November 10, 2012.

30. See DiMaggio's (1982) discussion of both the centrality and marginality of the cultural entrepreneur in relation to the setting up of the Boston Symphony Orchestra.

31. Thomson 1981.

32. Leech-Wilkinson 2002:238.

33. Taruskin 1995:96–97.

34. Kerman 1985:229.

35. From Peter Phillips' blog: http://tallisman.wordpress.com/2009/01/08/what-we-really-do, accessed July 18, 2012.

36. This is regrettably no longer always the case today, with universities becoming increasingly risk-averse "no" places.

37. See Cohen and Leventhal 1990; Zahra and George 2002.

38. Galton 1914:230–1, quoted in Ehrlich 1985:77.

39. The Royal Academy of Music was founded in 1823; the Royal College of Music in 1883.

40. Ehrlich 1985:105–106.

41. Godlovitch 1998:1.

42. Andrew Pinnock: interview with author, May 29, 2003.

43. Trevor Pinnock: interview with author, October 13, 2012.

44. Haynes 2007:43.

45. Roberts 1978:3.

46. Andrew Parrott: interview with author, December 3, 2003.

47. Alison Crum: interview with author, November 10, 2012.

48. The Early Music Centre opened in January 1976. It ran the Early Music Network, with c.100 concerts per year, and the Early Music Centre Festival, an annual series of 7 concerts in London.

49. Andrew Parrott: interview with author, December 3, 2003.

50. Haskell 1988:195. It is notable, for example, that The Tallis Scholars now run summer courses themselves in Uppingham, Sydney, and Seattle. See http://www.tsss.uk.com, accessed May 23, 2013.

51. Bennett 2008:62.

52. See Bennett 2008:81.

53. My italics.

54. Source: http://www.vam.ac.uk/vastatic/wid/ead/acgb/acgbf.html, accessed March 12, 2012. In 2010 the Arts Council introduced a new 10-year strategic framework for the arts. This encapsulates its new mission in terms of championing, developing, and investing in the arts.

55. The RAAs were established between 1956 (South West) and 1971 (Eastern). Following the Wilding Report (1989) they were restructured and consolidated into 10 Regional Arts Boards by 1992. Two years later, the Arts Council of Great Britain was dissolved and separate Arts Councils for England, Scotland, and Wales were formed.

56. Morrow Collection, box 1, King's College London.

57. From a copy of *Recorder & Music* 4(6) in the Morrow Collection, box 1, King's College London.

58. According to a publicity leaflet in 1978-79, the Network aimed "to extend early music throughout Great Britain and over the next three years aims to invite most of the major early music groups from this country and abroad to perform." (Source: Morrow Collection, box 2, King's College London.)

59. In Directory of British Early Music Groups, published in 1981 by the Early Music Centre (p.3).

60. Thomson 1978:60.

61. Morrow Collection, box 2, King's College London.

62. Kenyon 1984b.

63. Sir Nicholas Kenyon: interview with author, November 12, 2012.

64. Andrew Pinnock: interview with author, May 29, 2003. The ideal for many early music ensembles was to secure what amounted to subsidized rehearsal, i.e., fully-funded live concert opportunities en route to the recording studio. However, what was marketable on CD wasn't always marketable to live concert audiences. Placing subsidy with promoters rather than ensembles strengthened the promoters' repertoire negotiating position. As Pinnock puts it, "programming decisions taking more account of live audience interests were the hoped-for policy result."

65. Sir Nicholas Kenyon: interview with author, November 12, 2012.

66. Andrew Pinnock: interview with author, May 29, 2003. See Pinnock 2007 for related discussion of rent-seeking behavior in the arts.

67. Sir Roger Norrington: interview with author, June 23, 2004.

68. Sir John Eliot Gardiner: interview with author, November 6, 2012. It is interesting to note that the English Chamber Orchestra (in many respects the working model of a freelance chamber orchestra most similar to the period instrument orchestras) has long sought to make a positive virtue out of its "private" status. It includes the statement, "The orchestra receives no support from the Arts Council England" in its program notes. (See Chong, 2010:154; also Chong and Trappey 2001.)

69. Jeremy West: interview with author, November 10, 2012.

70. See Björkegren 1995 for a discussion of the two competing strategies ("aesthetic" and "commercial") applied by arts decision-makers with the aim of reducing uncertainty.

71. Blaug 2001: 132. Abbing (2002) raises the interesting idea that rather than a lack of subsidy being the problem for the arts, it is precisely the government's support of the sector that has maintained the "exceptional" economy of the arts—a situation that fails to benefit most artists.

72. See Baumol and Bowen 1966; Benedict 1991; Blaug 1976, 2001; Frey 1997, 2003; O'Hagan 1998; Peacock 1969, 1993; Throsby 1994.

73. Heilbrun and Gray 2001:222.

74. Ibid., 226.

75. Sir Nicholas Kenyon: interview with author, November 12, 2012.

76. Kenyon 1976:443.

77. Ibid.

78. See Castañer and Campos 2002 for a discussion of innovation in the performing arts.

79. Sir Nicholas Kenyon: interview with author, November 12, 2012.

80. See http://www.artscouncil.org.uk/media/uploads/portfolio_summaries/music.pdf, accessed July 17, 2012.

81. To put this in perspective, the Academy of Ancient Music's annual report for the period 2009–10 showed total income of £1,184,164, of which £412,148 was "voluntary income" (including a one off grant of £120k from ACE in 2009–10). Source: AAM website: http://www.aam.co.uk/media/Files/Resources/Corporate%20Info/annualreportv21lowres.pdf, accessed September 28, 2012.

82. Rooley 1978:64–65.

83. Kenyon 1976:445.

84. Sir Nicholas Kenyon: interview with author, November 12, 2012.

85. The infrastructure of professional classical music performance more generally was, of course, a supportive structure for Early Music at a systemic level.

86. See Pirnay et al. 2003 for a discussion of "spinning out" knowledge as the "third mission" of the university sector. See also the HEFCE Research Evaluation Framework REF "Part 2D Main Panel D Criteria" (http://www.hefce.ac.uk/research/ref/pubs/2012/01_12_2D.pdf, accessed May 21, 2013) for a discussion of what criteria constitute "impact." Early Music's achievements certainly appear in a most favorable light when set against the criteria listed.

87. Pearson 2012:10.

88. Ibid., 11.

89. Sir Nicholas Kenyon: interview with author, November 12, 2012.

CHAPTER 8

1. Reith 1925:3.

2. In North, Richard, D. (1999). Millenium Babes, *The Independent*. Available at: http://www.richarddnorth.com/archive/journalism/music/millenium_babes.htm, accessed July 31, 2012.

3. Frith 1998:39.

4. Ibid., 41.

5. The BBC's "Mission" is: "To enrich people's lives with programmes and services that inform, educate and entertain." See http://www.bbc.co.uk/aboutthebbc/insidethebbc/whoweare/mission_and_values, accessed May 24, 2013. More substantively, the public purposes of the BBC are as follows: (a) sustaining citizenship and civil society; (b) promoting education and learning; (c) stimulating creativity and cultural excellence; (d) representing the UK, its nations, regions and communities; (e) bringing the UK to the world and the world to the UK; (f) in promoting its other purposes, helping to deliver to the public the benefit of emerging communications technologies and services and, in addition, taking a leading role in the switchover to digital television. Source: BBC Charter. Available at: http://downloads.bbc.co.uk/bbctrust/assets/files/pdf/about/how_we_govern/charter.pdf, accessed July 25, 2012.

6. Born 2005:27.

7. Roche 1979c:821.
8. Carpenter 1997:103.
9. Roche 1979c:822.
10. In Carpenter 1997:165.
11. Wright 2008:7.
12. The number of "Early" pieces performed in each season rose from zero in 1960 to 10 in 1971–3. "Baroque" from 1 in 1960 up to 10 in 1972 (and 5 in 1973); see Wright 2008.
13. Wright 2008:9.
14. Ibid., 8.
15. Ibid., 10.
16. Donington 1983.
17. From a biography of Denis Stevens. Available at: http://www.baroquemusic.org/DenisStevens.html, accessed November 16, 2012.
18. Carpenter 1997:103–104.
19. Morrow Collection, box 3, King's College London.
20. See Kingsbury 1988 on talent, or Csikszentmihalyi 1999; Martin 2009 on creativity.
21. Marriner 1971.
22. Clifford Bartlett: interview with author, November 25, 2003.
23. In Carpenter 1997:104.
24. David Munrow's early career work for the Royal Shakespeare Company would have provided a perfect opportunity to explore music "in context."
25. See Hughes 1954; Hughes and Abraham 1960; Day et al. 2004 for further discussion.
26. Carpenter 1997:265. Munrow had first approached the BBC in 1966, highlighting his interest in "organising programmes of early music." The first pilots of *Pied Piper* were recorded in May 1971. According to Arthur Johnson, the show's producer, it was Christopher Hogwood who initially suggested approaching Munrow about this new program (see Carpenter 1997:265–266).
27. Sir Nicholas Kenyon: interview with author, November 12, 2012.
28. Chris Sayers: interview with author, November 25, 2003.
29. Sir Nicholas Kenyon: interview with author, November 12, 2012.
30. Kenyon 1976:447.
31. Thomson 1976:254.
32. Christopher Hogwood: interview with author, January 10, 2003.
33. One can only speculate as to whether performers with loyalty to other early music orchestras at the time (chiefly those led by Pinnock, Norrington, and Gardiner) would have found Hogwood's central involvement in this idea to be at all problematic.
34. The relationship between the BBC and the music profession has often displayed a degree of strain, with disputes and strikes—see Wright 2008 for discussion.
35. Sir Nicholas Kenyon: interview with author, November 12, 2012.
36. Interestingly, John Eliot Gardiner's father, Rolf, was heavily involved in folk music and dance. He was in charge of the Cambridge Morris men, which he toured to Austria and to the Baltic States, as well as to the Musikheim in Frankfurt an der Oder.
37. Lucie Skeaping: interview with author, November 10, 2012. Since 1984, Maddy Prior has performed regularly with The Carnival Band, which began as an offshoot of The Medieval Players theatre company. The Band's founder, Andy Watts, is principal bassoon with The Orchestra of the Age of Enlightenment.
38. Upton 2012:4.
39. Frith 1998:41.

40. MacKinnon 1993:53, quoted in Frith 1998:41.

41. MacKinnon 1993:40, quoted in Frith 1998:41.

42. Frith 1998:40.

43. This has continued to present marketing problems for conductor-less orchestras such as the OAE—see Wallace 2006.

44. John Bickley: interview with author, August 5, 2003.

45. Colin Kitching: interview with author, May 4, 2004.

46. Laurence Cummings: interview with author, January 9, 2012.

47. Frey and Pommerehene 1989.

48. Jeremy West: interview with author, November 10, 2012.

49. King 2003. Some other important British independent record labels with early music catalogues include Chandos, Collegium Records, CRD, Linn, Meridian, and Nimbus.

50. Simon Perry: interview with author, November 25, 2003.

51. Jolly 1992.

52. Chris Sayers: interview with author, November 25, 2003.

53. Concentus Musicus Wien was founded by Nikolaus Harnoncourt in 1953, and is regarded by some as being "largely responsible for launching the authentic instrument movement." See http://www.bach-cantatas.com/Bio/Concentus-Musicus-Wien.htm, accessed February 18, 2011.

54. Chris Sayers: interview with author, November 25, 2003.

55. Sir John Eliot Gardiner: interview with author, November 6, 2012. For a wider discussion of the "overly greedy multinationals" who came to dominate the classical music industry see Norman Lebrecht's *When the Music Stops* (1996), which devotes over 550 pages to a discussion of the "corporate murder of classical music."

56. Peterson 1997:206.

57. See Kenyon 1984a:2.

58. See Taruskin 1995:90.

59. Peterson 1997:4.

60. Bourdieu 1993: 83-84.

61. Andrew Pinnock: interview with author, May 29, 2003.

62. "Hogwood at 70", *Gramophone* podcast, transcribed by the author.

CHAPTER 9

1. Bakhtin 1984:265.

2. Schonberg 1967:23–24.

3. Page 2013:43.

4. Amongst the most prominent music directors of the extended first wave of the modern early music revival are Gardiner, Hillier, Hogwood, Morrow, Munrow, Norrington, Parrott, Pinnock, Phillips, and Rooley. One might also include Bolton, Brown, Christophers, Goodman, Goodwin, Hickox, Holloway, Holman, Kraemer, Lalandi, McCreesh, McGegan, Medlam, Page, Pickett, Roblou, Skeaping, Standage, Thorby, and Wallfisch; as well as second/third wave figures such as Adams, Bicket, Carwood, Chandler, Cummings, Curnyn, Egarr, Faultless, Hollingworth, King, Manze, Podger, Solomon, and Wickham. Alongside these are a number of ensembles that are not led by any individual, but have nonetheless featured in the early music movement, including the Rose Consort of Viols, The Hilliard Ensemble, Gothic Voices, His Majestys Sagbutts and Cornetts, Fretwork, and OAE.

5. Morrow Collection, box 12, King's College London. My italics added.
6. Morrow Collection, box 3, King's College London.
7. Maureen Garnham: interview with author, March 10, 2003.
8. Trevor Pinnock: interview with author, October 13, 2012.
9. Ibid.
10. Sherman 1997:391.
11. Ibid., 401.
12. Rose 2013:129.
13. Shiner 2001:115.
14. Ibid.
15. DiMaggio 1982:377.
16. Davies and Ford 1998:13. See also Ellmeier 2003; Rae 2005; and Swedberg 2006.
17. Bilton 2006:6.
18. Weatherston 2009: 52.
19. Stokes et al. 2010:35.
20. Wennekers and Thurik 1999:46–47.
21. Sir Roger Norrington: interview with author, June 23, 2004.
22. Sir John Eliot Gardiner: interview with author, November 6, 2012.
23. Trevor Pinnock: interview with author, October 13, 2012.
24. Andrew Parrott: interview with author, December 3, 2003.
25. Christopher Hogwood: interview with author, January 10, 2003.

26. Andrew Pinnock: interview with author, May 29, 2003. In this context it is interesting to note that having been in such groups as the Clerkes of Oxenford, The Tallis Scholars, and The Sixteen, early music singers of the caliber of Deborah Roberts, Sally Dunkley, Tessa Bonner, Don Greig, Charles Daniels, Robert Harre-Jones, and Angus Smith went on to cofound their own groups, including The Orlando Consort (1988) and Musica Secreta (1990). One might conjecture that they now had the experience and the confidence to do what they had not done 10 or 15 years earlier. By this time, some of these musicians were also very experienced musicologists and editors; Sally Dunkley, for example, had produced many of the editions used by The Tallis Scholars. Alongside singing, Dunkley describes "Editing, studying, writing and talking about 16th-c music [as] the other main element of [her] work (which generates rather modest profits, though lots of artistic satisfaction)." See http://www.thesixteen.com/page/3102/Sally-Dunkley/18, accessed May 24, 2013.

27. See Aldrich (1999) for a related discussion from an evolutionary perspective.

28. Brookes 1976. Incidentally, the conductor Roy Goodman (Brandenburg Consort, The Parley of Instruments, London Handel Orchestra, and the Hanover Band) is an experienced yachtsman, and in the summer of 2010 he completed a 2,800 mile solo circumnavigation of the UK and Ireland.

29. From Peter Phillips blog: http://tallisman.wordpress.com/2009/01/08/ what-we-really-do, accessed July 18, 2012.

30. Alison Crum: interview with author, November 10, 2012.
31. Trevor Pinnock: interview with author, October 13, 2012.
32. Ibid.
33. Sir Roger Norrington: interview with author, June 23, 2004.
34. Andrew Parrott: interview with author, December 3, 2003.
35. Ibid.
36. In Haladjian 2002.

37. Clifford Bartlett: interview with author, November 25, 2003.
38. Sir John Eliot Gardiner: interview with author, November 6, 2012.
39. Ibid.
40. Pinnock 2013:18.
41. Sarasvathy 2008:17.
42. Ibid.
43. Ibid., 15.
44. Clifford Bartlett: interview with author, November 25, 2003.
45. Andrew Parrott: interview with author, December 3, 2003.
46. From an interview with Brian Robins 2004 for *Goldberg*.
47. Bernard Thomas: interview with author, November 9, 2012.
48. From an interview with Brian Robins 2004 for *Goldberg*.
49. Trevor Pinnock: interview with author, October 13, 2012.
50. Turner 1969:41.
51. Ibid., 27.
52. Shepard 2011:6. See also Huizinga 1949; Hyde 2008 [1998].
53. Sutton-Smith 1997.
54. Schechner 2006[2002]:89.
55. Huizinga 1949:8.
56. Schechner 2006[2002]:89.
57. Bourdieu and Wacquant 1996:76.
58. See also Caillois 2001 on "mimesis."
59. Sutton-Smith 1997:10.
60. Ibid.
61. Sutton-Smith 1997:11.
62. Ibid.
63. Ibid.
64. Ibid.
65. Weber 1905 [1930].
66. See Weber 1909 [1978]; Weber 1946/1968.
67. Trevor Pinnock: interview with author, October 13, 2012.
68. From Sweeting 2007.
69. Rooley 1990:2–3.
70. Stearns 2011.
71. Sir John Eliot Gardiner: interview with author, November 6, 2012.
72. Ibid.
73. Sir John Eliot Gardiner and Philip Pullman Interview on *Front Row* (Radio 4), Tuesday December 13, 2005.
74. Sir Roger Norrington: interview with author, June 23, 2004.
75. Brown 1976:289.
76. It is interesting to note that (like Hogwood) Munrow was a "natural" radio presenter, unlike some early musicians. For example, Michael Morrow clearly found the recording process rather difficult, as this letter from BBC's Peter Dodd makes clear: "But something happens to some voices—yours is one—when a microphone is involved. I was not the only one of the opinion that your stresses and inflexions were wrong…I don't wish to engage in a slinging-match about it, but I do think that it's a pity you won't have another go at these programmes. They could be so much better." (Morrow Collection, box 3, King's College London.)

77. The Pied Piper of Hamlyn tells of how the piper casts a spell over the children of the town and leads them away, never to be seen again. There is some speculation as to whether this was based on a real historical event.

78. Hyde 2008:7.

79. Wistreich and Potter 2013:25.

CHAPTER 10

1. Wallace 2006:24.
2. Genesis 27:11.
3. This was the title of a 1973 film starring Ryan O'Neal and Jacqueline Bisset.
4. Archer 1996 [1988].
5. Ibid., 158.
6. Kenyon 1990.
7. Especially Taruskin 1995; Kivy 1995.
8. Crutchfield 1988:19.
9. Zaslaw 1992.
10. Baumann 2007:48–49.
11. Scardaville 2009:368. See Baumann 2001; Becker 1982; and DiMaggio 1982 for more discussion of this "triad of factors."
12. Bourdieu 2002:16.
13. Kenyon 1988:5.
14. Kenyon 2009.
15. Christopher Lawrence: interview with author, August 5, 2003.
16. In Wallace 2006:61.
17. Available at: http://www.abo.org.uk/user_files/ABO%20Publication%20Downloads/ABOChamberVision_web.pdf, accessed August 23, 2012.
18. Irving 2013:83. For his part, Andrew Parrott also talks of a "new orthodoxy," but he has something different in mind, i.e., that performers of early music "bear no real responsibilities towards its composers, only towards themselves and today's audiences." (Parrott 2013:37.)
19. Bernard Thomas: interview with author, November 9, 2012.
20. Robbins Landon 1982.
21. See Roche 1979a–d.
22. Winter 1984.
23. Robbins Landon 1982.
24. Lucie Skeaping: interview with author, November 10, 2012.
25. NEMA 2009.
26. Pinnock 1992:523.
27. Bernard Thomas: interview with author, November 9, 2012. Elizabeth Roche (2013:64) observes that the move from LP to CD was not altogether favorable to earlier repertoire: "With a continuous playing time roughly half as long again as the average for a double-sided LP, the CD format has been a boon and a blessing where opera and oratorio recordings are concerned, but it is less well suited to the shorter pieces which comprise so much of the medieval and Renaissance repertory."
28. In Pinnock 1992:523.
29. Christopher Hogwood website: http://www.hogwood.org/biography, accessed December 20, 2012.

30. Brown 1991:248. See also Taruskin 1995:168 on "speculative forward encroachment."
31. Holden 2012:15.
32. Kenyon 2013:6.
33. Dulak 1993:45.
34. Sir Nicholas Kenyon: interview with author, November 12, 2012.
35. Over 1,500 letters were sent out to professional, semi-professional, and amateur Members of the National Early Music Association (NEMA) in the UK. In addition, nine of the leading early music orchestras and choirs distributed the survey to their performers. A total of 566 responses were received, representing a 35.5 percent response rate. Of these, a total of 538 complete and useable questionnaires were obtained, of which 480 were from performers and 58 from instrument-makers. 41 percent of the performers were professional; 15 percent semi-professional; 44 percent amateur. A summary of findings was published in the *Early Music Performer* (the Journal of the National Early Music Association) October 14, 2004.
36. See Bourdieu 1984; 2002.
37. Cohen and Snitzer 1985:82.
38. Ibid., 83.
39. Ibid., 83–84.
40. Trevor Pinnock: interview with author, October 13, 2012.
41. Bernard Thomas: interview with author, November 9, 2012.
42. 87 percent of early musicians in NEMA's 2009 Survey Report had a degree (N.B. n=115 and most were amateurs).
43. Pinnock 1992.
44. This point is particularly telling in the context of my call for a more holistic assessment of authenticity.
45. Morrow Collection, box 2, King's College London.
46. Alison Crum: interview with author, November 10, 2012.
47. Sir John Eliot Gardiner: interview with author, November 6, 2012. According to Gardiner, "Learning as you earn" was a phrase coined by Emanuel (Manny) Hurwitz, the first leader of the Goldsbrough (later the English Chamber) Orchestra in 1960.
48. Alison Crum and Bernard Thomas independently emphasized this point in interviews with the author at the Greenwich International Early Music Exhibition, 2012.
49. Wallace 2006:67.
50. Monteverdi website: http://www.monteverdi.co.uk.
51. Holden 2012:13.
52. Ibid., 14.
53. Ibid.
54. See, for example, the *BBC Music Magazine*'s list of the 50 greatest classical recordings, which include: Bach *B Minor Mass* (Harnoncourt & Concentus Musicus, 1968), Allegri *Miserere* (Phillips & The Tallis Scholars, 1980), Handel *Messiah* (Hogwood & AAM, 1980), Monteverdi *Vespers of 1610* (Gardiner & EBS/Monteverdi Choir, 1989), and Von Bingen *A Feather on the Breath of God* (Page/Kirkby & Gothic Voices, 1981). Source: http://wpr.org/music/BBC-Music-Top-50-1201.pdf, accessed May 25, 2013.
55. It should be noted that in 2009/10 the Academy of Ancient Music's Annual Review (available at: http://www.aam.co.uk/media/Files/Resources/Corporate%20Info/annualreportv21lowres.pdf, accessed May 25, 2013) reported CD royalties comprising just 1 percent of income. Despite many commentators implying that the music industry is synonymous with

the recording industry, there exist music industr*ies* (plural), with live performance remaining very much at the heart of musicians' activities (see Cloonan 2007 for discussion in the context of popular music; also Frith et al. (2013) on live music in Britain).

56. Hennion 1997:420.
57. Genesis 27:37.
58. A letter in the Morrow Collection, box 3, King's College London.
59. I can't resist making a connection here to Classic FM's (launched 1992) *Smooth Classics* program "designed to ease away the stresses and strains of the day…with the world's most beautiful music." (Source: http://www.classicfm.com/radio/shows/smooth-classics, accessed May 25, 2013.)
60. Haynes 2007:8.
61. Brown 1991:248.
62. Kenyon 2009.
63. Cummings: interview with author, January 9, 2012.
64. See, for example, Norrington's interview with Paul Wegman Taylor, 2010. Available at: http://podiumnotes.org/2010/08/20/an-interview-with-sir-roger-norrington-part-1, accessed August 19, 2012.
65. Cohen and Snitzer 1985:43.
66. Alison Crum: interview with author, November 10, 2012.
67. Brown 2004:2.
68. Pinnock 1992:523.
69. Kenyon 2009.
70. Sir Roger Norrington: interview with author, June 23, 2004.
71. Andrew Parrott: interview with author, December 3, 2003.
72. Laurence Cummings: interview with author, January 9, 2012.
73. See Holden 2012:15.
74. "Hogwood at 70", *Gramophone* podcast. It is interesting, in passing, to note that Paul Goodwin (Associate Conductor AAM 1996) and Andrew Manze (Associate Director AAM 1996; Artistic Director TEC 2003–2007) have both moved on to pursue conducting careers beyond the specialist Early Music field.
75. See Stokes and Wilson 2010.
76. Hogwood at 70 podcast.
77. Morrow Collection, box 4, King's College London.
78. Pinnock 1992.
79. NEMA 2009:1.
80. Alison Crum: interview with author, November 10, 2012.
81. NEMA 2009:1.
82. Ibid., 29.
83. NEMA 2012.
84. Sir John Eliot Gardiner: interview with author, November 6, 2012.
85. Early Music 41(1).

CHAPTER 11

1. Mailer 1971:241.
2. Dahl 1991.
3. The hallmark of an immanent critique is that "it takes its departure from within the accounts it seeks to situate, correct or replace…to demonstrate either that an account is

theory-practice inconsistent or, if consistent, beset with...problems that are insoluble in its own terms." (Hartwig 2007:106.)

4. There is widespread disagreement over exactly when "modernity" started and/or finished, and indeed what it comprises. I follow Bhaskar in treating it as a whole, albeit comprised of three distinctive traditions: the *philosophical discourse of modernity*, "which arose in the wake of the consolidation of the bourgeois revolutions of the 17th and 18th centuries;" *high-modernism*, which is an "avant garde movement aesthetically within western European culture, which arose between the revolutions of 1848 and 1917"; and the thesis of *modernization*, "which arose after 1945 in the aftermath of the second world war with the birth of the newly independent ex-colonies." (Bhaskar 2002a:25–26.)

5. Weber 1905.

6. See Nietzsche 2001 [1882], "God is dead."

7. Harvey 2010:40.

8. Raymond Leppard: interview with author, January 5, 2012.

9. Leppard 1988:78.

10. The "underinterpreted," "objective" approach of Hogwood and AAM's Mozart *Symphonies*, for example, has been widely discussed in this respect—see particularly Eric van Tassel's review of the complete Mozart set in 1984 (van Tassel 1984:129).

11. Bostridge 2011:17.

12. From *Dirk Gently's Holistic Detective Agency* (1987).

13. Tymieniecka 2000:3.

14. http://www.patrickcurry.co.uk, accessed July 14, 2012.

15. http://www.harnoncourt.info/index_en.php/article/articleview/1407/1/15, accessed December 21, 2012.

16. Harnoncourt's explicit reference to "religiousness" and the "divine" is representative of a belief that many do not share, but this does not change the underlying nature of the argument here. See also Graham's *The Re-enchantment of the World* (2007), in which he discusses the relationship between art and religion, expressing the view that only religion can "enchant the world."

17. Sir John Eliot Gardiner: interview with author, November 6, 2012. See also Hyde 2007.

18. Bennett 2001:5.

19. Oxford Dictionaries.com. See also Bettelheim's 2010 [1976] *The Uses of Enchantment*, which explores the meaning and importance of fairy tales, particularly in the context of childhood development.

20. Bennett 2001:5. See Stone-Davis 2011 on enchanted mode of attention.

21. Jenkins 2000:29.

22. See Hay 2007 on "relational consciousness" as a property of spirituality.

23. In philosophical terms this is a characteristic feature of what would be described as our "nonidentity." See Bhaskar 1993; 2002a.

24. Frith 1998:39.

25. Belloc 1937:67.

26. Bennett 2001.

27. I am not saying that we cannot experience enchantment in/through (abstract) ideas in general; rather I am drawing attention to the illusory (i.e., "magical") nature of acquiring money *per se* as a source of enchantment.

28. Bhaskar 2002a:202. Bhaskar explains that "the false theory depends on, presupposes in practice, the true one; even though the false one may dominate and even occlude the alethically

true component of the totality which is that particular TINA formation." (Bhaskar 2002a:202.) In *Dialectic* (1993:117) he offers the fullest definition of TINA formations as "internally contradictory, more or less systemic, efficacious, syntonic (and...regressive) ensembles...displaying duplicity, equivocation, extreme plasticity and pliability and rational indeterminacy (facilitating their ideological and manipulative use). Moreover, they generate a characteristic range of paradoxes and effects."

29. Norrie 2010:109.

30. Adorno 1967b:123.

31. Tolkien 1988:49–50. See also Marina Warner's (2011) *Stranger Magic,* which provides further fascinating insights as to magic's inherent connection to constructive and imaginative thought, and of "dreaming the impossible."

32. Quoted in Curry 1999 from the *Journal of the Pagan Federation,* Pagan Dawn, 124, Lammas 1997.

33. Bhaskar 1993:60.

34. Hartwig 2007:372.

35. See Leadbeater and Oakley 1999.

36. See Rae 2005 on cultural diffusion.

37. Quoted in Harvey 2010:89.

38. Barenboim 2008 (book title).

39. Harvey 2010:88.

40. See Dreyfus 1983; Leech-Wilkinson 2002.

41. See Irving 2013 on "Historicizing performance practice"; or Rose 2013 "Towards the digital future."

42. Benjamin 1968.

43. See Lounsbury and Glynn 2001.

44. Kimmel 2000:200.

45. See Schumpeter 1934.

46. Harvey 2010:58.

47. Wallace 2006.

48. Sir John Eliot Gardiner: interview with author, November 6, 2012.

49. Peterson 1997.

50. Kimmel 2000:201.

51. Schechner 2006.

52. Barenboim 2008:52.

53. From *The Dry Salvages*. This explanation is philosophically problematic to the extent that it requires transcending our necessarily dualistic world—where performers and musical works are demonstrably separate and different things. Far from being the subject of some esoteric mystical theory, however, the evidence of an actually existing nonduality (i.e., the possibility of being "at one" with music, with nature, with other people, indeed with ourselves) is all around us in our everyday lives and actions (see Bhaskar 2002a; Bhaskar and Hartwig 2010 Chapter 8; Hartwig 2007, entries on "meta-Reality," "dualism," and "co-presence"). "Imagine deciding how one is going to drink a glass of water or formulate a sentence—at some point one must just drink it or speak it; at that point the action is basic; there is no duality involved—in that aspect of one's being one just is one with one's activity" (Bhaskar 2002a:201). So nonduality is a necessary condition for any consciousness or self-consciousness.

54. From *A Sketch of the Past* (1938). In Schulkind 1985.

55. We are all born with capacities, e.g., to learn Japanese. Whether we turn these capacities into capabilities, e.g., actually being able to speak and read Japanese, depends upon a range of factors, including our own motivations, skills, behaviors, upbringing, and "life chances."

56. Kernis and Goldman 2006:344. See Boltanski and Chiapello 2007 and Fleming 2009 for related discussions concerning the role of authenticity in the capitalistic workplace.

57. Barenboim 2008:20–21. Anthony Rooley's discussion of 17th-century *Sprezzatura* also offers a telling conception of the relationship between discipline and freedom. *Sprezzatura* (the art of spontaneity) results from *Decoro* (hard work). Furthermore, a "divine grace", *Grazia*, "touches a performance in which *Decoro* and *Sprezzatura* are in perfect balance." (In Garner 2011:192–193.)

58. My position appears to be at odds with that of Kivy (1995), who argues that his conception of "authenticities" "do not—cannot—converge, either in practice or in principle" (p.7).

CHAPTER 12

1. Kimmel 2000:206.
2. Sartre 1988:104.
3. Trevor Pinnock: interview with author, October 13, 2012.
4. See Small 1998 on "musicking."
5. Dewey 1934 [2005]:2.
6. Kenyon 2013:6.
7. See Dewey 1934.
8. It is worth observing that a major goal behind the current development of higher education courses in "creative" subjects, including the performing arts and design, is to help those involved bridge the divide between so-called "t-shirts" and "suits"; in other words, to help them communicate with each other.
9. Roy Bhaskar's seminal work on the *Dialectic* (1993) is subtitled *the pulse of freedom*. I am struck by the connection here to "pulse" in music, the heartbeat that keeps us "marching ever onwards" (Martha Graham in de Mille 1991:264).
10. Engen 2007:9.
11. See Butt 2002.
12. From English Heritage website: http://www.english-heritage.org.uk/about/interactiveo, accessed December 21, 2012.
13. Butt 2002:217.
14. See Fergusson's *The Sack of Bath*, 1973, which Butt describes as a "hysterical, yet path breaking study."
15. Bauman 1992:x–xi.
16. Nor should we reify "modernity" here; it is always real live human beings who are mediating these ideas through their everyday practices.
17. Catherine Mackintosh: interview with author, April 29, 2004.
18. Grout 1973: 538.
19. Ibid., 539.
20. Jenkins 2000:19.
21. These italicized terms are used by Paolo Knill (2005) in the context of expressive arts therapy.
22. Knill 2005:78.
23. This, of course, is a characteristic of all professions. Higher education, for example, is very good at producing professors.

24. The Arts Council continues to use "excellence" as a primary criterion for funding—see McMaster 2008.

25. Morgan 1988:78.

26. Ibid.

27. Knill et al. 2005.

28. Schechner (2006: 52) defines "performance" as "Ritualized behavior conditioned and/or permeated by play."

29. Knill 2005:83.

30. Levine 2005:45.

31. Kimmel 2000:198. It is helpful here to read Hjorth 2005 on creating spaces for play (heterotopia) as a central condition of the organizational entrepreneurship process.

32. Kimmel 2000:198.

33. Knill 2005:83.

34. Ibid., 76.

35. See Wenger 1998.

36. Stokes 2006:back cover.

37. See Knill 2005:77.

38. Curry 1999:10. This link to the "earth" is particularly evident in respect of Sir John Eliot Gardiner's life as both a farmer and a musician. Gardiner attributes his energy for music-making to "the landscape...from farming."

39. See Lévi-Strauss (1970) on the distinction between "the raw and the cooked."

40. Gardner 1993.

41. The "T-shaped skills" model, which encourages both a depth (specialism) and breadth (generalism) of education for any individual, is a helpful starting point here.

42. Cohen and Snitzer 1985:21.

43. See Shiner 2001:115.

44. Jeremy West: interview with author, November 10, 2012.

45. Dewey 1934 [2005]:26.

46. See Scharmer 2009 on "presence-ing."

47. See Kabat-Zinn 2004 on mindfulness meditation.

48. Phelan 1993.

49. Laurence Cummings: interview with author, January 9, 2012.

50. Hartwig 2007:84. See also Bhaskar 2002a:259.

51. Eliot 1975:38-39, quoted in Taruskin 1995:106.

52. In Schmied 2000. My own emphasis added.

53. Tosi 1743 [1978]:183–184.

54. Sir Roger Norrington: correspondence with author, November 7, 2012.

55. Sir John Eliot Gardiner: interview with author, November 6, 2012.

56. Ross 2009.

REFERENCES

Abbing, Hans (2002). *Why Are Artists Poor? The Exceptional Economy of the Arts*. Amsterdam University Press.

Ackroyd, S. and Fleetwood, S. (2000). *Realist Perspectives On Management And Organisations*. Routledge.

Adler, Guido (1924). *Handbuch der Musikgeschichte*. Schneider.

Adorno, Theodor W. (1967a). [1981] Bach defended against his devotees. In *Prisms*, Trans. S. and S. Weber, 133–146. [First published in German in 1951.] MIT Press.

Adorno, Theodor W. (1967b). [1981] Perennial fashion—Jazz. In *Prisms*. Trans. S. and S. Weber, 119–132. [First published in German in 1951.] MIT Press.

Adorno, Theodor W. (1973). *The Philosophy of Modern Music*. Seabury Press.

Adorno, Theodor W. (1976). *Introduction to the Sociology of Music*. Trans. E. B. Ashton. Seabury Press.

Adorno, Theodor W. (1989). [1936] On Jazz. *Discourse*, 12(1):44–69.

Adorno, Theodor W. (2003). [1973] *The Jargon of Authenticity*. Routledge Classics.

Adorno, T. and Horkheimer, M. (1972). *Dialectic of Enlightenment*. Trans. J. Cumming. Continuum.

Aldrich, Howard (1999). *Organizations Evolving*. Sage.

Alper, N. O. and Wassall, G. H. (2006). Artists' Careers and Their Labor Markets. In *Handbook of the Economics of Arts and Culture*, eds. V.A. Ginsburgh and D. Thorsby, 813–64. Elsevier.

Ansdell, Gary (2005). Being who you aren't: Doing what you can't: Community music therapy & the paradoxes of performance. *Voices: A world forum for music therapy*, 5(3).

Aoyama, Eriko (2004). *Noah Greenberg and the New York Pro Musica: The Career, Reception and Impact*. MA Thesis, Division of Research and Advanced Studies of the University of Cincinnati.

References

Archer, Margaret S. (1995). *Realist Social Theory: The morphogenetic approach*. Cambridge University Press.

Archer, Margaret S. (1996). [1988] *Culture and Agency. The place of culture in social theory*. Cambridge University Press.

Archer, Margaret S. (2003). *Structure, Agency and the Internal Conversation*. Cambridge University Press.

Archer, M. S., Bhaskar, R., Collier, A., Lawson, T. and Norrie, A. (1998). *Critical Realism: Essential Readings*. Routledge.

Arnold, Denis (1981). Introduction. In The Directory of British early music groups. Early Music Centre.

Arnold, Denis (1983). *The New Oxford Companion to Music*. Vols.1&2. Oxford University Press.

Arts Council England (2003). *Ambitions for the Arts: Summary 2003-2006*. Available at: http://www.artscouncil.org.uk/publication_archive/ambitions-for-the-arts-2003-2006/, accessed May 28, 2013.

Atkinson, David M. (2007). *Thinking the Art of Management. Stepping into 'Heidegger's Shoes'*. Palgrave Macmillan.

Austin, J. L. (1964). *Sense & Sensibilia*, ed. J. G. Warnock. Oxford University Press.

Baines, Anthony (1957). *Woodwind Instruments and their History*. Norton.

Bakhtin, Mikhail (1984). *Rabelais and His World*. Indiana University Press.

Barenboim, Daniel (2008). *Everything is Connected. The Power of Music*. Weidenfeld & Nicolson.

Barker, H. and Taylor, Y. (2007). *Faking it: The Quest for Authenticity in Popular Music*. Norton.

Barone, T. and Eisner, E. W. (2012). *Arts Based Research*. Sage.

Barthes, Roland (1978). [1967] The Death of the Author. In *Image, Music, Text*, ed. S. Heath, 142–148. Hill and Wang.

Bartlett, Clifford (1983). Early music and the critic. *Early Music*, 11(1):149.

Bartlett, C. and Holman, P. (1975). Giovanni Gabrieli: A Guide to the Performance of His Instrumental Music. *Early Music*, 3:25–32.

Bauman, Zygmunt (1992). *Intimations of Postmodernity*. Routledge.

Baumann, Shyon (2001). Intellectualization and art world development. *American Sociological Review*, 66(3):404–426.

Baumann, Shyon (2007). A general theory of artistic legitimation: How art worlds are like social movements. *Poetics*, 35(1):47–65.

Baumol, W. and Bowen, W. (1966). *Performing arts—the economic dilemma: A study of problems common to theater, opera, music and dance*. MIT Press.

Becker, Howard (1982). *Art Worlds*. University of California Press.

Belloc, Hilaire (1937). *An Essay on the Nature of Contemporary England*. Sheed & Ward.

Benedict, Stephen (1991). *Public Money & the Muse*. W. W. Norton.

Benjamin, Walter (1968). The Work of Art in the Age of Mechanical Reproduction. In *Illuminations*, ed. and trans. H. Arendt, 214–218. Fontana.

Bennett, A. and Peterson, R. A. (2004). *Music Scenes: Local, Translocal and Virtual*. Vanderbilt University Press.

Bennett, Dawn (2008). *Understanding the Classical Music Profession: The Past, the Present and Strategies for the Future*. Ashgate.

Bennett, Jane (2001). *The Enchantment of Modern Life. Attachments, Crossings, and Ethics*. Princeton University Press.

Bennett, Mary (1991). Robert Goble. From *The Thursley Chronicle* 1991. Available at: http://www.gobleharpsichords.co.uk/Robert_Goble_Biog.pdf, accessed September 30, 2012.

Bent, Margaret (2013). 40 years on. *Early Music*, 41(1):7–8.

Berman, Marshall (1970). *The Politics of Authenticity. Radical Individualism and the Emergence of Modern Society*. Atheneum.

Bettelheim, Bruno (2010). [1976] *The Uses of Enchantment: The Meaning and Importance of Fairy Tales*. Vintage.

Bhaskar, Roy (1975). *A Realist Theory of Science*. Leeds Books.

Bhaskar, Roy (1989). *The Possibility of Naturalism: A Philosophical Critique of the Contemporary Human Sciences*. 2nd edn. Harvester Wheatsheaf.

Bhaskar, Roy (1993). *Dialectic. The Pulse of Freedom*. Verso.

Bhaskar, Roy (1997). On the ontological status of ideas. *Journal for the Theory of Social Behaviour*, 27(2/3):135–47.

Bhaskar, Roy (2002a). *Reflections on Meta-Reality. A Philosophy for the Present. Transcendence, Emancipation and Everyday Life*. Sage.

Bhaskar, Roy (2002b). *The Philosophy of Meta-Reality, Vol.1, Meta-Reality: Creativity, Love and Freedom*. Sage.

Bhaskar, R. and Danermark, B. (2006). Metatheory, interdisciplinarity and disability research: a critical realist perspective. *Scandinavian Journal of Disability Research*, 8(4):278–297.

Bhaskar, R. and Hartwig, M. (2010). *The Formation of Critical Realism*. Routledge.

Bilton, Chris (2006). Cultures of management: Cultural policy, cultural management and creative organisations. Paper presented at the *Management of culture/Culture of management seminar 8*, Cultural Industries Seminar Network, Warwick Business School, June 28. Available at: http://www2.lse.ac.uk/geographyAndEnvironment/research/AP_CulturalIndustrySeminar.aspx#Belfast%20Seminar.

Bilton, Chris (2007). *Management and Creativity: From Creative Industries to Creative Management*. Blackwell Publishing.

Björkegren, Dag (1995). *The Culture Business: Management Strategies for the Arts-related Business*. Cengage Learning EMEA.

Blacking, John (1973). *How Musical is Man?* University of Washington Press.

Blaug, Mark (1976). *The Economics of the Arts*. Martin Robertson and Company. [Reprinted in 1992, by Gregg Revivals.]

Blaug, Mark (2001). Where are we now on cultural economics? *Journal of Economic Surveys*, 15:123–144.

Blume, Friedrich (1950). *Two Centuries of Bach: An Account of Changing Taste*. Trans. Stanley Godman. Oxford University Press.

Boltanski, L. and Chiapello, E. (2007). *The New Spirit of Capitalism*. Verso.

Born, Georgina (2005). *Uncertain Vision: Birt, Dyke And the Reinvention of the BBC*. Vintage.

Born, Georgina (2010). The social and the aesthetic: For a post-Bourdieuian theory of cultural production. *Cultural Sociology*, July, 4(2):171–208.

Born, G. and Barry A. (2010). Art-Science. From public understanding to public experiment. *Journal of Cultural Economy*, 3(1):103–119.

Bostridge, Ian (2011). *A Singer's Notebook*. Faber and Faber.

Bourdieu, Pierre (1984). *Questions de Sociologie*. Minuit.

Bourdieu, Pierre (1993). *The Field of Cultural Production*. Polity Press.

Bourdieu, Pierre (2002). *Distinction: A Social Critique of the Judgment of Taste*. Routledge.

Bourdieu, P. and Wacquant, L. (1996). *An Invitation to Reflexive Sociology*. Polity Press.

Boydell, Barra (1982). *The Crumhorn and Other Windcap Instruments of the Renaissance*. Frits Knuf.

Brett, P. Wood, E. and Thomas, G. C. (1994). *Queering the Pitch: The New Gay and Lesbian Musicology*. Routledge.

Brighton, A. Pearson, N. and Parry, J. (1985). *The Economic Situation of Visual Artists*. Calouste Gulbenkian Foundation.

Brookes, Oliver (1976). Tributes to David Munrow, *Early Music*, 4(3):377. [Also by Sir Anthony Lewis; Nigel Fortune; James Bowman; James Tyler; Andreas Holschneider; Arthur Johnson; Jasper Parrott; John Willan; John Currie; Christopher Monk; Meirion Bowen; Robert Donington; Jeremy Noble; Anthony Mulgan (376–380).]

Brown, Clive (1991). Historical performance, metronome marks and tempo in Beethoven's symphonies. *Early Music*, 19(2):247–260.

Brown, Clive (2004). Guest Editorial, *Early Music Performer*, October 14: 2–3.

Brown, Howard Mayer (1973). London Pro Musica surveyed, *Early Music*, 1(2):115–117.

Brown, Howard Mayer (1974). Review. *The Musical Times*, 115(1572), February.

Brown, Howard Mayer (1976). Instruments of the Middle Ages and Renaissance: In memoriam David Munrow. *Early Music*, 4(3):288–293.

Brown, Howard Mayer (1978). Introduction. In *The Future of Early Music in Britain*, ed. J. M. Thomson, XIII-XV. Oxford University Press.

Brown, Howard Mayer (1988). Pedantry or liberation? A sketch of the historical performance movement. In *Authenticity and Early Music*, ed. N. Kenyon, 2:27–56. Oxford University Press.

Brown, Rachel (2003). *The Early Flute. A Practical Guide*. Cambridge University Press.

Bruno, Malcolm (2007). *The Musical Explorer*. Available at: http://www.malcolmbruno.com/pdfs/pdf_parrott.pdf, accessed July 18, 2011.

Burney, Charles (1789). *A General History of Music*. Harcourt, Brace and Co.

Butt, John (2002). *Playing with History*. Cambridge University Press.

Caillois, Roger (2001). *Man, Play and Games*. University of Illinois Press.

Campbell, Margaret (1975). *Dolmetsch: The Man and his Work*. Hamish Hamilton.

Carpenter, Humphrey (1997). *The Envy of the World. Fifty Years of the BBC Third Programme and Radio 3*. Phoenix Giant.

Carter, B. and New, C. (2004). *Making Realism Work*. Routledge.

Castañer, X. and Campos, L. (2002). The determinants of artistic innovation: Bringing in the role of organizations. *Journal of Cultural Economics*, 26: 29–52.

Catch, John R. (1999). *The Viola Da Gamba Society. A Brief History 1948–1998*. The Viola Da Gamba Society.

Caves, Richard E. (2000). *Creative Industries: Contracts between art and commerce*. Harvard University Press.

Chong, Derrick (2010). *Arts Management*. Second edition. Routledge.

Chong, D. and Trappey, R. (2001). Privately held and managing well: the English Chamber Orchestra at 40. *International Journal of Arts Management*, 3(2):16–26.

Church, Michael (2013). L'Allegro, il Penseroso ed il Moderato, Gabrieli Consort/McCreesh, St. John's Smith Square, London. *The Independent*, May 11.

Churchill, N. C. and Lewis, V. L. (1983). The five stages of small business growth. *Harvard Business Review*, 61(3): 30–41.

Clark, Burton R. (1998). *Creating Entrepreneurial Universities: Organizational Pathways of Transformations*. IAU Press.

Cloonan, Martin (2007). *Popular Music and the State in the UK: Culture, Trade or Industry?* Ashgate.

Cohen, J. and Snitzer, H. (1985). *Reprise: Revival of Early Music*. Little, Brown & Company.

Cohen, W. M. and Levinthal, D. A. (1990). Absorptive capacity: A new perspective on learning and innovation. *Administrative Science Quarterly*, 35(1):128–152.

Collingwood, Robin G. (1938). *The Principles of Art*. Oxford University Press.

Cook, Nicholas and Everist, M. (1999). Analysing performance and performing analysis. In *Rethinking Music*, ed. N. Cook and M. Everist, 239–61. Oxford University Press.

Couldry, Nick (2010). *Why Voice Matters: Culture and Politics After Neoliberalism*. Sage.

Coussemaker, Edmond de (1852). *Histoire de l'Harmonie au Moyen Age*. V. Didron.

Coussemaker, Edmond de (1865). *L'Art Harmonique aux XIIe et XIIIe siècles*. A. Durand.

Croce, Benedetto (1922). *Aesthetic As a Science of Expression and General Linguistic*. Trans. D. Ainslie. The Noonday Press.

Crutchfield, Will (1988). Fashion, Conviction, and Performance Style in an Age of Revivals. In *Authenticity and Early Music*, ed. N. Kenyon, 19–26. Oxford University Press.

Csikszentmihalyi, Mihaly (1996). *Creativity*. Harper Collins.

Csikszentmihalyi, Mihaly (1999). Implications of a systems perspective for the study of creativity. In *Handbook of Creativity*, ed. R. J. Sternberg, 313–338. Cambridge University Press.

Csikszentmihalyi, Mihaly (2002). *Flow. The classic work on how to achieve happiness*. Rider.

Curry, Patrick (1999). Magic vs. Enchantment. *The Journal of Contemporary Religion*, 14(3):401–412.

Curry, Patrick (2008). Enchantment in Tolkien. In *Tolkien's The Lord of the Rings: Sources of Inspiration*, eds. S. Caldecott and T. Honegger, 99–112. Walking Tree Books.

Dahl, Roald (1991). *The Minpins*. Jonathan Cape.

Darsø, Lotte (2004). *Artful creation: Learning-tales of arts-in-business*. Samfundslitteratur.

Dart, Thurston (1954). *The Interpretation of Music*. Harper Collins.

Davies, A. and Ford, S. (1998). Art capital. *Art Monthly*, 1(213):12–20.

Davies, Stephen (2001). *Musical Works & Performances. A Philosophical Exploration*. Oxford University Press.

Day, T. Tietze, G. and Vlček, H. (2004). Histories in sound: Disseminating medieval music. In *Proceedings of the Conference on Interdisciplinary Musicology Graz/Austria*, eds. R. Parncutt, A.Kessler and F. Zimmer, April 15–18. Available at: http://www.uni-graz.at/richard.parncutt/cimo4/CIM04_paper_pdf/Day_Vlcek_Tietze_CIM04_proceedings.pdf, accessed August 3, 2012.

de Mille, Agnes (1991). *Martha: The Life and Work of Martha Graham*. Random House.

DeNora, Tia (2000). *Music in Everyday Life*. Cambridge University Press.

Dewey, John (1934). [2005] *Art As Experience*. Perigee Books.

Dewey, John (1989). Art as experience. In *John Dewey: The later works*, ed. J. Boydston, Chapter 10. Southern Illinois University Press.

Dickens, Charles (1859). *A Tale of Two Cities*. Chapman & Hall.

DiMaggio, Paul (1982). Cultural entrepreneurship in nineteenth century Boston. *Media, Culture and Society*, 4: 33–50. Reprinted in P. DiMaggio, [1986] Nonprofit Enterprise in the arts: Studies in Mission and Constraint: 41–61.

Dolmetsch, Arnold (1915). [2012] *The Interpretation of the Music of the XVIIth and XVIIIth Centuries*. Forgotten Books.

Donington, Robert (1963). *The Interpretation of Early Music*. Faber & Faber.

Donington, Robert (1975a). Foreword. In *Dolmetsch: The man and his work*. M. Campbell, ix–x. Hamish Hamilton.

Donington, Robert (1975b). Arnold Dolmetsch. *Early Music*, 3(3):236–239.

Donington, Robert (1983). Why early music? *Early Music*, 11(1):42–45.

Donington, Robert (1989). Review of 'Authenticity in Music' (Leppard). *Early Music*, 17(3):419–420.

Dreyfus, Laurence (1983). Early Music Defended against Its Devotees: A Theory of Historical Performance in the Twentieth Century. *Musical Quarterly*, 69:297–322.

Dreyfus, Laurence (1997). Postscriptum to Early Music Defended against Its Devotees: A Theory of Historical Performance in the Twentieth Century. [Originally published in *The Musical Quarterly*, 69 (1983), 297–322.] Polish translation by Magdalena Nowak, *Canor*, 19:27–39.

Duffin, Ross (2008). *How Equal Temperament Ruined Harmony: And Why You Should Care*. W. W. Norton & Co.

Dulak, Michelle (1993). The Quiet Metamorphosis of "Early Music". *Repercussions*, 2(2):31–62.

Dutton, Denis (2004). Authenticity in Art. *Oxford Handbook of Aesthetics*. Available at: http://www.interdisciplines.org/medias/confs/archives/archive_5.pdf, accessed May 22, 2012.

Eckhardt, J. and Shane, S. (2003). Opportunities and entrepreneurship, *Journal of Management*, 29(3):333–349.

Ehrlich, Cyril (1985). *The Music Profession in Britain Since the Eighteenth Century. A Social History*. Oxford University Press.

Eisner, Elliot (2002). *The Arts and the Creation of Mind*, Yale University Press.

Eliot, T. S. (1975). Tradition and the Individual Talent. In *Selected Prose of T.S. Eliot*, ed. F. Kermode. Harcourt Brace Jovanovich, Farrar Straus and Giroux.

Elliott, David (1995). Music Matters: *A New Philosophy of Music Education*. Oxford University Press.

Ellmeier, Andrea (2003). Cultural entrepreneurialism: on the changing relationship between the arts, culture and employment. *International Journal of Cultural Policy*, 9(1):3–16.

Engen, Rodney (2007). *The Age of Enchantment. Beardsley, Dulac and their Contemporaries 1890-1930*. In association with Dulwich Picture Gallery, Scala Publishers Ltd.

Etzioni, Amitai (1968). *The Active Society: A theory of societal and political processes*. Free Press.

Etzioni, Amitai (1993). *The Spirit of Community: Rights, responsibilities and the communitarian agenda*. Crown Publishers.

Etzkowitz, Henry (1998). The Norms of Entrepreneurial Science: Cognitive Effects of the New University-Industry Linkages. *Research Policy*, 27(8):823–833.

Etzkowitz, H. and Leydesdorff, L. (2000). The dynamics of innovation: from National Systems and "Mode 2" to a Triple Helix of university–industry–government relations. *Research Policy*, 29:109–123.

Evidence-Based Medicine Working Group (1992). Evidence-based medicine. A new approach to teaching the practice of medicine. *The Journal of the American Medical Association*, 268(17):2420–5.

Fabian, Dorottya (2000). Musicology and performance in practice: In search of a historical style with Bach recordings. *Studia Musicologica*, 41(1–3):77–106.

Fabian, Dorottya (2001). The meaning of authenticity and the early music movement: A Historical Review. *International Journal of the Aesthetics and Sociology of Music*, 32:2 (Dec):153–167.

Fallows, David (1995). Thomas Binkley, 1931-1995. *Early Music*, 23(3):538.

Faultless, Margaret (2010). Editorial. *Eighteenth Century Music*, 7(2):195–198.

Fellowes, E. H. and Westrup, J. (1941). [1969] *English Cathedral Music*. 5th rev. edn. Methuen young books.

Fellows, David (1981). David Munrow: a tribute. *Gramophone*, May:50.

Fergusson, Adam (1973). [1989] *The Sack of Bath—and After: A Record and an Indictment*. Extended edition. Salisbury.

Fétis, François-Joseph (1827). Découverte de plusieurs Manuscrits intéressans pour l'histoire de la musique. *Revue Musicale*, 1:3–11.

Ficker, Rudolph (1924-5). Formprobleme der mittelalterlichen Musik. *Zeitschrift für Musikwissenschaft*, 7:195–212.

Fine, Ben (1998). *Labour Market Theory: A constructive reassessment*. Routledge.

Fischer, Wilhelm (1957). Die sogenannte "Werktreue," *Wissenschaft und Praxis—Festschrift Paumgartner*, 12–21. Atlantis.

Fleetwood, Steve (2008). Institutions and social structures. *Journal for the Theory of Social Behaviour*, 38(3): 241–265.

Fleetwood, S. and Ackroyd, S. (2004). *Critical Realist Applications In Organisation and Management Studies*. Routledge.

Fleming, Peter (2009). *Authenticity and the Cultural Politics of Work: New Forms of Informal Control*. Oxford University Press.

Forkel, Johann Nicolaus (1788–1801). *Allgemeine Geschichte der Musik*. Leipzig.

Foucault, Michel (1967). *Of other spaces. Heterotopias*. Available at: http://foucault.info/documents/heteroTopia/foucault.heteroTopia.en.html, accessed December 13, 2012.

Freakley, Vivien (2000). *The artistic labour market and the rationality/ies of training actors and dancers*, unpublished doctoral assignment for the University of Warwick.

Freakley, V. and Neelands, J. (2003). The UK artist's world of work. *Research in Dance Education*, 4(1).

Frey, Bruno (1997). *Not Just for the Money*. Edward Elgar.

Frey, Bruno (2003). *Arts & Economics*. Springer.

Frey, B. and Pommerehne, W. (1989). *Muses and Markets*. Blackwell.

Frith, Simon (1998). *Performing Rites. On the Value of Popular Music*. [First edition 1996.] Harvard University Press.

Frith, S. Brennan, M. Cloonan, M. and Webster, E. (2013). *The History of Live Music in Britain, Volume 1: 1950–1967*. Ashgate.

Galenson, David (2007). *Old Masters and Young Geniuses: The Two Life Cycles of Artistic Creativity*. Princeton University Press.

Galton, Francis (1914). *Hereditary Genius*. Macmillan and Co.

Gardner, Howard (1993). *Multiple Intelligences: The Theory In Practice*. Basic Books.

Garner, Lesley (2011). *Life Lessons: Things I Wish I'd Learned Earlier*. Hay House, Inc.

Gaunt, Helena (2009). One-to-one tuition in a conservatoire: the perceptions of instrumental and vocal students. *Psychology of Music*, Society for Education, Music and Psychology Research:1–31.

Gerbert, Martin (1784). *Scriptores ecclesiastici de musica*. St Blasien.

Geulen, Eva (2006). *The End of Art. Readings in Rumor After Hegel*. Stanford University Press.

Gill, R. C. and Pratt, A. C. (2008). In the social factory? Immaterial labour, precariousness and cultural work. *Theory, Culture & Society*, 25:1–20.

Gilmore, J. H. and Pine II, B. J. (2007). *Authenticity. What Consumers Really Want*. Harvard Business Review Press.

Godlovitch, Stan (1998). *Musical Performance. A Philosophical Study*. Routledge.

Godlovitch, Stan (1999). Performance authenticity. Possible, practical, virtuous. In *Performance and Authenticity in the Arts*, eds. S. Kemal and I. Gaskell, 154–174. Cambridge University Press.

Goehr, Lydia (2007). *The Imaginary Museum of Musical Works. An Essay in the Philosophy of Music*. [Revised edition; first edition 1991]. Oxford University Press.

Goffman, Erving (1959). *The Presentation of Self in Everyday Life*. Doubleday.

Goldsbrough, R. and Goldsbrough, A. (1992). The early music renaissance: The pioneer work of Arnold Goldsbrough recalled by his son. *The Musical Times*, 133(1796):507–509.

Gollin, James (2001). *Pied Piper: The Many Lives of Noah Greenberg*, Lives in Music Series, no.4. Pendragon.

Gracyk, T. and Kania, A. (2011). *The Routledge Companion to Philosophy and Music*. Routledge.

Graham, Gordon (2007). *The Re-enchantment of the World*. Oxford University Press.

Grazian, David (2003). *Blue Chicago: The Search for Authenticity in Urban Blues Clubs*. University of Chicago Press.

Greiner, Larry (1972). Evolution and Revolution as Organizations Grow. *Harvard Business Review*, July-August, 37–46.

Grout, Donald Jay (1973). *A History of Western Music*. Revised Edition. Dent & Sons.

Guignon, Charles (2004). *On Being Authentic*. Routledge.

Guillet de Monthoux, Pierre (2000). The Art Management of Aesthetic Organizing. In *The Aesthetics of Organization*, eds. S. Linstead and H. Höpfl, 35–60. Sage.

Haladjian, Marguerite (2002). *John Eliot Gardiner*. Goldberg the early music portal, September.

Haney, Hal (1972). About Frank Hubbard (1920–1976), *Harpsichord*, 5(1) Feb–April [edited by B. J. Fine.] Available on the Hubbard Harpsichord website at: http://www.hubharp.com/fh_biography/fh_iview.htm, accessed March 1, 2012.

Harker, Dave (1980). *One for the Money: Politics and Popular Song*. Hutchinson.

Harker, Dave (1985). *Fakesong. The manufacture of British "folksong" 1700 to the present day*. Open University Press.

Harrison, Anthony K. (2008). Racial Authenticity in Rap Music and Hip Hop. *Sociology Compass*, 2(6):1783–1800.

Harrison, Anthony K. (2009). *Hip Hop Underground*. Temple University Press.

Harrison, Frank L.L. (1952). The Eton College Choirbook (Eton College MS 178). *International Musicological Society: Report of the 4th Congress*, Utrecht:224–232.

Harrison, Frank L.L. (1963). *Music in Medieval Britain*. Routledge and Paul.

Hartwig, Mervyn (2007). *Dictionary of Critical Realism*. Routledge.

Hartwig, Mervyn (2011). Bhaskar's Critique of the Philosophical Discourse of Modernity. *Journal of Critical Realism*, 10(4):485–510.

Harvey, David (2010). *The Enigma of Capital and the Crises of Capitalism*. Profile Books.

Haskell, Harry (1988). *The Early Music Revival: A History*. Thames & Hudson.

Hawkins, Sir John (1776). *A General History of the Science and Practice of Music*. Novello.

Hay, David (2007). *Why Spirituality is Difficult for Westerners*. Societas.

Haynes, Bruce (2007). *The End of Early Music*. Oxford University Press.

Heilbrun, J. and Gray, C. M. (2001). *The Economics of Arts and Culture*. Cambridge University Press.

Hennion, Antoine (1997). Baroque and rock: Music, mediators and musical taste. *Poetics*, 24(6):415–435.

Hennion, A. and Fauquet, J. (2001). Authority as performance: The love of Bach in nineteenth-century France. *Poetics*, 29:75–88.

Hesmondhalgh, David (2005). Subcultures, Scenes or Tribes? None of the above. *Journal of Youth Studies*, 8(1), March:21–40.

Hewison, Robert (1995). *Culture and consensus: England, art and politics since 1940*. Methuen.

Higgins, Kathleen M. (1991). *The Music of Our Lives*. Temple University Press.

Hirsch, Paul (1970). *The structure of the popular music industry: The filtering process by which records are preselected for public consumption*. Institute for Social Research, University of Michigan.

Hirsch, Paul (1972). Processing fads and fashions: An organizational set analysis of cultural industry systems. *American Journal of Sociology*, 77(4):639–59.

Hjorth, Daniel (2005). Organizational entrepreneurship: With De Certeau on creating heterotopias (or spaces for play). *Journal of Management Inquiry*, 14:386–398.

Hoffmann, E. T. A. (1919). Beethoven's Instrumentalmusik. In *Musikalische Novellen und Aufsätze*, ed. E. Istel, 69. Bosse Verlag.

Holden, Claire (2012). *Recreating early 19th-century style in a 21st-century marketplace: An orchestral violinist's perspective*. Paper given at the IMR seminar, 30th January, University College London, London. Available at: http://orca.cf.ac.uk/17241/1/Claire_Holden_IMR_Seminar_doc.pdf, accessed May 17, 2012.

Holschneider, Andreas (1980). Über alte Musik. *Musica*, 34, Kassel.

Hubbard, Frank (1965). *Three Centuries of Harpsichord Making*. Harvard University Press.

Hughes, Anselm (1954). *New Oxford History of Music, Vol. 2: Early Medieval Music up to 1300*. Oxford University Press.

Hughes, A. and Abraham, G. (1960). *New Oxford History of Music, Vol. 3: Ars Nova and the Renaissance, 1300–1540*. Oxford University Press.

Huizinga, Johan (1949). *Homo Ludens*. Routledge.

Humphries, John (2000). *The Early Horn. A Practical Guide*. Cambridge University Press.

Hyde, Lewis (2007). *The Gift: Creativity and the Artist in the Modern World*. Vintage.

Hyde, Lewis (2008). [First edn. 1998] *Trickster Makes This World: Mischief, Myth and Art*. Canongate Books.

Ibbotson, Piers (2008). *The Illusion of Leadership. Directing Creativity in Business and the Arts*. Palgrave Macmillan.

Irving, David, R.M. (2013). Historicizing performance practice: early music through time and space. *Early Music*, 41(1):83–85.

Jackson, C. Honey, S. Hillage, J. and Stock, J. (1994). *Careers and Training in Dance and Drama*. Institute of Manpower Studies.

Jackson, Roland (1997). Authenticity or Authenticities?—Performance Practice and the Mainstream. *Performance Practice Review*, 10(1) Art 2:1–10.

Jenkins, Richard (2000). Disenchantment, Enchantment and Re-enchantment: Max Weber at the Millennium. *Max Weber Studies*, 1:11–32.

Jolly, James (1992). Obituary: Peter Wadland. *The Independent*, Thursday, July 2.

Kabat-Zinn, Jon (2004). *Full Catastrophe Living. How to cope with stress, pain and illness using mindfulness meditation*. Piatkus.

Kelly, Thomas F. (2011). *Early Music A Very Short Introduction*. Oxford University Press.

Kemal, S. and Gaskell, I. (1999). *Performance and Authenticity in the Arts*. Cambridge University Press.

Kenyon, Nicholas (1976). The economics of early music. *Early Music*, 4(4):443–448.

Kenyon, Nicholas (1977). York Early Music Week 1977. *Early Music*, 5(3):435.

Kenyon, Nicholas (1978). Editorial. *The Early Music Gazette*, April:1.

Kenyon, Nicholas (1984a). Editorial. *Early Music*, 12(1):2.

Kenyon, Nicholas (1984b). Editorial. *Early Music*, 12(2):162.
Kenyon, Nicholas (1986). Editorial. *Early Music*, 14(3):322.
Kenyon, Nicholas (1988). *Authenticity and Early Music*. Oxford University Press.
Kenyon, Nicholas (1990). Editorial. *Early Music*, 18(1):2.
Kenyon, Nicholas (2006). Preface. In *Spirit of the* Orchestra, H. Wallace. Orchestra of the Age of Enlightenment.
Kenyon, Nicholas (2009). *Towards a revival of period dentistry?* Lecture marking the 25th anniversary of the Lufthansa Festival of Baroque Music, May 14th, St. John's Smith Square. Available at: http://www.lufthansafestival.org.uk/index.php?id=lecture-2009, accessed June 8, 2011.
Kenyon, Nicholas (2011). Early music is enjoying its moment. *The New York Times*, March 4.
Kenyon, Nicholas (2013). Introduction. *Early Music*, 41(1):5–6.
Kerman, Joseph (1985). *Musicology*. Fontana Press.
Kernis, M. and Goldman, B. (2005). From thought and experience to behaviour and interpersonal relationships: A multicomponent conceptualization of authenticity. In *On building, defending and regulating the self: A psychological perspective*, eds. A. Tesser, J. V. Wood and D. A. Stapel, 31–52. Psychology Press.
Kernis, M. and Goldman, B. (2006). A multicomponent conceptualization of authenticity. *Theory and research, Advances in Experimental Social Psychology*, 38:283–357.
Kiesewetter, Raphael Georg (1834). *Geschichte der Europäisch-abendländische Musik*. English translation 1848.
Kimmel, Lawrence (2000). The Aesthetics of Enchantment. In *The Aesthetics of Enchantment in the Fine Arts*, eds. M. Kronegger and A. Tymieniecka, 189–208. Kluwer Academic Press.
King, Robert (2003). Ted Perry. Founder of Hyperion Records. Obituary, *The Guardian*, February 13.
Kingsbury, Henry (1988). *Music, Talent and Performance: A Conservatory Cultural System*. Temple University Press.
Kirkpatrick, Ralph (1965). Foreword. In *Three Centuries of Harpsichord Making*, F. Hubbard. Harvard University Press.
Kivy, Peter (1995). *Authenticities: Philosophical Reflections on Musical Performance*. Cornell University Press.
Kivy, Peter (2002). On the historically informed performance. *British Journal of Aesthetics*, April, 42(2):128–144.
Knights, Francis (2013). Editorial. *Early Music*, 41(1):1–2.
Knill, Paolo J. (2005). Foundations for a Theory of Practice. In *Principles and Practice of Expressive Arts Therapy. Towards a Therapeutic Aesthetics*, eds. P. J. Knill, E. G. Levine, and S. K. Levine, Chapter 2:75–170. Jessica Kingsley Publishers.
Knill, P. J. Levine, E. G. and Levine, S. K. (2005). *Principles and Practice of Expressive Arts Therapy. Towards a Therapeutic Aesthetics*. Jessica Kingsley Publishers.
Koopman, Ton (1987). Some Thoughts on Authenticity. *Musick*, 8(3):2–6.
Lancaster, Helen (2004). Leading Musicians: Succession. *Australian Music Forum*, 10(3):41–44.
Langer, Susanne (1957). *Philosophy in a New Key*, 3rd edn. Harvard University Press.
Lawson, Colin (2000). *The Early Clarinet. A Practical Guide*. Cambridge University Press.
Lawson, C. and Stowell, R. (1999). *The Historical Performance of Music: An Introduction*. Cambridge University Press.
Lawson, C. and Stowell, R. (2012). *The Cambridge History of Musical Performance*. Cambridge University Press.

Leadbeater, C. and Oakley, K. (1999). *The Independents: Britain's New Cultural Entrepreneurs.* Demos.

Lebrecht, Norman (1996). *When the Music Stops. Managers, Maestros and the Corporate Murder of Classical Music.* Simon & Schuster.

Leech-Wilkinson, Daniel (2002). *The Modern Invention of Medieval Music: Scholarship, Ideology, Performance.* Cambridge University Press.

Leppard, Raymond (1988). *Authenticity in Music.* Faber Music Ltd.

Levine, Stephen K. (2005). The Philosophy of Expressive Arts Therapy: Poiesis as a Response to the World. In *Principles and Practice of Expressive Arts Therapy. Towards a Therapeutic Aesthetics*, eds. P. J. Knill, E. G. Levine, and S. K. Levine, Chapter 1:15–74. Jessica Kingsley Publishers.

Lévi-Strauss, Claude (1970). *The Raw and the Cooked.* J. Cape.

Leydesdorff, L. and Etzkowitz, H. (1998). The Triple Helix as a Model for Innovation Studies (Conference Report). *Science & Public Policy*, 25(3):195–203.

Lindholm, Charles (2008). *Culture and Authenticity.* Blackwell Publishing.

Lippman, Edward (1992). A History of Western Musical Aesthetics. University of Nebraska Press.

Lounsbury, M. and Glynn, M. A. (2001). Cultural entrepreneurship: stories, legitimacy, and the acquisition of resources. *Strategic Management Journal*, 22(6-7):545–564.

Lowenthal, David (1985). *The Past is a Foreign Country.* Cambridge University Press.

Ludwig, Friedrich (1902–3). Die mehrstimmige Musik des 14. Jahrhunderts. *Sammelbände der internationalen Musikgesellschaft*, 4-6:16–528.

Mackerness, Eric (1964). *A Social History of English Music.* Routledge.

MacKinnon, Niall (1993). *The British Folk Scene.* Open University Press.

Maconie, Robin (1990). *The Concept of Music.* Clarendon Press.

Mailer, Norman (1971). A course in film-making. *New American Review 12.* Simon & Schuster.

Marriner, Neville (1971). An English Musicologist. A Tribute By Neville Marriner, *Gramophone*, March 6.

Martin, Lee (2008). *Annihilating the ex nihilo: Critical Realism and Creativity.* Paper given at the International Association for Critical Realism Conference, King's College London, July.

Martin, Lee (2009). Critical realism and creativity: A challenge to the hegemony of psychological conceptions. *Journal of Critical Realism*, 8(3):294–315.

Mather, David (1997). Obituary: Bernard Wheeler Robinson. *The Independent*, August 19.

McGeary, Tom (1975). Frank Hubbard. *The English Harpsichord Magazine*, April 1(4).

McKinlay, A. and Smith, C. (2009). *Creative Labour. Working in the Creative Industries.* Palgrave Macmillan.

McLeod, Kembrew (1999). Authenticity within hip-hop and other cultures threatened with assimilation. *Journal of Communication*, Autumn 49(4):134–150.

McMaster, Brian (2008). *McMaster Review: Supporting excellence in the arts—from measurement to judgement.* Arts Council England.

Mellers, W. and Martin, P. (1987). Foreword. In *The Masks of Orpheus. Seven Stages in the Story of European* Music, W. Mellers, vii–ix. Manchester University Press.

Melly, George (1970). *Revolt into Style: The Pop Arts.* Penguin.

Menger, Pierre-Michel (1999). Artistic Labor Markets and Careers. *Annual Review of Sociology*, 25:541–574.

Menger, Pierre-Michel (2001). Artists as Workers: Theoretical and Methodological Challenges. *Poetics*, 28:241–254.

Menger, Pierre-Michel (2006). Artistic Labor Markets: Contingent Work, Excess Supply and Occupational Risk Management. In *Handbook of the Economics of Arts and Culture*, eds. V. A. Ginsburgh and D. Thorsby, 766–806. North-Holland.

Mertin Josef (1986). *Early Music Approaches to Performance Practice*. Trans. Siegmund Levarie. Da Capo Press.

Meyer, Leonard B. (1956). *Emotion and Meaning in Music*. The University of Chicago Press.

Moeck, Hermann (1971). *Zur Geschichte von Krummhorn und Cornamuse*. Moeck.

Monk, Christopher (1973). Where the wind blows. *Early Music*, 1(1):34–36.

Montagu, Jeremy (1976). *Making Early Percussion Instruments*. Oxford University Press.

Montagu, Jeremy (2007). *Origins and Development of Musical Instruments*. Scarecrow Press.

Moore, Alan (2002). Authenticity as Authentication. *Popular Music*, 21(2):209–223.

Morgan, Robert P. (1988). Tradition, Anxiety, and the Current Musical Scene. In *Authenticity and Early Music*, ed. N. Kenyon, 57–82. Oxford University Press.

Morrison, Richard (1979). Marketing early instruments. *Early Music* 7(4) Gazette:7.

Morrow, Michael (1978). Musical performance and authenticity. *Early Music*, 6(2):233–246.

Munrow, David (1976). *Instruments of the Middle Ages and Renaissance*. Oxford University Press.

Neel, Boyd (1950). *The Story of an Orchestra*. Vox Mundi.

Negus, Keith (1996). *Popular Music in Theory An Introduction*. Polity Press.

NEMA (2009). *NEMA Survey Report*, National Early Music Association. Available at: http://www.tvemf.org/NEMA/NEMA_survey_report.pdf, accessed August 23, 2012.

NEMA (2012). *The Early Music Yearbook & Performers Directory 2012*, National Early Music Association.

Nietzsche, Friedrich (1968). *The Will to Power*. The Vintage Press.

Nietzsche, Friedrich (2001). [1882] *Nietzsche: The Gay Science*. Cambridge University Press.

Norrie, Alan (2010). *Dialectic and Difference. Dialectical Critical Realism and the Grounds of Justice*. Routledge.

Nowotny, H. Scott, P. and Gibbons, M. (2003). Introduction: "Mode 2" Revisited: The New Production of Knowledge. *Minerva*, 41:179–194.

O'Brien J. and Feist, A. (1995). *Employment in the arts and cultural industries: an analysis of the 1991 census*. Arts Council of England.

O'Dea, Jane W. (1994). Authenticity in musical performance: Personal or historical? *British Journal of Aesthetics*, 34(4):363–375.

O'Hagan, John (1998). *The State and the Arts: An Analysis of Key Economic Policy Issues in Europe and the United States*. Edward Elgar.

O'Shaughnessy, Arthur W. E. (1874). *Music and Moonlight: Poems and Songs*. Chatto and Windus.

Packwood, Angela (2002). Evidence-based policy: Rhetoric and reality. *Social Policy & Society*, 1(3): 267–272.

Page, Christopher (1993). The English a capella renaissance. *Early Music*, 21(3):453–472.

Page, Christopher (2013). Credo. *Early Music*, 41(1):43.

Palmer, Russell (1947). *British Music*. Skelton Robinson.

Parrott, Andrew (2013). Composers' intentions, performers' responsibilities. *Early Music*, 41(1):37–42.

Paul, John (1981). *Modern Harpsichord Makers. Portraits of nineteen British craftsmen & their work*. Victor Gollancz Ltd.

Peacock, Alan (1969). Welfare economics and public subsidies to the arts. *Manchester School of Economic and Social Studies*, 4:323–35.

Peacock, Alan (1993). Paying the Piper. *Culture, Music and Money*. Edinburgh University Press.

Pearson, Ingrid E. (2012). By Word of Mouth: Historical Performance Comes of Age. *Performance Practice Review*, 17(1):1–15.
Peirce, Charles (1883). *Studies in Logic, by Members of The Johns Hopkins University*. Little Brown.
Perks, R.W. (1993). *Accounting and Society*. Chapman & Hall.
Peterson, Richard A. (1976). The production of culture: A prolegomenon. In *The Production of Culture*, ed. R. Peterson. Sage.
Peterson, Richard A. (1997). *Creating Country Music: Fabricating Authenticity*. University of Chicago Press.
Peterson, Richard A. (2005). In search of authenticity. *Journal of Management Studies*, 42(5):1083–1098.
Peterson, R.A. and Anand, A. (2004). The production of culture perspective. *Annual Review of Sociology*, 30:311–334.
Phelan, Peggy (1993). *Unmarked: The Politics of Performance*. Routledge.
Philip, Robert (2004). *Performing Music in the Age of Recording*. Yale University Press.
Pinnock, Andrew (1992). Early Music in Europe conference, April 10–12. *Early Music*, 20(3) August:523.
Pinnock, Andrew (2006). Public value or intrinsic value? The arts-economic consequences of Mr Keynes. *Public Money & Management*, 26(3):173–180.
Pinnock, Andrew (2007). The Gramppian Hills: an empirical test for rent-seeking behaviour in the arts. *Cultural Trends*, 16:277–294.
Pinnock, Trevor (2013). Reflections of a 'pioneer'. *Early Music*, 41(1):17–21.
Pirnay, F. Surlemont, B. and Nlemvo, F. (2003). Toward a typology of university spin-offs. *Small Business Economics*, 21:355–369.
Poole, Steven (2013). Give me the real thing. From vintage clothes to worries about Beyoncé lip-syncing, why is our culture so obsessed with the pursuit of authenticity? *New Statesman*, March 1–7:24–28.
Potter, John (no date) *Early music*. from John Potter's website. Available at: http://www.john-potter.co.uk/blog/category/early-music/, accessed February 22, 2011.
Rae, David (2005). Cultural diffusion: a formative process in creative entrepreneurship? *International Journal of Entrepreneurship and Innovation*, August 6(3):185–187.
Reid, Louis A. (1969). *Meaning in the Arts*. Routledge.
Reisz, Matthew (2012). Dissatisfied, A Review of What are Universities For? (Collini). *Times Higher Education*, February 23rd.
Reith, John (1925). [1991] Memorandum of information on the scope and conduct of the broadcasting service. In *A Social History of British Broadcasting*, eds. P. Scannell and D. Cardiff, 7. Wiley-Blackwell.
Riemann, (Carl) Hugo (1905). *Handbuch der Musikgeschichte I/2*. Breitkopf und Härtel.
Riemann, (Carl) Hugo (1908). *Kleines Handbuch der Musikgeschichte*. Breitkopf und Härtel.
Robbins Landon, H.C. (1982). Editorial essay on 250th anniversary of Haydn's birth. *Early Music*, 10(3):298.
Roberts, Deborah (1978). Training the professionals. *The Early Music Gazette*, April:3.
Robinson, Bernard (1985). *An Amateur in Music*. Countryside Books.
Robinson, Jenefer (1997). *Music and Meaning*. Cornell University Press.
Roche, Elizabeth (1979a). Early Music on Records in the Last 25 Years-1. *The Musical Times*, 120(1631):34–36.
Roche, Elizabeth (1979b). Early Music on Records in the Last 25 Years-2. *The Musical Times*, 120(1633):215–217.

Roche, Elizabeth (1979c). Early Music and the BBC-1: World War II to 1957. *The Musical Times*, 120(1640):821–823.

Roche, Elizabeth (1979d). Early Music and the BBC-2: 1957 to date. *The Musical Times*, 120(1641):912–914.

Roche, Elizabeth (1989). Early Music: Its Revival and Interpretation. *Music & Letters*, 70(3), August, 382–384.

Roche, Elizabeth (2013). A polyphonic Mass is not a symphony: some occupational hazards of recording early music. *Early Music*, 41(1):64–67.

Roche, J. and Roche, E.(1981). *A Dictionary of Early Music*, Faber Music Ltd.

Rogers, Nigel (1984). The singer's view. *Early Music*, 12(4):524.

Rooley, Anthony (1978). Education. In *The Future Of Early Music in Britain*, ed. J. M. Thomson, 64–66. Oxford University Press.

Rooley, Anthony (1990). *Performance: Revealing the Orpheus Within*. Element Books.

Rooley, Anthony (2009). A case for the pickled larynx. *Singing music from 1500 to 1900: style, technique, knowledge, assertion, experiment*. Proceedings of the National Early Music Association International Conference, in association with the University of York Music Department and the York Early Music Festival, at York, July 7–10. Available at: http://www.york.ac.uk/music/conferences/nema/rooley/, accessed August 4, 2012.

Rose, Stephen (2013). Towards the digital future. *Early Music*, 41(1):129–130.

Rosen, Charles (1990). The Shock of the Old (A Review of Authenticity and Early Music: A Symposium). *The New York Review of Books*, July 19.

Ross, Alex (2009). *The Rest is Noise. Listening to the Twentieth Century*. Harper Perennial.

Rowland, David (2001). *Early Keyboard Instruments. A Practical Guide*. Cambridge University Press.

Rubinoff, Kailan (2013). A revolution in sheep's wool stockings: early music and '1968.' In *Music and Protest in 1968*, eds. B. Kutschke and B. Norton, Ch.14:237–254. Cambridge University Press.

Ruskin, John (1866). *The Crown of Wild Olive*. Wiley.

Ryan, Jane (1999). Obituary, Francis and June Baines. *Early Music*, 27(3):508–509.

Salter, Lionel (2012). [2000] Gustav Leonhardt obituary. Harpsichordist at the heart of the early music movement. *The Guardian*, January 17th.

Samson, William (1979). Acoustics, appearance and authenticity—Are our priorities right? *FOMRHI Quarterly*. Bulletin 16, July, Communication 216:34.

Sarasvathy, Saras (2001). Causation and Effectuation: Toward A Theoretical Shift from Economic Inevitability to Entrepreneurial Contingency. *Academy of Management Review*, 26(2): 243–288.

Sarasvathy Saras (2008). *Effectuation*. Edward Elgar.

Sartre, Jean-Paul (1988). *What is Literature? And Other Essays*. Harvard University Press.

Sayer, Andrew (1992). *Method in Social Science*. 2nd edition. Routledge.

Scardaville, Melissa (2009). High art, no art: The economic and aesthetic legitimacy of U.S. soap operas. *Poetics*, 37:366–382.

Scharmer, Otto (2009). *Theory U: Leading from the Future as it Emerges*. Berrett-Koehler.

Schechner, Richard (2006). [First edn 2002] *Performance Studies. An Introduction*. Routledge.

Schering, Arnold (1914). *Studien zur Musikgeschichte der Frürenaissance*. Kessinger.

Schmied, Ernesto (2000). *Frans Brüggen*, Interview for Goldbergweb.com, June.

Schonberg, Harold, C. (1967). *The Great Conductors*. Simon & Schuster.

Schubert, Thomas W. (2009). A new conception of spatial presence: Once again, with feeling. *Communication Theory*, 19:161–187.

Schulkind, Jeanne (1985). *Moments of Being*. 2nd edn. Harcourt Brace & Company.

Schumacher, E.F. (1973). Organisation and Ownership. *Small is Beautiful: A study of economics as if people mattered*, Blond & Briggs.
Schumpeter, Joseph (1934). *The Theory of Economic Development: An Inquiry into Profits, Capital, Credit, Interest and the Business Cycle*. Trans. R. Opie. Harvard University Press.
Scott, M. and Bruce, R. (1987). Five stages of growth in small business. *Long Range Planning*, 20(3):45–52.
Scruton, Roger (1997). *The Aesthetics of Music*. Oxford University Press.
Seabright, Paul (2012). How to defend universities, A review of Stefan Collini's "What are universities for?" March 7th. *Times Literary Supplement*.
Sharpe, R.A. (1974). Ideology and Ontology. *Philosophy of the Social Sciences*, March, 4(1):55–64.
Shepard, Benjamin (2011). *Play, Creativity, and Social Movements*. Routledge.
Sherman, Bernard, D. (1997). *Inside Early Music. Conversations with Performers*. Oxford University Press.
Shiner, Larry (2001). *The Invention of Art*. University of Chicago Press.
Small, Christopher (1987). Performance as ritual: Sketch for an enquiry into the true nature of a symphony concert. In *Lost in Music, Culture, Style and the Musical Event*, ed. Avron Levine White. Routledge and Kegan Paul.
Small, Christopher (1998). *Musicking: The meanings of performing and listening*. Wesleyan University Press.
Smith, Adam (1776). *The Wealth of Nations*.
Stearns, Patrick (2011). Tough, thorny alt-conductor Sir John Eliot Gardiner follows his own tempo, *Inquirer*, November 13. Available at: Philly.com.
Steiner, Rudolf (1973). *Karmic Relationships*. Vol. VII. Trans. D.S. Osmond. Rudolf Steiner Press.
Sternberg, R. and Lubart, T. (2007). The concept of creativity: Prospects and paradigms. In *Handbook of Creativity*, ed. R. J. Sternberg, Chapter 1:3–15. Cambridge University Press.
Stevens, Denis (1989). Review of Authenticity and Early Music: A Symposium, and The Early Music Revival A History. *Early Music*, 17(3):415–419.
Stokes, D. and Wilson, N. (2010). *Small Business Management & Entrepreneurship*. CENGAGE.
Stokes, D. Wilson, N. and Mador, M. (2010). *Entrepreneurship*. CENGAGE.
Stokes, Patricia (2006). *Creativity from Constraints*. Springer.
Stone-Davis, Férdia (2011). *Musical Beauty. Negotiating the Boundary between Subject and Object*. Cascade Books.
Stowell, Robin (2001). *The Early Violin and Viola. A Practical Guide*. Cambridge University Press.
Strati, Antonio (2000). The aesthetic approach in organization studies. In *The Aesthetics of Organization*, eds. S. Linstead and H. Höpfl, 13–34. Sage.
Sutton-Smith, Brian (1997). *The Ambiguity of Play*. Harvard University Press.
Swedberg, Richard (2006). The cultural entrepreneur and the creative industries: beginning in Vienna. *Journal of Cultural Economics*, 30:243–261.
Sweeting, Adam (2007). The greatest soprano never to sing a note of Verdi. *The Telegraph*, May 24.
Taruskin, Richard (1982). On letting the music speak for itself: Some reflections on musicology and performance. *Journal of Musicology*, 1(3):338–349.
Taruskin, Richard (1984). The Limits of Authenticity: A Discussion: The Authenticity Movement Can Become a Positivistic Purgatory, Literalistic and Dehumanizing. *Early Music*, 12(1) February:3–12.
Taruskin, Richard (1988). The pastness of the present and the presence of the past. In *Authenticity and Early Music*, edn. N. Kenyon, Chapter 6:137–210. Oxford University Press.

Taruskin, Richard (1995). *Text & Act*. Oxford University Press.

Taruskin, Richard (2007). Foreword. In *The Imaginary Museum of Musical Works. An Essay in the Philosophy of Music*, L. Goehr, v–viii. Oxford University Press.

Taruskin, R. Leech-Wilkinson, D. Temperley, N. and Winter, R. (1984). The limits of authenticity: A discussion. *Early Music*, 12(1):3–25.

Terry, Richard R. (1907). *Catholic Church Music*. Greening & Co. Available at: http://media.musicasacra.com/pdf/terry.pdf, accessed May 28, 2013.

Thom, Paul (2011). Authentic Performance Practice, In *The Routledge Companion to Philosophy and Music*, eds. T. Gracyk and A. Kania, 91–100. Routledge.

Thomas, Bernard (1977). Renaissance music in modern notation. *Early Music*, 5(1):4–11.

Thomson, J.M. (1973). Introduction to first edition. *Early Music*, 1(1):1.

Thomson, J.M. (1974). Editorial. *Early Music*, 2(1):1.

Thomson, J.M. (1976). Editorial. *Early Music*, 4(3).

Thomson, J.M. (1978). *The Future of Early Music in Britain*. Oxford University Press.

Thomson, J.M. (1981). Editorial. *Early Music*, 9(1):10.

Thomson, J.M. Sothcott, J. Fallows, D. and Page, C. (1994). Michael Morrow, 1929–94. *Early Music*, 22(3) August:537–539.

Throsby, David (1994). The production and consumption of the arts: A view of cultural economics. *Journal of Economic Literature*, XXXII:1–29.

Throsby, David (1996). Economic circumstances of the performing artist: Baumol and Bowen thirty years on. *Journal of Cultural Economics*, 20:225–240.

Tolkien, J. R. R. (1988). [1964] *Tree and Leaf*. Unwin Hyman.

Tosi, Pier Francesco (1743). [1978] *Observations on the Florid Song; or, Sentiments on the Ancient and Modern Singers*. Minkoff Reprint.

Townley, B. Beech, N. and McKinlay, A. (2009). Managing in the creative industries: Managing the motley crew. *Human Relations*, 62(7):939–962.

Towse, Ruth (1992). The earnings of singers: an economic analysis. In *Cultural Economics*, eds. R. Towse and A. Khakee, 209–17. Springer-Verlag.

Towse, Ruth (1993). *Singers in the marketplace: The economics of the singing profession*. Clarendon Press.

Towse, Ruth (1995). *The economics of artists' labour markets*. Arts Council of England.

Towse, Ruth (1997). *Baumol's Cost Desease: The Art and Other Victims*. Edward Elgar.

Towse, Ruth (2006). Human Capital and Artists' Labour Markets. In *Handbook of the Economics of Arts and Culture*, eds. V.A. Ginsburgh and D. Thorsby, 865–894. Elsevier.

Trilling, Lionel (1972). *Sincerity and Authenticity*. Harvard University Press.

Turner, Victor (1969). *The Ritual Process*. Aldine.

Tymieniecka, Anna-Teresa (2000). Toward the aesthetics of enchantment, In *The Aesthetics of Enchantment in the Fine Arts*, eds. M. Kronegger and A. Tymieniecka, 3–20. Kluwer Academic Press.

Upton, Elizabeth (2012). Concepts of authenticity in early music and popular music communities. *Ethnomusicology Review*, 17:1–13. Available at: http://ethnomusicologyreview.ucla.edu, accessed May 28, 2013.

Vannini, P. and Williams, J. P. (2009). *Authenticity in Culture, Self, and Society*. Ashgate.

Van Tassel, Eric (1984). Untitled review. *Early Music*, 12(1):129.

Villa, Paola (1986). *Structuring of Labour Markets*. Clarendon Press.

Vulliamy, Ed (2005). £1m legal bill rocks a musical institution: Classical record firm at risk after court defeat, December 23. *The Guardian*.

Wallace, Helen (2006). *Spirit of the Orchestra*. Orchestra of the Age of Enlightenment.
Warner, Marina (2011). *Stranger Magic: Charmed States & the Arabian Nights*. Chatto & Windus.
Wassall, G. H. and Alper, N. O. (1992). Toward a Unified Theory of the Determinants of the Earnings of Artists. In *Cultural Economics*, eds. R. Towse and A. Khakee, Chapter 18: 187–200. Springer-Verlag.
Weatherston, Dawn (2009). Nascent entrepreneurship and music students. In *Dialogues in Art and Design: Promoting and Sharing Excellence*, ed. D. Clews, 50–57. ADM-HEA/GLAD.
Weber, Max (1905). [1930] *The Protestant Ethic and the Spirit of Capitalism*. Trans. Talcott Parsons. Unwin Hyman.
Weber, Max (1909). [1978] *Economy and Society: An Outline of Interpretive Sociology, Vol.1*. University of California Press.
Weber, Max (1946/1968). *Economy and Society, Volumes 1 and 2*. eds. G. Roth and C. Wittich. University of California Press.
Wenger, Etienne (1998). *Communities of Practice: Learning, Meaning, and Identity*. Cambridge University Press.
Wennekers, S. and Thurik, R. (1999). Linking entrepreneurship and economic growth. *Small Business Economics*, August, 13(1):27–55.
Westrup, Jack (1967). *Introduction to Musical History*. Hutchinson.
Williams, Jonathan D. (2007). 'Tha realness': In search of hip-hop authenticity. CUREJ, University of Pennsylvania. Available at http://repository.upenn.edu/curej/78, accessed September 30, 2012.
Wilson, Nick (2007a). Applying critical realism: re-conceptualising the emergent English early music performer labour market. In *Contributions to Social Ontology*, eds. C. Lawson, J. Latsis, and N. Martins, Chapter 18:304–323. Routledge.
Wilson, Nick (2007b). *Explaining Labour Market Emergence: The Case of Early Music Performance in the UK*. Unpublished PhD thesis. Kingston University.
Wilson, Nick (2009). Learning to manage creativity: An occupational hazard for the UK's creative industries. *Creative Industries Journal*, 2(2):179–190.
Wilson, N. Hart, M. and Kitching, J. (2008). It's the evidence stupid: Doing and legitimising policy research. *31st Institute for Small Business and Entrepreneurship (ISBE) Conference: International Entrepreneurship—promoting excellence in education, research and practice*; November 5–7, Belfast.
Winter, Robert (1984). The most unwitting foes of the Romantic piano may be those well-intentioned curators who lend their instruments for recording sessions. *Early Music*, 12(1):21–25.
Wiora, Walter (1967). *Alte Musik in unserer Zeit—Referate und Diskussionen der Kasseler Tagung*. Bärenreiter.
Wistreich, R. and Potter, J. (2013). Singing early music: a conversation. *Early Music*, 41(1):22–26.
Wolf, Johannes (1913). *Handbuch der Notationskunde I*. Breitkopf & Härtel.
Wright, David (2008). Concerts for coteries, or music for all? Glock's Proms reconsidered. *The Musical Times*, 149(1904):3-34.
Young, James O. (1988). The concept of authentic performance. *The British Journal of Aesthetics*, 28:228–238.
Young, James O. (2005). Authenticity in Performance. In *The Routledge Companion to Aesthetics*, eds. B. Gaut and D. Lopes, 2nd edn., 501–12. Routledge.
Zahra, S. and George, G. (2002). Absorptive Capacity: A Review, Reconceptualization, and Extension. *Academy of Management Review*, 27(2):185–203.
Zaslaw, Neil (1992). Editorial. *Early Music*, 20(2):194.

INDEX

Abraham, Gerald, 145
Academy of Ancient Music (AAM), xi, 23,
    230n17
  and Authenticity$_2$, 31–32
  formation of, 30, 57, 70, 76, 78, 81–82
  funding of, 137, 248n81, 255n55
  leadership of, 35, 161
  and L'Oiseau-Lyre, 151, 155, 224
  loyalty of performers to, 32, 147, 158
  See also Egarr, Richard; Hogwood,
    Christopher
Academy of St Martin in the Fields, 21, 23, 35,
    70, 75
Accademia Monteverdiana, 23, 144
  See also Stevens, Denis
Adorno, Theodor, 11, 13, 37–38, 46, 123, 198,
    202–203
aesthetic(s), 6, 7, 22, 38, 153–154, 170, 180–183
  knowledge, 40, 124, 126, 180, 214–215
Aldeburgh Festival, 70
Alte Musik. *See* early music
amateur(s), 13, 22, 78, 98, 184, 228
  and Authenticity$_1$, 107, 162, 186
  as critique of Early Music, 14, 26, 95, 104,
    223
  early music-making, 20, 22, 59–64, 100, 102

and move towards professionalism, 57, 75,
    79, 154, 179–180, 193–194
  vs. professional music-making, 5, 7–8, 18,
    33, 83–84, 148, 170, 191, 204–205, 212, 226
  rhetoric of Early Music, 9–10, 59
American early music, xii, 60–61, 65–66,
    72–73, 132, 153
Amsterdam. *See* Hague, The (Conservatory)
anachronistic dissonance, 67
Anderson, Nicholas, 146
anti-clash diary. *See* under-supply
Archer, Margaret, 177–178, 195
Arne, Thomas, 81, 155
Arnold, Denis, 28–29, 94–95, 142, 144
Ars Nova. *See* Parley of Instruments, The
art
  vs. artisan, 102, 124, 158–159, 212, 223
  and authenticity (*see* authenticity (in
    performing music))
  discourse of value, 9, 17, 123, 135, 141–148,
    153, 156, 223–224
  doing, 6, 7, 18, 43, 125, 180, 211–217, 221,
    223, 226
  Early Music as, 4, 44
  and education, 28, 123, 130, 132, 137, 161,
    170, 222–223, 226

279

art (Cont.)
    and enchantment, 213, 216–217
    vs. entertainment, 164, 200–201
    and knowledge, 53, 124–125, 137, 222–223
    and living, 7, 53, 102, 198–200, 202, 204, 213–215, 221–224, 228
    and nature, 221–222
    -science, 18, 50, 124, 129–130, 224, 226
artistic legitimation. *See* mainstreaming
Arts Council, 17, 25, 60, 123, 127–128, 132–138, 161, 224, 247n54
arts, the, 28, 33, 132–137, 159, 165, 195, 224
    characteristics of, 82, 126, 137, 202, 205
auction houses, 106–107, 115
audiences, 4, 9–10, 49, 53, 125, 129, 138, 150, 177, 180, 194, 218
    and the BBC, 143, 145–146, 155
    and enchantment, 210–211, 213, 215
    power over, 14, 148, 152, 203–204, 207
    and the "unfamiliar", 13, 206
Austrian early music, xii, 20–21, 25, 63
authenticities, 33, 41, 57, 59, 75, 211, 258n58
authenticity (in living)
    and the authentic self, 7, 13, 18, 27, 37, 42, 49, 53, 172, 195, 203, 211, 213, 215, 227
    and "being authentic", 6, 43, 196, 210–211, 221
    and enchantment, 199, 210–211, 213, 226
    and epistemology, 39, 45–46, 51, 210, 227
    and imagination, 13, 40, 42, 46–47, 96, 170, 172, 219–220, 223, 225, 257n31
    and ontology, 40, 45–47, 50–51, 152, 210, 226, 237n80
    personal, 37, 41–42, 48–49, 51, 125, 166, 211, 213, 215, 227, 245n9
    "real", 16, 125, 197, 211, 226
    utopian nature of, 11, 217
authenticity (in performing music)
    and art, xi, 6–7, 18, 38, 41, 43, 53, 209, 212, 215, 221, 225–226
    the case for, 36–38, 44, 50, 53, 104–5, 182, 235n34
    critique of, 11–15, 38–43, 45, 73, 152, 183, 188, 198, 206, 217
    the cult of, 20, 38
    discourses of, 7, 14–15, 33, 38–39, 142, 144, 152–154, 156, 191–192, 210, 225, 227
    dispositional (historical), 16, 50–51, 105, 124–125, 152, 204, 210–211, 214, 220, 225–226, 232n69

expressive, 38
fabricating, 75, 125, 153, 210
in folk music, 148–149
vs. "HIP", 45, 180–181, 192, 227
historical, 13, 20–21, 41–43, 49, 52, 124–125, 170, 209, 215, 222, 235n16
ideology of, x, 9, 12, 14–15, 42–43, 73, 87, 112, 148, 154, 156, 177, 179, 183, 191, 207, 209, 218, 220
and innate musicianship, 5, 67, 95, 197, 209
instruments and instrument-making, 72, 99, 103–105
of intention, 4, 5, 9, 38, 41–42, 51, 53, 95, 154, 236n58
and interpretation, xii, 95–96, 128, 152, 193, 236n59
the limits of, 43, 58, 88, 137
and the market, 45, 138
movement, 14, 39, 43–45, 129, 134, 153, 172, 191, 206, 219, 250n53
nominal, 38
and notation, 26, 50, 93–95, 125
and the performing arts, 38
of practice (practical), 41, 51, 167
rhetoric of Early Music, 8, 14–15, 59–61
and rough edges, 180, 189–190, 206
of sound (sonic), 41, 51
Authenticity$_1$, 28, 61–68, 96, 128, 171, 180, 182, 186, 189–190
    characteristics of, 36, 59, 75, 100, 107, 131, 135, 162, 187, 204
    definition of, 17
Authenticity$_2$, 61, 69–75, 128, 190, 205
    characteristics of, 59, 75, 100, 135
    definition of, 17
    move towards, 61, 75, 99, 101, 186, 194
authentic performance movement. *See* Early Music (movement)
avant-gardism, 60, 64–65, 143, 219
Aveling, Valda, 103

Bach, Johann Sebastian, 7, 9, 41, 59, 70, 72–73, 76, 80, 84, 102, 131, 153, 182
    Art of Fugue, 214
    Brandenburg Concertos, 46, 126
    Cantatas, 21, 34, 85, 155, 171
    Christmas Oratorio, 79
    Mass in B Minor, 48–49, 79
    Passions, 19, 79
    Suites, 85

Index

Bailey, Robert, 103
Baines, Anthony, 106, 243n33
Baines, Francis and June, 64
Barbican Centre, 8, 193
Barenboim, Daniel, 205, 211
Baroque, 3, 230n6
   early, 28, 59, 128, 143–144, 182–183, 186, 204 (*see also* Authenticity$_1$)
   pitch, 9, 72
   pop, 67
   repertoire, 10, 17, 30, 36, 59, 63, 69–70, 75, 95, 177, 188–190
   style, 31, 183
   See also Authenticity$_2$; instrument(s)
Bartlett, Clifford, 25, 39, 64, 97–99, 107, 145, 164, 166, 215
Bate, Philip, 99, 106
Bath Festival, 70, 80, 163
Beckett, John, 28–29, 142, 144
Beethoven "experience", 87, 172, 224, 234n30
Beethoven, Ludwig van, 3, 41, 87, 94, 119, 172, 182, 224
being and becoming, 5, 48, 219, 228
Belloc, Hilaire, 202
Benjamin, Walter, 206
Bennett, Clive, 142, 144
Bergmann, Walter, xii, 145
Bhaskar, Roy, 15–16, 48, 204
Biber, Heinrich, 74, 214
Bicket, Harry, 29, 35, 79, 188
Bickley, John, 58, 149–150
Biennial International Conference on Baroque Music, 128
Binkley, Thomas, 21, 66, 72
Birtwistle, Harrison, 61, 64–65
Bishop, Christopher, 27–28, 150–151, 215, 224
BIS Records, 100
Black, Virginia, 101
Boorman, Stanley, 95
Bostridge, Ian, 198
Boulanger, Nadia, 63, 65, 73, 85, 144, 227
Boyd Neel Orchestra, 35, 70
   See also Neel, Boyd
Brahms, Johannes, 33, 35, 87, 182
Bream, Julian, 69, 71, 105, 218
Brighton Early Music Festival, 131, 136, 149
British Broadcasting Corporation (BBC), 17, 30, 63, 108, 127, 140–147, 154–155, 248n5
   Baroque Orchestra (Early Music Orchestra/Training Orchestra), 146–147

   music library, 97
   Music Restored, 146
   orchestras, 82, 146, 162
   Pied Piper, 27, 146, 172, 249n26
   Proms, 8, 76, 83–84, 120, 143–144, 155, 181, 193
   Radio 3 music department, 65, 71, 83, 88–89, 96, 98, 100, 142–146, 151, 163
   Radio 3 (Third Programme), 8, 27, 66, 83, 142–143, 145–146, 151, 155, 164
   Singers, 83
   Spirit of the Age, 146
   The Early Music Forum, 146
   The Early Music Show, 146, 148, 182
   The Young Idea, 146
British Council, 67, 74, 134, 187
Britten, Benjamin, 66, 70–71, 182–183
Brown, Clive, 183, 191
Brown, Howard Mayer, xii, 19–21, 28, 31, 98, 172
Brüggen, Frans, 21, 25, 73, 148, 227
Bryanston Summer School, 63
Burnett, James, 215
Burton, Anthony, 146
business angels, 91, 138, 154–155, 159, 209, 224
Butt, John, 13, 22, 29, 80, 216
Bylsma, Anner, 25, 73

Cape, Safford, 66
capitalism, xi, 11, 13, 18, 197, 202–209, 212, 217, 223–224, 231n36
Cardinall's Musick, The, 36, 171, 183
Chickering (Boston), 73
choristers and choirs, 26, 79, 84, 149, 185, 190
Christie, George, 71
Christie, William, 73
Christophers, Harry, 29, 98, 130, 171
City Waites, 23, 148
Civil, Alan, 82
class, 4, 60, 163, 184
   See also social capital
Classical music
   period, 182, 232n7
   profession, 4–6, 8–10, 32, 90–92, 132, 142, 154, 163, 177–178, 218
   repertoire, 3, 17, 31, 59, 65, 69, 75, 87–88, 140, 177, 188, 190 (*see also* Authenticity$_2$)
Classic FM, 9, 255n59
"class of '73", 28, 33, 35, 76–83, 86–87, 89, 147, 158, 179

Clemencic, René, 73
Cohen, Joel, 57, 76, 101–102, 185, 191, 223
collegium musicum, 64, 68, 128–129
Collegium Musicum 90, 23, 31
   See also Hickox, Richard; Standage, Simon
Comberti, Micaela, 65
commercial
   discourse of value, 17, 141–142, 149–154, 156, 159
   influence on repertoire, 180, 182–184, 206
   rhetoric of Early Music, 8, 10–11, 37, 59, 61
   See also market
compromise, 14, 15, 72, 77, 105, 150, 167, 178, 191, 195, 198, 204, 212
Concentus Musicus Wien, xi, 21, 23, 152, 250n53
   See also Harnoncourt, Nikolaus
Consort of Musicke, 23, 64, 74, 157
   See also Rooley, Anthony
copying, 19, 27, 243n36
   Xerox photo-, 93, 97–98
copyright, 39, 49–50
CRD Records, 79
creative
   co-, 82, 124, 165, 167
   constraints, 220, 225–226
   decisions, 90, 145
   destruction, 172, 208
   individual(s), 82, 145, 165
   industries, xii, 82
   knowledge, 123–124
   labor, 57
   rhetoric of Early Music, 8, 12–13, 33, 45, 59, 61, 172
   unbalance, 143
creativity, 12–13, 108, 125, 154, 170, 172, 200
   communicating, 126–127, 159, 170
   and musicology, 68, 208
   recognizing, 125–127, 137, 144–145, 159, 170
   resourcing, 50, 126–127
critical realism, xi, 15–16, 45–46, 125, 201, 210
   dialectical, 16, 18, 48–49, 51, 124, 126, 138, 215, 225, 258n9
Cruft, John, 136
Crum, Alison, 64, 131–132, 187, 191, 194
cultural economy, 17
cultural production, 6, 10, 16, 38, 126, 139, 152–154, 179, 198, 203, 209–210
   Bourdieu's theory of, 141, 153

culture vs. commerce, 11, 18, 152, 165, 192, 204, 207, 226
Cummings, Laurence, 33, 100, 150, 190, 192, 226

dance, 59, 62, 67–68, 77, 95, 129, 146–148, 182–183, 190, 214
Dartington Summer School, 63, 65, 73, 143
Dart, Thurston, xii, 21, 24–26, 29, 68, 71–72, 74, 103, 145, 164
   and musicology, 75, 94–96, 128, 190
   and Philomusica of London, 70
Davies, Robert (Bob), 101, 102
Decca, 30, 70, 89, 151, 155, 162
   Gold Label, 66
   L'Oiseau-Lyre, 30, 81, 151, 162, 224
Deegan, Robert, 101
Deller, Alfred, xii, 29, 71, 145, 152
Dent, Edward, 21, 29, 100
Deutsche Grammophon (DG & DGG), 34, 66, 155
   Archiv Produktion, 65–66, 79, 165, 185
Dewey, John, 3, 48, 180, 213
dialectic. See critical realism: dialectical
diplomatics, 95
disenchantment, 6, 8, 123, 202, 215
   of the world, 13, 18, 196–199, 216–217, 224, 226
dogmatic, 5, 52, 67, 95, 170
   vs. creative, 45, 61, 74
   HIP, nature of, 75, 162, 192, 201
   rhetoric of Early Music, 8, 11–14, 59, 211, 225
Dolmetsch, Arnold, xii, 28, 43, 106
   the artisan, 102, 223
   background, 29, 73
   and the cult of authenticity, 20, 38, 104
   and Early Music, 20–21, 62–63, 75, 101, 216–217
   and the Haslemere workshop, 63
   and historical musicology, 96, 101, 182
   influence of, 95, 105, 223
   pioneer, 10, 25, 101, 147
   and the United States of America, 65, 73
Dolmetsch, Carl, 104, 243n32
Dolmetsch, Mabel, 147
Donington, Robert, xi–xii, 20, 28–29, 68, 93, 95–96, 215
Douglas, Basil (Management), 71, 73, 79

Dowd, William, 102
Dreyfus, Laurence, xii, 19, 29, 86, 179
Druce, Duncan, 61, 65
Dunkerley, John, 81, 155
Dutch early music, xii, 25, 73, 81, 148, 187
Dyson, Ruth, 101, 151

early music
  and contemporary music, 60, 64–65, 136, 183, 219
  definition of, x, 3–4, 19
  editing, 17, 48, 50, 92, 95, 97, 124, 145, 214, 222, 224, 251n26
  and mediation, 97
  and nature, 74, 221–222, 228
  re-enchanting, 196–202, 210–211, 215–221, 228
  revival, 9, 11, 14, 19, 21, 59, 62, 66, 94, 96, 99, 100, 123, 134, 138, 148, 205, 223
  sound, 9, 25–26, 52, 62, 66–68, 73–74, 84, 94, 102–103, 107, 147, 180–181, 189–190, 227
  and vibrato, 34, 68, 107, 190, 191
Early Music Centre (EMC), 64, 74, 94, 97, 100, 113, 117, 132, 134, 170, 183, 220
  formation of, 58, 133, 247n48
Early Music Consort of London, 10, 12, 23, 28, 59, 75
  formation of, 19, 27
  leadership of, 162, 166
  recordings, 68, 80, 151, 190, 205
  See also Munrow, David
Early Music in Europe Conference, 183, 186
Early Music Exhibition, 98, 107, 149, 179, 194
Early Music Journal, xi, 43, 58, 88, 100–101, 107, 128–129, 179, 195, 229n4
  adverts from, 110–120
Early Music (movement), x–xii
  achievements of, 177–195, 212, 227–228
  as community of practice (CoP), 220
  contradictions of, xi, 4–5, 8, 11, 18, 53, 173, 178, 204–209, 211–212, 216, 226
  and education, 127–132, 161
  funding, 132–139, 140–142, 150–156
  a "helpless situation", as response to, 218–219, 228
  ideology (*see* authenticity (in performing music))

incubating, 144, 155
and instrument-making, 100–105
and knowledge (seven claims), 123–126, 129–30
life course of, 16, 22–36, 58, 169
pioneers, xii, 4, 8, 11, 25, 30, 61, 74, 124, 157–158, 160, 163, 195, 209, 228
professionalization of, 62–75, 76–78, 82–88, 90–92
rhetorics of, 7–15
robber barons, 192, 208
roots of, 20–22
tensions and disagreements in, 83, 158, 166
See also authenticity (in performing music): movement
Early Music Network, 58, 117, 133–134, 247n48, 247n58
Early Music News, 97
Early Music Review, 97
Early Music Shop, 10, 19, 100–101, 107, 111
  See also Wood, Richard
Early Music Today, xi
Eastwood, Jennifer, 134
École de Musique Ancienne, 73
Edwards, Warwick, 29, 33
Egarr, Richard, 73, 80
Elder, Mark, 91
Elgar, Edward, 182
Eliot, T.S., 211, 226
Elsen, Gijs, 193
emancipation, 7, 42, 197, 204
emergence, 17, 53, 210, 212, 222, 226
  and creativity, 168
  and cultural entrepreneurship, 17, 159
  of Early Music, 9, 15, 44, 153–154, 165, 215
  and enchantment, 201, 206, 211, 214
  labor market (*see* labor market: emergence)
  and performing music, 41, 46–47, 49, 53
EMI's *Reflexe* and *Electrola* series, 27, 66, 80–81, 151, 163, 224
enchantment, 7, 53, 96, 196, 198–202, 206, 209–228, 257n27
  age of, 216–217
  vs. disenchantment, 8, 18, 204
  vs. magic, 201–204, 207–208, 210–213, 217, 221, 226
  See also disenchantment; re-enchantment
English *a capella* heresy, 31

English Baroque Soloists (EBS), 23, 30, 32, 76, 79, 164, 188
   and Bach Cantata pilgrimage, 155
   See also Gardiner, John Eliot
English Chamber Orchestra (ECO), 21, 23, 35, 71, 247n68
English Concert, The (TEC), xi, 23, 31, 158, 188
   formation of, 28, 30, 57, 76, 78–79
   funding of, 134, 137
   leadership of, 35, 193
   loyalty of performers to, 32, 147, 161, 163
   recordings, 165, 185
   See also Bicket, Harry; Pinnock, Trevor
English Consort of Viols, 63–64, 106
English Opera Group, 70–71
Enlightenment, xi, 6, 13, 90, 102, 124, 167, 197, 208, 217, 226
   See also Orchestra of the Age of Enlightenment (OAE)
entrepreneurial decision-making, 160, 165–166
   causation and effectuation, 166
entrepreneurship, xi, 5, 108, 123, 159–160, 165–168, 170–172, 226
   cultural, 5, 11, 17–18, 139, 157–173, 207–208, 212, 220–223, 227, 231n38, 246n30
Erato, 151
Evidence-Based Performance (EBP), 13, 34–35, 73, 96, 124, 129, 154, 181
expressive arts therapy, 219–221

Fallows, David, 25, 64, 66, 214
Faultless, Margaret, 181
Fellowes, Edmund, 96, 100
Fellowship of Makers and Restorers of Historical Instruments (FoMRHI), 99
Fires of London, 65
Fischer, Ivan, 90–91
Fiske, Roger, 145
fixing (orchestras), 63, 83, 134, 160
flow, 200, 225
folk music, 67, 68
   clubs, 148–149
   discourse of value, 17, 141–142, 148–149, 153, 156
   and early music, 60, 66–68, 73–75, 147–148, 153, 190
   festivals, 149
   Moravian, 74

revival, 147–148
   South American, 74
   Yugoslav, 67
freelance music and musicians, 57, 86, 93, 137, 147, 171, 247n68
Future of Early Music in Britain, The, 58, 128, 133, 137, 147

Gabrieli Consort & Players, 23, 30, 83, 183
Galliard Harpsichord Trio, 30, 78–79
Galpin Society, 99, 243n32
Garcin, Michel, 151, 215
Gardiner, John Eliot, 89–90, 98, 130, 143, 158, 188, 227–228
   authenticity, views on, 39, 164–165
   and Bach Cantata Pilgrimage, 26, 34, 155, 171
   and enchantment, 200
   and entrepreneurship, 159–160, 165–166, 171
   funding, views on, 135, 152
   and Monteverdi *Vespers*, 26
   musical excellence, views on, 85, 172
   musical training of, 29, 63, 75, 162
   music and nature, views on, 74
   as pioneer, 195, 209
   recordings, 79, 151
   See also English Baroque Soloists (EBS); Monteverdi Choir; Monteverdi Orchestra; Orchestre Révolutionnaire et Romantique (ORR)
Gardiner, Rolf, 63, 228
Garnham, Ben, 71
Garnham, Maureen, 71, 79, 86, 158
Gaveau (Paris), 73
German early music, xii, 19–21, 63–64, 68, 71, 93, 100–101, 105, 128, 187, 195
Gimell, 80, 151
Glasgow International Early Music Festival, 33
   See also Edwards, Warwick
Glock, William, 63, 80, 143–145, 215
Glyndebourne Festival Opera, 32, 70–71, 76, 91, 193, 208
Goble, Robert, 102, 104, 215
Goebel, Reinhard, 21, 72–73
Goehr, Lydia, 40–41, 45–47, 214
Goff, Tom (Thomas), 69, 72, 102–104
Goldsbrough, Arnold, xii, 71, 145

Goldsbrough Orchestra, 21, 23, 35, 71
    See also English Chamber Orchestra (ECO)
Goodman, Roy, 31, 251n28
Gothic Voices, 23, 30, 75, 88, 151, 171, 183, 190, 224, 233n20
    See also Page, Christopher
Gough, Hugh, 105
Greater London Council, 133
Greenberg, Noah, 21, 66, 72, 104
Greenwich Early Music Festival. *See* Early Music Exhibition
Grisewood, Harman, 143

Hacker, Alan, 29, 61, 65, 81
Hague, The (Conservatory), 21, 25, 131
Hall, Richard, 64
Handel, George Frideric, 7, 21, 40, 46, 59, 63, 76, 84, 91, 100, 151, 153, 190, 206
Hanover Band, 23, 31, 83, 188
Harnoncourt, Alice, xi, 21
Harnoncourt, Nikolaus, xi, 21, 25–26, 30, 32, 72–73, 90, 96, 151, 165, 199–200
harpsichord-makers, 72, 101–105, 112, 144
    See also instrument-making; instrument(s): harpsichords
harpsichord players, 20–21, 26, 30, 70, 72–73, 78–79, 103, 131, 151, 214, 218
Harrison, F.L., 96, 145
Harwood, Ian, 105
Haskell, Harry, 19, 64, 66, 132
Haydn, Joseph, 3, 15, 59, 87, 144, 147, 153, 182
Haynes, Bruce, 8, 14, 35, 131
head vs. heart, 4–5, 18, 73, 199, 211, 214, 226
Hedger, Eric, 194
Hegel, Georg Wilhelm Friedrich, 37, 202
heritage, x, 33, 67, 127, 138, 216
    musical, 5, 191, 216
Herreweghe, Philippe, 73, 185
Hickox, Richard, 31, 80, 84
Hildegard of Bingen, 88, 140, 151, 190, 224
Hilliard Ensemble, 23, 58, 75, 83, 171, 183
Hindemith, Paul, 21, 64
hiring. *See* labor market
His Majestys Sagbutts and Cornetts, 23, 30, 36, 128, 135, 151, 171, 223
    See also West, Jeremy
historical instrument collections, 99, 106–107

historically informed performance (HIP)
    and authenticity, 14–15, 37–53, 98, 125, 138, 152–154, 189–192, 209–211, 225, 227
    characteristics of, 4, 8, 26, 158, 181, 214, 230n8
    and democratic principles, 32, 89–90, 171, 192, 205, 207
    and dogmatic rhetoric of Early Music, 11
    and evidence, 34–35, 67, 73, 75, 141
    and heritage, 216–217
    industry, 10, 22
    and instruments, 72, 99–108, 189
    limits of, 31, 33, 87, 182–184
    and modern players, 82, 188
    movement (*see* Early Music (movement))
    and ornamentation, 49, 75, 94, 96
    orthodoxy, 6, 42, 177–181
    pragmatic approach to, 32, 82, 130, 152, 162, 166, 187
    research & development (R&D), 77, 138
    second/third wave, 31, 251n4
    training, 84–85, 127–132, 184–188
historical performance movement. *See* Early Music (movement)
HMV's *History of Music in Sound*, 66, 145
Hoffmann, E.T.A., 41
Hogwood, Christopher, 32, 36, 73, 80, 88–90, 98, 158, 190
    authenticity, views on, 12, 75, 183, 191–192
    background, 27–28, 30, 149
    and the BBC, 146–147
    and entrepreneurship, 159, 161, 166
    musical training of, 29, 74–75
    performance, views on, 82, 84, 107
    and Peter Wadland, 30, 81, 151, 155, 162
    recordings, 76
    and scholarship, 11, 70, 128, 170
    and succession, 35, 193
    See also Academy of Ancient Music (AAM)
Holden, Claire, 39, 183, 188
Holman, Peter, 64, 78, 88, 131
Holschneider, Andreas, 79, 155, 165, 215
Holst, Imogen, 63, 70
Howes, Frank, 100
Hubbard, Frank, 69, 72, 102, 104–105, 215
Hughes, Paul, 81–82
Hunt, Edgar, xii, 29, 106, 131, 243n32
Hyperion Records, 39–40, 49, 88, 97, 151
    See also Perry, Simon; Perry, Ted

I Fagiolini, 60, 183, 238n20
inauthenticity, 6, 18, 72, 125, 189, 204, 206, 238n22
　vs. authenticity, 7–8, 13, 37, 50, 209, 215, 225
　"jargon of authenticity", understood as, 7, 198, 203
　See also disenchantment; TINA formation
innovation, 17, 77–78, 126–127, 135, 159, 165, 208
　classical music, 4
　early music as, 123, 126, 133, 136–138
　knowledge claim, 124
instrument-making, 17, 60–63, 71–73, 99–107, 111–112, 115, 123–125, 195, 223, 246n22
　and craft tradition, 11, 17, 73, 99, 102–104, 223
　and DIY kits, 10, 101, 105, 204, 223
　and early musicians, 194, 220–222
　and quality, 101, 103
instrument(s)
　authentic, 9, 26, 72, 93, 99, 103, 105, 152, 191
　Baroque, 20–21, 65, 67, 72, 81, 85, 100–101, 104, 108, 131
　brass and woodwind, 21, 27, 82, 85–86, 93–94, 99–101, 106–107, 166
　clarinets, 65, 72, 107–108, 164
　Classical, 72, 100–108, 186
　harpsichords, 58, 72, 223
　horns and trumpets, 82–83, 85–86, 106–108, 182, 188
　lutes, 66, 71, 99, 105, 108, 162, 218
　Medieval and Renaissance, 9, 27, 68, 100, 107, 172, 186, 230n30, 245n80
　oboes, 85, 91, 164
　"old", 10, 14, 52, 58, 62, 82, 84, 91, 94–95, 100–101, 103–108, 129, 137, 189, 194, 205, 214, 217, 223
　strings, 62–63, 81–82, 93–94, 107, 164, 182, 186, 191
　viola da gambas, 21, 62–64, 73, 101, 131
Isserlis, Annette, 64, 76, 89

Jacobs, René, 73
Jarman, Heather, 82, 85
Jolly, James, 82
Jones, Geraint, 101
Jones, Trevor, 64, 65
Jurowski, Vladimir, 91

Kant, Immanuel, 7
Kent Opera, 58, 63, 163
Kenyon, Nicholas, xi, 11, 29, 39, 70, 190, 193
　amateurs, views on, 63, 83–84
　and the Arts Council, 134, 136–137
　authenticity, views on, 42, 84–85, 88
　and the BBC, 144, 146–147
　Early Music, views on, 8, 22, 34, 43, 57, 76, 178–180, 183, 192
　and the OAE, 91
　and Period Instrument Orchestra Enquiry, 134
　"R&D function", views on, 124, 138
　scholarship, views on, 128
　training, views on, 184
Kessler, Dietrich, 106
Keynes, John Maynard, 224
Keyte, Hugh, 83, 98, 144, 146, 151, 163, 214
King, Robert, 29, 166–167
King's Consort, The, 23, 30, 83, 166–167
King's Music. See Bartlett, Clifford
Kirkby, Emma, 29, 75, 80, 98, 100, 170, 190
Kitching, Colin, 63, 65, 83, 150
Kite, Christopher, 183
Kivy, Peter, 33, 41, 49, 51, 211, 215
knowledge
　Mode 1, 124, 129
　Mode 2, 124, 144
Koopman, Ton, 41–42, 58, 73
Kramer, Timothy, 65
Kuijken
　brothers, 21, 73
　Sigiswald, 89–90

labor market, xii, 17, 76–77, 82, 86–87, 90, 187
　emergence, xi, 240n6
　flexible system, 187
　lack of churn, 187–188
　processes, 82–88
　and succession, 193
Lake District Festival, 70
Lam, Basil, 71, 142, 144, 146, 214
Landowska, Wanda, xii, 20, 25, 65, 72–73, 102, 232n9
Lassus Ensemble, 144
Lassus, Orlande de, 71, 164
Lawson, Colin, 107–108

leadership, 53, 180, 189, 216
  of early music groups, 25, 63, 70, 82, 157–158, 161, 192–193
  See also entrepreneurship: cultural
Leech-Wilkinson, Daniel, xii, 12, 45, 74, 96, 129, 154, 179
Leonhardt, Gustav, 21, 25–26, 30, 32, 48, 49, 72–73, 90, 96, 165
Leppard, Raymond, 14–15, 26, 29, 71, 74, 100, 197–198, 232n15
London Baroque, 23, 30
London Baroque Players, 87
London Choral Society, 71
London Classical Players (LCP), 23, 31–32, 63, 76, 87, 134, 160
  See also Norrington, Roger
London College of Furniture, 105, 244n51, 244n59
London Orchestral Concert Board (LOCB), 133, 136–137
London Philharmonic Orchestra, 32, 242n62
London Pro Musica, 80, 98, 105–106, 116
London Symphony Orchestra, 78, 227, 241n62
Lufthansa Festival of Baroque Music, 23, 35, 70, 149, 180–181
Lute Society, 63, 105
luthier(s), 38, 71, 103–105

Mackerras, Charles, 90, 163
Mackintosh, Catherine, 25, 29, 62–64, 74, 89, 106, 108, 131, 217
magic, 18, 169, 196–198, 200, 203, 231n48
  decline of, 13, 216
  See also enchantment
mainstreaming, x, 17, 20, 75–76, 86, 120, 144, 177–178, 195
  artistic legitimation and, 33, 128, 133, 145, 152–155, 162, 179–181, 193
  authenticity and, 152–154
  and the OAE, 32, 90–92
  syncretism and, 178, 195
Malcolm, George, xii, 26, 103
management and managers, 5, 11, 130, 184–185, 202, 214, 223
  of artists, 58, 71, 73, 79, 149–150, 158, 165, 200, 202
  and cultural entrepreneurship, 157–165, 192–193
  general, 80, 98, 142, 145, 152, 180, 187, 193

  of orchestras, 80–83, 90, 180–181, 193
Marcus, Marshall, 29, 89–91, 193
market
  for Authenticity$_1$, 107
  context, 4, 7, 13, 20, 24, 46, 125–126, 160, 167, 197, 202–203, 208–209, 221
  and cultural entrepreneurship, 160, 207
  for Early Music, 6, 14, 17, 45, 58, 80–81, 87, 132, 138, 152, 179, 182, 209–210
  failure, 135, 138
  and musical work, 52
  push and *pull*, 77–78, 80, 87–88
  and relationship with high culture, x, 8, 11, 85, 138, 153, 180, 183, 192
  and universities, 129
  See also commercial; culture vs. commerce; neoliberalism; TINA formation
marketing, 4, 14, 45, 69, 91, 129, 149, 152, 167, 192, 207–209
marketization, 225
Marriner, Neville, 21, 29, 70, 75, 81, 145, 232n15, 239n61
Marx, Karl, 202–205, 208
Mason, Tim, 61, 65, 89, 91
Maxwell Davies, Peter, 64–65, 98
McGegan, Nicholas, 131
Medieval and Renaissance Conference (Med-Ren), 128
  musicology relating to, 12, 31, 74, 95
  repertoire, 3, 10, 25, 59, 81, 88, 148, 183, 186
  See also Authenticity$_2$; instrument(s)
Melkus, Eduard, 21, 87
Mellers, Wilfrid, xiii
Meridian Records, 151
Mertin, Josef, 69, 73, 93, 96
meta-Reality, 16, 258n53
Meyer, Ernst, 71
mindfulness, 226
modernist rhetoric of Early Music, 8, 13–14, 40, 44–45, 59, 61, 64, 141, 170, 198
modernity, xi, 13–15, 18, 60, 89, 123–125, 197–199, 202–204, 209, 217, 256n4, 258n16
  post-, 8, 15, 45, 47, 192, 199, 216–217
  See also disenchantment; market: context
Moëck, 21, 101
Monk, Christopher, 26, 29, 101, 194
Monkman, Francis, 101
Montagu, Jeremy, 69, 106

Monteverdi Choir, 8, 23, 26, 33, 35, 83–84, 134, 155, 188, 254n50, 255n54
  See also Gardiner, John Eliot
Monteverdi, Claudio, ix, 27, 50–51
  Il Ballo Delle Ingrate, 63
  L'Incoronazione di Poppea, 58, 71
  L'Orfeo, ix, 50, 71
  Vespers, 26, 143, 164, 167, 255n54
Monteverdi Orchestra, 8, 23, 26, 134, 164–165, 188
Morrow, Michael, 10, 27, 32, 59, 66, 83, 98, 133–134, 187, 194
  authenticity, views on, 25, 37–38, 163, 171
  background, 29, 103–104, 162
  and the BBC, 144–145
  Early Music, views on, 27, 80, 137, 157
  and entrepreneurship, 166, 171
  and folk music, 67–68
  originality of, 25, 190
  See also Musica Reservata
motivation, extrinsic vs. intrinsic, 8, 11, 77–78, 103, 149–150, 152, 202
movers and shakers. *See* Early Music (movement): pioneers
Mozart, Wolfgang Amadeus, 3, 36, 59, 66, 84, 87, 147
  (Da Ponte) operas, 32, 76, 91
  Requiem, 37, 182
  symphonies, 31, 85, 146, 185
multiplier effect, 136, 221
Munrow, David, 10, 26, 32, 58, 104, 150, 194, 224
  and authenticity, 74–75
  background, 27, 29, 66, 74, 149
  BBC and television, 143, 145–146, 172
  and Early Music, 19, 25, 80, 100, 157
  and entrepreneurship, 159, 162, 165–166
  and folk music, 74
  and "Munrow effect", 27–28, 81, 91, 172–173
  performances, 59
  recordings, 68, 80, 190, 205
  See also Early Music Consort of London
Musica Antiqua Köln, 21, 23
Musica Antiqua of London, 64, 171
Musica Britannica, 100
musical works, 15–16, 40–41, 45–50, 96, 228, 236n46
  and authenticity, 8, 39, 199, 211, 225–226
  imaginary museum of, 8, 46–47
  and performance, 42, 49–53, 97, 208, 213–214
  See also werktreue; work-concept
Musica Reservata, 10, 23, 59
  distinctive approach and sound of, 25, 67–68, 80, 190
  and entrepreneurship, 133, 166, 171
  performers with, 27–28, 80, 106, 144, 157, 182, 187
  and professionalization, 83, 98, 193
  See also Morrow, Michael
Music Camp (Pigotts), 61, 63
music clubs, 30, 142, 149–150
music colleges (conservatories), 9, 24, 57, 70, 123, 149, 230n29
  Continental, 20, 21, 25, 66, 68, 87, 131–132, 187
  Guildhall School of Music & Drama, 58, 131, 183
  and HIP, 6, 17, 31, 33, 64, 130–132, 136, 139, 142, 177, 184, 186–188, 208
  and recognizing creativity, 127
  Royal Academy of Music, 33, 91, 97, 100, 106, 131, 150, 246n39
  Royal College of Music, 33, 106, 131, 151, 246n39
  Trinity College of Music, 131
music critics, 4, 39, 44, 48, 68, 88, 96–97
music(k)ing, 102, 244n48
musicology and musicologists, xiii, 11, 19, 21, 25, 39, 45, 65, 71, 73, 94–96, 99, 127, 182
  "Cambridge", 70
  cultural, 46
  ethno-, 3, 127, 132
  historical, 8, 12, 19, 31, 62, 67, 75, 95–96, 129–130, 194, 197, 214, 217–218, 222, 227
  and knowledge, 123–124, 129, 144, 154, 181, 218
  new, 40
  and performance, 21–22, 66, 75, 88, 126, 129, 144, 155, 159, 163, 177, 183, 208
  See also performer-scholars; scholar-performers
Music Party, 65
Myall, Norman, 103

National Centre for Early Music (NCEM), 34, 137, 183
National Early Music Association (NEMA), 58, 182, 194

regional fora, 33, 136, 194
National Lottery, 33, 137
National Youth Orchestra (NYO), 91, 149
natural necessity, 47, 51–52, 210, 212
  See also truth
negative capability, 172
Neel, Boyd, 58, 70
neoliberalism, 7, 24, 209
networking, 91, 103, 106, 160, 163–165, 223
New Age, 59–60, 238n20
New Social Movements (NSMs), 8, 60, 216
New York, 43–44, 57, 65–66, 104, 146
New York Pro Musica, 66
  See also Greenberg, Noah
Noorman, Jantina, 26, 190
Norrington, Roger, 32, 75–76, 89, 98, 130, 224
  and the Arts Council, 134–135
  and Authenticity$_2$, 31, 87
  authentic performance, views on, 53, 58
  background, 63, 71–73, 143
  and entrepreneurship, 160, 166
  and Evidence-Based Performance, 34, 73
  and the OAE, 90, 134
  performing music, views on, 83, 163, 192
  and play, 88, 172
  and pure tone, 34, 191
  and Stuttgart Radio Symphony Orchestra, 34
  See also London Classical Players (LCP)

oil crisis (1973), 23–24
"old" vs. "new", x, 9, 12–13, 18, 136–137, 183, 208, 211, 213, 226–227
Orchestra of St John's (OSJ), 61, 65, 239n38
Orchestra of the Age of Enlightenment (OAE), 25, 35, 63, 81, 134, 171, 188
  and Early Music's coming of age, 208–209
  funding, 137
  launch of, 17, 23, 32, 65, 88–91, 178
  marketing, 91, 207
  naming of, 209
Orchestra of the 18th Century, 148
Orchestre Révolutionnaire et Romantique (ORR), 23, 33, 35, 164, 188
  See also Gardiner, John Eliot
Ord, Boris, 21, 29
organ scholars, 79–80
original instruments. See instrument(s)
"outsiders", 20, 163

overcoming separation, 5, 16, 212
Oxbridge. See University: Oxbridge
Oxford Early Music Group, 80

Pachelbel's Canon, 152, 206
Page, Christopher, 29, 68, 88, 146, 151, 171
Pallis, Marco, 63–64, 106
Parley of Instruments, The, 23, 30, 64, 88, 131
  See also Holman, Peter
Parrott, Andrew, 78, 98, 144
  and the BBC, 151
  and class, 163
  and entrepreneurship, 161, 166, 171
  historical performance, views on, 84
  and Munrow, 80–81
  and Musica Reservata, 25, 28
  and Oxford, 28–29, 65, 80
  and Tippett, 70
  training, views on, 131–132
  See also Taverner Choir, Consort & Players (TCCP)
Parsons, Geoffrey, 103
Pay, Antony, 65, 89, 91
Pears, Peter, 66, 70–71
performer-scholars, x, 35, 139, 144, 146, 169, 183
  See also scholar-performers
Period Instrument Managers Meetings (PIMMs). See under-supply
period instrument movement. See Early Music (movement)
Period Instrument Orchestra Enquiry, 134
period performance. See historically informed performance (HIP)
period style. See historically informed performance (HIP)
Perry, Simon, 151
Perry, Ted, 88, 140, 151, 215, 224
Philips Records, 144
Phillips, Peter, 28–29, 50, 79–80, 130, 151, 162, 171
Philomusica of London, 23, 26, 35, 70
  See also Dart, Thurston
Pickard, David, 193
Pinnock, Andrew, 25, 60, 99–100, 131, 134, 154–155, 187, 194
Pinnock, Trevor, 32, 71, 75, 78–79, 82, 88, 90
  background, 28–29, 73–74, 149, 163
  and entrepreneurship, 159, 161, 166–167

Pinnock, Trevor (*Cont.*)
   and Galliard Harpsichord Trio, 30, 78–79
   HIP, views on, 37, 74, 78, 85, 170, 213
   recordings, 79, 165, 185
   rivalry, 83, 158
   and Royal College of Music, 131, 218
   and succession, 35, 193
   See also English Concert, The (TEC)
Plato, 37, 40, 126, 221
play, 19, 157, 185, 220
   and cultural entrepreneurship, 17, 158, 168–173
   -ful music-making, 27, 88, 228, 259n28
   space, 6, 13, 43, 84, 139, 156, 168, 218–221, 223, 228, 259n31
   vs. work, 8, 13, 205
Pleasants, Virginia, 101
Pleeth, Anthony, 78
Potter, John, 12, 74, 173
Poulton, Diana, 105
power, 7–8, 11, 42, 129, 141, 147, 159, 202, 210, 214, 221
   and art, 204
   causal, 45, 47, 52, 125
   labor, 76–77, 82, 197
   and magic, 203–204, 210
   political, 24
   rhetoric of play, 169–172
power$_1$, 204
power$_2$, 204, 210
Preston, Simon, 26, 80, 103, 190
Preston, Stephen, 78
promoting. *See* labor market
promotion and promoters, xii, 11, 24, 35, 85–86, 147–150, 181, 200, 222
   and authenticity, 37, 152, 154
   economics of, 133–134, 202, 247n64
   and the OAE, 91, 209
   and the promoter subsidy model, 134
   self-, 162
Pro Musica Antiqua of Brussels, 66
Protestantism, 48, 68, 197
publishing and publishers, 64, 97–98, 182, 194, 214, 222, 224
Purcell, Henry, 63, 70, 151
Purcell Quartet, 23, 74
pure tone, 34, 191
Puyana, Rafael, 73

quality, 5, 28, 101, 103, 133, 164, 167, 187, 194
   guild-like, 5, 68, 131, 218

radio broadcasts, 67, 77, 94, 127, 142–147, 159, 218, 222
   A Feather on the Breath of God, 88, 151
   influence on Early Music, 73, 140, 205
   The Play of Daniel, 66
Radio 3. *See* British Broadcasting Corporation (BBC): Radio 3 (Third Programme)
Raglan Baroque Players, 23, 30, 134
Rameau, Jean-Philippe, 71, 151
Rattle, Simon, 29, 32, 76, 90–92, 182, 191, 208
Rawson, John, 102, 105
record companies, 17, 34, 49, 66, 79, 88, 100, 138, 140–142, 144, 150–152, 155, 167, 194
   executives of, 15, 30, 79–80, 151, 155, 158–159, 163, 168, 200, 202, 209, 218, 222
   motivation of, x, 8, 11, 14, 24, 45, 81, 90, 100, 140, 145, 151, 165
recorder, 106, 133
   makers, 20–21, 62, 100, 102, 223
   music for, 67, 80
   players, 21, 26, 33, 106, 148, 162, 194
   society, 62
   teaching, 33, 131
recording(s), 3
   authenticity and, 14–15, 138, 152, 154, 182, 192, 206
   contract (and deals), 70, 79–80, 91, 151, 159–160, 163
   early music, 6, 10, 59, 66, 83–84, 180, 183
   engineer(s), 80, 151, 155
   funding, 85–86, 127, 138, 150, 155, 164
   importance of, 76, 89, 135, 150–152, 194, 205
   industry, 34, 143, 150–151, 155, 180, 185, 191, 207
   influence of, 30–31, 65, 73, 148, 152, 165, 180, 189–191, 206, 223
   and relationship with live music, 146–147, 206
   and relationship with musicology, 100, 126, 137
   series, 10
   session (and studio), 70, 97, 127, 137, 147, 155, 164, 171, 178
   and synchronicity, 180, 188–191, 206
   technology, 6, 34, 66, 140, 189, 205–207

re-enchantment, 5–6, 16, 152, 158, 213, 215, 218, 221, 228
  the art of, x, 7, 18, 43, 212–215, 222, 226
  and classical music, 18, 51, 126, 213–214, 218–221
Regional Arts Associations (RAAs), 133, 247n55
Reith, John (Lord), 140, 142–143, 152
religion, 46, 197–202, 219, 256n15
resource leverage, 84, 160, 166–167, 179
revolutionary, x, 25, 57, 60–61, 75, 91, 148, 153, 181, 195
  lure of technology, 205–207
  rhetoric of Early Music, 8–9, 59–61
rewarding. *See* labor market
rite of restoration, 219–220
Roberts, Deborah, 131
Robinson, Bernard, 63
Robson, Anthony, 91
Roche, Elizabeth, 19, 59, 66, 87, 146, 182
Roche, Jerome, 29, 128
Romantic
  period, 33, 232n7
  repertoire, 3, 31, 59, 75, 87–88, 183
Romanticism, 20, 41, 44, 46, 62, 131, 158, 183, 216–217, 220, 223
Rooley, Anthony, 29, 58, 64, 73–74, 105, 107, 137, 157, 170, 173
Rose Consort of Viols, 23, 30, 36, 64, 171
Rubio, David, 69, 71–72, 104, 215
Ruskin, John, 3, 15

Sacher, Paul, 20, 68, 232n8
Sadler's Wells Theatre, 70
Samson, William, 103
Sartre, Jean-Paul, 37, 212, 220
Savall, Jordi, 73, 131–132
Sayers, Chris, 89, 146, 151, 215
schola cantorum. *See* collegium musicum
Schola Cantorum Basiliensis, 20, 66, 68, 79
scholar-performers, 12, 22, 139, 144, 169
  See also performer-scholars
Schütz Choir, 23, 63, 83
  See also Norrington, Roger
Schütz, Heinrich, 63, 71
Scottish Early Music Consort, 23, 33, 148
Sharp, Cecil, 67
Shuttleworth, John, 151
Sixteen, The, 23, 171, 183, 190

Smith, Steve, 80, 151
social capital, 96, 159, 161–162
Sothcott, John, 25
South Bank Centre, 25, 59, 87, 144, 193–194, 224
  Purcell Room, 30
  Queen Elizabeth Hall, 27, 90–91, 133
  Royal Festival Hall, 35, 71, 103, 147
spiritual(ity), 16, 46, 142, 197–198, 214, 216, 222
spotting opportunities, 77, 159–160, 164–165, 179
Skeaping, Lucie, 148
Skeaping, Roddy, 65
Springhead, 63
Standage, Simon, 31, 65, 78, 158
Steiner, Rudolf, 24
Stevens, Denis, xii, 29, 68, 96, 142, 144–145, 214–215
Stevenson, Mark, 101, 105
Stour Music Festival, 70–71, 152
Studio der Frühen Musik, 21, 66, 238n14
  See also Binkley, Thomas
superstar culture, 9, 86, 148, 192, 207
survey of British early music performers and instrument-makers, xii, xv, 184–186, 254n35

Tallis Scholars, The (TTS), xi, 50, 131, 166, 171, 183, 255n54
  and entrepreneurship, 162, 247n50, 251n26
  formation of, 23, 28, 76, 79–80
  and Gimell, 80, 151
  distinctive sound of, 190
  and university, 130
  See also Phillips, Peter
Taruskin, Richard, xi, 16, 33, 51, 226
  authenticity, views on, 37–45, 153, 217, 236n58
  critique of Early Music, 11, 13, 39–40, 64, 170, 236n65
  and English HIP, 75
  influence of, 15, 53, 191
  and musicology, 129
  and "self-consciousness" of Early Music, 31, 179
  Text and Act, x–xi, 8, 11, 16, 33, 37–45, 53, 211, 213, 228
Taskin, Paul, 105

Taverner Choir, Consort & Players (TCCP), xi, 83
  and entrepreneurship, 161, 166, 171
  formation of, 23, 70, 76, 80–81
  funding, 134
  mix of amateurs and professionals, 84
  See also Parrott, Andrew
teaching and teachers, 49, 64, 66, 73–74, 84, 105, 127–132, 147, 218–219
  and access to instruments, 99, 101, 108
  individualized tuition, 9, 149
  influence of, 28, 64, 73, 181
technology, 6, 52, 77, 127, 130, 197, 205–207, 213
  and compact disc, 23, 31, 140, 190, 206
  and LP, 66, 123, 140, 189, 205
  See also recording(s): technology
Teldec, 21
  Das Alte Werk, 66
Telefunken, 66
temperament, 72, 94, 221
Terry, R.R., 96
Thatcher, Margaret, 132, 202–204, 209
The 24 Violins, 78
Third Programme. *See* British Broadcasting Corporation (BBC): Radio 3 (Third Programme)
Thomas, Bernard, 80, 98, 105, 181–182, 185
Thomson, John (J.M.), 25, 27, 68, 129, 147, 229n4
Thorby, Philip, 171
Tilney, Colin, 73
TINA formation, 18, 203–209, 212, 215, 219, 224, 257n28
Tippett, Michael, 69–70, 80, 163, 183
Tobin, John, 71
Tosi, Pier Francesco, 227
touring, 34, 80, 134
training. *See* labor market
truth, 5, 16, 199, 212, 224
  alethic, 52–53, 210, 237n101
  of musical works, 53, 96
tuning, 85, 94, 206, 221
TV broadcasts, 145

under-supply, 31, 82–83, 150, 158, 160, 166, 187
unions (Equity, Musicians' Union), 62, 83–84

universities, 57, 60, 66, 73, 136, 142, 144, 149, 158, 163, 177, 186, 198
  and collegium musicums, 64, 68
  as knowledge-producing institutions, 17, 24, 123–124, 127–130, 138, 159, 222
  as "play" spaces, 139
University
  of Birmingham, 106
  of Cambridge, 21, 26–29, 68, 72, 74, 130, 164, 167, 186, 190
  of Durham, 128
  of Edinburgh, 106
  King's College London, xii, xvi, 26, 95, 128, 157
  of Leicester, 27
  of London, 97
  of Nottingham, 95, 128
  The Open, 80
  Oxbridge, 26, 28, 79, 149, 161, 167, 185–186
  of Oxford, 21, 28–29, 65, 68, 79–80, 98–99, 106, 130, 144–145, 163
  of York, 128
Urtext editions, 17, 97, 237n85
Utrecht Early Music Festival, 150, 181

venture capitalists, 155
Vienna Viola Da Gamba Quartet, 21, 73
  See also Harnoncourt, Nikolaus
Virgin Classics, 91
Vivaldi, Antonio, 21, 59, 76, 143, 206
Von Huene Workshop, 102

Wadland, Peter, 29–30, 81–82, 151, 155, 162, 215, 224
Wagner, Richard, 87, 182
Warburton, Ernest, 146
Ward Clarke, Jennifer, 65
Warnock, Felix, 81, 89–91, 193
Waterfield, Polly, 64
Wearing, Clive, 29, 142, 144
Weber, Max, 13, 170, 196–198, 202, 204
Wenzinger, August, xii, 72
werktreue, 11, 16, 41–42, 45
West, Jeremy, 29, 128, 135, 223
Westrup, Jack, 21, 29, 68, 96, 100
William Byrd Choir, 83

Wood, Richard, 100–101, 103, 107
Woolley, Dennis, 103
work-concept, 40–42, 45–46
   See also Goehr, Lydia
Wulstan, David, 28–29

York Early Music Festival, 23, 35, 43, 58, 114, 136, 149, 181
Yorkshire Arts Association, 133

Zaslaw, Neil, 146, 179